AMERICA'S MOST-WATCHED CELEBRITY AS YOU'VE NEVER SEEN HIM BEFORE!

He has been seen by more people more often than anyone else in American history—an estimated 8 million people per show for nearly thirty years! In a career begun at the dawn of television, he's hosted and hob-nobbed with the world's most famous personalities—politicians, singers, comedians, actors, musicians, artists, athletes, authors. But who is Johnny Carson, *really?*

King of the Night answers that by taking you out of the TV studios, into the homes and hearts of those who know him best, and finally into the mind of the witty media maven himself. Based on over 700 interviews, here is an intimate, no-holds-barred close-up of the man and his world—the glamour and glitter, the dark side of fame, and the sacrifices only a legend such as the King of the Night has known.

AS SEEN IN *GOOD HOUSEKEEPING*, *THE NATIONAL ENQUIRER*, AND NEWSPAPERS COAST TO COAST!

Read the raves for the ultimate Carson biography . . .

"NEARLY ALWAYS JUICY . . . sensational tidbits . . . a quintessentially American story."

—*The New York Times*

"REVEALING!" —*USA Today*

"Not a stone is left unturned!"

—*The Washington Post*

"Excellent dissections of Carson's business life . . . The most moving parts of the book are about Jody, Johnny's first wife." —*Chicago Tribune*

"A striking authenticity . . . bitingly written, free of overt malice."

—*Boston Herald*

"THE LIFE AND TIMES OF AMERICA'S FAVORITE TALK-SHOW HOST . . . Carson has enjoyed unprecedented affection from a notoriously fickle audience." —*Time*

"EXPLOSIVE . . . SENSATIONAL . . . SIZZLING . . . SHOCKING!" —*National Enquirer*

"THE CLOSEST THING TO A DEFINITIVE BIOGRAPHY OF CARSON, AN ENIGMA IF THERE EVER WAS ONE. . . . Readers will appreciate Leamer's extensive research, documentation, and above all, fairness to his subject."   —*Variety*

"This may well stand as THE MOST AUTHORITATIVE OF THE UNAUTHORIZED CARSON SURVEYS . . . the strongest, most deeply researched."   —*Kirkus Reviews*

"Neither a flattering puff piece nor Carson-bashing . . . A REVEALING AND ENTERTAINING ACCOUNT."   —*Library Journal*

"EXHAUSTIVELY RESEARCHED . . . Leamer digs deeper and strikes a richer lode of paydirt than previous Carson excavators."   —Liz Smith

"TERRIFIC . . . [a] very undull vivisection."   —Gossip columnist Cindy Adams

"What a melancholy, tragic story this book is!"   —Jack Paar

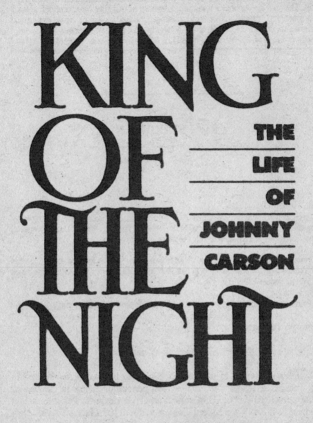

KING OF THE

THE
LIFE
OF
JOHNNY
CARSON

NIGHT

LAURENCE LEAMER

SMP

ST. MARTIN'S PAPERBACKS

TO
RON FRIEDMAN

Interview with Johnny Carson and Ed McMahon, by Timothy White, originally appeared in *Rolling Stone*. Copyright © 1987 by Timothy White. Used by special permission of the author. All rights reserved.

Permission granted to quote from "Life Is Beautiful." Music by Fred Astaire. Lyrics by Tommy Wolf. Copyright © 1974 and 1977 by WOLFLAND (ASCAP). International copyright secured. All rights reserved.

Published by arrangement with William Morrow and Company

KING OF THE NIGHT

Library of Congress Card Number: 89-31201

ISBN: 0-312-92256-6

Printed in the United States of America

William Morrow edition published 1989
St. Martin's Paperbacks edition/July 1990

10 9 8 7 6 5 4 3 2 1

AUTHOR'S NOTE

When I began this book, I wrote a letter to Henry Bushkin, Johnny Carson's attorney, asking to interview Carson. Bushkin replied that Carson would not cooperate because he would be writing his own autobiography. "Certainly your previous books demonstrate the quality of writing which you are capable of and his decision is not to be taken as a reflection upon your work," Bushkin wrote. "I know you can appreciate his position and I wish you the best with your book."

As I proceeded with my research, I often experienced what I took to be a strange ambivalence on Carson's part. One of his old friends, Bob Lehman, told me that Carson had exclaimed, "That son of a bitch has talked to everybody!" Lehman proceeded to give me information directly from Carson that seemed to have been intended to help my research.

Then, one evening, I dropped into the piano bar at the Westwood Marquis to say hello to Bill Baker. Baker had played with the New Yorkers in the fifties on several shows with Carson, and was still working as a piano player. I had already interviewed the musician. Baker told me that Carson had recently called him, after over thirty years of no contact, and suggested that he *not* talk to me.

A few days before Christmas 1987, Mary Jane Trokel, Carson's longtime lover and friend, went to see him at *The Tonight Show*. Trokel told me later that she had confided to Carson that she was talking to me, and she suggested that he do the same. According to Trokel, Carson did not appear upset that she had been interviewed; he even said that he was thinking of talking as well.

I had Carson's home telephone numbers, but I had never called him. A few months later I wrote Carson a letter requesting an interview and telling him that I would be calling. When I telephoned, the housekeeper answered and told me to try again later. When I called again, Alexis Mass Carson answered the phone. The new Mrs. Carson told me that her husband would not be giving me an interview and that I should stop calling their house.

In late October 1988, when I was finishing the manuscript, I decided to try once more. Carson answered the phone. He could not have been more civil. I asked him for an interview. "Well, I'll tell you why I'm not gonna," he said. "And I wish you luck with the book. I intend to sit down and do my own book, and there's no reason why I should give you what I'm going to use myself." We discussed the possibility of him checking out facts in the manuscript, but in the end I wrote Carson once again, putting in a final request for an interview. I said that I would not be pursuing him any further but would leave it to him to contact me if he wanted to do an interview. I never heard from him, and I went ahead and finished the book.

I was fortunate in that most of the important people in Carson's life did speak, either on- or off-the-record. I have many hours of tape-recorded interviews with Jody Carson, the first Mrs. Carson. Jody had never talked candidly to anyone about her marriage, and it was a highly emotional experience for both of us. I wish her well and I hope that she finds the tranquillity that she has sought for so long.

I also became acquainted with the second Mrs. Carson, Joanne. She was unwilling to grant me an interview about Carson. On the few occasions when she did talk about him, she spoke in positive and affectionate terms. In writing about the second Mrs. Carson, I also had access to an extensive series of interviews conducted by Eirik Knutzen, a syndicated television columnist.

The third Mrs. Carson, Joanna, was cordial and forthcoming. She responded to my many questions, even if at times she found them irrelevant or intrusive.

I have many fond memories of people I met doing research on this book: walking around Avoca, Iowa, with Marion Weinmann; having lunch with Al Bruno at his farmhouse in upstate New York; spending an evening with Jerry Solomon in Lincoln, Nebraska; dining with Mrs. Morrill, Jody Carson's mother, on Mother's Day at the American Legion in North Platte; joking with Joan Rivers during a weekend in Las Vegas; sitting with Tiny Tim in his Mustang convertible; hearing Trudy Moreault perform at a New York club; taking tea at Trumps with Mary Jane Trokel.

I cannot possibly thank all the people who were helpful. Although I cannot publicly acknowledge my many off-the-record sources, I want them to know how much I appreciate their assistance.

I would like to thank the following people for their help: Ray Abruzzese, Karima Akef, Steve Allen, Norris Anderson, Helen Andrews, Jules Arceneaux, Nick Arnold, Larry Ashmead, James Aubrey, George Axelrod, Shlomo Bachrach, Dr. Robert Baird, Bill Baker, Joan Barthel, Gordon Baskin, Ed Becker, Tony Bennett, Phil Berger, Milton Berle, Harry Benson, Mary Jane Beckenhauer Bentley, Stu Billett, Joey Bishop, Paul Block, Alicia Bond, Ben Brady, Bill Brennan, Cate Breslin, Mark Breslin, Bill Bridge, Michael Brouman, Al Bruno, Ann Buchwald, George Burns, Judy Bushkin, William Butterfield.

Jerry Calhoun, Carmen, Rose Mary Carroll, Rick Carson, Chevy Chase, Rafael Chodos, James Cochran, Bob Coe, Raphael Cohen, Vance Colwig, John Condon, Bruce Cooper, Jill Corey, Jim Crenshaw, Perry Cross, Arthur Crowley, Senator Ed Davis, Mary Lou Dawson, John Delgatto, Milton DeLugg, Duane Demaree, Jan de Ruth, Dee

Devoe, Edwin Doll, Elizabeth Dougherty, Marcia Fessler Drozd, Peggy Leach Ebles, Jack Eglash, Fred Egley, Nora Ephron, Chris Fager, Lola Falana, Don Fedderson, Irving Fein, Phillip Feldman, Margaret Ferraro, Billy Fine, Richard Fischoff, Orvie Fisher, Shirlee Fonda, June Foray, Arlene Francis, Val Friedman, Mike Fuehrer.

Mort Galane, Lila Garrett, Mabel Gaskill, Steve Gelman, Lorraine Beckenhauer Gipe, Michael Gold, Cal Gooden, Hal Goodman, Fay Gordon, Robert Goulet, Henry Gradstein, Arlo Grafton, Mort Green, Gael Greene, Richard Gully, Bob Hall, Buddy Hammer, Stanley Myron Handelman, John Harlan, Barbara and John Haslom, Tim Healy, Leana Heath, Skitch Henderson, Bob Hoag, Judge William Hogoboom, Chuck Howser, Fred and Diane Huffman, Dorothy Hundley, Marsha Hunt, Sandy Ignon, Stan Irwin, Christopher Jackson, Seaman Jacobs, Eddie Jaffe, Dick Kane, Roy Kammerman, Arthur Kassel, Marilyn Katleman, Fred Kayne, Walter Kempley, Joe Kirshenbaum, Al Klink, Alex Kolis, Sandi Kopler, Mirko Kontic, Natalie Kosbubal, Paul Krassner.

Bob Lardine, Dr. Alan Landers, Peter Leeds, Bob Lehman, Eric and Leza Lidow, Jim Logan, Roy London, Mary Ann Lopat, Adrian Lowell, Tanena Love, Steve Mallory, Pat McCormick, Cal McKinley, John J. McMahon, Bob Means, Mr. and Mrs. Keith Meiniger, Felix Mirando, Jr., Nat Miles, Ferris Mack, George Manning, Aileen Mehle, Dorothy Melvin, Bob Meyer, Michael Miller, Bob Mockler, Scott Morris, Jack Narz, Jim Nauman, Mr. and Mrs. Victor Nelson, Marsha Neuberger, David Niven, Jr., Steve North.

Mollie Parnis, Bob Patty, Jerry Petievich, Tom Poston, Dale Raasch, Roy Ratliff, Phil Ramey, David Rayfiel, Marjorie Reed, Trudy Moreault Richards, Joan Rivers, Betty Rollin, Marion Rosenberg, Ronnali Rosenfeld, Stanley Ralph Ross, Ashley Rothchild, Alan Rothenberg, Red Rowe, John Sacco, Pat Sajak, Larry Sanford, Alan Schnapper, Irving Schneider, Dick Scott, Ken Schwartz, Wally Seawell, Tom Sheils, Shelly Schultz, Susan Seton, Mrs. Daniel Seymour, Dutch Shutler, Hank Simms, Jadranka

Skenderovic, Danny Simon, Merrill Sindler, Red Skelton, Jerry Solomon, Don Spencer, Mrs. Mary Stark, Gary Stevens, Maco Stewart, Joyce Susskind.

Dr. Ed Tauber, David Tebet, Rudy Tellez, Jeanne Prior Tellez, Craig Tennis, Tiny Tim, Maynell Thomas, Charles Thone, Marge Alexis Todd, George Tricker, Mary Jane Trokel, William Turner, Linda Ulrich, Bobby Van, Harriet Van Horne, Michael Vollbracht, Jennie Walker, Marion Weinmann, Mort Wells, Roger Welsch, Phil Weltman, William Wenke, Julia Wolcott, Dr. and Mrs. Benjamin Wolstein, Shirley Wood, Bob Weiskopf, Merle Workhoven, Gil Wyman, Joseph Yablonsky.

I am indebted to a number of journalists for their assistance: Scott Malone, Dan Moldea, Dave Robb, Bill Knoedelseder, Donna Rosenthal, Elizabeth Mehren, Daniel Akst, Karen Jackovich, Chuck Conconi, Tom Shales, Eirik Knutzen, Al Delugach, Brian Linehan, Paul Rosenfield, Peter S. Greenberg, Sam Rubin, Larry Grobel, Tom Goldstein, Steve Tinney, Rudy Maxa, James Seymore, Donald Nielson, and the late Ned Day. I am grateful to Timothy White for allowing me to quote 350 words from his 1979 *Rolling Stone* interview with Carson.

I was assisted by various research librarians, including William Hifner at the *Washington Post*; Debra L. Hammond at *Playboy*; librarians at the *Las Vegas Sun*, the Lincoln Center Library for the Performing Arts, the Library of Congress, the Graduate Research Library at UCLA; the Corning Public Library, the Avoca Public Library, the Norfolk Public Library, the Omaha Public Library, collections at USC, and the Santa Monica Public Library. I also utilized the IQUEST on-line information service.

When I began *King of the Night*, I received a phone call from David Shumacher, a young journalist in northern California, offering his research services. In the many months that I have worked on the book, Shumacher's help has been invaluable. He has an amazing ability to locate information and sources. Among his many contributions to this book, he located Jody Carson through a tedious search of public records and scores of phone calls. He never failed me as a researcher, and he has never failed me as a friend.

My wife, Vesna Obradovic Leamer, did most of the library research. It is no wonder that she sometimes feels that she is allergic to Xerox paper and old newspapers. Without her insight, inspiration, and caring, the book would still be unfinished.

Harvey Ginsberg edited the manuscript with the detailed concern that is his trademark. Joy Harris can always succeed as a therapist, or motivation expert if she tires of being an agent. Ken Norwick, my literary attorney, is never more than a phone call away.

I have dedicated the book to Ron Friedman, who belies the axiom that Los Angeles is a place where it is impossible to make a true friend.

ONE

" Live from Hollywood! *The Tonight Show* starring Johnny Carson, the twenty-fifth anniversary. This is Ed McMahon, along with Doc Severinsen and the NBC orchestra, inviting you to join Johnny as we celebrate twenty-five years of late-night entertainment. . . . And now, ladies and gentlemen, HEEEEERE'S JOHNNY!"

Johnny Carson stepped from behind the multicolored curtain wearing a tuxedo. The five hundred guests rose from their seats in Studio 1. They clapped, screamed, whistled, and hooted exuberantly. Johnny walked forward to a star marked on the studio floor. Carl "Doc" Severinsen salaamed, twirling his hand downward from his forehead. McMahon paid homage too, pressing his hands together and bowing as if to a royal personage.

The camera panned across the audience, capturing snapshots of middle America. A family from Louisiana. A couple from Pennsylvania. A retired man from New Jersey. Two sisters from Seattle. Most of the audience had come to southern California on vacations. They had made this pilgrimage to *The Tonight Show* as important a part of their itineraries as Disneyland or the Universal Studio tour.

This morning, October 1, 1987, close to a hundred of the guests had been standing in line at the NBC studios in Burbank waiting for tickets when a major earthquake hit Los Angeles. Even that didn't dislodge them. Then this

afternoon they had stood in the heat of the San Fernando
Valley for two hours or more before ushers let them into
this cool sanctuary.

The applause didn't end, but rose from crescendo to crescendo. No one else in show business or public life received
such a nightly homage. In an age of disposable celebrities
Johnny had come into American homes over five thousand
times. He had been seen by more people on more occasions
than anyone in American history. He had become a fixture
of American life, a part of the cultural furniture. This evening alone, over 21 million people were watching the show.

Johnny exuded boyish impishness, but his face was as
weathered as an old Nebraska barn. He smiled warmly, but
his posture sent out a far different message. He stood as if
he had been jolted backward and had been frozen there,
forever pulling away from anyone who got near to him.

At the age of sixty-one, Johnny was the ultimate creature
of television. He had begun his career in Omaha in 1949,
the first summer that television went on the air in Nebraska.
He had worked in Los Angeles and New York as the networks had grown into the most powerful communications
medium ever known. Now, the networks had begun to decline, viewers lost to cable networks and videotape re-
corders. It was unlikely that any other performer would ever
have the same hold over the American night.

Johnny finally raised his hands and gently motioned for
quiet. "That is very sweet of you," he said. "Did you
intentionally stand, or were you thrown out of your seats?"

Johnny's monologue had a rhythm to it that was like a
favorite song whose chords brought forth memories of good
times. The audience sometimes laughed at the mere sound
of his voice.

"Oral Roberts felt the quake this morning," Johnny said.
That wasn't the punch line, but it was enough to set the
audience laughing. Roberts had said that if his flock didn't
contribute $4.5 million, God "could call him home," pre-
sumably a reference to heaven. For months Johnny had been
satirizing the faith-healing evangelist. His jokes had helped

to make Roberts a figure of widespread derision. Now the mere mention of his name was a joke. "Oral turned to his wife in bed and said, 'Oh, honey, the check must have bounced. . . .' "

Johnny moved on, line after line, hardly waiting for the laughter to die down. "People are not used to seeing me in prime time," he said, gesturing with his hands. "Imagine President Reagan tuning in now and saying to Nancy, 'Well it's eleven-thirty, I should have been asleep two hours ago.' "

In Washington Johnny's nightly political jibes were repeated the next morning all over the capital. If he joked about a politician regularly, it was as ominous a sign as finding a dead fish on your doorstep in Sicily.

Johnny created the illusion of daring. He was, in fact, a comedic politician, attuned to his viewers, leading them wherever they wanted to go. He had unchallenged power as long as he did not attempt to use it. Nightly he listened to the laughs and the groans from the live audience. They told him what was funny and what wasn't, who could be laughed at and who couldn't be.

In America ideas and values changed as quickly as hemlines and hairdos. Believe anything too deeply, strike too rich a characterization, and one was doomed to become passé. Johnny changed his jokes as he changed his wardrobe, never as hip as L.A., never as traditional as Omaha.

Johnny's monologues were part of the *Zeitgeist*. One day social historians will turn to his quips and commentaries in trying to understand popular American culture in the last third of the twentieth century.

"Would you have believed twenty-five years ago that now, today, in '87, we'd be seeing condom ads on television?" Johnny said, turning to another favorite arena of humor. "Now the next time you hear Ed say, 'On your way home pick up a six-pack,' he may not be referring to Budweiser."

In the show's early years Johnny had peppered the program with sexual banter and innuendo rarely heard on television. He was the comedic equivalent of the birth-control pill, helping to popularize America's sexual revolution. There are no revolutions without casualties; Johnny had made divorce a laughing matter, focusing on his own three ex-wives.

"Thank you for being with us," Johnny said as the NBC orchestra cut into *The Tonight Show* theme and Ed announced the sponsors. The red light went off, and the first barrage of commercials played silently on the monitors.

Johnny stood alone facing the studio audience. For an instant this was no longer Johnny Carson, television star, but a man standing there, and the audience squirmed uneasily. Usually someone shouted out a greeting. Johnny always said a few words.

"Thank you, you're going to make this a pleasure," Johnny said, setting off another round of applause. "Where were you all this morning about seven-forty-two?" he asked, referring to the time of the earthquake. A score of people shouted out the same answer: waiting for tickets for the show.

"I felt so calm because of this guy at Channel Four," Johnny said, shaking his head. Kent Shocknek, the morning anchorman, had distinguished himself by ducking under the desk during one of the aftershocks. "He dived under the desk and came up d-d-d-d-don't . . . don't . . . don't," Johnny stuttered. Then he mentioned a female reporter on the local station. "I think the most frightening thing was seeing Linda Alvarez without her makeup."

Johnny walked over and sat down at his desk next to Ed McMahon. For a program that brought in up to 17 percent of NBC's entire profits, *The Tonight Show* had a set that was surprisingly modest. The painted backdrop was of a gray stone fence and a Leroy Neiman–like blue sky, speckled with flashes of yellow. In front sat a jungle of potted palms and plants.

Johnny's desk looked as if it could have come from the office of a junior accountant, the chairs from rent-a-furniture. But on television they looked classy.

The two men sat quietly waiting for the light over the camera to come on again. Johnny usually began the show chatting with Ed before doing one comedy bit or another. This evening was different. Television is full of hoked-up celebrations, celebrity roasts, and award shows, but a quarter-century of dominating late-night television was an achievement worth noting.

"We have spent a lot of these evenings together," Johnny said to the sixty-four-year old announcer. Johnny hated the typical show-biz talk show where performers who hardly knew one another affected an instant intimacy, according hugs and accolades and words of perfumed adulation to mere acquaintances. Ed had been Johnny's announcer for twenty-nine years, his foil and shield, his claque, his laughter punctuating the night. "I cannot imagine doing this show without you. You have been an absolute rock all these years."

Johnny could have made this anniversary show a compilation of *his* greatest moments. But when others looked good, he looked better. So this evening began not with excerpts from Johnny's performances, but with a series of clips from some of the great American comics who had appeared on *The Tonight Show* over the years. As routines with Groucho Marx, Red Skelton, Jack Benny, George Burns, and Bob Hope played on the monitor, Johnny lit a cigarette and sat back. He laughed and laughed. Then, when he showed himself in 1964 singing "Our Love Is Here to Stay" off-key with an exuberant Pearl Bailey, he half collapsed with glee. It was not like a politician admiring himself on television, but like a man watching another person.

The Tonight Show was the great hub of the entertainment industry. No matter where performers were going, they almost always stopped to sing a song, tell a tale, play a number or two. Johnny introduced a series of clips. Judy Garland. Liza Minnelli. Diana Ross. Itzhak Perlman. Luciano Pavarotti. Benny Goodman. Buddy Rich. Louis Armstrong. Johnny could have chosen a hundred others as well.

Not only entertainers appeared on the show. *The Tonight Show* had revealed to politicians the value of playing "themselves" in a few minutes of calculated casualness. Ronald Reagan, Richard Nixon, and Martin Luther King, Jr., all lightly bantered with Johnny.

In Hollywood the stars of films exist in a higher firmament than do mere television stars. Johnny was the exception. Wherever he traveled to parties and gatherings among the Hollywood elite, he received a recognition and deference as great as any movie star. He belonged as the host of the Academy Awards. He was a success beyond success. He had lived half a dozen lifetimes on television. More money, more talent, and more energy had been spent trying to defeat him than any other performer in history. Dick Cavett. Joey Bishop. Merv Griffin. Alan Thicke. David Brenner. Joan Rivers. They had come in droves, and he had turned them all back.

The staff and NBC personnel usually watched the taping of the program with only modest interest. This evening, however, they stood backstage mesmerized in front of the monitors, as if even they were having a new vision of the program.

Most comedians considered their first appearance on *The Tonight Show* as a professional coming-of-age. Johnny could have shown clips from most of the major new comics of the last quarter-century. He cut the number down to five. Johnny's guest hosts, Jay Leno and Garry Shandling, were automatics. So was David Letterman, since Carson Productions owned his program. That left room only for clips from Eddie Murphy and Steve Martin.

Then Johnny played some of his own routines, and he was as funny as any of the other comedians. He was brilliant when all was not right with his world, when talking birds wouldn't talk, a pie in the face ended up as a pie on the forehead or the chest, an animal relieved itself on his arm.

These anniversary shows had become an annual ritual each October. Usually little or no time was spent reliving moments with politicians or classical musicians or jazz greats, and the humor had a heavy diet of pie-throwing and slapstick. This evening, however, was an encyclopedia of American popular culture for the past quarter-century. It was not simply a bunch of clips, the best of Carson. It was an homage to an extraordinary achievement.

"It has been a fabulous journey for me personally," Johnny said as the hour and a half drew to a close. "And without sounding mawkish, about a year ago I was going to hang it up on the twenty-fifth year of this show. I don't know why. Maybe twenty-five years is enough. And I found out I was having so much fun doing the show that we decided to stick around for a while. So if you stick around for a while, we'll stick around for a while to do the show for you."

When the applause subsided, Johnny ended the program with Fred Astaire singing "Life Is Beautiful," a song whose music Astaire himself had composed. *The Tonight Show* staff could have looked through every foot of video in the vaults and not found a more stylish way to end the twenty-fifth-anniversary show. Astaire personified a peculiarly American kind of class. In the clip Astaire sat next to Johnny and sang with the casual elegance and understatement a song that is now *The Tonight Show*'s ending theme:

> "Life is beautiful in every way
> Life is lovely as a spring bouquet
> Since I fell in love with you."

The show was over, but every year Johnny gave an anniversary party for the staff and production company. He usually held it at the Beverly Hills Hotel, a pink stucco palace on Sunset Boulevard where as many deals as affairs are consummated. This year Johnny's nephew, Jeff Sotzing, *The Tonight Show*'s associate producer, suggested holding the party on the *Queen Mary*. The giant British liner had come to its final resting place as a tourist attraction in the industrial port of Long Beach, thirty-six miles from Burbank. Johnny liked the idea, and the night after the anniversary show the party was held far from the Polo Lounge.

In Hollywood, wealth has been democratized, and many of the three hundred employees arrived in rented limousines. When they got out, a young lady in a tuxedo greeted them and took their pictures as if they were stars themselves. Then they walked along a red carpet, lined by velvet cords, and up a narrow escalator.

Johnny's company had taken over the entire second deck of the former Cunard liner, and had hired a security force worthy of a president. Plain-clothes and uniformed agents stood alert at the elevator, the escalator, the stairs leading up to the Queen Mary Hotel. Over the years Johnny had received death threats, but the security force was equally alert to attempts by journalists and other outsiders to crash the party.

Magazine editors were ready to put Johnny on the cover of their publications for the twenty-fifth anniversary. Television producers prepared to interview him for their networks. Newspaper editors offered major profiles in Sunday papers. Almost no one in Hollywood would have turned down such publicity, but Johnny did not give a single interview.

Johnny hated public affairs, even when he knew most of the people. But he played a worthy host, arriving before his guests. He staked out a corner of the bar beside his new wife, Alexis Mass, and did his best with the aimless chitchat.

When the camera is off, Johnny seems diminished, washed out. He looks like the tenth copy of a videocassette. He is five-feet-ten-and-a-half-inches tall, but if it is possible to be a short five feet ten and a half, he is it. He is thin, almost scrawny, at 170 pounds, with the muscular physique of an athlete fifteen years his junior, yet his face and hazel eyes show every one of his years. His most unusual feature is his elegant long hands, a surgeon's or a pianist's hands.

Alexis Mass was the Cinderella bride of the moment.

Thirty-seven-year-old Alex had been detailed like a Beverly Hills Porsche, polished and glazed from the bottom of her designer shoes to the tip of her long, frosted hair. She appeared the beautiful young woman on Johnny's arm, but underneath the relentless glamorizing was the fresh-faced, healthy look more common to the slopes and bars of Aspen than to the salons of Bel Air and Beverly Hills.

Johnny had a drink or two. Then he and Alex and the guests walked into the Grand Salon for dinner. When the *Queen Mary* sailed between New York City and Southampton, the three-deck-high, 143-feet-long salon was the first-class dining room. It is an exquisite room, the largest ever built on a ship, paneled with golden-brown Peroba and Maple Burr.

In the center was a large dance floor and a band that played the up-tempo jazz that is Johnny's favorite music. Set throughout the room were round tables for ten. Each table had a large floral centerpiece, linen napkins in the water glasses, and a gift for each guest, a German clock embossed HAPPY 25TH ANNIVERSARY THE TONIGHT SHOW.

Except for Johnny's table, the dinner places were not reserved. The Carson production and NBC employees found their levels. The prop men sat with their kind. The musicians sat with the musicians.

Johnny and Alex took their places. Behind them stood an immense map of the Atlantic Ocean that hung halfway down the room. To their left sat Ed McMahon and his young wife, Victoria. To their right sat Fred "Freddy" de Cordova, the *Tonight Show*'s executive producer, and his wife, Janet; they had been on the *Queen Mary* on its final journey to Long Beach in 1967. Doc Severinsen, the band leader, sat with his wife, Emily. Johnny's lawyer and closest friend, Henry Bushkin, was at a nearby table with his then-current love, Mary Hart, the co-anchor of *Entertainment Tonight*.

In Hollywood a young wife is as necessary an accoutrement to celebrity as capped teeth. Thus, except for Janet de Cordova, these were all thirtyish ladies, a generation younger than their husbands.

Looking out on the assemblage, Johnny did not see a particularly urbane gathering. Most of the guests were dressed like the crowd at the Norfolk, Nebraska, country club where Johnny's dad used to play golf. As for Johnny, he may have had his own line of clothing and his name on the best-dressed lists, but he was wearing a blue blazer and gray bell-bottoms, a style that went out of fashion with Nehru jackets and love-ins.

This was an anniversary, after all, an occasion for reflection. At many of the tables there was an undertone of melancholy, regret. Since General Electric had taken over the network two years ago, the whole atmosphere at NBC had changed. At times the place resembled an air-conditioned sweatshop.

Even as the guests ate their Cornish hen and poached salmon, other *Tonight Show* employees, cameramen and technicians, walked the picket line, on strike against NBC. Several men in the room planned to retire early. Whether people blamed GE, the economy, or the decline of the networks, NBC would never be the same. Future evenings like this would be rare indeed.

When dessert was finished and the champagne was being poured, Freddy or Ed could have risen and given a toast to Johnny. But Johnny hated such things, and it was his party. So he stood up, strode quickly across the dance floor, and stood before the microphone.

"I want to thank you for coming," Johnny said as his champagne glass tilted dangerously to the side. If he had been the executive of a small company, he would have cursed himself and vowed to take a lesson in public speaking. "A toast to twenty-five years of us."

An outsider might have thought that Johnny seemed estranged and distant. But these people with whom he worked knew that this was as openly emotional as he became.

Johnny thanked the young woman who had put the evening together. Then he turned to a different subject. "If you look at the back of your chairs, you'll see at each table there's one chair with a star on it. The person who has the chair gets to take the floral arrangement home."

Johnny continued to talk, but people all over the room clambered up and started searching behind their chairs.

When the room finally quieted down, Johnny's thin voice barely carried across the cavernous room. "We're passing around chips for the casino," Johnny said. "So you can gamble if you want, or dance to the band."

Johnny made a second toast as perfunctory as the first; with that, the formal part of the evening was over. He went back and sat down next to Alex. Then he got up abruptly, and with a curt twist of his neck motioned his young bride to follow him. He moved off toward the Windsor Room. He left Alex in the casino and headed off by himself toward a room with the simple appellation "Gentlemen."

Like most celebrities, Johnny hated going to public rest rooms. He had insisted on a private bathroom on *The Tonight Show* years ago. This evening he made it to the row of five gleaming urinals before most of the other guests. Two men sidled up next to him, filling the two empty spots.

"It's a wonderful evening," Johnny said as he looked down at the white enamel.

"Yes, it's a wonderful evening," said the middle-aged gentleman to the left.

"Wonderful evening," said the gentleman to the right. "Simply wonderful."

As Johnny zipped back up, the gentleman on the left turned his head toward him, then looked down at the business at hand and shook his head admiringly. "You sure pee faster than you used to," the man said.

Johnny didn't acknowledge the compliment. He turned and walked out of the men's room, stiffing the attendant who stood with his brace of towels and perfumed scents.

Back in the Windsor Room Alex was at one of the blackjack tables. Johnny sat down beside her. A dealer and three players were already seated at their table. No one else came to join them. No one rubbernecked, and despite subtle glances toward Johnny, the other guests maintained the illusion that he was just another player.

Johnny's youngest son, Cory, didn't even approach his father. Nor did Rick, his middle son. Ed McMahon stood in his impeccably tailored blue suit at the edge of the room. He did not play. He wasn't drinking. He looked as impassive as the rent-a-cops.

Johnny's guests had been given little bags full of play chips marked $500, $100, $25, $5, and $1. The big winners for the evening would be able to exchange the chips for fondue dishes and CD players.

"I don't know how to play blackjack," Alex said, looking at her new husband.

Johnny had played Las Vegas enough to pick up a few pointers about the game. Although he earned $20 million a year, he played for small stakes. He explained to Alex that the secret wasn't to try to hit 21, but to make the dealer lose.

"No, dear, the dealer has a small card there," Johnny said with pedagogical zeal. "You got a five there. Don't draw on a fourteen."

Nonetheless, Alex asked for another card, and proceeded to win the hand. Johnny continued playing conservatively, using his Las Vegas savvy. Twenty minutes later he had gone bust, losing all $2,500 in chips.

Johnny didn't sit watching Alex win hand after hand. He got up and walked over to one of the other tables. He took the cards from the dealer and began a series of card tricks.

Johnny was comfortable when he performed. It was better than chitchat, better by far. He was in control. He spread the cards on the felt table, and in one motion turned them all over, and back again. Then he pulled the four queens from the deck, reinserted them, and shuffled the pack again. One by one, he pulled the queens from the deck. After appropriate oohhing and ahhing, Johnny did a second trick.

"Now, Snooky, I want you to pick a card," Johnny said to Snooky Young, the band's longtime trumpet player. As

Young listened, he moved his body back and forth on the stool. "Remember which it was, in what order."

Snooky Young was not about to screw this up. He methodically counted until he came to the fifth card. A ten of diamonds. He gave the deck back to Johnny, who shuffled it.

"Now what card was it?" he asked the black musician.

"It was the fifth," Snooky said.

Johnny slapped down a three of spades. "There's your card," he said.

A grimace of worry crossed Snooky's face. "No, it was a ten of diamonds."

"You fucked up, Snooky," Johnny said. "You fucked up."

Then he turned to another young man. This time the trick worked. He did a couple more tricks, and left to a polite round of applause.

As Johnny began doing magic at the next table, the dealer whispered to the seated players, "You saw how he did it." It was half a question, half a statement.

"Yeah, of course," said one of the men. "He was dealing from the bottom."

"Yeah . . ." the dealer said, and went on to discuss exactly how Johnny had accomplished his "magic."

Johnny had performed his tricks. But the guests had created the greater illusion. They had let Johnny believe that he had fooled them. Johnny went through life meeting overwhelming deference. His days were full of gentle pleasantries. People laughed at his jokes, even if they weren't always funny. They applauded his magic tricks, even if they had them figured out.

Johnny moved on to a third table, where his son Rick and his date were seated. Rick had been trouble, a lot of trouble. Booze and drugs. Drugs and booze. He was thirty-five years old, and he never had done much with his life. Johnny gave Rick work with his company. He also gave each of his three sons thirty-five thousand dollars a year.

Rick's long page-boy hair had started to turn gray. He was slightly overweight, and he had a somewhat bloated resemblance to his father. Johnny did the same tricks as at the other tables. Doc Severinsen stood watching, applauding and laughing as he did on *The Tonight Show*.

"Now, Rick, I want you to take a certain number of cards out of the deck," Johnny said. "Remember how many. I'll turn my back."

This was Rick's moment. All his life Johnny's second son had hungered for his father's affection and attention. He peeled off five cards, stuffing three of them down the breast of his date, the other two down the dress of the lady to the right.

Johnny turned back. "Now, I'm going to lay the cards down one by one. When I come to the same number of cards that you took out, just remember that card. Don't say anything. Just remember."

With his elegant, manicured hands Johnny began taking the cards from the top of the deck. One card. Two. Three. Four. Five.

"That's it," Rick said proudly. "It was the fifth card."

"No," Johnny said, mildly exasperated. "You weren't supposed to tell me, Rick. That's the whole point."

"Oh, sorry." Rick shrugged.

"We'll do it again," Johnny said, and turned his back to the table. "You understand now. Just don't tell me which one."

This time Rick pulled six cards from the deck, evenly dividing them between the bosoms of the two women.

Johnny turned back and began to lay down the cards. One. Two. Three. Four. Five. Six.

"That's it!" Rick exclaimed triumphantly, as if he had solved a great puzzle. "That's it! Number six."

"No," Johnny said, his voice streaked with disdain. He looked at his son with a coldness that could have turned him into a block of ice. Then, without a word, Johnny whirled and left the table.

Silence. Finally Rick spoke. "It was really complicated,"

he said, his eyes scanning the other players, looking for understanding.

"Yeah," Doc Severinsen said.

Johnny joined Alex again. Then he stood and wandered around the room. He had known some of the people here for a quarter of a century or more. Yet he seemed so alone, so distant.

Kenneth Tynan, the late British writer, compared Johnny to F. Scott Fitzgerald's Jay Gatsby. Tynan wrote, "Gatsby, like Carson, is a Mid-westerner, a self-made millionaire, and a habitual loner, armored against all attempts to invade his emotional privacy."

Johnny also bore a certain resemblance to another great figure in American literature: James Tyrone in Eugene O'Neill's *Long Day's Journey into Night*. As a brilliant young actor, Tyrone had started playing the same popular role over and over again, as Johnny had played his ("That god damned play . . . it ruined me with its promise of an easy fortune. I didn't want to do anything else, and by the time I woke up to the fact I'd become a slave to the damn thing. . . .") Tyrone's wife became a drug addict, and his sons lived in the darkness of his shadow.

But of course Johnny was not doomed, drunken James Tyrone. Nor was he Jay Gatsby. He was Johnny Carson, toast of America, king of the night.

Johnny Carson stood on the garage roof in a clown's costume, looking as if he were about to cry. Johnny was supposed to be funny, but he couldn't get his mouth and words to work together. He gnawed on his tongue and looked down on the folks spread out on the pasture behind the Brennans' house. Mercifully he stepped back from the edge, and ended his first public performance.

Every summer the children put on a circus at Bill Brennan's house. That was just one of the summer activities in Avoca, Iowa, during the early 1930's. The town had only twelve hundred inhabitants, but plenty of adventure for a boy of seven or eight.

Johnny and the other boys played in the cool darkness under the Carsons' front porch. They went fishing on the banks of the East Nishnabotna River, south of the Fred Holtz Bridge, using tree branches for poles and worms for bait. One time before going fishing, Johnny borrowed a nickel from his dad to buy wieners at Blust Meat Market to roast, so it wouldn't matter whether they caught any fish or not.

Each summer the Conroy Brothers Show came to the fairgrounds, a real circus with ponies and trick mules and dogs and goats and aerial acts, and—best of all—free tickets passed out by the merchants along Main Street. The air show visited Avoca one year too, with tickets for a penny.

And of course there was the Fourth of July, the biggest holiday of all, with fireworks and picnics and one year a big boxing show, with a thousand people cheering the fighters on. Then, in August, came the county fair, complete with a rodeo and a four-piece Indian band.

Even if nothing else was happening at the fairgrounds, the swimming pool was there. Almost as long as a football field and far wider than one, the Avoca pool was one of the largest in Iowa. Season tickets for children were $1.25, and on those sweltering days of August, Johnny and the rest of the kids lived in the pool.

Johnny was a scrawny, taciturn boy with inquisitive hazel eyes. His ears stuck out like antennae from the side of his long head. He had his father's lanky build, his mother's narrowly set eyes, pointed chin, and nose.

Johnny's father, Homer L. "Kit" Carson, was local manager of Iowa and Nebraska Light and Power. On long summer evenings Johnny would go down to the ball field and watch his dad lead the Light and Power team in the "kitten" softball league. In June 1932, when Johnny was seven, his dad's team defeated Walnut 5 to 3. " 'Kit' has a 'sneak' ball that looks good, but is bad," noted the *Avoca Herald*. "He keeps it about six inches above the ground, and sneaked over a strike because the umpire does not know whether it is knee high or not, and 'Kit' has a sneaking idea it is a strike and occasionally sneaks one over on the batter."

Johnny watched his dad on the tennis court too. In the summer of 1933 Kit played Edwin Doll for the town championship. Doll had just graduated from high school, and Kit was spotting Doll about fifteen years in age. On that sweltering afternoon the smart money would have been on youthful stamina over experience. Johnny and his little brother Dick shagged balls, but only for their dad. As they scurried back and forth, young Doll chased after his own balls. Before he realized quite what had happened, Doll was walking off the court the loser, and the three Carsons were walking home triumphant.

* * *

Home was a large two-story white frame house on the corner at 725 Cherry Street. Johnny's mother, Ruth E. Carson, was a proper lady with a dramatic flair, and she ran her house as if she were the captain of a warship. She loved Johnny and his little brother, Richard, but she loved their older sister, Catherine, more. Mrs. Carson had wanted to have more daughters, and she coddled Catherine.

When Kit and the boys returned from a softball game, Ruth might put in a few moments of what the neighbors called "henpecking." She was as much the manager of this world as Kit was of Light and Power.

"The father was a wonderful guy," remembers Bill Brennan, who is two years older than Johnny. "He was conservative. The mother, Ruth, was more the extrovert. She was very good as a contortionist. There were parties where she would bend over and do a few tricks. It was good-natured fun. Sometimes my mother said that Kit would be fussed, mildly embarrassed at something Ruth would say. I think John's theatrical stuff comes from the mother's side."

The Carsons are an old American family, with roots in England and Ireland. Genealogists have traced the Carson ancestors as far back as 1521. In that year Thomas Kellogg was born in the English village of Debdon, Essex. A century later Daniel and Bridget Kellogg traveled to the American colonies and settled in Connecticut. Their offspring moved westward, drawn by hopes for a better life, for land and money. They settled in towns and countryside in Indiana and Nebraska.

In Nebraska Emiline Kellogg married Kit's grandfather, Marshall Carson (born c. 1833). Marshall's ancestors remain unknown, but he had more adventurous blood than most of the Kellogg clan. He and his bride traveled to the rude frontier of western Nebraska, where he staked a barren gold claim.

Marshall eventually settled in Logan, Iowa. There, Johnny's father was born in 1899. After a stint in the service during World War I, Kit took an uncle's advice and entered the University of Nebraska to study dentistry. After a year he left to join a crew stringing up electric transmission lines. This was a man's work, tough and dangerous. Among these rough-hewn, rowdy men, Kit was a rarity. He was soon called down from the lines to a managerial position. As lean and sparing in words as in appearance, he was a fair man with the workers and the clerical staff.

Ruth Hook, the woman Carson met and married in 1922, was born in Bedford, Iowa, in 1901. Better educated than her husband, she had attended Simpson College in Indianola, a rare feat for a woman of her generation. Originally Irish, the Hooks were also an old American family, arriving in America from London in 1668 and settling in Maryland.

If there are no esteemed explorers, no legendary storytellers, no men and women of historic vision in the Carson and Hook clans, there are also no horse thieves or murderers. Johnny's father was not related to Kit Carson, the legendary western hero, but the nickname stuck to him.

The Carson family was full of hardworking tillers of the land. Legend had it that Mrs. Carson was related to Captain James Hook, who may have served with George Washington at Valley Forge. Hook lost a slice of his ear to an assailant's knife; the good captain, a man of the Old Testament, proceeded to bite off his adversary's ear. Another ancestor, Judge James Hardy, a quixotic Iowa jurist, might well have found that Captain Hook had meted out appropriate justice.

Though the Carsons were not regular churchgoers, Johnny was nominally a Methodist. The Carsons were not active in civic groups, nor were they especially social. They minded their own business, and in the value system of Avoca, that was a high virtue.

When outsiders see the small towns and large farms of the Great Plains, they assume that the roots of the people are as deep as the wells. The Carsons, though, were a transient family, moving from place to place as Kit was transferred from one executive position to another. Although his earliest memories are of Avoca, John William Carson was born seventy miles away in Corning, Iowa, a town of about eighteen hundred people, on October 23, 1925. In Corning the Carsons lived in an upstairs apartment before renting a tiny square house on Main Street.

Johnny was scarcely a toddler before the Carsons were off again, to Clarinda, forty miles to the southeast, and then to Red Oak, thirty miles to the northwest. These towns had their broad main streets where the farmers came on Wednesdays and Saturdays. Each had its courthouse, and they were all stops on the railroad line. And they had their proud boosters.

John Wayne was born in Winterset, another southwest Iowa town. This was truly John Wayne country, a land of flag-waving, God-fearing, churchgoing, hardworking, provincial, patriotic people. They were at times intolerant of those of a different hue or culture, but their locale had been a stop on the Underground Railroad. They were conservative, but they were also a spawning ground for the militant farmer movements; indeed, today Corning is the headquarters of the National Farmers Organization. They were at times disdainful of the poor, but they could be monumentally generous toward those in need, stricken down by illness, age, or bad luck.

As a people, they are extraordinarily reticent, secretive even, about personal matters. If decency and good manners are part of this reticence, a shade of hypocrisy is there too. Appearance is the truth that matters. A man bought his liquor in the next town, and sinned with the shades down. Memory was supposed to be a sieve that drained out all that was petty and small, leaving only a few sweet anecdotes. One talked of the present as of the past, as if the world were made of pleasantries. Inquisitiveness was rudeness.

Few people in these towns remember the Carsons. Mabel Gaskill, who baby-sat for Johnny in Corning when he was a year and five months old, recalls him only as a "cute little kid," the parents as "lovely people." Helen Andrews, a neighbor, recollects only where they lived, and where they came from. Jim Logan, whose mother played bridge with Ruth Carson in Red Oak, recalls nothing either.

Johnny's parents were born and bred among these people, and their eldest son shared many of their traits. To learn the truth about a person, one did not ask baldly for the facts. As often as not, humor was the vehicle of truth. Even today, if one sits in the coffee shops or the American Legion halls, one hears a sly, subtle humor. Humor is a whole different medium of communication. When a man leaves the table, he is sometimes knifed in the back, not by a steely blade but by barbs that are just as sharp and just as destructive of his reputation.

Johnny started kindergarten in Red Oak, where his father was the local superintendent of the Iowa and Nebraska Power Company. He had been in school only a month when the family moved to Avoca, forty-five miles to the north.

Kit Carson was not only a leading citizen, he was the manager of a company whose product was universally wanted, a product that dramatically changed the life of the people of Avoca and the countryside. Electricity and gas brought magical possibilities to the farmer: food that did not spoil, irons that did not have to be stoked with coals, light that was almost as bright as day, and steady heat in the winter. Kit Carson wasn't like the banker, or the storekeeper, whose presence reminded people of debts and obligations and hungry stomachs.

The Carsons lived on the good side of town, and felt little of the Depression. Most others in Avoca and elsewhere were not so fortunate, and the more affluent townspeople did what they could to help. In the winter of 1932 they sent a railroad car of hay to the people of Armour, South Dakota, for their stock, and received a letter back telling of "women and children almost starving." Out in the countryside the banks foreclosed on farm after farm. In May 1933 about a hundred farmers went to the courthouse in Le Mars, to accost the judge who had signed many of the foreclosure notices. They grabbed Judge C. C. Bradley from the bench and took him out into the countryside to see their lands. They covered him with axle grease and said that they would hang him, and then they choked him until he fainted.

If a boy had seen that, or heard his father tell such tales, he would remember. But Johnny has no such tales to tell. His boyhood friends Bill Brennan and Marion Weinmann didn't suffer, either, during the Great Depression. But they can talk for hours of those who did.

Johnny's most vividly recalled memory of Avoca is the day he invited Peggy Leach to the movies. He was only eight, and the Carsons thought that their son was a bit precocious. "Mrs. Carson telephoned and said Johnny was going to ask Peggy on a date," remembers Mrs. Leach, who lives in the same house on Main Street in Avoca as she did half a century ago when Johnny came to call. "She said, 'We're not going to make anything of it.' "

Johnny remembers that he ran home from the theater leaving Peggy stranded. The object of Johnny's affection has a different memory. "I'm sure he stayed for the movies," says Peggy Leach Ebles. "Catherine, his sister, went with us. I remember the afternoon very plainly. He had on a black turtleneck sweater and knickers. I don't remember a thing about his running away."

Johnny had no opportunity to pursue his friendship with Peggy Leach. Soon afterward, the Carsons left Avoca. "It was third grade, and we had a going-away party in the room," says Peggy Leach Ebles. "He was sitting on one of those old-fashioned desks."

The departure of Johnny's father was notable enough to merit an article on the front page of the *Avoca Herald*: "H.L. 'Kit' Carson who has been the manager of the local office for the Iowa-Nebraska Electric Light and Power Company has been given the management of the company's office in Norfolk, Nebraska. This is a very nice promotion for Mr. Carson, and goes to prove where a young man is willing to work and give good honest service to his employer, there is a better opportunity ahead for him. Mr. Carson came to Avoca about three years ago. . . . He has served his com-

pany well. Norfolk is one of the largest towns in which the
Iowa-Nebraska Electric Light and Power Company is serving the people. It is considered one of their best towns and
the change from Avoca to Norfolk means much to Mr.
Carson.''

No moving van carried the Carsons' possessions to Nebraska. Instead, Orvie Fisher hosed out one of the Jacobson
Brothers' stock trucks. "We washed it out as clean as we
could get it," Fisher says. "We had moving pads and we
tarped it.''

On an October day in 1933, the Carson family drove due
westward. The farmers had harvested the land, and the barns
and silos were heavy with bounty. Nebraska is one of the
most rural states in America, and the Carsons saw only a
few small towns. The state had only two cities with pop-
ulations over twenty-five thousand, Omaha and Lincoln.

As the car approached the outskirts of Norfolk, the family
was entering what to them was a big city. With a population
of slightly over ten thousand, Norfolk was the sixth-largest
city in the state. The town wasn't simply a stop on the rail
line, it was a depot for three railroads: the Chicago, St.
Paul, Minneapolis & Omaha; the Northwestern; and the
Union Pacific.

Norfolk was set amid fertile farmland in the Elkhorn River
Valley. To the east and south stood other good-sized towns,
but westward lay hundreds of miles of rolling grasslands,
prairie land without a major town.

Farmers and ranchers and village merchants drove scores
of miles to trade and talk in Norfolk. The *Norfolk Daily
News* billed itself as "the best country daily in America."
The thousand-seat Granada Theater was a secular temple
with ornate fixtures and decorations. WJAG was one of the
first radio stations in the country, beaming out across the
plains with a thousand watts of power. The town even had
a professional baseball team, the Norfolk Elks, of the Nebraska State League.

Kit Carson drove down Norfolk Avenue to the Norfolk

Hotel, the finest structure in town—depot for such bus companies as the Corn Belt, the Arrow Stage Lines, and the Yellow Diamond, and nightly stop for traveling salesmen and visiting dignitaries. The Carson family was put into rooms on the top floor of the four-story brick building.

Years later Johnny remembered how he had looked down and thought that he had never seen such a city. This Main Street was twice as wide as Avoca's, with scores of cars parked perpendicular to the curb. He finally pulled back from the window and got ready for bed. He tried to sleep, but he lay awake for hours.

The next morning Mrs. Carson marched eight-year-old Johnny down to the Grant Elementary School and entered him in the third grade.

As they had in Avoca, the Carsons lived on the good side of town, in a house at 306 S. Sixteenth Street. Norfolk was settled in part by Germans, and the Carson dwelling had the stout structure that a provincial *Bürgermeister* would have approved. It was a two-story, three-bedroom frame house, dwarfed by the elm trees along the avenue. The home even had that midwestern luxury a sleeping porch. Johnny and Dick shared a room together, while their sister, Catherine, had her own bedroom.

Norfolk, founded in 1866, was only a generation beyond the frontier. The oldest house in Norfolk, built in 1868 or 1869, sat on a lot a few blocks from the Carsons' home. The Wild West lived in Norfolk in the person of Dr. Richard Tanner, the famous "Diamond Dick" of dime novels. Dr. Tanner drove his Model-T down Norfolk Avenue and told tales of frontier shoot-outs. Another citizen, Fred Patzel, brought fame to his hometown when he won the 1926 national hog-calling championship. His prize-winning call was to have been broadcast over WJAG. Alas, when Patzel let out his historic holler, he knocked the radio station off the air.

WJAG considered itself the voice of the farmer, and the farmer was particularly interested in two things: weather and crop prices. This was a land of such extremes in climate as to make a Quaker swear. In summer you baked, and in winter you froze, and in spring you worried about the floods. Old-timers could remember a plague of grasshoppers, and the high-water mark from the flood of 1912 still stood on many buildings in downtown Norfolk.

The Nebraska climate was a mark of regional pride, the stuff of tall tales. But nobody joked about the Dirty Thirties. For half a decade Nebraska had been cursed by drought or near-drought. In 1934 only 14.31 inches of rain fell on the state, the least since 1864. The rich soil was turning to powder and dust, blowing in great dark clouds across the prairie. With the crash of 1929, wheat that had brought sixty-seven cents a bushel now brought only twenty-eight cents, corn once worth a dollar a bushel now sold for eight cents.

This was not the Carsons' world though, and soon Johnny was as comfortable in Norfolk as he had been in Avoca. He did his Popeye imitation and made the kids laugh. He and his friends went to the YMCA, where Chief Moore, the longtime head of the Y, led the boys in sports and games. Johnny was a scrawny, feisty lad, whose enthusiasm did not quite overcome his lack of prowess.

In the summers Johnny went camping by Black Bridge and the Elkhorn River. The river was two miles from town, and the boys hooked wagons to the back of their bicycles and pedaled out there to stay for two or three days at a time. They hung on the railroad bridge when the trains came by. They fished for supper, went skinny-dipping, built camp-fires, and watched the stars in the brilliant summer sky.

On Sunday evenings Johnny spread himself out on the floor in the living room in front of the console radio to listen to *The Jack Benny Show*. Monday morning he came into the schoolyard. While the other kids talked about one half-remembered joke or another, Johnny went through the whole routine, joke by joke.

"There comes a time or a moment when you know in which direction you're going to go," Johnny reflected in a 1979 *Rolling Stone* interview by Timothy White. "I know it happened to me when I was quite young. I think it's when you find out that you can get in front of an audience and be in control. I think that probably happened in grade school, 5th or 6th grade, where I could get attention by being different, by getting up in front of an audience or even a group of kids and calling the attention to myself by what I did or said or how I acted. And I said, 'Hey, I like that feeling.'

"When I was a kid, I was shy. And I think I did that because it was a device to get attention. And to get that reaction is a strange feeling. It is a high that I don't think you can get from drugs. I don't think you could get it from anything else. The mind starts to do things that you didn't even realize it could do. I suppose it's the manipulation. I suppose it's the sense of power, the center of attention and the me-ism. And performers have to have that. That's one of the things that goes against the grain of being brought up that you should be modest; you should be humble, you shouldn't draw attention to yourself. Well, to be an entertainer you gotta be a little gutsy, a little egotistical, so you have to pull back sometimes when people say, 'Well, he's stuck-up.' Stuck-up is only another word for self-conscious. You aren't stuck-up. You are aloof because you aren't very comfortable so you put up this barrier."

The fraternity of boyhood has its own rude democracy, of the leaders and the led. Johnny was never the most popular, never the boy chosen first for teams and games. He put people down. Even that first year he had called out on the playground, "Don't pick Gertrude, she walks like a duck." By third-grade standards, Johnny's remark was witty enough, a comment that stuck to one, a badge of humiliation, a remark that was still painfully remembered half a century later.

A neighbor across the street from the Carsons considered Johnny "the orneriest kid in the neighborhood." Another neighbor, Mrs. Stella McNeely, remembered him as "a little snip, just a bully. John Carson used to be in my living room a lot, and he pushed my boys around. They were younger, so he could get by with it. They didn't mind. But I did.

And I still have a hole in my front window from his BB gun.''

Although it was little solace to Mrs. McNeely, Johnny aimed his BB gun closer to home as well. "We were very big on BB guns," recalls his brother, Dick. "One Christmas, Johnny and I took our BB guns and shot all the balls off the Christmas tree.''

For a mother who doted on her pretty daughter, Johnny and Dick were a boyish plague. One year Johnny raised a pair of white rats, who took seriously the biblical injunction to go forth and multiply. Soon there were twenty rats, then fifty, finally a hundred, until Mrs. Carson declared a moratorium. Another time Mrs. Carson wallpapered the living room. A couple of weeks later Johnny threw a large, juicy grapefruit at his brother. Dick ducked, and the grapefruit splattered down the wall and fireplace, ruining the wallpaper.

Johnny's worst trouble as a boy was an incident unknown to his parents. "I hooked a ring from a dime store," he recalled years later. "You know, all kids shoplift something at some time or other. The guy caught me and he threatened to take me over to my father, but he didn't. He just bawled me out and took the ring back, and I never tried it again.''

Johnny did not spend his days tormenting the young, destroying wallpaper, peppering the town with BB pellets. When Alan Landers entered junior high school, Johnny watched out for the younger boy. "He picked me up and took me to school with him and showed me around," Dr. Landers remembers. "That was one nice thing.''

Johnny had a certain physical courage as well. "I was walking home with Johnny from elementary school," recalls James Cochran. "This bigger boy, Dick Fowler, jumped out from behind the bushes and said he was going to whip me. I was bigger than John, but he stepped in front of me and said, 'No, you aren't going to touch him.' He kept me from getting my ass whipped.''

Johnny no longer wore jeans with uneven cuffs, and ragged sneakers. He was neat, almost meticulous, in appearance. "I sat in front of him in grade school," says Lorraine Beckenhauer Gipe. "He was so fastidious. I used to comb my hair. It bothered him. He asked me to stop it."

Johnny was becoming a handsome young man, suffering few blemishes of face and manner. His ears no longer seemed to stick out. He carefully brushed his brown hair back. His oval eyes were highlighted by long eyelashes. He was still without an ounce of fat on his frame.

As Johnny entered adolescence, he sought adventures greater than bicycling out to Black Bridge. One Sunday when he was thirteen, he and two other boys sat smoking cigarettes in a friend's living room. The three were puffing away when they heard a horrid sound: an automobile pulling into the driveway. Johnny and the second youth scurried out the front door at the precise moment that the parents entered through the back door. "I was trying to wave the smoke away, and my parents came in and the room is full of smoke," said the other participant. "They were mad at me. One of the things they said was, 'Don't hang out around with that Carson. He's no good, nothing good is ever going to come from him.' Probably he was the instigator, but I was a willing collaborator. We were all willing."

Johnny had an aura of unpredictability. Bill Bridge, who was Dick Carson's close friend, puts it somewhat differently: "There's a mean streak in John."

Johnny was a boy with many friends but with no best friend. "I have a feeling that he just had goals and dreams that he probably never shared with anybody," said Larry Sanford, one of his friends. "He never got that close to people. I don't know who is close enough to have known all his thoughts and dreams and drives."

At the age of twelve, Johnny was playing at the McNeelys' house. Ten-year-old Phil McNeely had come back from visiting a cousin in Omaha, bringing with him a deck of marked cards and a catalog from a magician's supply house. Johnny was mesmerized.

"It showed exactly how [to do tricks] with a kit of stuff

from some mail order magic house in Chicago,'' Johnny remembered. "So I sent for it. I started making the things I needed and it was fascinating. I spent hours at it. Magic became my all-consuming interest.''

Children often dabble with magic, mastering a few tricks to be paraded out before acquiescent guests by adoring parents. Johnny's interest went far beyond that. He practiced hours on end, to the complete disregard of other childhood avocations. "He could be a pest,'' his mother remembered. "He was always going around, asking, 'How does this look?' 'Did you see that?' It didn't make any difference if he was interrupting. It seemed like he was always at your elbow with a trick.''

Johnny needed a stage name. Of course, there already was the Great Houdini, that master of a thousand escapes. And a magician called "Mortoni'' had performed in Norfolk. Johnny would be the Great Carsoni. He had a different persona now, an exotic identity, a whiff of the Orient, a touch of Italy. He sent away for a fifteen-dollar ventriloquism course. That too was magic. If he could project his voice, he could become someone else.

For Christmas Mrs. Carson gave her eldest son a magician's table with a black velvet cloth on which she had embroidered a name in big Oriental-looking letters on the velvet: THE GREAT CARSONI. Johnny had never "seen anything more beautiful.''

A magician's success depends in part on mechanical perfection, on movements and techniques flawlessly executed. Johnny went nowhere without his cards. "Take a card, take a card,'' became his signature greeting, a phrase that years afterward would be a family joke.

When the Carsons visited potential colleges for Catherine, they left Johnny standing in front of a full-length mirror practicing his tricks. When they returned a few days later, they walked in the door and there stood Johnny, in front of the mirror.

"Mother, do you suppose he's been right there all this time?'' Catherine asked.

As he performed for shanghaied audiences of friends and family, he developed his own little patter. A few years before, he had stood tongue-tied on Bill Brennan's roof, unable to play the clown. But it was not that hard for Johnny to be funny when his chatter was only a distraction, a sleight of words to distract the audience from his sleight of hand.

This element of humor required a stage presence and a confidence beyond that of most amateur magicians. Johnny did the classic trick where he cracked a raw egg in his top hat, and—Abracadabra!—pulled a cake from the hat. Only the Great Carsoni turned over the hat and a messy glut of broken egg fell on the stage.

"Johnny had excellent audience control even at that age," recalls James Cochran. "He was a darn good magician. But that trick caused him to spend all he got just to clean the hat. Whenever he got a spare dollar, he would buy a new trick."

For an amateur performer, all Norfolk was a stage. Of course, the townspeople listened to *Fibber McGee and Molly* or *Amos 'n' Andy* on the radio. But they didn't sit six hours a day in front of the television. To a remarkable extent they made their own entertainment. They didn't catch the Atlanta Braves or the Chicago Cubs on cable; they went out to the ballpark to watch the Elks.

The Great Carsoni performed frequently. Johnny did his tricks before his mother's bridge club. The parishioners enjoyed the efforts of the Great Carsoni at the Methodist Church socials. He got up on the pool table at a friend's house and did his act. Johnny put on shows in his basement. The kids came and paid their pennies and thought their money well spent.

"I can't say I ever *wanted* to become an entertainer," says Johnny. "I already *was* one, sort of—around our house, at school, doing my magic tricks, throwing my voice and doing the Popeye impersonations. People thought I was funny; so I kind of took entertaining for granted. . . . It was inevitable that I'd start giving little performances."

At the age of fourteen, Johnny made his professional

debut at the Rotary Club. He wore a black silk shirt on the back of which his mother had sewn a white rabbit. He was paid three dollars. He would have had to mow half the lawns on T Street for that amount.

All the Carsons understood the value of the holy dollar. Kit instilled in his children a belief that frugality was next to godliness. Years later Johnny's grandfather, Christopher M. Carson, noted approvingly that his grandson "used to keep track of every dime he made." That was something of an exaggeration, but Johnny was a boy who worked and saved, delivering furniture, ushering at the Granada Theater, and putting on his magic act.

The Carson family lived well. In 1937 Kit bought Johnny a top-of-the line Schwinn bike for $38.75 minus $10.00 credit for an old bike. Many farm families around Norfolk would have been glad to have earned that much cash in a month. Kit even had a movie camera to take pictures of the family, an unthinkable extravagance for most families in the late 1930's.

The Carsons were highly respected in Norfolk, and they seemed to have all the virtues of their society: sobriety, discipline, responsibility, caring. They were not a family that wasted valentines of affection on each other. "Nobody in our family ever says what they really think or feel to anyone else," Dick Carson has said.

Mrs. Carson was the emotional center of the family. "His mother was very domineering, very sarcastic," says Jody Wolcott Carson, who became Johnny's first wife. "I heard stories that she broke a whole set of dishes on the kitchen wall. She was the real force in the family, the real matriarch."

Johnny did not talk to his mother and father the way some sons did. For the Carsons, what was left unsaid was more important than the words spoken. Ruth Carson was not a woman who praised her sons. No matter what they did, no matter how great their achievements, she met them usually with silence, as if they had somehow fallen short. Her daughter, Catherine, had given her the first and greatest joy of motherhood, and Johnny and Dick never quite measured up.

At times Ruth Carson seemed to want to put her eldest son down, to make Johnny feel insignificant and unworthy. To Johnny, his mother *was* womanhood, and as he entered adolescence, it would be no wonder if he found it difficult to treat women with caring and trust.

Unlike many firstborn sons, Johnny did not have a mother who made him feel special. He was hungry for approval. In his magic shows and public antics, Johnny received an open affection and applause that he did not receive at home.

Johnny had moments of great emotional turmoil. "He told me of this nightmare he had ever since he was a little boy," Jody Carson says. "There was this white line down the middle of this road. He had to keep following it forever, faster and faster and faster. That made him wake up screaming. It terrified him. His folks would put him in a cold bathtub of water when he had the nightmares. But once you get on that white line, you have to keep going."

"John was kind of a loner," says Charles Howser, a school-mate and now a Norfolk mortician. "He was always funny. He kind of made his own space. He was all by himself even when he was with the guys. You'd have six people in a group walking into school and he'd be by himself. Yet in school he liked to be the center of attention."

Johnny's personality was a brew of shyness and cocki-ness. He drew out of himself, to act upon the world. He knew what he could get away with, how far he could push. In class he projected his voice to the far corners of the classroom, destroying the decorum of learning in a moment. He was the prankster, and it took a shrewd adult to catch him at his act. When his mother walloped him, he could make her laugh and soften the blows. With girls he knew that gentle humor was sweeter than perfumed words.

Johnny was always testing himself, testing the world, playing his tricks and then retreating back into himself. One time Johnny and a friend were paid twenty-five cents an hour to paint the light poles in Norfolk green. "We had paint left over," Johnny remembers, "and we painted a number of other things, among them a car."

In chemistry class Johnny won the nickname the Carbide Kid, and not for any devotion to organic chemistry. He created a concoction of potassium carbide and water. When the teacher left the room, Johnny set the brew on top of a Bunsen burner, and filled the laboratory with soot. On another occasion he created a more volatile mix of chemicals. "He somehow put hydrogen sulfide into the school's ventilating system," John Busch, a friend and classmate, recalls. "That cleared out the school in a hurry." The smell was so bad that the students were given the rest of the day off.

Johnny considered that his most notable prank. Not only was it audacious, but he and Busch were never found out. Time and again in high school Johnny pulled off his capers, sticking his finger into the face of propriety, then running away undetected.

Unlike Jack Benny and most of the other comedians Johnny listened to on the radio, his humor did not grow out of the wellspring of poverty. He was not laughing where he might easily have cried. He was not attempting to forget a childhood in the ghettos of Brooklyn, or Philadelphia, or a journey in steerage from Dublin. Nor was he the witty raconteur of the country-club set.

Johnny's humor was full of guile and cunning, the humor of a young man not willing to accept the decorum and rituals of society. It was a way, too, of seeing life, of confronting truths that he could not deal with directly. He turned his classmates into an audience, laughing at the more inept or credulous teachers. He always stopped an inch from the precipice. With Miss Jennie Walker, the mathematics teacher and a stern disciplinarian, he couldn't risk throwing his voice. He had to settle for a witticism or two. One day Miss Walker drew a baseball diamond on the blackboard for a geometrical problem.

"John?" she asked.

"Miss Walker," he replied, "how can I solve the problem when I don't know what teams are playing?"

Miss Walker didn't mind Johnny's occasional jokes. "He'd always do everything he could, but he always knew when it was enough," she says. "He wasn't a bother."

Johnny's act was not without its detractors. "Johnny was a pain in the ass," says Dale Raasch, a classmate. "He would disrupt everything by practicing his ventriloquism in class. He was practicing magic too, always striving for attention, a pain in the ass."

Raasch was one of only a few farm boys at Norfolk High School. "When we came to town to join these people, maybe Johnny thought we smelled like cow shit, and maybe we weren't so sophisticated," says Raasch in a voice still tinged with bitterness. "So he knew me, but only when he needed like to have me vote for him for a cheerleader or something. This town is quite cliquish, and he was considered part of the upper echelon."

The rites of passage at Norfolk High were simple enough: booze and cars and sex were the holy trilogy, sometimes together and sometimes alone.

When Johnny was about fourteen, he and his buddies rolled the Carsons' automobile out of the driveway and took it for joyrides. "His dad had a '39 Chrysler and my dad had a '41 Chrysler," recalls Duane Demaree, a friend and schoolmate. "We'd have a bunch of kids and we'd have our cars. A time or two we got out on Highway 275 and we'd see who could beat whom. I'd win the first mile, and since his car had overdrive, he won the last mile."

In Norfolk the chosen arena for fame and heroism was not the back-country roads or amateur theatricals but the athletic field, and the favorite sport was football. Johnny didn't have too much interest in sports. In physical-education class, his instructor, Fred Egley, considered him an "average boy." Once Egley bawled out Johnny and Harold Schultz for malingering in the locker room, where Johnny was showing off with card tricks.

As a senior, Johnny attempted the most uncharacteristic act of his high school career. He went out for the football team. For three years he had watched the team from the stands, and he had decided to seek a modicum of glory before graduating. "The first time I ran with the ball and got tackled, the next thing I remember is the coach looking down in my face and asking if I was all right," Johnny remembers. "He recommended that I give my full extra-curricular time to other activities."

According to Mrs. Carson, Johnny bet a friend five dollars that he would make the team. "He even bought some football shoes," she recalled. "But he came home after about the second practice and decided that he was getting his hands stepped on too much. He couldn't risk injuring those hands because of the magic tricks. The magic was more important. But, oh, how he hated paying off that five-dollar bet."

Johnny was more successful at the sexual challenges of adolescence. In Norfolk there were the good girls and the bad girls. The bad girls were usually dealt what were considered bad cards: plainness, naiveté, an undue desire to please. If they were dealt a decent hand, they didn't understand the nature of the game: to play was to lose.

Johnny and his buddies thought that sex was something you got by tricking or fooling or taking advantage. "As in all small towns there are certain 'nice' girls, girls that you marry—and girls that you do not," said Johnny. "Well, there was this girl, I'll call her Francine, and Francine, well 'put out'—at least that's what was going around. I finally got up enough nerve to ask her out, she said yes, and you can imagine my excitement . . . Mount Vesuvius! But then I had to overcome a problem—protection. I went up to the drugstore counter and the druggist yells, 'Well, John, what can I do for you?' Luckily then he saw that I had Francine waiting outside in the car and he knowingly handed over the goods. I remember I had, as we used to put it, a 'swell' time."

Johnny and his buddies did not "date" the bad girls. They screwed them. Then they told their buddies about it.

"One of our friends fixed Johnny up with his girlfriend's cousin," recalled Bob Hall, a schoolmate. "He said he took her home after school, and he realized, 'Oh, my God, I've got to get a condom.' When he got back with the condom, good God, every blind in the house was pulled. It was about five o'clock in the afternoon. He was always funny, telling about it, always working his routine."

Johnny had his nice girl too. Her name was Mary Jane "Janie" Beckenhauer, and she was two years younger than he was. She was one of the prettiest girls, pert, well-dressed, the perfect date for the prom or the football game. "It was a high school romance," Mary Jane Beckenhauer Bentley remembers. "He was so good a dancer that I couldn't keep up with him on the dance floor. That was back when the jitterbug was big, and Hi-Y dances were something everyone wanted to go to. I used to go to those dances with him, and sometimes to the movie. Actually John went out with girls fairly regularly. He wasn't a sit-at-home. But he was very quiet, not at all forward. I went with him a long, long time before he kissed me."

Johnny acted totally different toward Janie than toward "Francine." Nor did she see the brash, joke-cracking young man that his male friends knew. Johnny cared for Janie, and there were those who thought that one day they would marry.

Even Janie was not exempt from Johnny's pranks. One summer Johnny's dad hired his son and his buddy, James Cochran, to work for the power company. "John and I are digging this ditch," remembers Cochran. "It's pretty muddy. And along comes Janie, a very fair-haired, pretty little girl. She always looked like she had just stepped out of heaven. She had a new doggy, a white dog. And here she comes, with her new dog. She turned her head, and John picked the dog up and stuck it in the middle of the mud hole. When she turned around, there was her dog covered with mud. And I don't think yet she knows how the dog got there."

* * *

On December 7, 1941, the day the Japanese bombed Pearl Harbor, Johnny was working as an usher at the Granada Theater. The Bob Hope film *Nothing but the Truth* was playing.

Until then, Norfolk had been largely isolated from the world. Now, in the *Norfolk Daily News* Johnny read harrowing accounts of soldiers who had recently been schoolmates. One young man had survived the sinking of the USS *Northampton* in the Pacific. Another local GI was a hero of the Battle of Guadalcanal. As Johnny walked the streets of Norfolk, he saw soldiers on leave and navy fliers taking courses in ground and flight instruction at the junior college.

The high school students helped the war effort by putting on a scrap-metal drive. Johnny and his friends descended on peaceful Norfolk, ravaging neighborhoods for every last bit of metal. "Johnny was the instigator for our class," recalls John Busch. "Somewhere, somehow, he got hold of an old Model-T flatbed truck. We went all over town collecting scrap iron. Johnny never told us where he found this truck. To this day, I still don't know."

The Great Carsoni was full of magic. "One night John couldn't collect a crew," says Chuck Howser. "So he went out alone, and in the morning, there in the parking lot of Norfolk High was a big hayrick. You know how big a hayrick is? It takes a tractor to move it. How John got that thing to the school parking lot no one knows and he never did tell, but later that day a very mad farmer showed up and hauled it away."

Johnny and his friends laughed for weeks. But the lady who found her fence missing, and the farmer who had to waste half a day retrieving his equipment, didn't find it very funny.

In his high school years Johnny had managed to create an identity for himself as a performer—as a magician and as a comedian who used humor to gain attention. If he mocked the society around him, he understood the parameters of the permissible. He was never kicked out of class, never sent up to the principal's office.

As graduation approached, Johnny took honors for his humor, if for nothing else. He graduated 54th in a class of 141. He was a "B" student, not good enough to be one of the twenty seniors named to the National Honor Society. He didn't win the Good Citizen Award or any scholarships, either. But on that day when the honors were given out, he put on his magic act and, along with Larry Sanford, read a funny radio skit titled "Portia Faces Death."

Johnny was the class historian, and in the school yearbook he plied his adolescent wit: "I, John Carson, being of sound mind and body (this statement is likely to be challenged by my draft board and the high school faculty), deem it advisable to give you the lowlights of 1942 and 1943. I can visualize 20 years from now when you sit by the radio (listening to Roosevelt) with the old 1943 Milestone in your trembling hands, and as you glance over these remembrances, you will say to your son—'I wish I could get hold of that #?$))&/ Milestone Staff.' And then your little son will look at the Milestone and say meekly—'Boy does this stink.' Be that as it may, I have hereunto set my hand to the task of giving you a month by month, drip by drip account of Norfolk High School activity during the year. If you like this account, tell my friends (my friends include my mother and others who have asked that their names be withheld)."

When the yearbooks arrived and Johnny saw his first published humor, he took the book around to be signed by students and teachers. He gave the book to Miss Walker. She had her difficulties with Johnny's jokes in class, but she looked kindly on him. "You have the ability to make people laugh," she wrote. "You will go far in the entertainment world."

Larry Sanford shared similar sentiments. "John, if you don't get killed in the war," predicted his classmate, "you'll be a hell of an entertainer some day."

THREE

Johnny had a few months before entering the navy, and in the summer of 1943 he hitchhiked to California. After seeing what a uniform could do, he went to an Army-Navy store and purchased a navy air-cadet uniform. Johnny was a shy, small-town boy, but in a uniform he became another person. He was no longer seventeen-year-old Johnny Carson from Norfolk, Nebraska. He was a handsome future aviator, entitled to all the perks. He even danced with Marlene Dietrich at the Stage Door Canteen in Hollywood, a fantasy of GIs from North Africa to the South Pacific.

Johnny went down to San Diego to watch Orson Welles, the legendary director, perform a magic show. He had *become* Johnny Carson, navy air cadet. He didn't lurk in the corners of the auditorium. He volunteered to be sawed in half, and walked up to the stage.

That evening two MPs asked Johnny for identification, and when he had none, he was charged with impersonating a member of the armed forces. He had chosen a uniform to which he would soon be entitled, and he was let off after paying fifty dollars' bail.

Johnny enlisted to become a pilot, but the navy shipped him instead to the midshipmen's school at Columbia University in New York City for naval-reserve officers' training. From there he was transferred to Millsaps College in Jackson, Mississippi, where he spent the academic year, earning sixty-one credits toward a college degree.

Johnny had thought he would be fighting the Germans or Japanese. Instead, his main battle was with engineering textbooks, his main danger getting caught out after curfew. Millsaps College was rigidly conservative, and the navy had ruled hands off the coeds. But the town was full of southern belles who found glamour in a navy uniform, even one attached to a midwestern accent.

Johnny and a friend, Jules Arceneaux, bartered their abilities as entertainers for privileges that the other men didn't have. The two men put on shows for the troops, and Johnny continued to develop as a performer, working diligently at his craft. "We were putting on a show at a hospital one night," remembers Arceneaux. "There were a bunch of fellows in wheelchairs and a bed. Johnny was doing his magic tricks, telling his jokes, and he wasn't getting much response. Everyone was serious. Finally he made an American flag appear and said, 'Now clap, damn you!' It broke the ice. Everyone started clapping and laughing."

Johnny came home on leave. "One night we went to a basketball game in Wayne, Nebraska," recalls Jim Cochran. "We came home after the game. Johnny was driving his dad's car, that '39 Chrysler. Johnny did not see the sign where the state highway ends in Norfolk. We came upon it very fast. John went straight on through and into the cornfield. I don't know how many times and how far it rolled, but the car was destroyed. I can't believe that they got that baby fixed."

Johnny was not hurt.

After almost two years in the navy Johnny was shipped out to the South Pacific to serve on the USS *Pennsylvania*. On August 6, 1945, while his troopship steamed westward, the United States dropped an atomic bomb on Hiroshima. Three days later an American plane dropped a second atomic bomb on Nagasaki. As the Japanese sued for peace, their soldiers continued a few futile attacks. On August 12, they torpedoed the *Pennsylvania* as it sailed off Okinawa. On August 14, the last day of the war, Johnny arrived on the crippled ship.

As he had missed the stark realities of the Great Depression, so too had he missed combat experience in World War II. Like most young men, Johnny might be forgiven for mistaking good health and good fortune for immortality. Now, though, he was faced with a task that changed his attitude toward life and death. He saw an image of war far different from the newsreels and war films that he had seen at the Granada Theater.

The Japanese torpedo had wreaked havoc on the *Pennsylvania*. "It practically blew off the stern and killed twenty guys," Johnny has recalled. "So she headed into dry dock at Guam. I was assigned to damage control, I guess maybe because I was the youngest officer and the most recently arrived. And my first assignment was to go down into that hole in the stern and supervise the bringing out of those twenty corpses and their personal effects. Jesus, that was an awful experience. They'd been down there eighteen days by that time, and I want to tell you, that was a *terrible* job."

The *Pennsylvania* sailed slowly to Seattle. There, nineteen-year old Johnny was put in charge of a troop train. "Jesus, what an experience," Carson remembers. "There I was, the only officer in charge of a whole train of enlisted men heading back to places like Memphis, Atlanta, Augusta . . . They didn't give a shit for anything by that time. One officer in charge of eight or nine cars full of guys who had been in service ten or fifteen years, enlisted men, and all of us riding day coach. We bought our own food from military supply depots and guys were assigned as cooks and they cooked right on the train.

"One time they hooked a car full of nurses on to our train, and we had to have a Marine guard on that little platform between the cars, or there would have been a real rape-athon. Another time once we were stranded in Fargo, North Dakota, for several days. Now, Fargo is one of the *coldest* goddamned places in the country, and there we were in the middle of a snowstorm, stuck. And I couldn't think of anything else to do, so I gave the guys liberty. Can you imagine? There are three to five guys who just *disappeared*—never been heard of since. No kidding, a few guys just simply dropped out of sight—I never saw 'em again.''

The train was full of bodies too, and that stench of death traveled with him back across the continent. There were the cooking odors, the bodies, the sweat of hundreds of soldiers, the curses and taunts and boasts of men who were through with war.

Johnny has rarely talked of this journey, and he never talks of his cargo of bodies. Jody Carson, however, says that for years afterward he was haunted by that stench of death.

The war might have been over for many of his charges, but not for Johnny. He was shipped back to the South Pacific, to Guam. The 202 square miles of the island had been one of those bloody stepping-stones on the way to Japan, the mountainside scoured by the tongue of flamethrowers and the tattoo of shells.

Guam had no Stage Door Canteen, no movie stars, but the chow was regular and so was the mail. Johnny sent away to Chicago to a mail-order house for a dummy that he named Eddie. Although he was not part of a unit that entertained the troops, Johnny had plenty of opportunity to perform.

The comedian is the most vulnerable of performers. His audience judges him joke by joke, moment by moment. When that other high-wire performer, the trapeze artist, falls to the net, the audience gasps in appreciation for the worthiness of the attempt. When the comedian fails, he or she is met only with the disdain of silence, or by a hundred muffled groans.

As the Great Carsoni, Johnny had come onstage as a magician, not a comedian. If his jokes failed, they were simply part of his patter. In Guam he could always hide behind Eddie, his dummy, but military audiences are the most generous of all, applauding jugglers, mimes, tenors, and saxophonists of mediocre talent, and a fledgling comedian as well. "I was the only officer in the enlisted men's shows," Johnny recalls. "What'd I do? I'd knock the officers."

Johnny made the GIs laugh. As he did, he learned to feel an audience, each member of which had different emotions and hungers, that came together as one. These people had to be wooed, fed, seduced, and pampered. They could roar their approval, a sound sweeter to a novice performer than words of love or the tinkle of silver coins. But they could turn on you, or ignore you, or forget you. Sometimes they had to be slapped or warned or chastised. He was not learning this lesson in a dank nightclub in Newark or Toledo in front of a score of drunks after sitting in a dressing room where the only thing to read is the graffiti on the walls. Instead, he was among young men who were a cross-section of America, young men who laughed because laughter was better than feeling melancholy or homesick or sorry for themselves.

Johnny spent many hours practicing his craft, trying out routines and jokes. His duties as an ensign included decoding messages. Early one morning he delivered a coded message to James Forrestal, the secretary of the navy.

"I walked in with this thing, and there was Forrestal with the admiral, having breakfast," Johnny recalls. "He asked me my name, and if I planned to stay in the Navy. I said 'No, sir,' and he asked what I wanted to do after I got out of the service. Well, I hadn't really given it much thought myself, but I had to say something. So I said I'd always been interested in being a magician and entertainer. Forrestal said, 'Can you show us some tricks?' And the admiral pulled out a deck of cards from somewhere. And there I was, after being up all night, at six or seven in the morning on Guam, doing card tricks for the admiral and the Secretary of the Navy."

Before long, Johnny was sailing home on the *Pennsylvania*. There was no longer any danger of torpedoes, and Johnny used his skill as a ventriloquist to throw his voice around the deck, giving imaginary orders, sending sailors scurrying fore and aft. He had done the same thing at Norfolk High, but he was much better at it now.

> Come-a runnin, boys,
> Don't you hear that noise
> Like the thunder in the skies
> How it rolls along
> In the good old song
> For the sons of Ne Bras Ki.

The thousands of spectators at Busch Stadium for the Homecoming game stood with their heads bowed during the singing of "The Cornhusker." That tradition was still alive, but in the fall of 1946, when Johnny entered the University of Nebraska, almost everything else was changing.

Lincoln is the capital and second-largest city in Nebraska, home to what people in the state call simply "the University." That fall a record nine thousand students enrolled at the school. Veterans flooded the campus, swaggering with life and its possibilities, money from the GI Bill filling their billfolds.

Johnny was "an outstater," from a place in the state other than Omaha or Lincoln. When he arrived from Norfolk, 111 miles to the north, he roomed with three of his Norfolk classmates.

The four men rented a modest two-room apartment on the third floor of a house about a mile and a half from campus. At the beginning of the term the lodgings had been clean. The four veterans had experienced enough KP for ten lifetimes. No one mopped, dusted, or straightened up. The squalor got so bad that one young man left before the first term ended.

The apartment had an antiquated toilet that sprayed the bathroom with mist. Johnny came up with a solution. One day he returned home carrying an umbrella, which he set down in the bathroom.

Another minor annoyance was not so easily solved. That was the Great Carsoni himself. At first Johnny's humor delighted his friends. It was almost like getting Jack Benny or Bob Hope as a roommate. There are only so many jokes though, so many times you can hear the same routine. The roommates would have cried foul if John Busch, a future dentist, had lined them up for flossing each morning. But it took them the longest while to realize that Johnny wasn't joking. He was working at his chosen vocation, and work was a bore, even if the work was comedy.

"I'd go down there for football games," remembers Bob Hall, a Norfolk friend. "I'd load up with booze. They'd say, 'Thank God you're here. He can try out his jokes on someone else.'

"He could take one joke and work it and work it and work it until it was right. Those guys got so sick of his routines, and the jokes. Everyone got sick of him working his jokes on them."

In the fall of 1947 Johnny pledged the Phi Gamma Delta fraternity. Like most veterans, he was less than enthusiastic about the more adolescent games of the fraternity system, particularly the week of hazing called "Hell Wcek." Most of the pledges at least pretended to go along. Not Johnny.

"Johnny was quick as a trigger with his mouth," recalls Jerry Calhoun, another pledge. "He had a kind of superior air. He didn't want to be involved in any rough stuff. He disappeared during Rush Week. It still bugs me, and I won't watch *The Tonight Show*."

Charles Thone, the pledge president, recognized that "Johnny didn't accept the fraternity system. He was a loner. He wasn't very popular." Thone could have thrown Johnny out, but he had the political instincts of a young man who would one day become the Republican governor of Nebraska. He knew that Johnny's abilities as a performer would be an asset to the fraternity.

For Phi Gamma Delta, the biannual Kosmet Klub shows were an important event. They were one of the great traditions at the university, dating back to 1911. Before the war the comic revues had received national attention. In 1936 newsreel crews from Fox, Paramount, and Universal News filmed the performance.

The Kosmet Klub shows had one subtle distinction that set them apart from other university theatricals. They were all-male shows, featuring the finest flowering of Nebraska youth in full, outrageous drag. After the shows the fraternity men packed away their heels and silks or shipped them back to Mother.

In the spring of 1947 Johnny had a leading role in the Kosmet Klub revue, playing a newspaperman in *Aksarben Nights*. That was his first major recognition at the university. In the fall show he had an even bigger role. Not only was he to play Cleopatra in the Phi Gam's skit "She Was Only a Pharaoh's Daughter, but She Never Became a Mummy," he was to be the master of ceremonies as well.

Johnny rehearsed diligently. In one scene Cleopatra went offstage to the bathroom, her exit punctuated by a humming falsetto and a loud flushing sound. In preparation Johnny and Dee Devoe, a fraternity brother, flushed the toilet again and again, with a recording microphone dangling down the bowl. They were satisfied only when they had a sound like the Hoover Dam breaking loose.

One evening Johnny and the cast went through the routine for the fraternity. The skit had a scene satirizing radio.

"Be sure to tune in tomorrow for another chapter in the life of a girl chariot rider," Johnny said. "Brought to you by the makers of Horatio beer, the beer that makes you want to get up and go. Drink Horatio beer in the can, or anyplace in your home.

"The time is eight-thirty. It's time to play that new quiz game 'Take it or Get Thrown to the Lions,' brought to you by the Sunshine Sandal Company. Now here's your genial quiz master, Dr. D."

The fraternity brothers broke into applause.

"Good evening, fellow Romans," said Johnny, sounding like the well-known quiz-show host Dr. I.Q. "Now, in the center tier."

"I have a glad . . . a gladiator, Doctor," a student yelled into the microphone.

"You've got the clap too," Johnny said, sotto voce, breaking up the crowd.

Johnny would not be joking about clap the night of the show. A faculty adviser ruled upon the skits before the big night, and woe betide the college thespian who went beyond the bounds of the script. The university was concerned with "good taste." The year before, Alpha Tau Omega had put on a skit, "Coon Court," that took place in "a police court filled with black-face policemen and featuring the dancing of sepia 'girls.' " The faculty were much more worried over sexual innuendo than any racist humor, and that skit won first prize.

On the evening of November 22, 1947, Johnny stood on the stage before five thousand Nebraskans gathered at the coliseum. As MC, he filled in between the skits with his own patter, and briskly moved the show along. Phi Delta Theta and Sigma Chi changed their skits, adding an emphasis on the bowels that even a proctologist would consider excessive. Afterward, the administration banned the two fraternities from the next year's show.

Johnny's remarks between the acts may have seemed ad-libbed, but he knew how far he could go in his sexual asides, how daring he could be in his humor. It was a dangerous age for a comedian, and Johnny almost never risked political jokes. He had a stock of jokes about other aspects of college life, but his best jokes were usually about sex, not bawdy burlesque stories, but witty allusions. He gave the thousands before him the feeling that here was a daring young man, but he kept within the boundaries of the permissible. Johnny was a success, and the Phi Gams won first prize for their skit that year.

That evening Johnny walked away a Big Man on Campus. He would never make the Big Red in football, but he was suddenly one of those students whom people looked at and talked about.

The fellows at the fraternity were always thinking of one

prank or another, and Johnny was usually involved. He called a sorority and pretended that he was the clerk down at the railroad station with packages to be picked up. In restaurants he paid the waitress. Then, when she started to put the money in the cash box, she noticed that the money was gone, whisked away by Johnny's sleight of hand.

In the Nebraska spring a young man's fancy turned to thoughts of panty raids. The students stood hollering and whistling outside the sororities waiting for the dainties to be hurled from the windows. Then they strung them up on a clothesline across Sixteenth Street. But, alas, the rope began to sag. And when a Greyhound bus passed by, it dragged the panties and the rope down the road.

When thoughts of panties were not in the air, the brothers strung up a gigantic slingshot made of old inner tubing and a piece of leather. They set water balloons into the sling, pulled it back, and let go, sending the balloons sailing hundreds of feet across the campus. "You can let those babies go and there's no way they can tell where it's coming from," recalls Dee Devoe. "Johnny used to do that."

A favored target for pranks was the despised ATO house next door. Late one night the pledges in Johnny's class crept over and hooked up the lawn sprinkler. Then a couple of them crept up to the second- and third-floor dorms carrying the hoses, and set the sprinklers down. On the given signal the sprinklers were turned on, and for a moment the drowsy ATO brothers thought that it was raining inside.

In the spring of 1948 many of the fraternity brothers joined in the largest protest the university had seen since the war. More than two thousand students marched on the capital demanding to see the governor. Even the combined efforts of the Lincoln riot squad, the fire department, and tear gas could not stop them. As the motley mob marched through the streets, bystanders shouted out, "Reds!" and "Commies!"

The students were protesting against no-parking regulations on Twelfth and R streets, on the edge of the campus. It might seem a benign cause, but who knew what dark Red spirit lurked behind the students? "What might have been laughed off as college spirit in days past is classed as a significant act of foreign influence in these days of world insecurity," editorialized the *Daily Nebraskan*.

For Homecoming the fraternities decorated their houses. The Phi Gams dressed up dummies of Nebraska's opponents, the Kansas Jayhawks, like dancing girls at a sideshow. "Hurry, hurry, hurry," blared Johnny's recorded voice to all who passed by. "For ten cents, the thin part of a dollar, come and see the girls dance. They're direct from Paris. You can't find a better bunch of girls. It's only ten cents. Come up and see them dance. First, they dance on one leg. Then on the other, and between the two they make their living. Hurry, hurry, hurry."

In 1947 the Carson family moved to Lincoln, where Kit became the district manager of the Consumer Public Power District. Johnny could live at home now, at least part of the time. The Carsons were hospitable people, and they let a Norfolk boy, Dick's friend William Butterfield, stay in the house when he started college. "That summer John was living at home," Butterfield says. "He was selling vacuum cleaners. I hardly got a solid meal, I was laughing so hard. Every day he told about the incidents of the day, going door to door."

Johnny may not have been an outstanding vacuum-cleaner salesman, but he did have a certain business acumen. "Gasoline was still rationed, so Johnny rallied us to build up a good business," reminisces Bill Wiseman, Jr., a classmate. "We pooled our gas-ration stamps and we supplemented our supply through various devious means—don't ask how—and we sold gas in beer bottles at 50 cents. Obviously, a fellow couldn't get very far on a beer bottle of gas, but at least he had some measure of mobility, and it took him and his girl to a quiet parking place.

"Then our stamps ran out and our other sources dried up, but Johnny got an inspiration. He had a jalopy that had finally collapsed and he didn't have the money to buy parts to repair it, so we all towed the car back to Phi Gam house where, of an evening, it was very dark, very quiet. Johnny rented out the car as a necking parlor for 25 cents an hour and did a rushing business. Privacy was guaranteed.''

Johnny majored in radio and speech, but his primary concern was perfecting his comic routines and his magic. Beyond that, his interest in the opposite sex had not deteriorated. One day in the student union a pretty coed mistook him for another student. Johnny was impressed enough by the vivacious young woman to learn that her name was Marge Alexis and that she was the daughter of his Spanish professor. Although Marge was a member of the Pi Beta Phi sorority, she lived at home, a mile from the Carsons' two-story brick colonial.

Johnny and Marge ended up dating steadily, a matter important enough to get into the gossip column in the *Daily Nebraskan*. ''Margie Alexis has evidently found the man of her life as she and John Carson are going steady,'' the paper noted. ''Being the magician that he is maybe John tricked her into it.''

Marge was a serious young woman. ''I would have been the 'nice girl,' '' Marge Alexis Todd recalls. ''My father was a professor. I went to church. I didn't drink or smoke. Johnny said that he would never go out with a girl who was kissable on the first date. I think he was serious about that. It shows how square he was. His family was very similar to mine. When the grandparents would come to visit, they would have to hide the bourbon.

''John gave me a family ring, a ruby, that I wore. We talked about getting married, but my mother was very much opposed. She said, 'He'll never amount to anything.' She said, 'He thinks he's better than other people.' I thought if anything he had a little inferiority complex. John would say, 'I don't think your mother likes me.' I said, 'No, she doesn't.' ''

In the fall of 1948 Johnny was master of ceremonies for the Kosmet Klub show and one of six candidates for Prince Kosmet. This was a popularity contest, and Johnny did not win. But between acts he entertained with his jokes, ventriloquism, and comments.

Johnny was so good at hosting the shows that he was automatically chosen for the coveted MC position. In the spring of 1949 when he stepped onstage, Johnny faced a minor crisis. The Kosmet Klub had hired the locally famous orchestra of Johnny Cox. But the band leader hadn't shown up.

"I'm afraid we have a problem," Johnny announced. He paused and gazed down at the band. "It looks like we've got ten men and no Cox."

Johnny was celebrated on campus for his wit and humor, and onstage he projected an image of gregariousness and warmth. But he was a young man without a close friend. His brother, Dick, was a fraternity brother, but the two Carsons didn't appear especially close, either. Johnny would go on double or triple dates with his fraternity brothers. He would regale the group. But Johnny's humor was a shield that kept the world at a distance.

When he wasn't rehearsing, Johnny didn't hang around Phi Gamma Delta. He did get to know the housemother, Mrs. Mae Minier, who had been a second "Mom" to hundreds of young men. During the war she had sent out her mimeographed "Bull Session Echoes from Mom's Room" to about six hundred former students. When Ernie Pyle, the war correspondent, found a soldier reading one of the letters, he wrote about "Mom" in his column.

Johnny seemed to be able to talk to "Mom" Minier better than to many of his peers. "He was always courteous, but he tended to business," Mom Minier remembered. "He took part in all the parties but he didn't go in for excesses. He was a hard worker. He would go out to entertain in different little towns to help his pay through school. I got him a job in my home town of Oakland entertaining for a businessman-farmers banquet. They were doubtful about having a university kid, but they had him up there and invited him back for different things."

John took part in some of the fraternity activities. As a

pledge, he was in the Grand Ballroom of the Hotel Lincoln for the annual dinner of the fraternity's secret society. Here, the brothers young and old met to dine on roast pig and to invoke mysterious rituals. The pledges sat in the center of the gathering. One by one, they went through an initiation ceremony that included kissing the rump of a stuffed pig. After the pledges performed on the pig's posterior, Johnny performed his magic show. Later there was always an unscheduled entertainer, usually a stripteaser from Omaha or parts east. "Long and loud was the merry making and it soon transferred to the lower regions of the chapter house where some of the brothers amused themselves in various ways," noted *Lambda Nu Today*, a fraternity publication.

The brothers were sworn to keep their rituals secret. As silly as these dinners seemed, they were serious acts of male bonding. The fraternity men who had graduated were often successful and ready to help the younger men.

The following year the fraternity held its annual dinner in the Blue Room of the Paxton Hotel in Omaha. Merle Workhoven, the MC, was a prominent announcer on WOW in Omaha. Another member, Bill Wiseman, was WOW's assistant station manager. His son, Bill Wiseman, Jr., was one of Johnny's fraternity brothers.

Johnny's magic show had become as much a part of the evening as the pig and the stripteaser. Afterward, Workhoven talked to Johnny. "I was very impressed," remembers Workhoven. "The next day I talked to the program director at WOW. I said, 'Say, there's a guy we should hire, because we're going to be going on TV pretty soon and the guy is a natural.'

"The program director said, 'Oh yeah, we already know about him. It's all in the bag. We've already made a commitment to hire him as soon as he graduates.''

Johnny's romance with Marge Alexis lasted no more than a year. Marge headed on to law school at the university, and Johnny headed back to the Pi Beta Phi house.

More than one young man on campus had arrived at the

Pi Beta Phi house anticipating a date with Joan "Jody" Morrill Wolcott. There, he would be told by a grieving sorority sister that Jody's grandmother had died and the poor girl was at the funeral home. A few minutes later another young gentleman might arrive to be told the same terrible news. Jody often scheduled two or three dates for the same evening. This habit had begun in high school, to her mother's dismay. She was totally democratic. She left with whichever young man arrived first.

Jody discovered that as a date the Great Carsoni was the anchovies of fraternity row, an acquired taste. "I said I'd never go out with him again," Jody says. "He lit my cigarette and burned my nose. He was so aloof, so superior, and almost mean. He called me for another date. I don't know, something else came up, and I wasn't there. He sent me this potty with a cactus in it and a card saying, 'Sit on this. It will remind you.' I thought it was clever. He planted it himself. It attracted my attention. I thought maybe he wasn't the person I went out with the first time. He was not terribly popular in college."

Jody Wolcott had the looks that were especially prized in the late 1940's. Scarcely over five feet tall, she had a pixielike quality to her that almost defined the word *cute*. She resembled Leslie Caron, the actress, and her beguiling, flirtatious manner had driven more than one young man to despair.

"Johnny was vulnerable and boyish," Jody says. "He was shy, but he covered it up with a very superior, scornful air that I sort of saw through. There were all sorts of fellows around saying I love you, all this and that. But I fell in love with John, who didn't do any of that stuff. I fell in love with the man that he was. I believed in him.

"John could talk me into about anything. I was a virgin and he talked me into going to bed. He talked me into letting him take these nude pictures. It wasn't showing an awful lot. I was sitting on a blanket, but it showed that I was nude. It was a terrible scandal. He talked me into going off with him to do magic shows as his assistant, and I was kicked out of the Pi Phi house. It wasn't that much fun living with my grandmother. I was so isolated, shut off from the other girls. I was almost kicked out of school. I had to go in front of the dean of women.

"Johnny's very persuasive. I don't think any other young man at the time could have gotten away with what he did with me. I was brought up in a very strict manner. I wouldn't have gone along with any of that. I trusted him. I thought I would marry him. He was very sweet when he fell in love with me. He was very dear.

"I had a sense of humor and I enjoyed watching him do his magic act, going around at milkmen's conventions and chicken hatcheries, things like that. And he was very exciting, a little bit different from the usual date you'd have, and quite domineering."

Jody was from North Platte, a tough, windblown town in western Nebraska that prided itself on a frontier heritage. She came from an old Nebraska family. As a young man, her great grandfather, Charles H. Morrill, had hired Buffalo Bill Cody to provide meat for the crews building the transcontinental railroad. Morrill had made a fortune as a banker and land speculator. Morrill County was named after him, as was Morrill Hall, the world-famous paleontology museum at the University of Nebraska, where Jody's grandfather had been a distinguished professor. Her father was a civil engineer whose professional pride was work creating Lake Maloney, outside North Platte. Her mother was a rarity for a woman of her generation, a former University of Nebraska student and a Pi Phi as well.

Growing up, Jody had felt lost between her older and young sisters. She had tried to be the dutiful daughter. As a teenager during the war, she had trudged down to the depot in North Platte as a part of an Episcopalian group and served coffee and sandwiches to the soldiers on the troop train. She had tried to be as responsible as her two sisters, but she was as high-strung as a hummingbird. Jerry Calhoun, one of her high school friends, was not alone in finding her "fun but a little bit flighty."

Jody's father had a speech impediment, making it doubly special for her to be with Johnny, who could make words dance, sing, and do somersaults. But at the university Jody wasn't simply Johnny Carson's girlfriend. She had a role in the 1948 *Co-ed Follies*. She was best known as a cartoonist with a cynical, witty view of life. She loved to draw, sketching the foibles of college society in cartoons featured in university publications. In one cartoon she pictured a diminutive coed during Rush Week, surrounded by grotesque, slack-jawed, cigarette-smoking sorority sisters telling the poor maiden, "You're just like one of us." Another cartoon showed a pledge hefting an enormous trunk on which sat a prickly-legged sorority sister.

Jody could have been a successful commercial artist, but Johnny became her all-consuming interest. She was a "good girl," but she had slept with Johnny. She had stood up innumerable dates, and now she was the one waiting for Johnny.

As Johnny's assistant, Jody went with him wherever he put on his show. Not only did she exude charm and youth, and carry doves and rings with perfect aplomb, but she was tiny and sufficiently acrobatic that she could squeeze into the black box when he sawed her in two. She listened to his jokes and routines a thousand times, never expressing boredom. She went to his room at the Carsons' home in Lincoln and sat while Johnny worked on his routines and his thesis.

Johnny was not a demonstrative sort. He did not profess his love, bring Jody candy or flowers, *show* that he cared. Her father was like that too, and so were many of the Nebraska men she had known. She loved Johnny and she knew that he loved her too, and he didn't have to tell her so.

Jody might have wondered more about Johnny's love if she had talked to her sorority sister Marge Alexis. Marge, who was now a freshman law student at the university, had not shown much interest in Johnny's career. She did not go onstage as his assistant. Yet Johnny sent her the flowers and gifts that he never gave Jody. And now he treated Jody in a manner that he would not have dared to treat his former girlfriend. "My sorority mother claimed that when Johnny and Jody were first together, he would leave her at the sorority house on the weekends," says Marge.

His senior year at Nebraska, Johnny served as master of ceremonies for the Kosmet Klub revues and performed at various functions. Three mornings a week he played in a western comedy, *Eddie Sosby and the Radio Rangers*, on KFAB, a Lincoln radio station. The program ran from 7:30 to 8:00 A.M. That meant he was fifteen minutes late to his eight o'clock Spanish class. His excellent memory enabled him to keep up with the class.

Johnny's main haunt on campus was the Temple Building, down the street from the fraternity. The old redbrick structure housed the speech and radio department and the university theater. The basement was a warren of studios and offices. Here, during Johnny's senior year the students experimented with a new form of communication: television. Stations had already gone on the air on the West and East coasts, but for Lincoln this was decidedly a first. Johnny played a milkman in *The Story of Undulant Fever*. The program was broadcast only as far as the theater on the floor above.

For Johnny, the real theater of the air was radio. When he prepared his thesis on "How to Write Comedy Jokes," he was talking about radio. Instead of merely writing a dissertation, he prepared a tape that included excerpts from his favorite radio performers and his commentaries. "I remember up in his bedroom listening to his tapes," Jody says. "He studied them all, their different mannerisms, how they timed it, the structure, how they got a laugh. He studied a lot of different people. He took a little bit from each one."

For months he worked putting together the tape. He taped Fibber McGee and Molly, Fred Allen, Milton Berle, Jack Benny, and Bob Hope. Since he was a young boy lying on his stomach in the living room in Norfolk, he had heard these programs. But he listened now as a performer.

"A good comedian can get you to buy his sponsor's products," Johnny said in his introduction. One could hardly imagine the youthful Charlie Chaplin envisioning a glorious day when the genius of his tramp would be used selling IBM computers. But Johnny understood the nature of the medium. Radio was there to sell as much as to entertain.

Johnny didn't simply listen and laugh when he turned on the radio. He was like an automobile designer learning about a car by taking it apart piece by piece. He understood the structure behind Jack Benny's jokes. He heard how Benny used timing, how he paused, punctuating the joke and drawing laughter out of the audience. To a novice, that silence would have seemed an eternity, but Benny dared to wait. Timing. Nobody was better than Benny. Johnny gave some examples on the tape.

He also explained how running gags work, and how to build a punch line with a signature phrase ("T'aint funny, McGee"). "There are many reasons for a top comedian's success, and one of the most important is in the writing of comedy shows," he said. That statement too showed how far Johnny was from many radio listeners, who assumed that their favorite comedians were ad-libbing, or at least writing their own material. He understood the collegial nature of radio comedy. There was always a team.

Johnny's thesis was not the clarion call of a young idealist ready to take on the world and change the nature of comedy. Johnny was a realist who understood much about the nature of the profession he was about to enter. He had learned from listening to Jack Benny all those years, playing those radio tapes over and over again, hosting the Kosmet Klub shows, appearing before milkmen's conventions and GIs. He was only twenty-three years old, but as he graduated from the University of Nebraska, he was already on his way to becoming a seasoned, knowledgeable performer.

• • • • • • • • • • • • • • • • • •

FOUR

---

pon graduation Johnny went to work for WOW, the most important radio station in Nebraska. Almost immediately, on August 1, 1949, *The Johnny Carson Show* went on the air each morning from eight-fifteen to nine o'clock. He played records, read the news, weather, and sports, and filled the rest of the time with his patter. He realized that he couldn't wing it every morning. At night he worked preparing routines and jokes. He had a sense of humor that the farmers, housewives, and businessmen appreciated. He was comfortable and comforting even if the audience found him at times a bit risqué.

These were heady times for a young man just out of college. Johnny had listened to the station as a boy and a college student. WOW was affiliated with the biggest network, NBC, and had a signal that went as far as eastern South Dakota, western Iowa, and northwest Missouri. His salary was only $47.50 a week. That was enough for a modest walk-up at the Drake Court apartments. It was enough, just barely, to get married on as well.

On October 1, 1949, the Reverend Seward H. Bean pronounced Johnny and Jody man and wife in a ceremony before 150 guests in North Platte's Episcopalian Church. As Jody walked down the aisle, Mrs. Wolcott thought that her daughter looked like a princess. Jody wore a wedding gown of ice-blue satin. A fingertip veil graced her brown hair. Johnny's parents were there, and his brother served as best man. He remained a man with few friends, even at his own wedding. He had two of his fraternity brothers, P. K. Ely and Jerry Calhoun, as ushers. They were local boys, and Calhoun didn't even like Johnny.

The reception was held in the Crystal Room of the Pawnee Hotel, the six-story structure that dominated the skyline of North Platte. Jody wore a smartly styled wool-garbardine suit and a white orchid when they left that day. They had no time or money for a real honeymoon. It was off to Omaha and the Drake Court apartments, and back to work.

"I had a Nebraska upbringing," Jody says. "I respected my father, but I was afraid of him. That made me a good wife. I expected John to be the boss. There wasn't any equality in our marriage, but I didn't expect there to be. It was all what John wanted. It was all John. That was all right with me. He selected my clothes. I was a captive. I had very few friends outside my marriage."

When Johnny arrived in Omaha, the great excitement was the prospect of television. In the summer of 1949 WOW-TV broadcast an engineering test pattern four hours every day. Those fifteen hundred residents with sets invited their friends over to watch the pattern. Those not so blessed traveled down to the air-conditioned Greyhound bus depot, where thirty-three sets had been set up to provide a preview.

The Omaha papers advertised TV receivers at prices ranging from $119.95 to $1,150. The *World Herald* was full of useful advice to prepare Nebraskans for the coming of television. "Don't buy a set with a screen too large for the room," the paper admonished. "There are some suggestions on set sizes. Seven inches for two viewers, 10 inch for three, 12 or 12½ for four and a 16 inch for seven."

The Omaha Power District advertised that "medical authorities do not consider television a threat to healthy vision." That didn't even begin to address the positive benefits of watching television. "Television is being singled out for its virtues," the paper trumpeted. "One of them is a curb on juvenile delinquency. In Scarsdale, New York, for example, juvenile delinquency sank nearly to zero as ownership of television receivers rose. Kids just weren't on the streets."

Johnny was present on August 29, 1949, when WOW-TV, the first station in a five-state area, went on the air. The dignitaries and station officials made the obligatory remarks. "Believe you me, that television set of yours is going to be the center of things in your home for a long time to come," an official said, with the same hyperbolic enthusiasm used in selling the flashy new Chevrolet, or a Frigidaire. Behind the scenes everyone was winging it. "They were planning to run a film made by Senator Taft," Johnny remembers. "It had to be on the air at 10 P.M. It was rushed on the air, the emulsion dripping, but we made it."

Nebraskans did not immediately begin to spend their evenings seated in front of their televisions. Although sales of the sets expanded dramatically, viewers had little to watch. The coaxial cable that brought the network shows live from New York City hadn't reached the Missouri River yet. Instead, the three local television stations showed kinescopes, which were films of the network shows shot off the screen. The contrast between the grainy, shadowy kinescopes and live television was so dramatic, and the national programming so meager, that stations filled up the hours with local programming.

Johnny had arrived at WOW at the beginning of the age of television. Everything was new, and everyone was a novice. The technical staff had to learn how to manipulate the snouts of the massive cameras. The sales staff needed to figure out the way to price the advertising. The news people had to get pictures to go with their words. The executives sought to fill all these hours. The viewers themselves switched back and forth, fiddling with their antennae until they got a clear picture.

One day Johnny walked past the notice board and saw a new directive. He was to host his own television program each weekday at 12:30 P.M. He decided to call the program *Squirrel's Nest*. He told jokes, did humorous interviews, but he had no time to prepare elaborate scripts. The show was only fifteen minutes long, but often it seemed as if he had to fill hours. "The trick was just finding something to do," Johnny remembers. "We had turtle races, one of the more exciting things. There was no money in television in those days but nobody cared because you were learning what it was all about."

Johnny was swimming in this new medium, bobbing up and down, almost sinking some days, then the next day diving in again. "We were all caught up in the idea that we were on television," Johnny remembers. "You'd just go in and they'd kind of roll a camera out and you were on the air. In one corner you had Martha Bohlsen and her set would be on one end, and the news set would be ten or fifteen feet away and Mel Hansen's farm set was there and Coffee Counter. Then I had my set. All five of the sets were set around the perimeter of the studio."

The sets were scruffy affairs made of pasteboard and cheap paint. But focus a camera on the sets and they became kitchens, living rooms, newsrooms.

Johnny discovered that television was not simply radio with pictures. "My experiences on radio didn't help me in TV at all," Johnny has said. "I learned a lot though, from doing my magic and ventriloquism acts."

As a magician and ventriloquist, Johnny had learned to appear fully involved with the audience while his attention was elsewhere. In television he had to produce the same illusion while he worried about cameras and cables. "There are so many things to keep in mind and cues to look for," said Fred Allen, the brilliant radio comedian who never successfully made the transition to television. "No sooner do I get going . . . than I get a hand signal to break it up. A television performer is surrounded by bloody commotion."

In a sense television had an intimacy that radio did not have. The stentorian tones of an old radio announcer sounded stiff and pretentious on television. Intense or highly stylized performers often blew themselves out, like a dinner guest who talks too much. Johnny's low-voltage, seemingly casual personality wore well. He looked far better on television than he did in person. In person he was, if anything, too thin, but the television camera put a few pounds on him.

Television was an intimate medium in another sense. It was like a family in which people knew each other so well that they only half listened. On radio the audience sat in front of their sets and grasped the nuances of Fred Allen's wit. On television such sophisticated, gentle humor was often lost, drowned in the machine-gun delivery of Milton Berle, the slapstick of Red Skelton, or the blaring humor of Jerry Lewis.

Johnny's image entered the living rooms of homes all over eastern Nebraska and western Iowa. Within the range of the WOW beacon Johnny was a famous man; beyond that range he was nothing. He was not famous as a general was famous, or a politician or a movie star. He was a trusted, familiar figure whose daily appearance insinuated him into the consciousness of his audience. When sponsors and businessmen and housewives and farmers came up to him, they talked to him as if they knew him.

When the red light was on, he constructed an illusion that was as great as any of the Great Carsoni's magic tricks. His words and gestures created the image of a spontaneous, witty, irascible, charming, devil-may-care character.

Those who worked with Johnny saw all that went into that illusion. "Most deejays walk in the door about the same time the guy they're relieving puts the new guy's theme on for him," says Workhoven. "In the mornings Carson was there an hour or more ahead of time. He would check the news wires and look over everything, looking for something that he could use on his show. He did his show, then he had his regular shift. I'd often do the news at ten P.M., and John would be there still recording things and working out skits and stuff. I've seen him put in an hour or so working on a thirty-second gag. Then it would just pop up in his show. Like it was a kind of throwaway. But he had been working on that sucker for an hour.''

The viewers in Nebraska and Iowa enjoyed Carson in part because his low-key humor was a part of the tradition of plains humor. The homesteaders and ranchers were a laconic lot. Their wit snuck up on you. For many of them, the biggest laugh was on themselves. They had fallen for the advertisements the railroad companies and others put out, talking about the abundance of the land and the opportunity. It was a far cry from the sod houses, the piercing cold, the relentless heat, the grasshoppers, the floods.

The settlers' reality was as large as the plains themselves. In their humor the settlers exaggerated the world around them. They created mythic frontier characters tenfold larger than life. They told of weather so terrible that even they had not experienced it. They prospered and suffered through a largely common fate, and they loved to prick pretensions, pull down those who fancied themselves better than anyone else.

Johnny was not a folk humorist. He was a performer and a masterful mimic. He picked up routines and techniques from the comedians that he heard and saw as if he were picking fruit from a tree.

In those months doing *Squirrel's Nest* Johnny developed much of the public personality that would become so familiar to viewers of *The Tonight Show*. Here, for the first time Johnny played wacky Professor Carson on "The Homework School of the Air."

"What should students eat for breakfast?" asked Bill McBride, the announcer.

"When you're young, it's important to have a good breakfast," Johnny said authoritatively. "We've talked to our experts and have come upon a breakfast to carry you through the day. We suggest that you start off with a nice plate of liver and onions. Follow that with a combination garlic salad, dill salad, and sour cream, and two or three slices of zwieback. That starts you and makes you feel good all through the day.''

"Thank you, Uncle John," said McBride. "Here's a question from Geraldine Ferdahunkin."

"Ferdahunkin?" Johnny asked.

"Is there any way to distinguish—and let's be real serious on this one—is there any way to distinguish between a relative quantity and a variable factor in chemistry?"

"Yes!" John said emphatically.

"That's 'The Homework School of the Air' for today."

When Johnny went home to the Drake apartments, he was a quiet, serious, sometimes dour young man. Even there, he worked, trying out routines and jokes on a wire recorder he had purchased.

To Johnny's colleagues at the station, Jody had become "the wife," a woman they knew hardly at all. "The pressures of the business began right away," says Jody. "I immediately started having babies. We were married in October, and the next November our first child was born. My diaphragm didn't work. We didn't experience life together as we had known it in college. We didn't even have a year until we were parents, and that's just very hard, especially when your husband is working all the time, and you don't have much money, and you keep having children. Pressures everywhere. Pressures of the family. Pressures of the job."

Jody enjoyed the times that she and Johnny went out together. They had friends from their college days who were not simply interested in Johnny. One time the Carsons went to the Omaha Club with John and Barbara "Zip" Haslom. Johnny reached into his pocket for some change and felt a hole.

"Hot damn, there goes my egg money," he said.

Once Johnny and Jody spent the evening in Lincoln. "We went into this restaurant," recalls Jerry Solomon, a fraternity brother. "He loved to confuse the waitress. And of course the waitress had seen him on his little show on television up in Omaha. He had the whole place in an uproar, and the waitress had all the orders mixed up. And by the time we got out of there, the place was a total disaster.

"But Johnny was always working. Always working. I respected him for that, because he was trying out new stuff, working his material. He used his friends and his environment to find out how his material was working."

"Do you think that I've got the talent to ever get anyplace?" Johnny asked Mort Wells, whose band played every weekday on the station.

"John, by God, I think you've got the talent to go as far as you are able to go," replied Wells, who thought that if Johnny had one weakness it was that he was too impatient. "Now you may have to have a lot of luck with it."

Wells had played for Meredith Wilson and the Armed Forces Radio Band, and Johnny respected the trumpet player. He often went with the band to play the Legion halls in Norfolk or Grand Island. He did his magic show when the group took a break. It was fun, but the extra money was even nicer. In 1951, after almost two years at the station, he was earning only $57.50 a week.

Johnny had his radio show in the morning. He had *Squirrel's Nest* at lunchtime. He did news programs and read the ads. He even shared the sportscasting duties on the first televised football game at WOW-TV, from his alma mater in Lincoln.

Johnny took whatever extra gigs he could get, including a kiddie show at the Orpheum Theater on Saturday morning. He had to dress in a cowboy outfit, but he couldn't afford to buy special clothes. Joe Kirshenbaum of Wolf Brothers Western Store lent him the costume. Kirshenbaum taped the soles of the fancy cowboy boots so the store could sell them as new.

If Johnny and his colleagues weren't making much money, they were having fun. One day just before the newscaster went on the air, Johnny and his buddies came into the control room and moved the clock ahead a few minutes. Then, as the newscaster began his report, they entered the studio, speaking loudly to one another. "We started to say things that I couldn't say here," Johnny says. "And we drove him crazy because he thought all of this was going out on the air and pretty soon it became a shouting match and terrible things were said back and forth and he almost dissolved and finally we had to tell him. So when he finally did go on the air, he was almost out of it by then."

Another time Johnny played a joke on one of the engineers. The man had a drinking problem. Even when he was supposed to be in the control room, he was not beyond making an emergency trip down to the Seven Seas bar near the back door of the station. On one occasion he came hurrying back, royally fortified with a shot of whiskey and a beer. He looked through the control-room window where Johnny was reading the news. *No sound. No sound.* He frantically twisted dials, turned switches. Within thirty seconds he was cold sober, as visions of unemployment danced through his head. Finally he realized that Johnny was merely mouthing the words, and the program had gone off the air.

Johnny hated the busywork of television. He was weeks late in filling out the announcer's logs. He made a twenty-cent personal phone call to Council Bluffs, hardly an act of major embezzlement. Yet he kept getting statements dunning him as if he had ripped off a fortune. Johnny walked across the street to the Douglas County Bank, where he hired the bank guard. "Please get a bag, put twenty pennies in it, and I want you to deliver it," Johnny said.

The guard entered WOW with gun drawn, and deposited the money bag on the desk of the shocked controller.

Johnny's most celebrated exploit involved saving the pigeons who roosted on the Douglas County Courthouse. The city council had decided to get rid of the birds. "I simply took the pigeons' side," Johnny remembers. "And I did a remote broadcast one morning. I got up on top of the building with a microphone. And I said, 'Just get me a record with some coos that sound like doves or pigeons.'

"So I went up and I asked the pigeons how they felt about this attempt to remove them. And then we would play the cooing and I would interpret what they said, that they were very saddened at the fact that the city government would try to move them off a public building. It got a lot of press and finally I think the Natural Gas Building or something like that offered to take the pigeons."

The record companies sent disk jockeys lists of questions for celebrities along with their prerecorded answers. This was a minor deception, and only the chronically naive believed that a singer like Patti Page was sitting in the studio talking to the local deejay.

Johnny devised some new questions for Miss Page.

"I understand you're hitting the bottle pretty good, Patti. When did you start?" Johnny asked.

"When I was six, I used to get up at church socials, and do it."

Johnny even made fun of WOW management. He told his radio audience that he had gone to see the general manager with his paycheck. "I said, 'Do you want to see something funny?'" Then Johnny pretended to open his pay envelope to the sound of cackling, sound-effects laughter.

Johnny remembers, "Another morning I opened my paycheck on the air and said, 'Let's see how much I got this week.' And I maybe had three or four coins and all you heard was 20 or 30 cents clanking out on the table. Drive them nuts with this kind of stuff. They were wonderful days."

Life was full of absurdities that Johnny was ready to point out. In January 1950 the USS *Missouri*, the battleship on which the Japanese surrendered, ran aground on a sandbar in the Chesapeake Bay. The navy would have been red-faced if the accident had taken place off Rio or Manila. But it was unspeakably embarrassing to have it happen so near to Annapolis, the home of the Naval Academy, and to Washington, the home of the Appropriations Committee.

Johnny, the ex-navy man, was only too willing to help the navy out of its plight. He staged a contest seeking the best solution. Alas, the landlubbers of the Great Plains could not seem to come up with a decent resolution. So Johnny offered his own answer. The navy should leave the ship sticking in the mud, but they should paint it white and turn it into a national monument.

As Johnny waxed rhapsodic, he was told that the secretary of the navy was waiting outside. Johnny knew when his buddies were putting him on. He would have been less surprised if Patti Page had been out there. "Good," he said, "tell him to get that boat out of the mud and report back here in twenty minutes."

Secretaries of the navy did not spend much time sitting around local television and radio stations. But this secretary of the navy, Francis P. Matthews, also happened to be the chairman of the board of WOW-TV. And when Johnny walked out of the studio after his show, there sat His Honor, in the livid flesh.

"The station manager told Johnny that he didn't want to hear the battleship mentioned again," Workhoven said. The world was full of leaders getting stuck in the mud, and Johnny moved his pointer on to other targets. To hold down inflation, the Truman administration decided on a wage freeze. Freezing Johnny's salary was like freezing a teardrop, and he decided to do a skit. He came on the air as if he were a reporter, standing outside the conference room where the board of WOW was meeting.

Johnny then entered the room to ask a few questions. As Workhoven remembers it, the only sounds were some drunken voices, glasses clinking, and riotous laughter.

"Hey, Frank, what do you think of the wage freeze?"

"Heeeerssh's ta the wage freeze," a drunken voice responded.

Johnny managed to get in the first names of other board members as well. They were all well in their cups, celebrating the happy news that their employees couldn't demand salary increases any longer.

This was daring material. What was most daring, almost foolhardy, was that Johnny was attacking his own company.

Johnny already had the topical humor that years later he would use with his monologues on *The Tonight Show*. He knew what people were thinking and talking about. The morning after a notorious criminal escaped from the courthouse near the station, Johnny began his morning radio show, "Kenneth, please call home." That afternoon he began his television program by having the camera zoom in on a lone candle burning in the window. "He never mentioned the name or anything," recalls Workhoven. "But for people who were aware of what was going on in the world, it was very funny. I know I laughed myself silly sitting there."

Johnny had fake letters that he answered on the air.

"What do you have to do to be in broadcasting?" one purported correspondent asked.

"Have an outside source of income," Johnny answered.

When Johnny and his material were right, *The Squirrel's Nest* had a giddy informality. Viewers felt that they were part of an extended family: crazy, wonderful Uncle Johnny and friends. After a while the show was televised later in the afternoon, and a group of teenagers showed up regularly. Johnny dubbed them the Dillinger gang. They laughed at every joke, deemed it a good day when they had leftovers from the cooking show to eat, and could even be persuaded to move pianos and furniture. One Easter when the boys helped Johnny color eggs on the show, they took the trolley home and bombarded passing vehicles with their seasonal weaponry.

Life was a little different in the Carsons' cramped third-floor walk-up. When Jody gave birth to a son, Chris, on November 7, 1950, her mother arrived to help. Mrs. Wolcott discovered that her duties included not only diapers and baby food, but also recording Jack Benny on the radio for Johnny.

On his Christmas show in 1950 Johnny had a great deal for which to be thankful. He had a loyal wife, a healthy new son, and a successful career.

"A lot of you people are probably watching this show for the first time today with your new Christmas television sets, and we hope this program won't let you down, and frankly we know it will."

Johnny introduced most of the WOW off-camera personnel, and a pathetic Christmas tree that looked as if it had been given a GI haircut.

"I don't mean to interrupt," one man said, "but it looks terrible."

"The tree?" Johnny asked.

"It's a nice tree, but there's nothing on it."

"It was a bargain, you know."

"Was it left over from last year?"

"Let's decorate it," Johnny said, changing the subject. "We don't have any lights, fellows. But we've got some decorations. We all do this together and hang the tinsel right."

As the men hung decorations as pitiful as the tree, they began to fight, pulling the tree back and forth.

"Hold it, hold it now, fellows, calm down!" Johnny yelled. "It's Christmas Day. All right, it wasn't a very expensive tree anyway. Let's go back and sit down and have some punch."

This only led to more squabbling, as did an attempt to open some presents. The group then set out to sing "Jingle Bells," and proceeded to desecrate the song.

"That was the WOW technical choir in their very joyous rendition of 'Jingle Bells,' " Johnny said solemnly. "And we hope that it has added a final touch to your Christmas holidays.

"The world is in quite a boxed-up situation, December, Christmas Day, 1950, and we certainly hope that by next Christmas in 1951 peace on earth and good will toward men will certainly be the thing."

War was raging in Korea, and in often subzero weather the Chinese were driving the United Nations and South Korean troops back down the Korean peninsula.

"I have a young son just six weeks old, and I certainly

hope that he and a lot of other young kids like him that are watching the show today and a little older, when they get to the age of the fellows on the program today don't have to live in the time that we're living in right now. We hope things are going to be better.''

As Johnny talked, his colleagues began throwing pies at one another. ''We'll see you next Wednesday on *Squirrel's Nest*,'' Johnny said as cream-filled pastry whizzed through the air. ''Till then, this is Johnny Carson, saying, Goodbye, everyone.''

F or months Johnny had been planning this trip. When his vacation came due in the summer of 1951, he packed his family into the secondhand Oldsmobile and headed west. He didn't intend to explore the Grand Canyon or spend days in the fond embrace of relatives. He had other things in mind. If he wanted to make it big in radio and television, he had to make it in California or New York.

Johnny and his colleagues at WOW-TV had shot a half-hour audition film. Unfortunately Omaha is known more for beef than broadcasters, and in San Francisco Johnny couldn't get past the receptionists.

One station did express some interest. After his interview Johnny and Jody sat in the Top of the Mark, the San Francisco restaurant on top of the Mark Hopkins Hotel. Johnny had to decide how much salary to ask. He fortified himself on several bourbons. Then he marched back to the station and asked for two hundred dollars a week. When he was turned down, he marched back out again.

In Los Angeles Johnny had somewhat better luck. Bill Brennan, his childhood friend from Avoca, was the program manager of KNXT-TV, the CBS affiliate. Brennan loved to talk about his boyhood days in Iowa. He had a voice that was like a warm hug. He was ambitious, not only for himself but for his friends. He promised Johnny that if an opening came up for an announcer, he would try to get him the position.

In the fall Brennan called Johnny. "John, I've got an opening on the announcer's staff," Brennan remembers saying. "It pays a hundred-fifteen dollars a week. It will get you in, and we'll try to develop something for you."

"Bill, that's good," Johnny said.

"There's only one bad thing. John, if you take it, and you don't have to, you'll have to start a week from Monday."

At WOW Johnny was not simply an announcer. He was a performer with his own show and a growing recognition in Omaha. That meant little if he had an opportunity to succeed in Los Angeles. He told the station he was quitting and packed up his belongings. He owed money to at least two of his friends at the station, but he forgot to pay them back.

A week later Johnny drove west alone, hauling a U-Haul behind the Oldsmobile. Jody was pregnant again, and the family would follow. In Oklahoma he ran into a blizzard. The tires blew out. The hitch came loose. By the time he reached Los Angeles, his fingers had stiffened from working too long in the cold.

That first evening in Los Angeles Johnny stayed at Bill Brennan's house. The next day he moved in temporarily with his aunt, left the trailer at a gas station, and went hunting for a place where his family could live.

This was not Nebraska, where the towns and villages are islands on the land, lost in the vast expanse of the plains. Los Angeles did not seem like a city but an endless array of villages. Johnny rented a duplex apartment in the San Fernando Valley, on the far side of the Hollywood Hills.

KNXT relegated Johnny to the worst hours and the most menial chores. He announced the time, weather, and call letters, and eventually did advertisements as well. On New Year's Day he had the unenviable chore of coming in to sign the station on the air at 8:00 A.M. When most people were watching the Parade of Roses, nursing hangovers, or eating with their families, he was sitting in the announcer's booth introducing everything from *Rhythm on Snow* to *Defense Theater*, doing plugs for future shows and public-service announcements for fire prevention and CARE. He didn't finish work until four-thirty. Only then could he begin to enjoy the holiday.

Johnny was far from the fame that he courted, more distant than in Omaha. There, he had been blessed with the patina of celebrity. Here, he was nobody in a city where obscurity seemed a moral judgment. Yet he could almost touch the famous. As he came into work early each morning, he drove along beside stars and directors on their way to the studios. At Kelbo's, Rand's Round-Up, and the other popular hangouts, he sat next to them. Even when he sat at home, he looked out the window and saw the hills above and the successful people who lived there. "I remember those first months in Hollywood when we used to look out over the hills, in the Toluca Lake area," Johnny says. "And I remember saying, 'Bob Hope lives right over there.' "

If Johnny and Jody were quite the young couple in Omaha, in Los Angeles they were as green as April corn. One evening they invited a group over to their place at 8:00 P.M. The guests assumed that they had been invited for dinner. Johnny poured drink after drink, but offered nothing more nourishing than potato chips. Finally one hungry guest mentioned food. Johnny drove to Love's Barbecue to pick up some ribs.

On another occasion Keith Meiniger, a fraternity brother, invited the Carsons to dinner. The Meinigers were house-sitting for a well-to-do doctor, and Keith told Johnny that the Japanese maid might answer the door. The Carsons were late, and Johnny hurried up to the front door of the large home. A lady answered the door. Johnny barged right through and went looking for Keith and his wife. When the man of the house saw this thin, hyperkinetic stranger running into his dining room, he directed him to the proper address, a block away.

Johnny got it right this time. After dinner the two couples drove into Los Angeles to attend the burlesque. Johnny had seen few agonies to compare to the burlesque comedian dying a slow, lingering death on the stage. He shouted out a remark from his table. The audience roared. Johnny gave the strippers bawdy new names and upstaged the whole show.

Johnny had given himself a year to make it in Los Angeles. If it hadn't worked out by then, he planned to move to New York and try there. He might seem a guileless young man, but he could not keep to his timetable without a full measure of shrewdness.

Johnny was in a position of considerable prestige even if he was dissatisfied. Radio announcers were the voice of the network, and they were chosen with care. Johnny was sufficiently proud the first time he did a coast-to-coast identification for the CBS Television Network that he telephoned his parents to watch.

Only four years before, on January 22, 1947, commercial television had begun in Los Angeles on KTLA. Bob Hope hosted the opening program. He read from a script in his hand, as he had on radio, and maneuvered uneasily in front of the cameras.

The audiences were endlessly forgiving. Viewers were used to radio, where *they* created Hope's car in their mind and visualized his house. Now, on television, they accepted a couple of chairs and a painted backdrop as a French café or a cut-out board as an automobile.

The coaxial cable hadn't reached Los Angeles. The stations had to come up with hours of local programming. This led to a carnival of the air, a bizarre, eclectic group of programs, a kooky distillation of Los Angeles in the early fifties.

Lawrence Welk and his Champagne Music emanated from the Aragon Ballroom, a sound as effervescent as an Alka-Seltzer. Those dreaming of more exotic climes only had to tune to Harry Owens and his Royal Hawaiians. Korla Pandit played mysterious chords on the organ, never saying a word the entire hour, a discretion that was in part the secret of his longevity. Those wanting to cool off with their music tuned in to Frosty Frolics, songs sung by ice skaters. The Continental provided on-air romance, with a moustache as well greased as his words of love. Professional wrestlers like Gorgeous George grappled on the air. Cars smashed together in a demolition derby. Humans smashed together as they careened around a wooden track on skates playing roller derby. And in an esoteric sport called moto polo, drivers in little cars knocked a big ball up and down a court.

Johnny started hanging out at Kelbo's Hawaiian Restaurant on Fairfax Avenue across from the new CBS Television City. The restaurant featured drinks in schooners as large as soup tureens, all festooned with cherries, pineapples, and gift-wrapped swizzle sticks. The drinks packed a wallop, and after a long day at the station many television people made their way across the avenue to the dark haunts of the bar. Everyone in radio and television drank, or so it seemed.

Bob Lehman, a radio producer in New York, got his start in television simply by sitting in the Nickelodeon bar, an industry hangout on Sunset Boulevard. A television producer who happened to be sitting next to him asked Lehman to put together a situation comedy on local television. For the first shows he simply wrote a story line, and the two actors winged it, ad-libbing their way through the half hour.

Lehman became friendly with Johnny, who was the occasional announcer on one of the first talk shows on television, *Backstage with N.T.G.* This was not the toughest duty in the world, since Nils T. Granlund garnished the program with gorgeous models and actresses.

When Granlund opened the show, saying, "We're really loaded tonight," it was a question of whether he was referring to the guests, the models, or himself. Once when Johnny was announcing *Backstage with N.T.G.*, Lehman returned to the station after filling up on high-test at the Jester Room.

Lehman was using scripts now, but he still played it loose.

On the night in question he meandered up to the cameraman standing behind the unwieldy instrument. The camera was less than three feet from Carson's face, shooting at him through a turret that was like a wide peashooter. "I shoved the cameraman out of the way and blew a big gob of smoke through the turret right into Carson's face," Lehman says, remembering the moment with immense satisfaction.

After it was over, everyone repaired to the bar to tell and retell the story. Johnny merited a place at the bar along with the others. By most standards he was doing well. In addition to his other duties, he was announcing a daily fifteen-minute show featuring the music of the New Yorkers, a popular three-piece combo. He was supposed to play it seriously, but Johnny could take the straightest line and twist it into a joke. "He was very funny," recalls Bill Baker, the piano player. "That's when he told everyone he was going to be the biggest thing in TV. I think he was serious."

When he hung out at Kelbo's, Johnny was not only having a good time. He was mixing with people he might need one day. "He had a lot of close friends, of buddies," Jody remembers. "They used to party after the show or rehearsals at Kelbo's. They would tell jokes and things like that. And time would go by. In those days it was a fellowship kind of thing. He was having such a good time that he didn't want to go home. We lived in the country too, far away."

Jody had shared Johnny's life in Lincoln and Omaha, but now she had been shunted aside. Their second son, Richard (Rick), was born on June 16, 1952, and she was nursemaid to two rambunctious, often unruly little boys.

When Johnny came home, she could smell the booze on his breath, and she suspected that he had other women as well. "When we first got to California, we were having coffee somewhere," Jody recalls. "He told me he had slept with the receptionist at WOW. I just looked at him, and I couldn't imagine why he would tell me. He said, 'Don't worry, everyone slept with her,' as if that would make it all right. Evidently the receptionist was sort of passed around. He was involved with quite a few people, starting from the beginning. He wasn't really involved though. It would get late and he'd get drunk, and I guess he took whoever was handy."

In September 1952 Jerry Solomon and Keith Meiniger showed up at the studio to go out drinking with their fraternity brother. Johnny was sitting on top of a washing machine, about to do a live commercial. But he appeared more interested in telling a story to his Nebraska friends.

As Johnny told his joke, the director signaled that airtime was only twenty seconds away. Johnny's hair was a mess. He casually ran his fingers through it, and went on with his story. Ten seconds. The director was frantic. Johnny continued his story. Five seconds. Johnny sat up straight and turned toward the camera, still talking to his friends. As the red light came on, Johnny started his spiel from memory, speaking as if nothing mattered in his life more than this washing machine that was his throne. As Johnny finished the commercial, perfectly on the mark, the red light went off, and he segued back to his joke.

Later that evening the three men sat at Kelbo's drinking. Johnny felt that he wasn't getting anywhere, and his year was almost up. He had a wife and two children, Chris and little Ricky. It wasn't cheap buying shoes and diapers and food. "John said he was working his tail off," recalls Solomon. "Even with us there, he was table-hopping. We're sitting at the bar and he would go off and talk to someone for fifteen minutes. He couldn't get a sponsor for a TV show. He was broke. He was down-and-out. He said he had a hard time meeting his obligations. I remember loaning him money, twenty dollars. I never got it back."

Dum-de-dum-dum. The organ played the familiar chords of *Dragnet*, the popular detective series.

"Ladies and gentlemen," said John Condon, a young announcer who had arrived at the station the same time as Johnny, "the program you are about to see is true, only the jokes have been changed to protect the station . . . KNXT, in cooperation with the itinerant yam pickers of southern California, *cautiously* presents . . . *Carson's Cellar*!!''

On Saturday evening at 7:00 P.M. on October 4, 1952, Johnny's program debuted on KNXT-TV. It was called *Carson's Cellar*, a pun on the bargain-basement nature of the show.

Carson made a few opening remarks and then proceeded into a half-hour satire of television. Satirizing television might seem like making fun of a child taking his first steps, but the material was wonderfully rich. This was what Johnny *knew*, and he had written a deft, wryly funny half hour.

Johnny came on as Liberace. He sat in front of a piano with the candelabrum blazing away. In later years Liberace would make fun of himself in routines that were kitsch classics. But in these days housewives swooned over Liberace and dreamed of cuddling up next to him, like a poodle, never imagining that the pianist played at a different piano.

"I have selected one of your favorite songs," Liberace aka Johnny Carson said, " 'When It's Strawberry Time in the Valley, I'll Get Rash over You.' "

The playing deteriorated into mayhem, and Johnny went on to impersonate a singing cowboy ("We're mighty happy to be comin' yur way with another eight hours of yur favorit requests.") He satirized commercials ("We're offering fur a limited time only a beautiful illustrated book titled *How to Perform Operations at Home*.") He introduced the three-member band, the New Yorkers, and made fun of them.

Then Carson introduced Condon, the announcer, as Mr. Harold Frankner. Condon spoke in sonorous tones: "As a representative of *TV Snow* magazine, it gives me a great pleasure to present Johnny Carson this award on behalf of the editors and publishers of *TV Snow*, for outstanding television artistry for 1952."

"I . . . I . . . hardly know what to say," Johnny stammered. "But this is only our first show on television."

"Well, Johnny, all programs receive some award after

they've been on the air for a while. We're presenting this award in the event that your program might not last any length of time. Congratulations.''

To the viewer who tuned in to *Carson's Cellar*, Johnny seemed hip and knowing. From the beginning the program had a savvy audience, alive to the nuances of Carson's satire. By the second week there was already a small studio audience.

Television was one big joke, as Johnny and his director, Bob Lehman, saw it. One week Johnny, with mock-solemnity, presented a public-service ad. He pretended to clean the insides of the viewers' television picture with a cloth. Television was so new that some viewers may have thought they were getting a free cleaning of their newfangled set.

One day the director called his star to suggest a skit on a late-night movie host. Johnny had never watched television that time of the evening. But when he did, he saw the possibilities. The skit began with some old silent-movie footage of a pilot landing his biplane and running into a building. The camera cut to Carson, as the movie host, who said that the pilot was in a hurry because it had been a cross-country flight. Then, after some more patter, he announced that they were going back to the film. Instead, they cut to film of the numbered academy leader that is at the beginning of films. The numbers flashed on the screen: 10 . . . 9 . . . 8 . . . 7 . . . 6 . . . 5 . . .

The studio audience was so used to technical problems on television that they didn't see it as a joke. "We had to run it twenty seconds," Lehman remembers. "I'm sitting shitting razor blades wondering if they're ever going to get it.''

Carson's Cellar was an orphan. The station dropped spot advertisements into the program, but *Carson's Cellar* didn't have a full sponsor, or a regular time slot.

Johnny wasn't exactly receiving a star's billing or salary. He earned an extra fifty dollars a week doing *Carson's Cellar*, but he had his full announcing schedule as well. He also had a budget of twenty-five dollars to pay for cande-labra, cowboy hats, and assorted other props.

Everyone on the show wanted to succeed, but they were going to have fun while doing it. Johnny and Bob Lehman were drinking and fishing buddies, and neither man let duties get in the way of a good time. Lehman's wife, Linda Williams, a statuesque woman, performed as a bit player. When the director needed a chorus line, he photographed his wife's legs through a prism, multiplying them into a line of legs more precise than the Rockettes.

John Condon was the archetypal announcer, as straight as a stand-up microphone, with a voice that resonated like an echo chamber. He served up his lines to Johnny like a pitcher throwing underhand to Mickey Mantle. He didn't get paid extra for his comic chores, but he enjoyed doing the show. So did the New Yorkers. They were as hip as Condon was straight, and Johnny played off them, as years later he would play off the band on *The Tonight Show*.

The New Yorkers not only played music, they performed in the skits. On one program Bill Baker, the piano player, lay on an operating table while Johnny changed his oil. As soon as the skit was over and the screen went black, Baker tore off the sheet and ran over to the piano in time for the musical cue.

Much of *Carson's Cellar* could have been dusted off and redone on *The Tonight Show*. Johnny had the beginnings of a topical monologue ("Some good news for the kids in Baltimore this week. The teachers are on strike.") He answered supposed questions from the viewers. He played a scatterbrained teacher, a familiar character too, as was the TV movie host, later reincarnated as Art Fern, the greasy matinee-movie host.

These were good times. "It was a different kind of feeling then," says Peter Leeds, a regular player in the skits. "You had a camaraderie, a relationship, a love, and a respect. There wasn't any strain. If you didn't make it, someone else would do it. If anything went wrong, you laughed it up."

When someone ran across the set, Johnny announced that it had been Red Skelton, doing a guest shot. It was a funny bit, the idea of a big star doing *Carson's Cellar*. But Skelton happened to be watching, and the next week he showed up for real.

During the week Phil Weltman was a hot young agent at the William Morris Agency. On weekends Weltman was usually just another guy at the beach, working on a tan. This weekend, however, Weltman lay in bed with the flu. He turned on television, and saw Johnny Carson. Weltman found himself laughing, forgetting his aching body. *If he can look that good to me in my condition, he must be just what they're looking for,* Weltman thought.

Weltman called KNXT and set up a luncheon with Johnny at the Brown Derby on Sunset and Vine. "As of now, I'm your agent," Weltman remembers saying. "You're going to get calls because people have seen us together. Tell people I represent you. They're probably going to call you in to have you sign a long-term contract. Tell them you won't sign anything."

Jack Hellman, the *Variety* television columnist, saw Johnny eating with Weltman at the legendary Hollywood restaurant. He wrote Johnny up in his column ("Carson is on his way and with the right kind of material and handling should go far.")

James Aubrey, the KNXT station manager, telephoned Weltman. Aubrey, a future president of CBS, was already on his way to earning his nickname: the smiling cobra. "Aubrey said either sign with us for three years or we're going to cancel the show," Weltman says. "John needed the money. I said, 'Don't worry about it.' "

Johnny had developed some heat. He was an original, and shrewder heads than his were figuring out his future. Weltman signed Johnny to a contract with the Ted Bates Agency. In the 1950's advertising agencies not only bought time on television, they produced entire programs. Thus, the Ted Bates Agency could almost single-handedly create a major new television personality.

American Home Products agreed to sponsor Carson. The advertising executives weren't particularly interested in the motley brew known as *Carson's Cellar*. They wanted a classier program with a classier title: *The Johnny Carson Show*. Johnny would need some writing help. Weltman used that as an opportunity for another William Morris client, Bob Weiskopf. The young comedy writer took the train out from New York to help write the thirteen-week program scheduled to be shown regionally in the western United States.

Lehman struggled to make the new show work. He understood the problems of advertisers. One day when he was running through the filmed commercials, Fred Allen, the radio comedian, walked into the control booth.

"When does my spot come on?" asked Allen. He was to be the guest star.

"Right after the Nair commercial," Lehman said brightly.

"No way am I going to come on after those Gabby Hayes legs," Allen deadpanned.

Allen wasn't serious, but the comedian had a point. What gagman could write better lines than: "Girls, have you got briar-patch legs? Try this test! Rub your hand along your leg. Feel that stubble—that bristly hair. If so, say 'goodbye' to briar-patch legs."

The advertising men in New York who spent their days writing such prose took themselves very seriously. The gentlemen from American Home Products had a much narrower vision of comedy than that which had appeared on *Carson's Cellar*. They were all for parody, but in good taste, and nothing sacrilegious, nothing that might cast aspersions against Arrid extra-dry deodorant and Nair.

"They hired me to produce and direct, and I lasted two weeks," Lehman says. "They didn't understand the philosophy of the show. They wanted to put on an orchestra and a girl singer. They wanted to make it like any variety show. I fought them for two weeks, and I quit.''

Johnny was already experiencing the bureaucracy of stardom, the entourage of agents, advisers, publicists, and hangers-on, all full of advice. He wanted to succeed, and these people knew more than he did, or so it seemed. ''Johnny was being very neutral,'' Lehman asserts. ''It was his first contact by a major national television sponsor. I'm sure that Johnny heard beautiful music.''

Although network television was still in its infancy, it already at times resembled a gigantic soup kitchen that would take the richest stew and water it down until it tasted like weak bouillon. While *The Johnny Carson Show* had some good skits and material, the program was not *Carson's Cellar*. From the opening line of the programs, the difference was apparent. *Carson's Cellar* had begun with self-deprecating wit:

> KNXT, DESPITE THREATENING LETTERS, CAU-
> TIOUSLY PRESENTS JOHNNY CARSON'S CELLAR.
> AND HERE'S THE GUY WHO HAS TO ACCOUNT FOR
> THIS HALF HOUR . . . JOHNNY CARSON.

The new show opened:

> THE JOHNNY CARSON SHOW! . . . BROUGHT TO
> YOU BY ARRID, THE DEODORANT THAT IS
> PROVED 53 PERCENT MORE EFFECTIVE THAN ANY
> OTHER LEADING BRAND IN KEEPING UNDERARMS
> DRY AND ODORLESS—AND HERE'S THE STAR OF
> OUR SHOW . . . JOHNNY CARSON.

Johnny did the best he could with the material, but much of the program was no more singular than the opening. ''The show wasn't that successful,'' says Weiskopf. ''It was borderline, and the ratings weren't that good.'' Weiskopf hardly remembers the show. Neither does Carson. When he talks of that period in his life, it is as if the original *Johnny Carson Show* never existed.

A year earlier Johnny had been the hottest new comedian in town, but by the summer of 1953 he was off the air. For a few short months television had made Johnny part of Los Angeles's aristocracy of celebrity. It wasn't like being a movie star, but he was *somebody*. Now, he was another performer looking for a new series.

In television when you worked, you worked with almost ceaseless energy. When you didn't work, you gave your greatest performance: maintaining the illusion of success and affluence. Johnny wasn't a star, but he was wise enough to realize that Los Angeles was a graveyard of careers, of aspirations gone wrong, of men and women of his generation for whom it was already over.

Johnny visited the home of a once-famous comedian. The man was spending his days sitting in his house calling his agent, trying to get a guest-appearance shot on television. "You look at a man like that," he said, "and it makes you want to cry."

In May 1954 Johnny got his first break on network television: host of a prime-time game show, *Earn Your Vacation*. The program was a dreary bit of business, and it lasted only through the summer doldrums. However, the show had one fringe benefit. The writers and performers could win more goodies than the contestants, by working in plugs for various products. Mention a certain whiskey on the air, and a case of the beloved beverage would arrive at one's door. Talk about a clothing company, and one had a new wardrobe. "None of us had any compunction about dropping a plug in," says Brennan, who produced the show. "One time we had eighteen plugs on, and Johnny thought it was getting a little bit much. Of course, he was taking booze and merchandise too."

Johnny needed exposure, for in television exposure was life. "One day after my two-hour talk show, Jim Aubrey asked to see me in his office,'' recalls Red Rowe, whose program was broadcast regionally on CBS. ''Aubrey said, 'We got this new guy Carson who we think has something to offer, but we don't have anything for him to do. Sales can sell him to a coffee account. If it's all right with you, we'd like to put him on at nine A.M. for five minutes, right after your show. We'll build him a little set, and he'll tell two or three minutes of jokes, and you stand around and laugh at his jokes.'

''So I'd sign off my show and they'd do a station break and he'd come on. The crew was still there. There would be a studio audience as well. Aubrey was, in effect, putting a plug on at the end of my show for a guy who was more ambitious than I was, though I was the guy making the money.''

Carson's Coffee Break appeared twice a week on KNXT. ''The longest 5-minute show on television,'' Johnny called it years later. ''Not even 5 minutes. I did a commercial—3 ½ minutes!'' Johnny needed money, especially since on November 2, 1953, Jody gave birth to a third son, Cory. Johnny earned more income and kept his comedic wits alive by writing for Red Skelton, CBS's top comic. Skelton, who billed himself as an American clown, was masterful at wringing the last laugh out of his characters and routines.

In the era before television, comedians might perform the same routine for years, from city to city, vaudeville hall to vaudeville hall. But in the television age the best material, the best lines, were gone in a moment. A comedian might come on a few times and burn himself out.

Television comedians didn't like to admit that they were dependent on writers. Some of them preferred not even to see the plebian scribes. Jackie Gleason had scripts shoved under the door of his hotel room, as if they had been created by room service. Red Skelton acted as if he employed writers as charity, a prod to his comedic genius. ''I used to write the show and the music for the background,'' Skelton says. ''They would hand this to the writers and they would punch it up. At the rehearsal I would try the different guys' lines, and end up with the original because I know myself better than anyone or I wouldn't have been on television for twenty years."

Skelton performed a very physical comedy. On August 18, 1954, he was rehearsing a skit in which he played a prisoner called "Inky" because he "ran out of the pen so often." The comedian ran toward the breakaway door. The door did not break away, and Inky lay unconscious.

"They took me back to the dressing room and I'm out for forty-eight hours," Skelton recalls. "But first they said, 'What are we going to do about the show?' I looked up and said, 'Get Johnny Carson. He knows the show backwards and forwards.' "

The producer called Johnny at home. "Tonight?" Johnny asked.

"Tonight. Now."

As he drove into the studio, Johnny composed a monologue in his head. Johnny's head was a filing system of jokes, something old, something new, something borrowed, and something blue. He put in a few surefire jokes, added lines that he thought would work for the Skelton audience, and he was ready.

Johnny told the audience about Skelton's accident. "Personally, the way I feel right now, I think Red's doctors should be doing this show," he said. In a sense Skelton *was* doing his show, since Johnny introduced kinescopes of the comedian's previous appearances.

Johnny did a credible job that evening. That he could do it at all on such short notice was the most important fact. Television needed performers who could work within the confines of time and routine, never missing a beat. Johnny was soon signed to a contract by CBS.

Johnny was a man of great ambition, but he enjoyed good times and good friends. In the privacy of his home he might be sullen and withdrawn, but with good drinks and good friends he could be funnier than on television.

Like most comics, Johnny was at his funniest when he

was with his peers. One evening he was at a bachelor party attended by many of the leading comedians in Los Angeles. Each was trying to top the other. Other entertainment was planned for the evening as well, to be provided by two young ladies of less than pristine reputations. As Johnny told his story, one of the young ladies entered nude from the bedroom. She sauntered up to Johnny as he continued to tell his story. Putting her arm around him, she brushed a breast against his shoulder. Finally Johnny noticed. He looked down and said, "Get away from me, you point-killing son of a bitch."

Johnny got the biggest laugh of the night. The other comedians understood the truth in Carson's comment; sex is great, but a good joke is better.

Several years later, when Johnny was better known, he flew to New York City to be the substitute host of a daytime game show. Johnny usually kept to himself, and he was sitting in his hotel room when the phone rang.

"Mr. Carson?"

"Yes?"

"J. B. Derkin of Derkin . . ." the voice said, reeling off a list of impressive sounding names. "I'm head of the Buick division. We've seen you this week and we'd like you to do a commercial for us. There's a new Buick and ten thousand dollars in it for you."

This was better than Vegas. Johnny could see himself tearing down the freeway in his snazzy new car.

"We're going to be taping these next Tuesday."

Johnny's heart fell.

"Mr. Derkin," Johnny said, trying to control his anguish, "I'm very flattered, but I can't be here."

"What?"

"I can't be here."

"It's just like you West Coast guys! You do a little piddling show there, and you come back here and you think you're big shots."

Johnny finally realized that "Mr. Derkin" was his friend Jonathan Winters, doing one of his impressions.

* * *

One night Johnny was having dinner at Kelbo's with Seaman Jacobs. Jacobs had started out in the business as a press agent, but he was now writing comedy for Carson and others. Johnny dumped some Thousand Island dressing on his salad. As he ate a bite of the salad, he grimaced. "I think I got a bad island."

At 2:00 A.M. one morning Jacobs and his wife, Margaret, heard an incredible thrashing sound out at the pool. The couple lived in the woods of Coldwater Canyon. They looked out the window to see what beast had stumbled into their backyard. There was Johnny, swimming in their pool. "He was half-smashed," remembers Margaret Ferraro, Jacobs's former wife. "He scared the hell out of us. He was out boozing, running around, womanizing. I guess he wanted to smell of chlorine and not another woman. And in the morning his shorts were lying on the poolside. His shorts were battleship gray. He should have kept them on when he was in the chlorine, and they might have been bleached."

On many occasions, though, the Carsons went out as husband and wife for liquor and laughter. Los Angeles had a great jazz scene in the fifties, and Johnny and Jody loved to go to the clubs and listen to the music. On weekends they sometimes went to Lake Arrowhead, a couple hours from Los Angeles, and along with the New Yorkers stayed with a wealthy couple in their immense house. The place was so large that the band set up in the fireplace to jam the night away with Johnny on drums.

"Jody tried to do everything to please him," says Mrs. Ferraro. "She had dark circles under her eyes. I remember one day we went to the drugstore to get some Erase to put under her eyes. She did everything to try to enhance her beauty for him, because she knew of his chasing. She was intimidated by him because he was so strict with the boys. When he walked in the house, he wanted Jody and the boys to bow and scrape, all in a line, to the right, like a little Hitler."

Jody and Johnny had three of the most energetic boys in Los Angeles, tireless, exhausting tykes. When the Carsons redecorated, they chose Naugahyde furniture that was practically indestructible. The children gave Jody little peace, and what free time she had, she wanted to be with Johnny. She made sure she was always there the night of his shows so that she could go to the party afterward. Tagging along behind Johnny wasn't easy, but it was better than staying at home.

"I knew that women were always throwing themselves at people like Johnny," Jody says. "You had a few drinks in you and some beautiful woman comes along and it's hard not to shack up. It doesn't have to do with your home or your wife. It's just there. When I wanted to go with John once, he said to me, 'Why take a ham sandwich to a banquet?' "

SIX

Not until almost a year after his appearance on *The Red Skelton Show* did twenty-nine-year-old Johnny get his own half-hour comedy on CBS. *The Johnny Carson Show* began on Thursday evening, June 30, 1955, as a summer replacement. It seemed like old times again. Bill Brennan was the producer. John Condon signed on as announcer, at $125 a week instead of the $25 he'd received doing *Carson's Cellar*. Johnny planned to use Jody occasionally too.

Brennan went to New York and hired Mort Green and George Foster as writers. The two had been working on *The Big Show*, one of the last big network-radio shows. Brennan impressed them. They liked the sheer warmth of the man. They listened intently to his tale of how Brennan and his boyhood friend, Johnny Carson, were going to have a hit.

Johnny had no end of things to worry about. "When I met John in college, he was very thin, almost scrawny, and very hyper," Jody says. "Before his first network show he was memorizing scripts. He bought weights. The sponsor insisted that he have his teeth capped. Up until then he never smiled with his mouth open. Instead of putting on temporary caps, he had to have all of his teeth ground down and capped in one week. I think he felt pain because of this." According to Bill Brennan, CBS agreed to pay for one tooth, but Johnny went ahead and had his entire mouth done.

George Gobel had begun his network career as a summer replacement, and he had become the most successful comedian on television. Now the networks and the sponsors were looking for "the new George Gobel," and Johnny was going to be it. Johnny was laid-back, but Gobel was so low-key that he seemed asleep. Johnny didn't want to be considered a pale Xerox copy of Lonesome George.

Johnny had sponsors, Revlon and General Foods, to deal with as well. Mort Green remembers Johnny's premiere very well: "I'm sitting in the control room with the sponsors. I can see the audience and I can see the stage. Carson walks on. 'Good evening, ladies and gentlemen.' Screams. I turn to this fellow and ask what's what. I say, 'Look at those people out there. They're not laughing.'

"The sponsor says, 'It's a laugh machine. We want to protect him.'

"I say, 'Let him suffer the slings and arrows. If the audience doesn't get it, that's beside the point.'

"The laugh machine was William Morris's idea. It was very unusual to use it on a variety show, but they did it."

Johnny thought of everything. The first week he did a parody of *Person to Person*, the Edward R. Murrow interview show, using his own family. The next week he parodied the popular game show *What's My Line?* Then he stopped doing parodies for a while. He had only so many TV shows to satirize, and he didn't want the audience to expect one every week.

He introduced Jody and the kids as his real family; his TV wife was Virginia Gibson. But he didn't want to do husband-and-wife skits every week. That could be another trap. He introduced a female vocalist. She received bad reviews and was gone, to be replaced by Jill Corey, a talented stylist who bore a striking resemblance to Jody.

A television production is a collegial activity, and a score of people were working to make *The Johnny Carson Show* succeed. The publicity people gave it their best shot. Johnny had never received much publicity before, but he had something rare to offer: the perfect family. In addition to using

Jody and the boys on his show, he let photographers and reporters come out to his new home in Encino to record life at the Carsons'.

Johnny and Jody appeared on the cover of *TV Guide*, a great coup for the young comedian. The cover photo showed the adoring Carsons sipping a soda like college sweethearts.

"All the time we were posing for publicity photos, the happy married young couple, when a whole other life was going on," says Jody. "I remember the night before the *TV Guide* came out, he didn't come home until four o'clock, drunk, lipstick all over him. It upset me, because I had to get the children ready for a publicity layout. They had to be washed and dressed, smiling and happy and posing, the happy, modern Carsons.

"Maybe it doesn't seem like much to a man, but timing matters. You have three little boys. You have to get them fed. You have to keep them clean. You have to keep the house clean. You have to iron the clothes. You have to do the dishes. That's the whole day. You get it done. You get your bath. And you're ready and the boys are all ready. Daddy's coming home. Then you wait and you wait."

"Carson was this nice guy from the Midwest who suddenly was surrounded by all this excitement and stardom and beauty," says Mort Green. "He gets his teeth fixed. Now his poor little wife, Jody, is in the toilet. We're sitting in Kelbo's when he should be home with his wife. And he's saying, 'Let's go out and party.'

"I'm here from New York without a wife, living at the Beverly Hills Hotel. And Carson's probably thinking, Say, hey, wait a minute, you're going back to the Polo Lounge and you're going to swing and there are going to be these beautiful hookers and other dames around. And oh Jesus, I'm going out to the valley."

Here he was then, the eminently likable Johnny Carson, funny man, family man, with a marriage falling apart and a show that wasn't working.

The Johnny Carson Show was a smorgasbord without any main courses. Jack Gould wrote in *The New York Times* that while Johnny was pleasant enough, "the rest of the show, unfortunately, was only too typical summer video fare . . . a routine girl vocalist, a conventional jazz unit, and a sketch about a guest who did not know when to go home."

CBS could turn the decibel level of the laugh machine up until it rocked the rafters, but that didn't help the ratings. During the fifties people talked about television. In offices and homes they discussed the comedies and the dramas, the variety shows and the sports programs. Television was live, the best of it, and that lent an added excitement. But almost nobody was talking about *The Johnny Carson Show*.

Johnny was doing his on-the-air training in front of a national television audience. "You've got to remember here's a guy who has never been in the borscht belt or the theater," Brennan says. "He's never had any acting training. He's a child of radio and television. So, anyway, we're groping around, trying to put the elephant through the porthole. He had very definite ideas about what he was and what he wasn't. He'd dig his heels in. He'd say, 'I don't do that kind of shtick.' He was also learning the word *shtick*. You got to remember he had lived a white-bread life, a pure Middle American middle-class life."

Jody saw Johnny's frustration the way no one else did. She saw him come home after the rehearsal when he was told a skit wasn't funny. She watched him as the writers changed, and the format changed, and still the show didn't seem to be working. Before the series ended, seven directors and eight writers came and went, each one full of promises.

Television had made Johnny. The medium could plunge him back into obscurity as easily as turning off a TV set. John Crosby of the *New York Herald Tribune* struck the most ominous note of all. "One of the young comedians being looked over [as another George Gobel] is Johnny Carson and I rather think that they won't find Gobel there,"

Crosby wrote. "Maybe three summers from now they'll be looking for Johnny Carson and by that time he'll be in Europe, looking at cathedrals, and they'll wonder where he went."

After the summer was over, heads began to roll on *The Johnny Carson Show*. Johnny had seen it before. When Bob Lehman had left the original *Johnny Carson Show*, Johnny had stayed out of the way. This time it was his oldest friend in Hollywood, Bill Brennan, who was fired.

Mort Green was in the barbershop at the Beverly Hills Hotel when he got a phone call from a CBS executive.

"Did you hear the news?" the executive asked, as Green remembers.

"No."

"Well, the network just fired Brennan."

"Does Carson know?"

"I don't know."

Green called Johnny from the barber's chair.

"John, I guess you know the news," Green said.

"Yeah," Johnny said, according to Green.

"Yeah?"

"Well, you know, in this business it's every guy for himself."

"Okay," Green remembers replying. "You can take your show and shove it up your ass, because I'm leaving, I'm going back to New York."

Green set out to find Brennan. "Brennan was a mess," says Green. "It was the way Carson treated him. On Monday I got a call from the new executive producer. They wanted my partner and me to stay on as producers and head writers. But I said the man who brought Carson here, and worked like a dog to get him here, you fire. I said I wouldn't want to work on a show where the star had treated a man the way Carson treated Bill Brennan."

"There were too many cooks telling me what to do and how to do it," Johnny said. "There was no central control.

The agency was putting people on without my knowledge, the scripts were being edited without telling me. I was sitting around like a dummy.''

CBS canceled the show after thirty-nine weeks. According to Jody, Johnny learned about it by reading *Variety*. A year ago he was on the cover of *TV Guide*, and now he was off the air. A year ago the critics had wanted to call him the new George Gobel, and now old Lonesome George was already on his way down, blown off the ratings by *Gunsmoke*.

Johnny was under contract to CBS, and the network relegated him to the world of daytime television. Within a couple months he was back on the air doing his own half-hour daytime show, still called *The Johnny Carson Show*. John Condon, his longtime announcer, would have liked to continue to work with him, but he sensed that Johnny didn't have much clout. He didn't ask for the job, and he didn't get it.

Johnny had loyal friends in people such as Condon and Lehman who liked Johnny for himself. Yet these very qualities made it unlikely that they would exploit their friendship by asking for work.

Johnny made the best of his demotion. "I'd have been wise to start out with an afternoon show, where the pace is easy and relaxed, and grown into nighttime TV," he told a reporter.

While the show didn't score in the ratings, either, it came far closer to displaying Johnny's abilities to advantage. He didn't knock you dead with his punch lines. He was more subtle, and tickled you like a feather.

One day Johnny was doing a favorite routine, "The Homework School of the Air," with his new announcer, Hank Simms. When Simms read the question to "Professor Carson," it was so funny that he began to laugh. Then the audience began to laugh. Simms laughed until tears rolled down his cheeks. The audience was convulsed. Everyone was laughing: the cameramen, the other performers, the soundman. Everyone but Johnny.

Simms finally got control of himself, biting his lips. It was time for Johnny to answer, though it was impossible that it could be as funny as the question.

The camera focused on Johnny's face, as solemn as a hanging judge. "Would you repeat the question, please?" Carson deadpanned.

Simms and Johnny became friends. "My wife and I were living in a lousy flat," Simms says. "One night John came over for dinner alone. There was another couple, who left early. There were eyes being passed back and forth, and this fellow figured he should get his little broad out of there. Then John said, 'I have to hit the road.' I said, 'Fine, but you better have one for the road.' I mixed him another Jack Daniel's and ginger ale, and we started telling stories. Finally my bride said to me, 'We've run out of ginger ale.' I said, 'Don't worry. Use Seven-up.' So we mix some more, and later she said, 'We've run out of Seven-up.' I said, 'Just put in club soda and a little sugar. He won't notice the difference.'

"We're still telling stories, and it's really getting late, two in the morning. My wife comes in and says, 'We've run out of club soda.' I said, 'Give him tonic, he won't know the difference.' So I poured him one. He took one sip and said, 'That's where I draw the damn line.'

"Anyway, it's three o'clock in the morning, and we have to be at rehearsals at eight. I said, 'You might as well stay the night.' So we get to rehearsal at ten o'clock. The director is hysterical because we're going on the air at eleven and John has a tongue that looks like the Sahara Desert. The show goes on, and he practically wings it because he didn't really rehearse it. And it was the funniest show in the whole series.

"He had a couple of Japanese gals with their ceremonial robes and obis in the back. They were showing him how to drink sake. They didn't have much English, and it was hysterical. Everyone knew it was ginger ale in the bottles. He's doing tremendous takes every time he takes a sip, crossing his eyes. After the show I said, 'John, that was a

wonderful acting job. I know you weren't feeling too great.
Everyone in the audience, and everyone at home, will think
that's actually sake.'

"He said, 'I got news for you. That was sake.' "

Johnny wasn't drinking only sake. "It was kind of my
duty over the weekends to keep him out of trouble," recalls
Cal McKinley of the New Yorkers, whose combo still
played for Johnny. "That was kind of ridiculous, because
I got in as much trouble as he did. He got kicked out of
places like the Cock and Bull on Sunset. One night he put
the make on a broad next to him, who happened to be the
bartender's girlfriend. At that time he was pretty expert at
jujitsu. The bartender came over the top of the bar, and
John threw him through the front door. We got out of there
just before the cops came.

"Our wives used to get pissed off at us. I'll never forget
taking him to my home to sleep one night. I'm trying to
get him into bed. We had twin beds hooked together at the
headboard. I got his clothes off and got him in bed, and he
fell down through the crack and ended up beneath the bed
on the floor. It must have taken me two hours to get that
SOB back on the bed. I finally get him on the bed, and he
goes to sleep.

"I'm in the kitchen making a Bloody Mary. And the
intercom comes on, and it's John, asking, 'Is this place on
Diner's Club?' "

There were many good moments on the daytime *Johnny
Carson Show*, but in four months it was gone. When
the show started, Johnny had compared himself to a ball-
player going down to the minor leagues for some seasoning. He had struck out once more, and it wasn't on the
Yankees.

Phil Weltman didn't shunt aside a client simply because
he had some bad luck. But no one was calling William
Morris desperate to sign Johnny, and Weltman was handling
a lot of other clients. Carson was a known commodity, the
star of a failed network program. Weltman used some of

his chits at the agency on Johnny's behalf, getting him a co-starring role with Carol Channing in *Three Men on a Horse* in the prestigious *Playhouse 90* series on CBS on April 18, 1957. But that was about it.

More than Johnny's professional life was in trouble. Those who saw Johnny and Jody together sensed that their marriage was doomed. At parties Johnny went off in one direction, flirting with women. Jody staked out a chair at the far end of the room, and drank and talked the evening away. Although Jody doesn't feel so, she acted something of a flirt herself. Jody's strained relationship with her father continued to reflect itself in her childish taunting of Johnny.

One evening the Carsons' good friends Jack and Mary Lou Narz went out to Don the Beachcomber with Johnny and Jody. The two couples downed a few drinks, and by the time they left they were flying. The group went to another favorite haunt, the Four Jokers, where they exploded into the club in a burst of conviviality and good cheer. Johnny loved to hear the Jokers playing their music. When the place closed up, Jack invited some other couples and the band out to his place in the valley.

The band brought their instruments. Jack and Johnny drove over to the Carsons' in Johnny's Porsche sports car to pick up his drums so he could sit in with the band.

The party lasted all night long. Jody had had a long day, and she went into a bedroom to lie down. One of the musicians sacked out on the bed beside her. When Mary Lou walked into the bedroom to go to the bathroom, she saw the two bodies. It appeared perfectly innocent, but she thought to herself, If Johnny sees this, there is going to be trouble.

At around dawn Johnny and Jody walked out on the back porch. He struck his wife, hitting her from one side of the face to another. Jack and Mary Lou had never seen a man hitting a woman before, and they didn't know what to do. As Johnny flailed away, Jody yelled loudly enough to wake the Narzes' children. Still he continued beating her as she backed out of the house into the driveway.

As the attack continued, Mary Lou thought to herself, He is going to kill her when he gets home.

Despite all that they had seen, the Narzes did not call the Carsons. In the 1950's physical abuse was the unmentionable, unthinkable vice, especially among people of Johnny's class and aspirations. No one knew how serious John's attacks in the privacy of their house were. But on that day Johnny Carson showed a side of himself that his friends didn't want to believe existed. "Many people can't take that over and over again," says Jody. "He could have accidentally killed me, and not have known about it until the next morning."

Jody's isolation was almost absolute. The darkest secret of her marriage was out, and no one had done anything, no one had cared. Despite the attacks, Jody wanted her marriage to continue. Johnny was the father of her children; she wanted to be part of his world. But she could tolerate him no longer, and Johnny and Jody separated.

Seaman Jacobs took Jody to dinner to talk to her about going back to her husband. "Johnny got very angry that I was dating his wife," says Jacobs. "And I don't think he ever believed me, that I was trying to be a good guy."

"I was seeing a psychiatrist who was also a marriage counselor," Jody says. "He said that John should leave because of the beating up and the drinking. The analyst said that I should date other people. Maybe he thought if John was jealous, he would change, but I was so vulnerable. I was thrust into the wolves of Hollywood.

"One night Johnny walked in and there was a man there in the living room. Johnny didn't like that very much. But I think it did help a little bit. He realized that it could happen. It was possible that we could become divorced.

"That evening he said he wasn't leaving. I was very glad to get back in the marriage. After that I got everything. I got a Plymouth convertible that was gold with wings. I went all out. I dyed my hair blond. I got a housekeeper. I got a mink stole. I did the whole thing to try to attract his attention, to make him jealous, to have him see what it felt like."

To win her husband back, Jody believed that she had to become like the women that she thought Johnny saw in Hollywood. She tried to grow away from *herself*, from Jody Carson, the daughter of Nebraska pioneers and a small-town girl; and also sought to grow away from *him*, from the John Carson she knew.

Johnny appeared to have no one left whom he could trust completely. He couldn't trust where Jody had been, whom she had seen. Even at home she seemed a woman trying to become someone else. Johnny had lost his oldest friend, Bill Brennan. He still had an agent, but he felt that Weltman had largely deserted him.

Carson decided to try a nightclub act. He wrote his own material and opened in Bakersfield, a farming town in the San Joaquin Valley. If CBS nighttime was the major leagues, then the Maison Jaussaud in Bakersfield for four hundred dollars a week was semipro softball.

Most comedians in the fifties had their rites of passage in the toilet clubs of America, harassed by loudmouths, heckled by drunks who dared them to be funny. Now, Johnny learned what it was like to be screamed at by tomato farmers.

Johnny perfected his routine and then invited his William Morris agent to make the journey to Bakersfield. Weltman might have ventured as far as the outer reaches of the San Fernando Valley, but he did not journey to the vegetable fields of central California. Instead, two junior agents showed up and monitored Carson's act from a corner. Another comedian might have been appreciative that even these two underlings had come. Carson felt abandoned.

That Johnny was not going to make it as a stand-up comedian was clear enough. CBS had not renewed his contract. He was out of work, with three kids, a big mortgage. He was fed up with William Morris.

At a party Johnny met Tom Sheils, a personal manager. Sheils had entered the business before World War II, when he was still a high school student in Connecticut. He and his classmate Al Bruno had hired a fledgling band for their

high school prom for $350. The band leader, a bespectacled
clarinet player called Glenn Miller, asked Sheils to manage
his band. By December 1944, when he was lost over the
English Channel, Glenn Miller was one of the biggest names
in the music business. Sheils had gone on to manage other
clients, including Miller's singing group, the Modernaires.
He had talked his old high school friend Al Bruno into
leaving the liquor business and becoming his partner, managing their clients out of New York City.

When Bruno and Sheils entered Johnny's life, they were
handling no one of Glenn Miller's stature, but they were
full of enthusiasm and energy. They wouldn't take the place
of an agent; but Johnny needed a catalyst for his career,
and he figured that Bruno and Sheils might be it.

In the spring of 1957 Carson wrote a letter to William
Morris discharging the agency. Phil Weltman had enough
clients so that he didn't have to worry about losing Johnny.
But he was hurt. "I always felt that our relationship was a
staunch friendship with the strongest kinds of loyalty," the
agent wrote Johnny. "To sum it up, Johnny, I am very
disappointed that you do not share the same faith and loyalty
in us that we have shown toward you."

With the help of Sheils, Carson auditioned to be the host
of a daytime television game show called *Do You Trust
Your Wife?*, which had originated on CBS a year earlier as
a prime-time evening show hosted by the ventriloquist Edgar
Bergen. Don Fedderson, the producer, remembers testing
Johnny before an audience waiting to watch *The Lawrence
Welk Show*. "John was so far above the others," Fedderson
says. "Whatever it was, he had that star quality that I at
least recognized."

Johnny was glad to be offered the job, a mark of how
far he had fallen. He had done a daytime variety/talk show
on CBS. But this was a game show. Moreover, it was on
ABC, the third network, which didn't even have daytime
programming. *Do You Trust Your Wife?* was going to have

the dubious honor of opening the network's day each afternoon at three-thirty, televised live from New York City.

All Johnny's friends got together one evening for a going-away party on the beach at Paradise Cove. Everyone roasted wieners, everyone drank, and everyone wished Johnny and Jody well.

Johnny rented a house outside New York City. Jody took care of settling the family, hoping that now everything would be different. But she saw ominous signs. "When we were unpacking, I found some magazines on the top shelf in his den of men beating up women, chained up and things," Jody said.

SEVEN

"**W**elcome to *Who Do You Trust?*" Johnny said amiably to Mike and Debbie Pollock. "What do you do for a living?"

"I'm with the City Center," Mike Pollock answered. "I'm one of the stage managers."

Johnny had his first success on national television. The show had become one of the most popular daytime programs. The original name, *Do You Trust Your Wife?*, had been changed so that unmarried contestants could be featured.

"How did you get started in show business?" Johnny asked, looking at the prepared questions. He had done the program live so many times from the Little Theater on West Forty-fourth Street that it was all routine.

"For a while I had to play in a burlesque house," Pollock replied, giving the answer he had been coached to give.

"You even *had* to," Johnny laughed. "I'll bet that took some coaxing. I had a job in burlesque myself once. I was a stagehand. I got ten dollars a week and all I could see."

Johnny was becoming known as one of the great ad-libbers in show business. The contestants were usually so struck by Johnny's wit that they laughed right along with the audience.

"What did you do after you left the burlesque?" Johnny asked, reading another prepared question.

"I had a very unusual job playing the French horn at the Bronx Zoo."

"Why did the Bronx Zoo need a French-horn player?" Johnny asked.

"It seems the alligators weren't mating and they had found out that the music of the French horn was stimulating to them. It made them more amorous."

Johnny made one of his patented takes, staring into space. "French-horn music makes alligators amorous," he said finally. "How in the world did they ever find that out? Did it work? Did the alligators seem to like music?"

"We got them pretty stimulated. I think they missed us when we left."

"What did you say when you left—'Stimulator, alligator'?" Johnny quipped, ad-libbing again. "How long did you stay on the job?"

"Just that one day. The zoo figured it had worked all right, so we quit."

"Darn good thing, or we'd all be up to here in alligators!" Johnny said, once again displaying his quick wit. "How many of you were there playing for the alligators?"

"There were four of us," Pollock said.

"Four of you! I suppose they needed one to play the horn and the other three to hold back the alligators."

As the live program continued, Roy Kammerman, the headwriter, sat in his office looking at his script. Kammerman and his staff had interviewed the contestants and prepared the questions and answers on the left-hand side of the page. This was the script that everyone on the show saw. But Kammerman's script was different. Written down the right-hand side were all Johnny's "ad-libs." Kammerman even wrote down Johnny's "takes." Indeed, the more spontaneous anything appeared, the more certain it was that Kammerman or another writer had prepared it beforehand. The day that Johnny knocked over the set as he roared around the studio in a little car was as scripted as a Molière comedy.

As the show proceeded, Kammerman checked off the

"ad-libs" one by one. Johnny skipped a one-liner. "That son of a bitch, why doesn't he do that line!" Kammerman yelled, banging his fist against the door. "That dirty bastard, why isn't he doing my lines?" Kammerman hit his fist so many times against the door or the wall that he had a mark across his hand.

Like many comedy writers, Kammerman would have liked to have been the one up there telling the jokes, counting the laughs. He wanted his name up in lights, not rolled down the screen at the end of the half hour so fast that even a mother could hardly read it.

Who Do You Trust? rose or fell on its humor. The program didn't want to be known primarily as a game show. America had just been scandalized to learn that contestants had been fed answers on quiz programs. Charles Van Doren, bearer of a great name in American cultural life, had been caught cribbing answers on *Twenty-One* while he won $129,000. Nor was Van Doren the only one to whom producers had given answers, all in the name of holy entertainment.

Television had reformed. But it was still considered all right for Johnny to be fed *his* answers. Groucho Marx depended on his writers too, on *You Bet Your Life*, and the public thought he was winging it. Television involved too many viewers, too many sponsors, too much money, to indulge in spontaneity. Johnny was a funny man, but he wasn't funny every afternoon at three-thirty—at least not without a script.

In some respects *Who Do You Trust?* was almost as much Kammerman's show as Johnny's. One of the highest-paid writers in daytime television, Kammerman reveled in his work. He knew that it wasn't easy always to give the script the right intonation. He appreciated the fact that Johnny's ability was in making the lines *his*. Taking what might sound downright dirty coming from anybody else and passing the words through the mouth of this good old small-town Nebraska boy was like running something through a laundromat.

To fool the ABC censors Kammerman often prepared a

special script pruned of carnal innuendo. He gave the real script to Johnny, whose sexual suggestions didn't seem excessive to the housewives of America.

Still, it drove Kammerman up the wall when Johnny goofed. Maybe he wasn't Shakespeare, but he stayed up half the night in his room at the Algonquin writing the bits, and he couldn't stand to have them blown.

Johnny was a creature of his cue cards. If the program ran thirty seconds or so short, David Lowe, the director, knew enough to roll the credits slowly, very slowly. Johnny didn't appear confident filling the time. As for the contestants, they had to be warned not to ad-lib. God forbid if an original witticism flashed through a guest's brain and he or she didn't have the good sense to keep quiet. As often as not, Johnny would abruptly end the interview by calling for the quiz. He seemed not to like having celebrity contestants, either; they were harder to control, and he didn't seem at ease with them.

Johnny almost never saw Kammerman, or any of the other writers. He isolated himself from the people with whom he worked. He had tried to get his friend Hank Simms to become the announcer. Simms had turned him down, and when the first announcer wasn't working out, Johnny called Simms a second time. Simms still refused. A few weeks later Johnny flew out to Los Angeles to sell his house. He showed up at the Simmses' one morning and knocked on the door. "Do you want the job or don't you?" he asked a half-asleep Simms when he answered the door. "This is as far as I go."

Simms laughed until he practically fell on the carpet. But he couldn't see moving to New York, not even for Johnny.

Johnny had gone East when much of network television was moving West. Television had been justly proud of dramas such as *Studio One* and *Playhouse 90* that were performed live from New York. Now, the networks were replacing most of these programs with series filmed on the West Coast.

Johnny had grown up in live local television, but that too

was shrinking, and with it, much of the early freedom. Old movies were cheaper, and the ratings were often as good. RKO and Warner Brothers had already sold big blocks of old films to television. In 1954 WOW-TV had shown live drama from New York every night. Two years later the station was showing 88 percent films.

When Johnny returned to New York, he interviewed Edward "Ed" McMahon, a Philadelphia television personality, for the job of announcer. McMahon took the train from Philadelphia. Johnny talked to him for five minutes while they watched workers change the marquee on the movie theater across the street. The interview was so brief and so uncommunicative that McMahon didn't realize he had the job.

McMahon, a husky thirty-five-year-old former marine aviator, may have been a local television star in Philadelphia; but at heart he was a salesman who knew his territory, and his territory was wherever he happened to be.

Ed's father was a salesman too. In Ed's childhood the family had moved from place to place, school to school, from a suite at the Mark Hopkins Hotel in San Francisco to a flat in Bayonne, New Jersey, from wealth to poverty, poverty to wealth. In college at Catholic University in Washington, D.C., Ed sold pots and pans door-to-door. He then became one of the aristocrats of the nickel-and-dime hustle, selling "the famous Morris metric slicer" on the Boardwalk in Atlantic City.

On his first *Who Do You Trust?* Ed tried not to sound nervous. He began announcing the show and the sponsor in a voice full of energy and confidence. Suddenly he realized that Johnny had set his script on fire. "It was my job to get everything right before the whole script charred to ashes in my hands," McMahon remembers. "I got it so I never missed a beat and it never even singed my hands."

Ed had to sell himself to Johnny day by day, show by show. He slowly developed one of the most subtly calculated personalities in television. Kammerman was the primary sculptor in shaping an image of Ed as an amiable lush with an IQ in the temperate range. ("You know, Ed started drinking on doctor's orders. The doctor was a drunk too.") Johnny insulted Ed, but with an underlying assumption of affection.

Ed became Carson's comedic foil; but he was not merely Johnny's straight man, he was his greatest enthusiast. "I was responsible for Ed's booming laugh," recalls Robert Coe, the announcer's longtime manager. "I said, 'Just exert a feeling of friendliness, a feeling of really thinking this guy is terrific, great to work for.' A lot of people say that's phony. It's not phony. It has grown so that now it's like breathing in and breathing out."

Johnny needed a drinking buddy too. That wasn't in the job description, but often in the afternoons the two men headed out to hit the bars. Ed was two years older than Johnny. He wasn't as close as Hank Simms, but he put up with Johnny as well off-camera as on-camera.

Johnny's relationship with Art Stark, the producer of *Who Do You Trust?*, was equally complicated, and more profound. Stark was a gruff, emotional man, so much a part of the New York show-biz world that he could have been born backstage. Before the Second World War, he and his first wife had been a dance team. After Pearl Harbor he had tried to join the armed forces, but was rejected because of a bad knee. He still could dance though, and he spent the war leading a USO troupe, primarily in the Pacific. Years later he told his second wife, Mary, that when he was flying home, he had dropped his dancing shoes out of the plane and vowed to become a writer.

Stark started writing for the pulps, churning out stories by the score. He worked on an early television program in New York, *Broadway Open House*, a precursor of *The Tonight Show*. He graduated to game shows, and a career in daytime television.

Art was in his early forties, with a mercurial temperament and an irresistible impulse to speak his mind about matters large and small. Unlike many producers, Art was not afraid of *his* star. He yelled at Johnny as he yelled at everyone else. Art was the doorkeeper to Johnny's presence and time, and he protected Johnny. If he was like a stern second father to Johnny, he was like a mother too, cautioning him, taking care of the details of his life.

Meanwhile, Al Bruno was promoting Johnny in numerous ways. "When Al Bruno took Johnny over, he became a property," remembers Jody. "He just pushed him. The phone would ring, and Johnny would pretend he wasn't in. He had John seen in all the spots, performing for different charities. He treated me as if I didn't matter. I remember once John hadn't been home for two days. I had seen him on the show. I called Al and asked if he knew where he was. I said I was worried. I didn't know. Reluctantly he said, 'All right, Jody, I'll see where he is.' "

Johnny's family lived in rented homes with rented furniture until settling into a palatial brick house on three-and-a-half acres in Harrison, outside the city. The *New York Daily News* ran a photo essay of the happy family. The photographer posed Chris, Rick, and Cory around their father's Porsche as "Jody waits patiently on the back porch for a 'hello' kiss from Johnny."

The three boys and their mother would have had to be patient, for Johnny was gone much of the time. In January 1958, after he had only been in New York a few months, he took over the lead in a Broadway comedy, *Tunnel of Love*, from Tom Ewell.

Johnny had no professional experience on the stage, and hardly any amateur experience, either. He was chosen not by the producers but by the ladies in the matinee audiences. These matrons had been given ballots to fill out, listing four or five possible leads. Overwhelmingly they had chosen Johnny, whom they knew only from his television show. It was a poll, then, not as much about Johnny as about the power of television.

Within a few years it would become common for TV stars to bolster fading Broadway shows, but in 1958 it was unusual. Johnny's co-star, Marsha Hunt, and the rest of the cast worried about working with a TV game-show host. But

Johnny knew his lines, and he had unquestioned aptitude for light comedy. If at times he played too much to the audience, sucking the laughs out like a stand-up comedian, that was easily remedied. Hunt found it peculiar that her onstage husband never talked to her during the ten weeks of the run. Although their dressing rooms were adjacent, Johnny merely murmured a greeting. "Once I admired his sweater and I said I wanted to get one for my husband," Hunt says. "We talked for two minutes, and that was our longest conversation."

Johnny might have parlayed his Broadway appearance into a successful career as a comedic actor. He did not pursue it, and the main legacy of his short-lived stint was an apartment in Manhattan. Jack Narz believed that one of Johnny's primary reasons for taking the part was so that he could have a place in New York to carry on a separate life.

For a time Johnny's romantic interest was a woman he had known in California, Jill Corey, the singer on the nighttime *Johnny Carson Show*. Even in California, staff members at CBS thought that they were involved.

Johnny and Jill had a great deal in common. Like Johnny, Jill was a big hit on television for the first time, one of the stars of *Your Hit Parade*, singing the top songs of the week. She was a small-town girl from Pennsylvania who didn't put on airs. "I always felt chagrined that he had a wife and children," Corey says. "You like someone and you think it's the right thing to do. There might be love going on, and he's not happily married. At one time I think we thought we were in love. I don't know if it was the small-town background, and we could keep our equilibrium, that's how we related.

"You have to give of yourself to have a close friend, and I think he was always shy and afraid to share that. I remember Johnny was drinking a little. He liked to battle when he had a few drinks. One night we went to see Sylvia Sims sing, and he got in a fight with people. I knew I didn't like to be with him when he was like that."

* * *

Jody didn't know about Jill Corey, though she had heard
rumors of women running in and out of his apartment. In
California Jody had friends, women she could talk to, but
here in the suburbs she knew no one. "It was so embarrassing to have the black-and-blue marks," she says. "It's
not something to be talked about. You might talk about it
when a person is a truck driver or works in a supermarket,
but when your husband is on television or a big businessman, someone with his reputation depending on his image,
it's different."

Jody began to drink more than she should have. Finally
she began seeing Dr. Edward Tauber, a prominent analyst.

"I wasn't in a position to validate those stories [about
abuse]" recalls Dr. Tauber. "But that doesn't mean I think
they were all fictitious. I was very concerned about her. I
felt very sorry that she was so harassed and felt so lonely
and helpless. She had a lot of trouble thinking straight.

"Jody wasn't able to master anything herself. She was
too out-to-lunch most of the time. She seemed like a lost
animal."

In his concern for Jody, Dr. Tauber went beyond the
confines of the fifty-minute hour. He called Mrs. Irma Wolstein, a commercial artist and the wife of a Manhattan psychoanalyst, and asked her to help. Mrs. Wolstein was a
woman who attracted the hurt and the needy. She found in
Jody a strange, sad being, a hummingbird with a broken
wing. She tried to set Jody up with her own art agent, but
that didn't work out. Then she sublet her studio to Jody so
that she would have a place to work. One night she dreamed
that the studio was destroyed. The next morning she went
to the studio on the Upper West Side. It was not destroyed,
but it was very messy, and she found but one picture in the
studio: a self-portrait of a drunken Jody.

Jody had a way of emotionally ingratiating herself, and
Mrs. Wolstein felt responsible for her. One day Jody suggested that the Wolsteins meet Johnny. Jody's narrow circle
of friends were almost all involved with therapy. Like many

people going through analysis, she placed the therapeutic experience at the center of her life. It was a new world for Johnny too, and when he walked into the Wolsteins' home, with its books, dark woods, and rich carpets, he could have been walking into a salon.

Mrs. Wolstein had heard many stories of Johnny, of his drinking, his attacks, his emotions. When he sat down in the living room, she noticed Johnny's eyes. They appeared red-rimmed and cold. "I'm afraid of cats," Johnny said, looking at the Wolsteins' pet.

This was not Johnny's scene, and it was a mark of how much he wanted his marriage to continue that he was even here.

"I don't know what Jody is so upset about," he said. "She can have anything she wants. If she wants to paint, she can paint. If she wants a studio, she can have it."

Dr. Benjamin Wolstein did not spend time around television personalities, and he observed Johnny closely. Inevitably the conversation turned to therapy.

"I don't want to go into analysis," Johnny said over dinner.

"Creativity is *not* neurotic," Dr. Wolstein said, attacking one of the clichés of the moment. "If you could unblock it, you could be even more creative."

"I don't want to touch it," Johnny said, his eyebrows rising. "I don't know where my creativity comes from, and I don't want to know."

The Wolsteins saw Johnny and Jody socially. They went to a party at their house where Jody danced on the table. They met the Carsons for drinks at Sardi's and other restaurants. The more time they spent together, the more Mrs. Wolstein thought that in a way Jody and Johnny were well matched. They both had drinking problems. Johnny seemed cold, self-involved, and may even have had a cruel streak. Jody was not cold, but she too appeared self-involved, and manipulative.

Dr. Wolstein had his own view of Johnny: "He has a terrible fear within him, a fear that if he ever lets go, he'll lose everything. He can't give anything. Anyone who wants anything from Johnny is lost. He has other affairs because he can never commit himself to anyone or anything. As soon as he has one woman, he has to have another.''

Johnny did not want a divorce. Even Jody felt that, after he blacked out during his drinking bouts, he might not even have remembered his attacks. But by now Johnny and Jody had picked at the scabs of their marriage until most of the caring had been bled away.

"The night Johnny told me I could have my divorce we were supposed to see *My Fair Lady*,'' Jody remembers. "But when I met him at Sardi's, he was sitting with Ed McMahon. He said, 'We aren't going to any play tonight.' We went from bar to bar. Everybody knew he was getting pretty dangerous. I was so paralyzed with fear. They were telling all these filthy jokes. I became more and more ill, and I wanted to leave. He kept throwing insults at me, telling me how awful I was.

"Suddenly he turned to me and said, 'You can have your divorce, but you're not getting the children and you're not getting any money.' I had never stood up to him much before. But I'd just had it. I pushed the table and I stood up and I said, 'Go fuck yourself.' He wasn't used to that.

"We went to pick up the car. All the way back he was cursing me. Oh, he was furious. He was very drunk. He got to the garage and said, 'I don't want to be responsible for what happens to you tonight driving.' This cab drew up and he shoved me in the door. I didn't have any money, but John shoved twenty dollars in my hands.''

Jody says that Johnny returned to the house at dawn. "He was terribly hung over. It was strange. He went up and lay down on the bed. Then he started washing the windows. I don't know why. I didn't know what to say to him. I went out with the boys to go shopping. I kept hoping he'd be gone when we got back.

"A few days later he wanted to make love. I said, 'Go ahead, it doesn't make any difference.' He said, 'How long

has this been going on?' I said, 'I don't know, a long time.'
He got up and picked up the television set, which was in
the corner of the bedroom. He picked up a set of pearls he
had given me. He walked out the door. Evidently he had
somewhere to go. He wanted to take anything he had.''

On September 30, 1959, Johnny and Jody separated legally, and Johnny moved into a one-bedroom apartment on
East Fifty-third Street. He had a couch and a chair, a table
for writing, a double bed for sleeping, a pan for boiling
water for instant coffee, three gray towels in the bathroom,
and a set of white Raymond Loewy china.

When Red Rowe, his old colleague from Los Angeles,
came to visit, he was impressed, though not by the decor.
''He had on a pair of faded blue jeans and nothing on top,''
Rowe recalls. ''There was a gal in the corner in leotards
having a beer. And everything in this wonderful apartment
was still in the boxes. It was like walking into a warehouse,
with these people drinking beer, running around half-naked.''

In 1959 separated and divorced fathers had not yet become
a species unto themselves, on weekends filling the zoos and
the children's movies with their charges. On Saturdays
Johnny drove out to Harrison in his Porsche to spend the
day with his sons. Johnny was not comfortable with the
idea of divorce, and the matter was kept as quiet as possible.
As for Jody, she felt that life was better now for her and
the boys. She says that though Johnny spent more time with
his sons than before, she felt he did not want to deal with
their problems, to be a real father. He wanted to be the
bountiful giver of good times and good gifts.

It was easy for Johnny to give Chris a BB gun, but not
so easy for Jody to attempt to monitor its use. It was easy
for Johnny to take the boys for a ride in his new boat, the
Deductible, not so easy to live at the house and deal with
their emotional problems.

''I don't think the relationship with the children was that
good,'' says Dr. Tauber. ''As I recall, the children oscillated
between him and her, depending on who would do more

for them. The children were tremendously opportunistic. They were having an awful lot of trouble growing up. I didn't see anything in the family structure that was conducive to encouraging any faith in life, or in anything else. It was all grab and grab and grab, as much as you can.

"I think the parents made very little effort to cool down and truly get in touch with anything. The children had nothing there."

The worst marriages do not end in divorce; the partners go on torturing one another until death do them part. Nonetheless, for a man who would eventually have four wives, Johnny was extremely slow in ending his first marriage. "That's the lowest I've ever felt, the worst personal experience of my life," he said later. "We'd been married ten years—since college, in fact. And children were involved—three sons. I think that's the worst guilt hangup you can have, when children are involved. But divorce sometimes is the only answer. I think it's almost immoral to keep on with a marriage that's really bad. It just gets more and more rotten and vindictive, and everybody gets more and more hurt."

Johnny's friends dismissed Jody by saying that he had outgrown her, that he had left her as part of the molting of stardom. But she was the one who sought the divorce, not Johnny.

In the first months of their separation, Jody's friends hoped that she would use her freedom to move beyond Johnny and their problems. But she flitted from place to place. She was forever calling her friends at the last minute, asking them to meet her at Sardi's or Danny's Hideaway, one restaurant or another. Although Irma Wolstein continued to be Jody's friend, she had the feeling that inside Jody was an emptiness that nothing could ever fill up.

According to Jody, Al Bruno set her up with dates. "There was this big man at CBS," recalls Jody. "Bruno said, 'You have to go out with this man. He's very, very rich. Think of the children. Do it for me.' So what the heck.

I met him in New York at the Brasserie. He was a skinny old man, a little shorter than I was. Immediately the hand goes on the thigh. This little man is determined that he's going to make a little time with me. I sort of fended him off as best I could. And I took the train back to Harrison. I told Al about it. He said, 'You have to overlook those things, you're a big girl now.' ''

Jody eventually did receive an assignment as an artist, to paint a mural for a midtown nightclub called Camelot. She painted an enormous dragon, its great body winding snake-like around a castle. In front of the dragon stood a small knight trying to fight his immense adversary and reach the castle. When Jody finished the painting, she looked at the dragon with its fangs and leering smile and realized that it was Johnny—before he had his teeth fixed. She looked again and she realized that she was the little knight.

As distraught as Johnny might be, he always had the elixir of work. Even if everything else in his life went wrong, he had applause and laughter. He began to appear regularly on various programs. He even subbed for Jack Paar on *The Tonight Show* for two weeks in 1958. Paar was not a co-median but a witty conversationalist who each night exposed his psyche. Johnny couldn't compete with that, but his low-key comedy worked as well in the late evening as it did in the afternoon. Johnny was so successful that he began to be touted for a nighttime show. "Jack was nice enough to say to me before going on his vacation, 'Good luck,' '' Johnny told Earl Wilson, the gossip columnist. '' 'You did the best job of any of them who replaced me the last time.' ''

Johnny shot an apple off Garry Moore's head on *I've Got a Secret*, a popular celebrity game show. He did a comedy routine on *The Perry Como Show*. He played several roles on *The United States Steel Hour*. He flew to London to host a television special in Great Britain. He gave interviews about television and comedy, making himself accessible, creating an image of a thoughtful, modest, multitalented young man.

Johnny was becoming a "personality." Through the repetition of his image on television, he became like one of these balloon characters at the Macy's Thanksgiving Day parade, floating high above the city.

Johnny was parceled out among a half-dozen different people. Of course, Bruno and Sheils got their 10 percent as managers, and later 15 percent, when Johnny dropped his new agent, MCA, which had been taking 10 percent of his new projects. But the unkindest cut of all was William Morris. The talent agency was receiving 10 percent even though it had nothing to do with getting Johnny the job on *Who Do You Trust?* or negotiating his contract. He had, however, still been under contract with Morris when he began hosting the game show. Johnny was a Nebraska boy. He thought that it was wrong to take money for something you didn't do, and the business with William Morris rankled him.

Johnny also had an accounting firm to pay, and they weren't cheap. Art Stark was paid by Don Fedderson, but professionally and emotionally the producer had a piece of Johnny. Roy Kammerman appeared to think of Johnny as a ventriloquist's dummy whose job was to mouth the writer's mortal lines. The public-relations people at NBC had their bit of Johnny too, setting him up for interviews.

As Johnny's career took off, Bruno hired a top-rated public-relations man, Gary Stevens, to promote Johnny. Stevens was a sophisticated urbanite who seemed out of place in the hurly-burly hustle of flackery, but he thought that Johnny was immensely talented. What struck him most was how out of it his newest client seemed. Johnny appeared uncomfortable in first-class restaurants. He dressed like a junior high school principal.

"Don't be overbearing," Bruno cautioned Stevens. "Let him guide what he wants to do. He's a little bit shy. He doesn't want the kind of publicity that most people would like. Just see that you're covered, that you're building a conservative image."

Bruno had already been very successful building Johnny's

image. He had helped his client get involved with the Friars Club and its "roasts." At these all-male gatherings comedians savaged one another in words of free-flowing invective, making attacks that were often hysterically funny. Nothing quite equaled the legendary Friars' party in New York City during Prohibition after a cockroach died in a glass of scotch. The good Friars, some of whom were hoping for a similar end, gave the late lamented a three-day wake, presumably observed by many of the deceased's relatives.

At the Friars' roasts those who believe that all comedy is a form of put-down, a display of superiority, would find ample evidence. Comedians such as Jack E. Leonard or Don Rickles had acts that consisted of roasting the world. Johnny had a nasty comedic streak too. The other comedians, appreciating this gift, elevated Johnny above the lowly category of TV game-show host. "He came out the hero at the Friars," Bruno recalls. "One time he introduced Lucille Ball as Lucille Testicle."

Johnny stood there looking like Tom Sawyer in a three-piece suit, and attacked the guests with his zingers. He hit Jack E. Leonard over the head with a verbal beanball, calling the insult comedian "the mean Mr. Clean." On another occasion Jan Murray mused sentimentally and interminably on the dread fate of children growing up unable to see the immortal Al Jolson. "They grew up while you were talking," Carson interjected.

Johnny had very little to do with *Who Do You Trust?* except showing up to host the show each afternoon. He hung out in his office, a cluttered hideaway above the Little Theater on Forty-fourth Street. For diversion he had his drums, and a bow and arrow and a bull's-eye on the wall.

For Christmas Johnny gave gifts such as tarnished cuff links to his co-workers. At the staff party Johnny appeared uncomfortable. He went into Art Stark's office and talked on the phone.

"One Christmas we gave Johnny an outrageously garish vest," remembers Stu Billett, a staff member. "It was a joke. When he said, 'Thank you, thank you,' we didn't know if he was being funny or not. He came to do the show and he had a white-on-white tie, a white-on-white shirt, with the vest on. And he went out on-stage. I mean, he was not a clothes horse.''

To his colleagues, Johnny was as distant as the outer reaches of Tibet. He never seemed quite comfortable with them. He was at his most free performing acts of physical daring or skill. One day he shot at a target with a bow and arrow while a champion archer looked on. He hit the bull's-eye. When he was about to perform on a trapeze, he pretended to be desperately afraid. But when he finally swung across the stage, he did so with grace and aplomb.

Charles Chaplin and Harold Lloyd were so brilliant at physical humor—at falling down the stairs, or failing to keep up on the assembly line—that the audience forgets it is watching acts of extraordinary dexterity. Johnny, who had not been athletic in school, took immense pride in his prowess, but he was not willing to do anything for a laugh. He wanted to be applauded for his dexterity or courage. He might play the buffoon for a moment or two, as long as the audience understood that here was a man up to the challenge.

As a comedian, Johnny was discovering that trying to be funny on network television was like conducting the New York Philharmonic from a phone booth. He could hardly move. He wanted to satirize Ma Bell. That was a no-no. The *Bell Telephone Hour* was a prestigious network program. He wanted to poke some fun at the government by pretending that the White House was run like a Madison Avenue advertising agency, a skit that would have been prophetic. That was a no-no too.

It wasn't just the network censors who were sensitive. He told a joke on one program about a dog lost by Mickey Cohen, a gangster. The next day an anonymous caller warned him, ''You just better watch your step.'' Even if he was making fun of dogs, cats, sundry animals, or politicians, he was sure to raise the wrath of one group or another.

Johnny knew that to be funny he had to ''tread on people's

toes.'' Yet whenever he did, he expected to be attacked by ''a nutty fringe waiting to be offended.'' Johnny felt that people were too on edge to laugh. ''You say to your wife, 'Hey, honey. Where'd you get the dress?' and automatically she says, 'So what's wrong with it?' ''

On *Who Do You Trust?* Johnny had nothing to do with the guests. Dealing with them was left to people such as David Rayfiel, one of the interviewers. Rayfiel was a young aspiring playwright who started to write a play about his experience. He gave that up. Almost thirty years later he co-authored the script to *'Round Midnight*, a film about a very different world of the late fifties, that of black jazz artists in Paris.

Rayfiel and the other interviewers listened to myriad stories. Doug and Myrtle Casement had hitchhiked to Las Vegas on their honeymoon. That was enough to get them on the show. Millard Hooper billed himself as the former professional checker champion of the world. That was bizarre enough to merit time with Johnny. Max and Will Berkowitz, twin undertakers from Cleveland, were rich subjects for bad puns. The show had ''normal'' people, but the staff sought out eccentrics: the two young men in the blue-dyed Eisenhower jackets who said they were from the planet Venus; the clairvoyant with a glass eye taped on his forehead; the lady who collected wishbones; the man in contact with Castro in his head.

The show was supposed to be funny, but sometimes it was the humor of a child laughing at something beyond understanding. Rayfiel discovered that if one probed too much, the humor often turned into something darker. Sometimes eccentricity was a gentle name for a terrible aloneness, or even madness.

The guests might write in requesting to be on the show, or Kammerman or Rayfiel or the others might spot them on the street or subway. Some of them wanted the money, though it was at most five hundred dollars. What they really wanted was to be on television, to be seen, to have their lives certified as interesting.

After Rayfiel interviewed the guests, Kammerman wrote the script. Those who were to appear were prepped, prepared question by question. Then, at three-thirty every afternoon, the red light went on, and Ed introduced the first couple. Johnny asked his questions, read his jokes, and played the game. Then the contestants were gone, and somebody new appeared before the camera.

When Johnny had his daily show from Los Angeles, he had come in each morning, rehearsed a little, done the show, prepared for the next show, and called it a day. Now, with the advent of television taping, it was possible to do a whole slew of shows in a day. It was hell on everyone and everything except for the bottom line.

Who Do You Trust? was still performed live most of the time. On Fridays, however, a second and sometimes a third show were taped. That way the staff could have a three-day weekend. After the three-thirty show Johnny and Ed headed over to Sardi's for a break. "How much can you drink in two hours, especially if you're talking business?" McMahon asked rhetorically a few years later. The answer, as any businessman could have told him, was a great deal. "The trouble was that Johnny, as he's said many times on the air, isn't the world's greatest drinking man. Give him three shots and he gets very frisky. And sometimes when we'd come back to tape the Monday show, tongues got tangled and things got said that had to be bleeped."

Even Johnny knew he had a problem. "We would go next door to Sardi's to have a small flagon of grape," he remembers. "And then we would come back to do a show at 6:30. And then we had one at 9:30 at night and I can remember coming in completely bagged. I'm not a good drinker, you know, two and three and I go bananas."

On one show Johnny kept asking the contestants the same questions again and again. Where do you come from? How long have you folks been married? McMahon found this very funny, but it was a private joke between him and Johnny.

Don Fedderson became so upset that he flew back to New

York. "I got a call to watch the show," the producer says. "I didn't see it, but I sure went back there fast, because if you don't control something like that you're in real trouble."

Johnny had not grown up in a family where his parents had a glass of wine or a beer with their evening meals. Liquor was one of the many forbiddens for a teenager in Norfolk. Booze meant tying one on with your buddies, rowdiness, joking, and crazy good times.

Johnny was not a heavy drinker in college, but in television in the fifties liquor was the drug of choice. In New York he found some new spots to replace Kelbo's and other hangouts. Sardi's was a favorite place. So was Danny's Hideaway. Johnny never cared much for food, but he enjoyed sitting at the bar, drinking and smoking.

On television Johnny was creating an image of Ed McMahon as a red-faced lush, boozing his way through life. Ed was a heavy drinker, but he had the capacity of a camel. Not only was Johnny looped on a couple of drinks, but his whole temperament changed. He was not always pleasant to be around.

"Johnny was heavy into liquor those days," remembers Ed McMahon's manager, Bob Coe. "I remember one night Frank Sinatra wanted to kill him. It was Johnny's general 'fuck you' attitude. He'd use these four-letter words to anyone, men, women, anyone.

"One night Johnny, Ed, and I were at a place on the West Side that was a Mafia hangout. Johnny had quite a bit to drink and he was really weaving. And he saw this attractive blonde. He went over to her and tried to pick her up. Well, this blonde was one of the girls of this top Mafia guy. And the owner of the place got hold of Johnny and just took him outside, because the guy would have killed him. Absolutely. And Johnny resisted. He didn't want to go."

"They all protected Johnny during those alcoholic years," says Harriet Van Horne, the longtime television columnist whose husband, David Lowe, directed *Who Do You Trust?* "Johnny would be dead or in jail or in a mental hospital if people hadn't looked after him. He was the worst kind of a drunk. He couldn't handle liquor at all. He'd get in fights. He'd get sick in public places. He'd insult important people. Ed McMahon was his nanny, his bodyguard. Ed is very big, and he'd pick Johnny up from the floor and take him home. Johnny is a very, very bad drinker. There's a dark side that would come out terribly when he drank. He got into serious trouble two or three times. It was always Ed McMahon who saved him.''

Johnny enjoyed Ed's company. He was not a comedian to whom the world consists of large audiences and small audiences. He didn't need a rat pack of boozing, backslapping buddies drinking his liquor and laughing at his jokes. An audience of one was fine.

Johnny was a loner, but a loner who was not comfortable being alone, a trait that was almost as effective at driving him to the altar as a shotgun would have been. Johnny's friends tried to fix him up. In the spring of 1960 Jack Narz was preparing to host a new nighttime game show called *Video Village*. Contestants rolled a giant die, and then moved along an enormous game board. Narz's assistant, twenty-eight-year old Joanne Copeland, accompanied the contestants on their quest. The task was slightly more arduous than turning vowels, and though Joanne was an intelligent young woman, she was chosen primarily for her decorative value, of which Narz was not unappreciative. He kept telling Johnny that he should go out with her.

Joanne says that it was her father, a business executive with Bechtel, who introduced her to Johnny. In March Johnny met Joanne and her father at Eddie Condon's, a popular hangout. After dinner, according to Joanne, the three went to her apartment. Copeland asked Johnny's advice on whether Joanne's younger sister should pursue a career as a violinist. He played a short tape.

"I think she should quit as soon as possible," Johnny said. Joanne decided then and there that this was the man for her.

In the spring of 1960 Johnny was still primarily a daytime game-show host, in the same immortal company as Ben Alexander, Fred Robbins, and Gene Rayburn. Johnny was one of those vaguely recognizable faces that people knew that they knew, but he was hardly a head-turner. A few days later Johnny took Joanne to dinner at P. J. Clarke's, an East Side restaurant and singles bar. "People are staring at me," Joanne said as they left.

"I think it's me they're staring at," Johnny said, looking at his date. Joanne believed that half the people in P. J.'s had put down their drinks to stare at the host of *Who Do You Trust?*

In the three decades of her life Joanne had managed the considerable feat of maintaining her romantic illusions. Back in the early 1950's Joanne had been engaged to an engineer who flew with her on Pan American when she was a stewardess. They had gotten married, but it had been quickly annulled, and she still fantasized what married life would bring.

When she was six months old, her parents divorced. For the next dozen years she was watched over by nuns in half a dozen convent schools, each summer staying with an aunt or uncle. Each fall, when her relatives sent her back again, she wondered what she had done wrong. When she was twelve, her father remarried, and she finally had a home.

Joanne attended San Mateo College before becoming a stewardess. She enjoyed ministering to the passengers, arranging their pillows, seeing that their seat belts were fastened, shepherding them across the Pacific.

On one of her trips to Hawaii she talked to a fascinating man who called himself Mr. Howard. He was on his way to Wake Island to consult on a government project. Joanne confided to this strange, rumpled man that she dreamed of becoming a movie star, but that, alas, dreams never come true.

When Joanne returned to Los Angeles in 1952, she had a message to call the RKO Studios. She was told that Howard Hughes was impressed with her. Although she did not see Hughes for some time, she was signed to a contract at RKO. Jane Russell was giving the studio trouble. Hughes had created the bosomy star, and he could create a new Jane Russell as well.

As a first step the studio sent Joanne to Wally Seawell, a prominent photographer. Jane Russell's gowns in *The French Line* were cut down so that they would fit Joanne's thin frame. A makeup artist worked on Joanne's features. And Seawell shot a spectacular series of photographs of a sensuous, sultry young woman.

Joanne learned that her romantic fantasies of a starlet's career were far different from the reality. She took acting lessons and screen tests, but after six months she had not even had a bit part.

Joanne decided to tell Hughes that she wanted to quit. As the two sat having dinner, the reluctant starlet told Hughes her decision. Hughes couldn't understand why anyone would give up such an opportunity.

"I thought movies were made in two hours," she said to Hughes. "To me, making films is the way I feel about lovemaking. If you're going to do it, do it! Don't put it in an inch and wait."

Hughes laughed. That he could understand. "What we have between us is our business and nobody else's," Hughes said, according to Joanne. "The minute it is somebody else's, we have no relationship."

Joanne took Hughes's phone numbers. Although she never saw him again, he called her many times in the next quarter century.

Joanne was a combination of contradictory traits. She was calculating yet embarrassingly naive. She was ambitious yet generous; manipulative yet thoughtful. She was a sexy television hostess, yet she was still a child of the convent who sought to rebuild her private world.

Joanne was five feet two inches tall and weighed less than ninety-five pounds, with high cheekbones and a frame as delicate as filigree. She also had a furious intensity that was sometimes too much for people. But for Johnny, here was a woman who seemed ready to devote herself to him and to his career. She brought over lamps and other furniture for his apartment, giving it a certain homeyness, and prepared food for Johnny's weekly poker games.

Early in 1961 Johnny moved into Joanne's building on York Avenue on the Upper East Side. His eighth-floor apartment was better by far than his old place. He had magnificent views of the East River, and Joanne was two floors below. In the enlightened spirit of bachelorhood Johnny was attempting to have romance, companionship, all the advantages of marriage without any of the disadvantages. Nonetheless, for a separated man uncertain about a second marriage, it was a curious step, like a compulsive eater taking a job in a bakery.

Joanne decorated Johnny's apartment. It was indeed *his* apartment, as one reporter, Roger Kahn, wrote, "notably free of feminine influences such as Ming vases in the foyer and nylons in the bathroom."

Johnny and Joanne hung out sometimes at Eddie Condon's, listening to jazz, but as the months went by, those occasions became rarer and rarer. Johnny seemed to be withdrawing even more into himself, with Joanne as his guide.

In the summer the couple sometimes journeyed by boat out to Art Stark's place at Amagansett on the south shore of Long Island. Ed also came, as did Stu Billett, the associate producer, and his girlfriend.

Summer on Long Island is a time of relentless socializing. Mary Stark was a stylish lady with East Side friends who weren't going to be overwhelmed by the presence of a game-show host. But she learned not to invite any outsiders when Johnny was there. Billett observed that, even when the half-dozen people in the room were all from the show, Johnny was uptight, squirming like a boy during the sermon at church.

Johnny and Joanne spent much time together. Joanne offered Johnny the gift of herself, but at times he seemed to buckle under the weight. She wanted the perfect relationship, the perfect romance. Unlike his first wife, Joanne had a career, an independent temperament, and the temerity to talk back to Johnny. Their fights were legendary, not for their number but because so many of them took place in public.

"There were a lot of arguments," Jack Narz recalls. "We would double-date. The four of us would be out in the country somewhere on his boat. He would get so pissed off at her that we'd get back onshore and he would take her to the train station and get her the hell back to New York."

Both Joanne and Johnny called Art Stark to discuss their relationship. In the strangest twist of all, Jody says that Joanne called her to ask help in snaring Johnny. "I helped her marry him," Jody says. "She would call me and cry because John was so mean to her. She said, 'What am I going to do? Dye my hair blond?' John sent me a big art chest and wanted to come back. I realized it would be the same thing all over. I really wanted her to marry him. I thought it would be good if he remarried. It would take the pressure off us. She said, 'I'm going to get married to get even with him.' But I don't think that was the reason she married him. Any courtship with John is going to be fraught with all sorts of emotional battles."

Even Bob Coe was not exempt from Joanne's ministrations. "She used to call me at least once a month, asking, 'Where's Johnny? Where's Johnny?' I said, 'I'm not Johnny's keeper.' She knew that Ed, Johnny, and I used to go out a great deal, so she figured I knew where he was every minute. Which, of course, I didn't. So I finally had to tell her off in a nice way. I'm not one of these rough, tough guys, but she was tough."

John and Joanne got into such a battle on their vacation in Florida that Joanne flew back early. On another occasion, when the couple went to the Bahamas, Joanne insisted on hauling home a stock of duty-free liquor. Johnny blew up over the delay at the airport.

Bruno thought that it would not be good for Johnny's

image to divorce Jody and marry another woman, especially not Joanne. "Johnny tried to dump Joanne, and I was the one that agreed to get rid of her," Bruno says. Johnny apparently changed his mind, for the relationship continued.

Despite all the problems, Joanne felt herself the most blessed of women for having Johnny. She sang Johnny's praises in lyrical bursts that no publicist would dare attempt. She was a woman who assaulted life with her goodness, rushing in with her ideas, attempting to redecorate not only Johnny's apartment but his life.

EIGHT

"*The Tonight Show* is coming up for a change," Johnny told Tom Poston early in 1962 as the two comedians rode in a taxi through Brooklyn. "Paar is thinking of leaving."

Poston and Johnny had become sufficiently friendly that they could talk frankly about their careers. Poston was doing well. He had already won an Emmy for his work on *The Steve Allen Show* and was a regular on *To Tell the Truth*, the celebrity game show that he and Johnny were doing today.

"I'd like to take a shot at it," Johnny said.

"Don't do it," Poston replied. Paar wasn't just another interchangeable talk-show host. Paar was a phenomenon.

"Why not?" Johnny asked.

"No way!" Poston exclaimed. "Nobody can follow Jack. You've got to let somebody else take it. He'll bomb. Then you'll come in. You'll be compared to the bomber, and not the king of the night."

It was not Paar but Steve Allen, the first host, who was largely responsible for creating *The Tonight Show*. When Johnny arrived in Los Angeles in 1951, people were still talking about Allen's talk show on KNX radio. The program had begun in 1948 as a late-night, half-hour disk-jockey show. Allen was wonderful ad-libbing. His witticisms and zaniness pushed the music aside. Soon he had his own audience, and an hour each evening for a comedy interview show that was a spiritual precursor of *The Tonight Show*.

Allen went to New York, where, on September 27, 1954, he began hosting *The Tonight Show*. The program was the brainchild of Sylvester L. "Pat" Weaver, the president of NBC. Weaver's grand design for television was "to create an aristocracy of the people, the proletariat of privilege, the Athenian masses." The Athenian masses made no appearance, though millions did start watching Weaver's other creation, *The Today Show*, once Dave Garroway acquired J. Fred Muggs, the irresistible chimpanzee. And they began watching Steve Allen on *The Tonight Show* as well.

A decade earlier it would have been unthinkable that people would stay up until 1:00 A.M. to watch a television program. But Steve Allen was convincing them otherwise.

Allen had no stand-up monologue. As the show opened each evening, the bespectacled comedian sat at a piano. He played some music, perhaps introduced Steve Lawrence and Eydie Gorme to sing a song. He might do a man-in-the-street interview with Don Knotts, Louis Nye, or Tom Poston, three of his regulars.

One evening Allen dived into an enormous tub of Jell-O. Another time he plunged into a vat of hot water dressed in thousands of tea bags. He roamed among the audience to talk to perennial guests such as Joe Interleggi, "the Human Termite," who liked nothing better than to bite into a good two-by-four. Sometimes Steve walked out of the back door of the theater to interview passers-by. One evening he dressed as a police officer and waved down passing autos. "Sorry, sir, but this is the border patrol, and we're making a spot-check for contraband," he told a taxi driver.

"What band?" the man asked.

"I just wanted to know if you're smuggling any fruits or nuts."

"No. Absolutely not!"

"Drive on! And remember, the life you save may not be worth it."

NBC decided to give their late-night star a shot at the big

time: a Sunday night slot opposite *The Ed Sullivan Show*, one of the top-rated programs on television. After less than two-and-a-half years, on January 25, 1957, Allen hosted his last *Tonight Show*. Although *The Steve Allen Show* did moderately well and the comedian went on to win many accolades, he never again matched that early television triumph on *The Tonight Show*.

As a replacement, NBC aired *America After Dark*, a dreary tour of nightspots and high life that put all but insomniacs to sleep. The program was so bad that not only did viewers turn off their own sets, but it was said that they went next door to turn off the neighbors' sets. When *America After Dark* proved a disaster, NBC hurriedly decided to resurrect *The Tonight Show*, with Paar as host.

Television was about time, nothing but time. Airtime that at the late hour had been next to valueless could be made worth millions of dollars. Johnny had helped ABC to assert sovereignty over the midafternoon when he hosted *Who Do You Trust?* The networks were charging into the Sunday ghetto of cultural programming with football games, and one day they would even attack the early morning hours with news programs. But for now, *The Tonight Show* was the frontier, and Jack Paar was the weapon.

Paar's career paralleled Johnny's in certain respects. He had begun in radio before the Second World War. While Johnny was gingerly joking about his superiors on Guam, Paar was already famous throughout the South Pacific for his humorous attacks on officers ("The captain himself is censoring the mail again this week—so let's cut down on the big words"). After one USO show he was threatened with court-martial. Following the war, Paar had a short-lived career in Hollywood. He wasn't a movie star. He tried hosting a couple game shows. He failed with a daytime television program, *The Morning Show*. He wasn't right for that time, either.

The resuscitated *Tonight Show* was the perfect format for Paar's talents. When he first became its host on July 29, 1957, he created what Johnny called "the most talked about show on television.'' He permanently changed the late-night habits of millions of Americans.

Paar took his private neuroses and turned them into a public spectacle. As he began his monologue each evening, the 8 million viewers were waiting not for bon mots or thigh-slapping humor, but for Jack's catharsis of the moment. He might walk off the show, break into tears, steamroller a guest, insult a politician or a commentator, or threaten to quit altogether.

The viewers had never been to such a party before, and they watched by the millions. The French singer Genevieve spoke in hilariously fractured English. Dody Goodman, a scatterbrained onetime actress, talked about her life. Cliff Arquette played Charley Weaver, a grumpy old fellow from the mythical town of Mount Ivy.

Paar pushed the permissible boundaries of television farther than they had ever been pushed before, discussing such matters as his daughter's first bra or attacking Dorothy Kilgallen and other columnists. He had a genius for public rancor. He praised Castro's Cuba and stood at the Berlin Wall. He made stars of his regulars and then fired them. He pouted and he swooned and he introduced Middle America to sophisticated guests like Oscar Levant and Alexander King. He talked with Senator John F. Kennedy, Albert Schweitzer, and Mrs. Eleanor Roosevelt, and other notables who spoke on serious subjects in a serious manner.

At its best, Paar's show seemed like an American salon. It was often a great show, and an emotionally trying one for Paar. He had threatened to retire more often than Frank Sinatra ever would, but by early 1962 he was serious.

Johnny was funnier than Paar, but *The Tonight Show* wasn't simply a matter of jokes. It involved holding together the longest time period in television, an hour and forty-five minutes each evening, from 11:15 P.M. to 1:00 A.M.

If Johnny took over *The Tonight Show*, he would be violating every axiom he had learned about television. He saw how the networks took anything that was popular—a game show, a western series, a comedian—and sought to clone it. "Bad programming drives out good programming" was the Gresham's law of television. Soon the original was gone as well as its imitators. Johnny believed that "a new funnyman should appear as often as possible—once a week—during his first year on TV. But after that he should be seen less frequently." Do what Bob Hope did, a few specials a year. That way the audience still wanted you. "It's almost impossible to do a live show every week and keep people with you," he said. "Even if you have the best material in the world, people get tired of looking at you."

NBC considered Johnny a quick-shooting ad-lib artist, the Matt Dillon of comedy. Mort Werner, the NBC vice-president who was courting Johnny to replace Paar, believed that he didn't "need prepared material or rehearsals," unaware that *Who Do You Trust?* was quite possibly the most heavily scripted game show on the air.

Of course, Johnny wasn't solely a creature of his writers and cue cards. He wrote his own material for the Friars and other performances. But that wasn't the same as coming up with zingers night after night when he knew he *had* to be funny. Not only that, but he had to be funnier than Paar; he wasn't about to flash his psyche whenever things got dull, or wave one political flag or another.

Johnny had something else going for him. He was a WASP in a profession full of Jewish comedians. The television executives knew that much of their audience was in Topeka and Peoria and Tulsa and other stations in the heartland, where the borscht belt was considered an item of apparel. They needed a host whom farmers in Oklahoma, salesmen in San Jose, and housewives in Binghamton would want to stay up for each evening, yet one worldly enough to maintain the interest of bankers in New Rochelle and brokers in Chicago.

When NBC first contacted Johnny, he said no. Any performer would have been flattered to be asked to replace Paar, but Johnny felt that he simply wouldn't succeed. Al Bruno tried to convince him that he was wrong. Agents and managers are professional optimists, but Bruno genuinely felt that Johnny could go to the top. He told Johnny that he was good, the greatest. He spent as much time selling Johnny to himself as to the networks.

NBC approached Johnny a second time, as soon as it became clear that Paar was definitely leaving. This time Johnny appeared interested. But ABC refused to allow him to abandon *Who Do You Trust?* until his contract ran out, in the fall of 1962.

Bruno was worried. "A lot of people forget that there was a little guy by the name of Merv Griffin," Johnny's former manager says. "I think Merv would have gotten the show if Johnny hadn't signed."

NBC decided that it was willing to wait for Johnny, and he signed a contract. In early March the announcement was made that in October Johnny would become the new host of *The Tonight Show*.

Johnny jumped into a cab to take him downtown. In the morning he had the temperament of a Genghis Khan. He asked only to be left alone.

The driver turned back to look at his semifamous passenger. "You know what you oughta do with that show?"

For that taxi driver, as for several million others, the real front-page news of the day was not some monkey business in Washington or rumblings in Southeast Asia. It was the fact that Johnny was taking over *The Tonight Show*.

Paar did not make the transition any easier by his manner of leaving, his body escorted out by a brace of famous pallbearers. Politicians and celebrities are excellent at funeral orations, especially when their grief is richly tempered by the happy realization that they will not have to deal with the person any longer. Paar's final show, March 30, 1962, was a canonization that seemed to bury not only Paar but the show.

Paar was not going to arrive too early for his own funeral. During the first fifteen minutes Jack E. Leonard introduced a series of the bereaved. Tom Poston, Sam Levenson, Selma Diamond, and others filed past the empty bier to pay their final respects. Then the band leader played the theme music from the show, as the mourners squirmed in their seats. Finally Hugh Downs, the announcer, read a selection about Paar from the bible of show business, *Variety*.

At eleven-thirty Paar stepped from behind the curtain to a standing ovation. The host began by proudly displaying an array of the products he had sold successfully, showing that, as kooky as he might seem, he still had his priorities straight. He talked about the past four-and-a-half years and showed some film clips.

Then representatives of America's aristocracy of celebrity appeared on film and tape to bid their fond adieu. Comedians: Bob Hope and Jack Benny. Politicians: Richard Nixon and Robert Kennedy, displaying Paar's political ecumenism. Actors: Charles Laughton and Tallulah Bankhead. A blessing from Billy Graham. A word from a technician on the show.

Finally Robert Merrill appeared on stage to sing a final selection. Although *Ave Maria* would have been almost as appropriate, the great baritone sang the famed aria of a tragic clown from Ruggiero Leoncavallo's *I Pagliacci*. Paar said his last good-bye, tears leaking down his cheeks like water from a garden hose. And then a lone slide appeared superimposed: NO MORE TO COME.

Johnny was fortunate that he didn't have to take over Paar's seat while it was still damp from his tears. Instead, a large group of hosts tromped through the NBC studios and tromped out again. Joey Bishop, Jerry Lewis, Soupy Sales, Jan Murray, Peter Lind Hayes, Mort Sahl, Steve Lawrence—at least seventeen different performers took their turn.

The guests earned only a few hundred dollars for appearing, and celebrities had always come on the show to promote themselves, but with a modicum of discretion. Now, hosts and guests relentlessly pushed their books, records, films—everything but home movies and T-shirts. The guest host might cut away for a couple minutes of relative subtlety known as paid advertising. But, alas, as the months went by, many advertisers packed up their wares and left.

Johnny continued cranking out *Who Do You Trust?* each week. In the months preceding his debut Johnny had a myriad of press interviews foisted on him. He would have been perfectly happy if the press had limited its duties to spelling his name right in the TV listings. But he needed publicity now, or so the publicists told him.

When he talked to reporters, Johnny didn't play the witty, charming Johnny Carson of television fame. He gave a series of dour, diplomatic interviews, as if he were the new head of state of some Balkan principality, where the slightest miscue would offend one group or another.

Bruno fretted that stories of Johnny's separation would ruin his richly contrived image of midwestern innocence. "About your wife," asked Roger Kahn, writing a story for *TV Guide*.

"We're separated," Johnny said, a crime not quite on par with ax murder or white slavery.

"Do you have to mention that?" Bruno interjected.

"There's no disgrace in being separated," Johnny said. "I'd like to see more honesty about marriage. I'd like more people to tell the truth. You know, 'We're not separated. We're living together. But we're miserable.' "

That was not exactly what Bruno had in mind, an attack on all the moral hypocrites. Lose them and you might not have an audience. Bruno was sufficiently worried about Johnny's image that, according to Jody, he begged her not to make excessive demands on Johnny, but to go quietly and economically away.

Johnny could not risk irritating the old king of the night. Paar was an emotional hemophiliac; scratch him and he bled all over the media. Johnny made a special point of praising Paar in his interviews. "Whether you like him personally or not had nothing to do with it, he did one hell of a job," he told the *New York World-Telegram*. In response to one question Johnny stated, "The only thing I can clearly remember about any of those fill-in assignments is that I met

Jack in his office and said, 'Hi, Jack!' I thought it was a very clever line. After all, I didn't want to overpower him. Beyond that I've had no dealings with him. I've never seen Jack Paar socially any place, and I was never a guest on the show when he was presiding. He might be an interesting guy to know. I just don't know. I really don't have the slightest idea what he's like.''

Johnny's most important job was to put together his own team, starting with an announcer sidekick. Those who watched his telegenic rapport with Ed McMahon on the game show each day assumed that Ed was his first choice, and Ed may have made the same assumption.

Johnny had other ideas. He called Hank Simms in California to feel him out. This was a quantum leap from being asked to be the announcer on a game show, and the two men talked at length. When Simms became seriously ill with colitis, the discussions ended.

Whatever Ed may have felt about Johnny's ambivalence, he had a more urgent personal problem. He was a lavish spender, building a palatial home in Philadelphia. He needed the money that the new job would bring. According to one source close to Johnny, Ed came to Johnny and earnestly asked that he be given the job. Johnny hated personal confrontations, and he ended up offering Ed the position. Ed was not only the second banana, he was the second choice. He was happy and grateful, but he had learned that with Johnny loyalty ran one way.

Johnny had been in television for more than a decade. By rights he should have had a Rolodex full of names of writers, producers, directors, and others he might call upon. Yet this man who was about to become America's number-one host knew practically no one. He needed a producer who would put *his*, Johnny Carson's, indelible stamp on the show. Art Stark was the obvious choice, but he was still under contract to ABC. So Johnny settled for Perry Cross, one of Paar's former producers, who was running the show during the interim. Cross would bring continuity to the job. As director, Johnny called in his brother, Dick, who had begun a career in television in California. Dick had been given an opportunity to try out with the guest hosts, and he had passed the test. As the new head writer, Johnny called Herb Sargent. "I'd worked on the show," says Sargent, "and he didn't know anyone else who had."

By August Johnny had chosen the top members of his team. He sat with a reporter discussing *The Tonight Show* and whether he would do a monologue. "It can be a trap," Johnny said, dragging on a cigarette. "We'll probably vary the opening.

"I swear I'm not nervous," Johnny said as he lighted a new cigarette. He looked down and saw that his old cigarette was still burning in the ashtray. "Who's nervous?"

On September 7, Johnny did his last show on *Who Do You Trust?* Johnny and his team of Cross, Sargent, Bruno, and his brother, Dick, flew down to Fort Lauderdale for a week of brainstorming and table-hopping. "We would sit around all day talking ideas and at night we'd go to a Polynesian restaurant and get drunk," Sargent recalls. "Not drunk but drunk enough so that if some dancing girl came over and offered to teach you the hula, you'd get up and do the hula. Johnny was very good at the hula."

Johnny was not the sort to bite his fingernails up to his knuckles. But no performer could possibly have been as relaxed as he appeared. Johnny was putting on a performance for his new team, and probably even for himself. That made it easier on Sargent and the others, but infinitely more difficult for Johnny.

As one of his last live appearances before *The Tonight Show*, Johnny flew out to Dallas to headline a B'nai B'rith banquet. "Tom Sheils called and said Johnny's scared shitless," recalls Jack Narz, who was also managed by Bruno and Sheils. "Tom said, 'He's as nervous as he can be. Would you meet him in Vegas? He wants to be around someone he knows. He's so frightened.' So afterward, he flew to Las Vegas. Tom and I spent the week calming him down."

* * *

Johnny knew that he would have an enormous audience for his first program. *The Tonight Show* was the only alternative to old movies. For several million people, it was as much a habit as brushing their teeth before bedtime. They were a mass audience, but by television's arithmetic not large enough to ensure that the show would continue. The Paar loyalists would be tuning in to see what the "new" Paar looked like. So would the curious, their interest stimulated by all the press coverage. And as always, there would be the crowds that formed waiting to see an accident happen.

On October 1, 1962, the tension was palpable in NBC's 6-B, the same studio that Paar had used. Perry Cross, the producer, sensed Johnny's apprehension but felt that his star would be just fine once he got over "the nervousness and the awesomeness and relaxed and the machine was rolling."

Gary Stevens, the publicist, stood backstage. Stevens, who had worked as a television producer in California, knew how nervous performers became doing live television. But even to him, the anxiety level this evening seemed incredible. Joan Crawford, a star who appeared only rarely on television, was so nervous that she seemed ready to cancel and walk out. She went to the ladies' room once, twice, half a dozen times. Even the technicians were terribly edgy. Stevens remembered other nights, other programs, and thought that this was the tensest television show he'd ever seen.

When Ed began warming up the audience, Johnny stood by himself in the hallway. Skitch Henderson, the musical director, saw Johnny there alone. He had gone through opening evening with Steve Allen, and he sensed how Johnny was feeling.

"Good luck, John," Skitch said.

Johnny said nothing. Skitch walked away thinking there had been a look of pure horror in Johnny's eyes.

When Shelly Schultz, one of his talent coordinators, observed Johnny coming toward the stage, he couldn't believe it. He was wearing a plaid jacket and Hush Puppies. Hush

Puppies! The new king of the night, and he looked as if he had just come off the bus from Pittsburgh.

To introduce Johnny this first time, NBC had prevailed on Groucho Marx, one of the true legends of show business, who was now better known as the host of the recent game show *You Bet Your Life* than for such classic Marx Brothers films as *A Day at the Races*.

Johnny walked from behind the curtain. He appeared as nonchalant as if he were out for his afternoon constitutional. But he thought to himself, What am I doing out here?

Johnny was going to be hosting this show every night. He didn't intend to come out here all whistles and sirens blowing, and knock 'em dead with material that sounded as if he'd worked on it for six months. He had to play it low key, even if he didn't get too many laughs.

"Now I'm aware of what you ladies must go through in a pregnancy," he said, referring to the six months' expectancy. "The difference is I didn't get sick.

"Jack Paar was king of late-night television. Why don't you just consider me the prince?" This was a distinction for which Gary Stevens claims credit, ensuring that at least verbally his client would not be considered a usurper. Johnny said that he was not going to represent each guest as his beloved old friend. This was a departure from Hollywood protocol, where friendship is defined as having sat next to one another on a talk show.

"I don't come from a show-business background at all," Johnny said, "in that I wasn't born in New York on the Lower East Side."

For his first show Johnny did not attempt to load up the hour-and-forty-five minutes with A-list celebrities. Instead, the program was a reasonable approximation of what his *Tonight Show* would become. Joan Crawford made it out of the ladies' room in time to sit down next to Johnny. The audience wanted a peep behind the star's mascara. For her part, Miss Crawford wanted to plug her new autobiography. She provided her peep. He gave the plug. And the show moved on. Rudy Vallee, the troubadour of the twenties, had a book to sell too, and Johnny and the singer went through the same routine. Johnny was a devotee of popular music, and he had one vocalist, Tony Bennett, plus another group, the Phoenix Singers. He introduced a bunch of clips of flubbed promos for the show. He talked with Mel Brooks, a young, relatively unknown comedy writer, who bantered relentlessly and seemingly endlessly with Johnny.

"I wonder how this thing is going to go?" Johnny asked Bennett as the red light went off. He thought a moment. "I wonder if it's going to go at all."

Some of the reviewers had the same question. "There was none of the free-wheeling frivolity, the titillatingly suggestive humor, the strong commentary, the boisterous what'll-he-do-next quality that so often sparked Paar's show," wrote the *New York Herald Tribune*. "He is not the showman his predecessor was. But perhaps he will come along."

Jack Gould in *The New York Times* sounded a more sympathetic chord. "Mr. Carson's style is his own. He has the proverbial engaging smile and the quick mind essential to sustaining and seasoning a marathon of banter . . . He began in an atmosphere mercifully free of impending crisis."

The one critic he had always wanted to please was his mother, and she gave him only a barely passing grade. "I thought it was interesting," Mrs. Carson told an interviewer. "I wasn't sure that John was the type for it. When Jack Paar had the show, it was more like an arena—so much controversy, all the time. John is a gentle, kind person. He's not controversial. But I think now maybe he'll do all right."

The public had its own opinion. For the first week the show had 40.9 percent of the audience, over 7.5 million viewers. That was an extraordinary beginning, better than Paar had done for most of his tenure. Chicago had been a big city for Paar. Yet Johnny scored a 16.4 rating in the Windy City for the first two months, more than the ratings of the city's three other channels combined. Paar had occasionally scored in the high teens when he was going through a binge of controversy, but Johnny was scoring as high as a 21 rating sometimes, or 58 percent of the viewers. The *Variety* reporter in Chicago couldn't figure it out. The show "hardly generates coffee klatsch discussion, the way the Jack Paar edition did, and gets almost no press."

Carson's success crept up on the world. Even his own talent coordinator, Shelly Schultz, was amazed by Carson's achievement. "Here was a man who wasn't great at talking to people, who didn't like to meet new people, who wasn't a great conversationalist, and he had the country on his knees because he was coming across right on the tube.

"I think that he is one of those rare phenomenal people who understood the medium," says Schultz, who is now an agent at ICM representing another phenomenal success, Eddie Murphy. "In a very unintellectual way he understood it for what it was. He settled in and played the game every night, and he became very likable. He wasn't one of those who overintellectualize the communications medium and had the danger of failing because you think too much."

For five years Johnny had honed his media personality and his humor on an endless number of interviewees on *Who Do You Trust?* He never swung for the fences. He peppered the field with base hits, turning even bloopers into singles. Home runs were dangerous. They ended up offending one group or another. He had learned what worked and what didn't work. He understood those matinee ladies of the television audience better than he had understood his own wife.

The Johnny Carson that the audience saw on *The Tonight Show* was as subtle and as complicated a personality as any in television. He sat there with one camera always focused on him, showing *his* responses. He almost always sided with the audience and its reactions, but even that was conditional. He might chastise the audience for not understanding a joke, making them want to laugh even more.

Johnny kept his distance from his material too. If a joke failed, he managed to convey to the audience that he hadn't written the material. Then he saved the joke, with a line that was not his, either. He was a magician of comedy, turning not water into wine but failed jokes into laughs. When he sat down and did a second comic bit, he could have continued using cuecards. Instead, he read off sheets of paper, pretending that this was the first time he was seeing the material. If the material was drawing groans, as often or not he would toss the sheets of paper away and go on to something else.

Johnny Carson was a patchwork of other performers. His takes were carbon copies of Jack Benny's. His character Carnac the Magnificent was similar to Steve Allen's classic Answer Man. The irascible old Aunt Blabby was almost a twin of Jonathan Winter's Maude Frickert. But Johnny made the audience forget these antecedents.

In a brilliantly intuitive fashion Johnny played to his various constituencies. By saying that he was not from a show-biz background, not from New York or the Lower East Side, he was telling the audience he was not going to threaten them with urbane ethnic jokes beyond their experience. When he risked offending one group or another— old people when he played Aunt Blabby, traditional moralists when he leered at a star's bosoms, conservatives or liberals when he made fun of politicians—he knew when to draw back short of the precipice, but short of the biggest laugh too. He was his own best censor. He was a cautious comedian.

He understood what mid-America found funny. "You have to tailor your material to the medium," he said. "I can look at a piece of material and know fairly well whether it will play and be amusing. You have to learn to be an editor. You experiment sometimes. I'm sure Mel Brooks is not a comic who reaches the great percentage of the audience. He's kind of wild—but when he's good, he's near genius. I'll put him on the show. I'm much safer with a Sam Levenson. He talks about kids and schools, and he won't offend. You just have to rely on your own judgment. If you do make a mistake, you'll find out soon enough— because suddenly you won't have an audience."

The Tonight Show slowly took on Johnny's image. Johnny was a solo act. Unlike Paar, he wanted no family of regulars around him. He gave out no tenure. In his monologue he didn't mention his divorce or his kids. Each evening he said a few words to Ed McMahon, and then the announcer played his game of musical chairs. "I begin each show sitting on the chair next to Johnny," McMahon said. "And then as the program progresses, I move on down the line until I'm completely out of the picture."

Johnny did skits reminiscent of his days on *Carson's Cellar* and *Squirrel's Nest*. He welcomed physical challenges, wrestling with Antonio Rocca, fencing with a champion, dancing a hula with Miss U.S.A. and a snake dance with the Augue and Margo dance team. He stood on the pitcher's mound at Yankee Stadium pitching to Mickey Mantle. One day he flew with the U.S. Air Force Thunderbirds, filming a sequence for *The Tonight Show*.

Another element of Johnny's humor was only vaguely apparent in these early years. He could make fun of his audience. He could put them down and they didn't care. Jody understood that as well as anyone. When he played Floyd R. Turbo, a hayseed reactionary, she knew that Johnny based the character on old farmers back in Nebraska. She knew too that probably nobody laughed harder than the people being caricatured.

Johnny had learned the parameters of the permissible back in Norfolk when he had put on his teachers, in the army attacking superiors, at Nebraska hosting the Kosmet Klub shows, doing television in Los Angeles and New York. At this late hour he made jokes that had rarely been heard on network television, and good old Peck's Bad Boy Johnny got away with it. He peppered the show with sexual innuendo, much as he had on *Who Do You Trust?* He had no second script to defeat the censors, and he depended on his double takes and expressive eyebrows as much as on language.

Anyone who thought that an easy task had only to ask Woody Woodbury, who had taken over for Johnny on *Who*

Do You Trust? Kammerman wrote the same jokes that he always had. But when they came out of Woodbury's mouth, they sounded positively dirty, and the new host stood looking like a leering burlesque comic. The show was eventually canceled.

Johnny had had marvelous training for hosting *The Tonight Show*. On *Who Do You Trust?* he had learned to make anyone interesting for a few minutes. He had a memory like a computer, and after a decade of doing television he had an immense store of jokes.

The king of the night was easily bored. That too he used to his advantage. Few terrors in public life compared with sitting next to Johnny on *The Tonight Show* as his eyes glazed over. He was usually polite to his guests, but they knew they had better be entertaining, or they would be gone before very many viewers got up to change the channel. If they were very good, he kept them on longer, even if it meant bumping another guest. "If you book three guests and something is going very, very well, you don't worry about the third guest," Johnny said. "You go with what's working."

Johnny was wonderfully empathetic talking to little old ladies and obscure eccentrics. He was not always at ease interviewing the major stars. Many of his celebrity guests came to sell a glamour that they often didn't possess, a humor that they rarely had. Carson knew all this, but whatever the stars did or said, he almost always tried to make them look good—as long as they did what they were supposed to do.

Only a few days into the show Red Buttons, a comedian and movie actor, set off on a soliloquy about politics and psychology that was as boring as it was interminable. Johnny's instant warning system went off. He sent silent signals to Buttons, but to no effect.

"You're kind of a redheaded Dr. Schweitzer tonight, aren't you?" Johnny said finally. With that, Buttons returned to the business at hand—to be amusing, and to pass on some minor Hollywood lore.

In February 1963 Sargent Shriver appeared to talk about the Peace Corps. Later in the year Dr. Robert Baird, an idealistic young doctor, became one of the first people to discuss the drug epidemic on national television. But it was rare indeed to have serious discussions on the show. When a politician was booked, it was usually a character like Sam Yorty, the fast-talking mayor of Los Angeles, who provided as many laughs as a stand-up comedian. Mayor John Lindsay went for laughs, talking about a dating computer for New York's parks. Lindsay said that a bachelor deposited his quarter and told the machine, " 'I'm sensitive, I'm single, I'm rich,' whereupon the machine mugs him."

Johnny attempted to steer the show away from the grim and the humorless. Yet in private he was very different. Johnny saw hypocrisy almost everywhere he looked, from civil-rights proponents who were "for it so long as it doesn't touch *them*" to those who were all for helping drug addicts as long as "they don't put up a hospital near *their homes*." He was a man without heroes, a curmudgeon who considered most people "afraid to express ideas which do not bow to popular opinion." He thought that America had gotten into a slough of mistakes in Vietnam, though no one watching *The Tonight Show* would have known.

For years Johnny had worried about the danger of overexposure. Although he was doing eight hours and forty-five minutes of television a week, he still adhered to his axiom. He allowed the other performers not only to shine, but occasionally to outshine him. He could play straight man. He exerted extraordinary discipline, letting someone else get the biggest laugh because when someone else scored, the show scored, and ultimately he scored more than anyone else.

"The ratings always sag when there's a replacement on for a time," Johnny said. "I think I do a hell of a lot better show—Jesus, that sounds terrible—but I think I do a better show because I have an affinity for editing and pacing. I make comedians look as good as I possibly can. This show is a combination of a lot of things—music, comedy, talk

—but you must have a personality around which the show revolves. The show depends on how he works with the acts, the way he performs; his attitudes and opinions are what carries this kind of show.''

Six weeks after he took over *The Tonight Show*, Johnny sat in the Rockefeller Center restaurant looking out on the ice skaters gliding around the rink. As he talked to a companion and ate a late breakfast of scrambled eggs and french fries, an old lady approached the table. When Johnny looked up, the lady asked for his autograph.

''It's for the little girl across the street from my home,'' the lady said. ''She just loves you.''

Johnny was with a reporter, and he was not about to tell the lady to let him have his breakfast in peace. He smiled his television smile, but he was already savvy enough at the business of fame not to start a conversation, not to ask what the little girl was doing staying up until 1:00 A.M. He wrote his name, and the lady left.

After the initial flurry of articles about the show, the newspapers and columnists weren't writing very much about him. He wasn't a subject of great fascination to the gossip columnists, either. But the press hardly mattered compared to the transcendent power of the tube. Wherever he went, people looked at him. He had wanted this fame, he had pursued it, but he hated the glad-handing, the way people burst in on him with an assumption of intimacy. He couldn't stand it when some guy would grab his arm, saying, ''Hey, Johnny, c'mere and meet my wife.'' He had even had one man ask him for an autograph at a urinal. People like that he would have loved to have punched in the mouth. He couldn't, though, because he knew that the headline would read, JOHNNY CARSON PUNCHES FAN IN THE MOUTH. After a while he insisted on a limousine so that he wouldn't have to brush against the public as he arrived and left NBC.

Everyone wanted something out of Johnny now—to be on the show. Rock-'n'-roll singers. Movie stars. Girl singers. Authors. Presidential candidates. To be near him, to touch him, to know him. Everyone also wanted to help him, to do something for him. That was fine and good, though Johnny was discovering that the difference between a helping hand and an outstretched palm is a twist of the wrist.

Perry Cross, the show's producer, understood the pressure Johnny was under, his constant preoccupation with the show. Cross had hired a young, enthusiastic group of writers, talent coordinators, and office staff. Although Johnny was only thirty-seven, he was considerably older than most of his colleagues. Even if he had been a sunnier, friendlier person, much of the staff would have treated him with the distance of age and authority. As it was, he wanted to be left alone in his office, to deal with Perry or his brother, Dick, or a few others.

It was a job churning out the shows, and Cross came in each morning at about nine-thirty or ten and didn't get home until one the next morning. The producer's theory was that the best way to produce a happy show was to have a happy staff. He acted, in Shelly Schultz's words, "like the social director of a resort in the Catskills."

Every afternoon Cross and Ed McMahon met with Johnny in his office. The producer carried a folder with research notes and the lineup for the evening's show. The three men drank vodkas and tonic, and talked and laughed. By this hour Johnny was usually in a halfway decent mood, and the liquor helped.

Johnny gave a far funnier, far freer show here in private than he would later on *The Tonight Show*. He might do an imitation of an NBC executive, or tell one outrageous story after another. Perry had a wild sense of humor, and he made Johnny laugh. He sometimes did his tap dance or his routine based on the comedy of Jack E. Leonard. Ed was full of stories too. Johnny loved to laugh, and Ed and Perry could break him up. And when the time came to go into the studio, the three men were ready.

One day after nine months or so, Perry Cross came to Johnny with news that risked upsetting this afternoon routine. Jerry Lewis had asked Cross to produce his new variety show on ABC. Cross loved doing *The Tonight Show*, but Lewis was offering a salary four or five times the one he received from NBC. Cross didn't want to leave Johnny. All he wanted was a raise.

Johnny could have asked NBC to give Cross his raise, but Cross didn't understand the man for whom he worked. Johnny didn't like to be bothered by such business. Ed McMahon had given his manager specific orders never to ask Johnny about money or contracts. Never.

Cross didn't know for sure whether Johnny interceded with NBC. But when the offer came back, he considered it little better than an insult. He looked at Johnny and Ed, and figured they were getting rich and he was getting nowhere. He told Johnny that he would be leaving.

The Tonight Show decided to have a going-away party for him. The Stage Door delicatessen catered the event with a big spread of hors d'oeuvres and cold cuts. The staff were a hard-drinking crew, and many bottles of liquor sat on the table as well.

Two of John and Dick's old Nebraska buddies, Bill Bridge and William Butterfield, were visiting, staying with Dick. They were enjoying themselves so much that Bridge backed up into a salad bowl, covering his behind with creamy dressing.

"How're you getting along?" Johnny asked Bridge as they stood in the center of the crowded room.

"Fine," Bridge said, sipping his drink, "but you know that fellow there, the assistant director, he won't talk to me."

Johnny looked toward one of the assistant directors who stood against the wall. "There's a reason," Johnny said. At that moment the assistant director slumped over and slid down the wall, dead drunk.

The time came for Johnny, in the noble tradition of corporate going-away parties, to bid Perry Cross good-bye in words sweeter even than the deli cakes. As Johnny stood in the center of the room, his minions shouted, "Quiet!"

and within seconds the gathering was as quiet as if the red light had gone on.

Johnny and Perry stood together, while the crowd waited in anticipation. "As you know, we're all here for Perry," Johnny said, looking at the producer. He spoke with understatement but with an undertone of emotion. "Perry is going with *The Jerry Lewis Show*.

"Perry," Johnny said, looking at the producer. Perry looked up at Johnny with modest anticipation.

"Perry, I want to say this. Fuck you, Perry."

In September *The Jerry Lewis Show* debuted and lasted three months. Cross ended up selling real estate in the San Fernando Valley.

As the new producer, NBC hired Art Stark at a considerably higher salary than Cross had received. Although *The Tonight Show* was getting better ratings than Paar, as John Horn of the *New York Herald Tribune* wrote on July 28, 1963, Johnny had "yet to create a distinctive 'Tonight' style of his own." Critics might be ignored, but even many of those working on the program felt that it needed direction.

Stark understood Johnny's insecurities and his dark, fluctuating moods. He saw it as his job to protect Johnny, to keep others away. Stark, who had labored in the fields of daytime television for many years, liked the idea of producing one of the most successful programs on television. He liked the money, the power, and the game.

From the day Art Stark walked in, he made it clear that he was the producer and his authority was not to be trafficked with. At one of the first staff meetings he had to decide how to replace a singer who had suddenly dropped out.

"I can get you Anita O'Day," said Bruce Cooper, one of the talent coordinators.

"Who the hell is Anita O'Day?" asked Stark about the jazz singer.

"You're producing one of the biggest shows in television and you don't know who Anita O'Day is?" Cooper said.

One man's candor is another man's belligerence, and

Stark didn't appreciate Cooper's remark. He was not going to ingratiate himself with the old staff. He made no effort to hide his dislike of Cooper, and he didn't seem to care that the talent coordinator didn't like him, either. The staff realized that Stark was not a man who wanted his authority challenged. The collegial atmosphere of Cross's short-lived regime did not end completely, but staff shenanigans were held in check. It was okay to joke and laugh, but it was all for one purpose: to make Johnny look good.

Johnny called Stark around noon every day to talk about that evening's show. Art had a meeting with Johnny each afternoon. When his star arrived in the offices at Rockefeller Center around 3:00 P.M., Art sensed his mood. If Johnny was in one of his black spells, Art had his own techniques to pick Johnny up. He would go back to the writers' offices and have them redo all the interview notes and introductions, making them positively obscene. Knowing that they had an appreciative audience of one, the writers penned jokes and dialogue of unadulterated filth. Johnny opened the manila envelope, and soon erupted in laughter. If Johnny had ever used the material on the show, he would have blown out half the sets in America. But the idea was to bring Johnny out of his funk, and usually it worked.

Art created a format for Johnny based in part on his experiences working on *Who Do You Trust?* To do the show night after night, Johnny needed a comfortable, predictable routine. In the afternoon Johnny read through the interview material and background information on his guests. As part of their job, the talent coordinators interviewed the guests and jotted down possible questions and themes.

Some stars could hardly say their full names if they weren't reading from a script. For them, the writers crafted questions and answers that Johnny stuck to as religiously as he had the scripts on *Who Do You Trust?* A few guests, like Eva Gabor, got out there and winged it. But most wanted a good idea of what Johnny was going to ask them. That way they had time to practice their spontaneity.

At around six o'clock Johnny received the monologue

material from the writers. Johnny and the writers read the papers and the magazines and watched the TV news programs as avidly as any news junkie. They picked out any topical item or story that they could twist into a joke. Unlike many television comedians, Johnny could have written his own material. He knew what he wanted, what Johnny Carson could say.

Johnny edited the jokes, shuffling their order, and then sent the monologue off to be put on cue cards. Johnny needed only a few key words. As he stood in front of the audience, he turned almost imperceptibly from left to right as he did one joke after another. Inevitably, some jokes didn't work, but nobody in show business was better at turning grimaces into grins. He was forever coming up with the most wonderful savers. ("Where were you when I raised the flag on Iwo Jima?") Although these lines seemed spontaneous, they were written by his staff, and Johnny never went out to do a monologue without his verbal life preservers.

In his office Johnny also worked on the skits that became a regular part of the show. They were written in blocks of dialogue, climaxed by a joke. "If one fails, Johnny just moves on to another," says Walter Kempley, who became the new head writer. "If none work, he can save it by stepping out of character."

As the show approached the seven-thirty taping, Johnny didn't say more than a few words to his guests, if he met them at all. That was another precaution. Johnny didn't want to pretend that he was hearing a story for the first time when he had just laughed at the anecdote in the Green Room, where the guests waited to go on.

Despite everything else he had to think about, Johnny had to work in all the commercials. As the midnight hour approached, Johnny was less like a host than an air-traffic controller at La Guardia Airport on a Friday afternoon. *Television Magazine* clocked the ten-minute period between 11:51:10 and 12:01:04. The seven commercials took up five minutes and fifteen seconds. Title cards and promotion added another twenty seconds. That left Johnny a meager four minutes and nineteen seconds.

Although Johnny and the staff took impish delight in attempting new material, they learned that at times their mass audience had to be led to the humor by the hand and taught how to laugh. On one occasion a comedian wanted to appear pretending to be John Glenn's father. The bit had endless possibilities. When Glenn orbited the earth in February 1962 he became a front-page hero across America. He was Davy Crockett, apple pie, and Buzz Corbett, space cadet, all wrapped up in one red-white-and-blue package. Johnny and the writers thought it would be hysterical, one outrageous line after another about what a miserable, god-awful little snit Glenn had been.

Johnny introduced the supposed Mr. Glenn with perfect solemnity. Comedians had died before on *The Tonight Show*, but this was suicide. The audience wasn't catching on, and Johnny could do nothing about it. They believed that the show had booked this old mountebank to come on and savage his son, America's greatest hero, in front of 8 million of his fellow citizens. The comedian realized what was happening, but he couldn't very well start telling mother-in-law jokes, or do a soft-shoe routine. He blundered on, as the hostility deepened and deepened. By the end that was not an audience out there, it was a lynch mob.

After the show the smell of death was so strong on the comedian that no one wanted to be near him. He never returned to do the show again.

Johnny always ran a risk when he didn't alert the audience to his jokes. Another time he introduced a uniformed Pinkerton man who carried with him the Star of India sapphire, one of the greatest jewels in the world. As Johnny took the famous jewel in his hand, he dropped it on the floor, and the paste sapphire shattered into a hundred pieces. Johnny didn't laugh. The Pinkerton man didn't laugh. The audience didn't laugh. Art Stark cut to a commercial.

For Thanksgiving Johnny and an actor bobbed for apples. Johnny ducked his head in the tub until finally he grasped a slippery apple in his teeth. Then the curtain closed. When it opened again, Johnny and his apple were gone. But the actor was still there, his head bobbing away as if he had drowned in a futile search for an apple. The curtain closed again. The show went on, but NBC received a slew of calls from offended viewers.

In 1965 the most famous of all *Tonight Show* comedic incidents took place during the appearance of Ed Ames, a popular television actor. Ames was playing the Indian Mingo on the television series *Daniel Boone*. He was to teach Johnny how to throw tomahawks at the image of a sheriff. Ames aimed carefully, and sent the lethal weapon sailing toward the plywood figure. The tomahawk landed in the poor sheriff's crotch.

Ames moved forward to retrieve the tomahawk, but Johnny grasped his arm and held him. That was the instinctive gesture that made the scene a classic. Johnny milked the laughs for minutes more, looking incredulously at the camera. Then, when the laughter was down to random giggles, Johnny turned to Ames and said, "I didn't know you were Jewish."

Not all of the proposed skits and bits ended up on the air. One time when the owner of a pet shop appeared as a guest, he left a parrot behind. The bird was supposed to talk, and that opened up a number of possibilities. After considerable discussion the staff members decided to teach the bird the phrase "Fuck you, prince." The parrot would be the ultimate animal act. They would have to bleep the F-word on the tape, but the audience would understand.

Shelly Schultz become the bird's trainer. When he was not interviewing celebrities and others, he sat in his small office peeling bananas and saying, "Fuck you, prince," over and over again to the mute parrot. Although the bird was a slow learner, he was very good at certain bodily functions. The staff learned to steer a wide berth from the room, which smelled like a bird cage.

The then-prince of the night was not so above the daily routine that he did not take a certain interest in a parrot that would say, "Fuck you, prince." Every week Johnny asked when the dress rehearsal would take place. Every week Shelly continued his lessons. Finally he told Johnny, "I think I got it."

Johnny came to Shelly's office for the great moment.

"Fuck you, prince," Shelley said.

"Fuck you, prince," came a disembodied, parrotlike sound from the general direction of the parrot. Johnny looked down where his brother, Dick, was squatting under the desk, rendering his best imitation of a talking bird. Even for the prince of late night, life was full of disappointments.

The audience thought that Johnny, Ed, and Skitch Henderson were buddies. Not only did Johnny and the musical director have no relationship at all, but Henderson was mildly disdainful of the show. He wanted to become a serious conductor, and he talked frequently about the more congenial atmosphere of Steve Allen's *Tonight Show*.

"After about a year Ed McMahon came up to me and said it's time for the three of us to go have a drink," Henderson recalls. "I am not a drinker, and Johnny has problems when he drinks. Neither of us were able to take care of ourselves if we drink. We went to Trader Vic's. Ed was late, and in our embarrassment we had two navy grogs. By the time Ed got there, we were totally sloshed. Many things were said that night that eliminated that invisible barrier. After that, I tried to be one of the troops, to be more supportive. I didn't agree with his musical tastes, Wayne King and Rudy Vallee, but I tried to understand what he wanted."

On August 17, 1963, Johnny took the step that many thought he never would take. On a sweltering Saturday afternoon he married thirty-one-year old Joanne in the Marble Collegiate Church on Fifth Avenue. Johnny had been host of *The Tonight Show* for almost a year. The famous and almost-famous would gladly have stacked the pews. One call from Gary Stevens and the street outside would have been full of newspaper photographers and the curious. The last thing

Johnny wanted was a media free-for-all. He went so far in protecting his privacy that he didn't invite even his own mother and father or Joanne's father and stepmother.

The ceremony took place not in the main church where Norman Vincent Peale preached the power of positive thinking each Sunday. The Reverend Donald W. Hoffman, the pastor, officiated in the small private chapel. Joanne usually dressed in slacks and a sweater, but today she wore a white silk dress subtly accented by roses. Thirty-seven-year-old Johnny wore a black suit. His brother, Dick, was the best man. Art Stark gave the bride away. Al Bruno was the only other guest.

Afterward, the small group went uptown to Johnny's apartment on York Avenue. Skitch Henderson, Rudy Vallee, and a few other guests arrived, but they hadn't even known that Johnny and Joanne were being married. The press found out anyway, and a group of photographers waited impatiently downstairs until the bride and groom agreed to be photographed.

One other detail of this marriage had taken place far away from the East Side of Manhattan. When Johnny decided to remarry, he needed to formalize his divorce. Al Bruno had dreaded seeing Johnny's name dragged through the sooty pages of the tabloids. So Jody agreed to fly down to Mexico to obtain a divorce. Jody had already settled with Johnny for 15 percent of his gross income, and for her the trip was a mere formality, like an appointment to have a tooth pulled.

"I flew down to Mexico in the late afternoon," Jody recalls. "I went to the lawyer that afternoon. I met the lawyer again the next morning. I signed the paper. The lawyer took me back to the hotel. I packed and took the flight back."

Marriage to Joanne changed Johnny's daily life very little. For him, as for most of the staff, *The Tonight Show* was the center of everything. Working on the show had all the intensity and pressure of a political campaign. Most of the people who put the program together were in their late twenties or early thirties and decidedly single. They partied almost as hard as they worked. If they were married when they joined the show, they often were soon divorced.

Johnny's writers were probably the least happy of the lot, but that was more the nature of writers than of *The Tonight Show*. Writing comedy under deadline is an unnatural act, and the staff had almost as many tics, idiosyncracies, and personal foibles as could be found in a ward at Bellevue. They also had a great deal of talent. In the early years Dick Cavett wrote a short while for the show. Marshall Brickman went on to write movies with Woody Allen. Ed Weinberger and David Lloyd became two of the top television writers and producers in Hollywood.

Johnny kept a cordon sanitaire between himself and the people who prepared his daily diet of wit. Walter Kempley, the head writer, was an anomaly on the staff, a married man with four children. He was the first of the writers to show up each morning, at around ten o'clock. Kempley filled his office with so many toys that it looked like the NBC outlet to F.A.O. Schwarz. In the morning he sat reading the newspapers, looking for items that Johnny might use. By the time of the noon staff meeting Kempley's wit was wide awake, and he and his fellow scribes stood at the door bombarding each other with sarcastic gibes and private jokes funnier than most of those they gave to Johnny. Then to work. As each finished his daily chore—the monologue, a skit, a routine at the desk, funny interview answers—they traipsed down to Johnny's office and left their typed material.

Johnny did not praise his subordinates. Silence was the highest accolade. Sometimes he wanted changes or more material. He rarely complained, but others performed that function. "The producers could hardly wait to tell you if anything bombed," Kempley said.

Whether the writing was good or bad or mediocre, that night's show was soon forgotten in the rush of new deadlines. Whenever the writers reminisced, it was usually the disasters they remembered. On one occasion a writer prepared a sketch commemorating the anniversary of Custer's Last Stand. In this version Colonel Custer, played by Johnny, survived after battling the last Indian to a standstill. The extra playing an Indian had to walk across the stage to Johnny, grapple with him, and fall to the ground. When the Indian reached stage center, he turned toward the camera. "Many moons ago," the actor said, beginning a lengthy soliloquy as Johnny watched incredulously. The speech ruined the skit, and the phrase "many moons ago" became a code word for impending disaster.

Only once in those early years did Johnny ever openly complain about his writers. That was on one of the annual trips to Los Angeles. The writers were New Yorkers who thought of the sun as the great electric light bulb in the sky. Here in southern California the sun, the sky, the warmth pulled irresistibly. After handing in their material, they went outside the NBC studio in Burbank and began tossing a Frisbee around in the parking lot.

"Where are the writers?" Johnny asked.

"They're out playing Frisbee," said Jeanne Prior, Johnny's stunning secretary.

Johnny was infuriated. He ordered the group back into the studio, where he berated them. "What the hell are you guys doing!" he yelled. "Out in the parking lot playing Frisbee when you're supposed to be working."

As the writers walked back to their offices, Johnny turned to his secretary. "What's a Frisbee?" he asked.

Jeanne had a unique relationship with Johnny. He joked about her on the show, creating an image of the classic blond bimbo whose greatest accomplishment in life is painting her nails. In fact, Jeanne lasted with Johnny because she was a woman of competence and discretion. She loved Johnny, as secretaries sometimes love their bosses. Johnny cared for Jeanne too. He watched paternally as she dated two men, Rudy Tellez and another talent coordinator. The writers and other staff members watched too, feeling that whichever man won Jeanne's hand would win Johnny's nod for rapid advancement.

Johnny had a unique relationship with Jeanne Prior. "In everybody's life there are four or five people who are important," she says. "He was one of those. I was twenty-five years old. My parents were dead. I was a young Catholic girl in the city. I had blond hair and I looked different than what I was. I needed protection. He did that for me, and in a way I did that for him. I kept people away. I ran interference."

Jeanne saw Johnny for seven years as he developed into an enormous star. "Except for the beginning years of his life, I don't think Johnny has ever been rejected," she says. "Just think of the fact of going around for thirty years and never being rejected by almost anybody, not waiters, not anybody. What do you think would be easier to live with, his life or the life most of us live? There is a cost, and that's why he insulates himself. He used to get in the car and go home."

The writers were perfectly comfortable keeping their distance from Johnny. The producer, however, decided that the staff should get together socially, and planned a gala evening at the Carsons'.

The evening was a bust. After a few drinks the writers and some other members of the group went out into the hallway and started shooting craps. Johnny didn't seem to mind, but that was the end of the socializing at the Carsons'.

One of those shooting craps that evening was Bruce Cooper. Despite his conflict with Stark, Cooper was one of the three talent coordinators who chose the guests. Occasionally Johnny had a say in this; but to keep from being badgered, he always said that the final decision was up to the producer and the talent coordinators, who put in extraordinary hours. They were at NBC during the day, and with the guests before and during the show. Afterward, they headed out to the theater and clubs, checking out candidates to appear on the show.

The talent coordinators were poorly paid, but they had the best seats on Broadway, the best tables at nightclubs, plus other benefits. Bruce Cooper booked Wilhemina, the famous model, and later married her.

One of the other talent coordinators, Mike Zannella, had begun as a seventeen-year-old cue boy on *Who Do You Trust?* Zannella was so star-struck that he had stood outside the theater one December as Johnny left after doing the game show. The teenager shyly handed his favorite television star a Christmas present. Johnny was touched, and Zannella became Johnny's special assistant. The young man's proximity to his idol only increased his awe. He began to dress like Johnny. When he got an apartment, he furnished it so much like Johnny's that Joanne named it "the Junior Carson apartment."

In the morning production staff meeting the talent coordinators often bickered over their assignments, fighting to be given the top guests. They assessed each potential guest with brutal frankness, with little room for dying legends or stars on a downward trajectory.

One day the group mused over how to deal with Little Stevie Wonder. He wasn't so little anymore. He wasn't such a great booking. No one on the staff had any idea that the adult Stevie Wonder would go on to become one of the great stars of his generation.

"How are we supposed to get this blind kid to come out and hit his mark, to do the song?" asked Rudy Tellez.

"I've got it," the producer said. "We'll use a set that looks like a ship's deck, put Stevie in a sailor's suit, and have him walk out holding onto the railing."

The Tonight Show provided valuable exposure to singers. In the first years of the show Johnny featured everyone from Jan Murray to Errol Garner, Homer and Jethro to Barbra Streisand. The show could put a book on the best-seller list, something that even ecstatic reviews or full-page ads might not be able to do. Gore Vidal, Harry Golden, and William Saroyan all shilled their latest. They were the most promotable authors in America, yet they had to face the harsh arithmetic of television. Because best-selling authors didn't interest a mass television audience the way a comedian or a singer did, they were usually relegated to the dead end of the show, hurried out of the Green Room in the last few minutes.

For comedians, *The Tonight Show* was the Holy Grail. If you made it on *The Tonight Show*, if Johnny passed his blessing on you, you were made. A first appearance on the show was high school graduation and oral exams all wrapped up together. Unlike Paar, Johnny didn't fancy himself the discoverer and nurturer of young talent. But if you were good, if you made Johnny laugh, then you got invited back, and maybe next time you got to sit down next to Johnny after your bit.

America first appreciated the comedic genius of Woody Allen on *The Tonight Show*. Redd Foxx's big break came there. Freddie Prinze attributed his career to his appearance with Johnny. Bill Cosby got much of his start on the show. Almost every important new comedian of the sixties and much of the seventies gained exposure and acceptance appearing with Johnny.

The hardest part was to get on, to appear that first time. Joan Rivers was one of those who beat at the door until her fists were raw. The thirty-one-year-old comedienne was relegated to grimy clubs in Greenwich Village, sundry work on *Candid Camera*, and the realization that maybe she wasn't going to make it. "Put her on as a comedy writer," Rivers's manager beseeched Shelly Schultz, the talent coordinator. "Use her in the death slot."

On February 17, 1965, Joan received a call that she would have a spot on *The Tonight Show* that evening. In the afternoon she sat with Schultz and outlined the areas that she would talk about, from being single to problems with her car. She walked onstage as the next-to-last guest of the evening wearing a black Jax dress, a string of pearls, and a pink boa. She was a bold, acerbic entertainer, who would have made many television hosts uncomfortable. Johnny had a genius for making a performer look good. It is the greatest gift that one performer can give another.

"He understood everything," Rivers wrote later. "He

wanted it to work. He knew how to go with me and feed me and knew how to wait. . . . He never cut off a punch line and when it came, he broke up. It was like telling it to your father—and your father is laughing, leaning way back and laughing, and you know he is going to laugh at the next one. And he did and he did and he did. . . . At the end of the show he was wiping his eyes. He said, right on the air, " 'God, you're funny. You're going to be a star.' "

Rivers was back on *The Tonight Show* two weeks later as the lead guest. She had worked years to become an overnight success, and she soon became one of Johnny's favorites.

Sometimes Johnny had problems that couldn't be blamed on the talent coordinators. One evening Susan Hampshire, a British actress, appeared on the show to promote *Living Free*, a film about lions in Africa. Columbia Pictures had come up with a lion cub from Lion Country Safari in Florida. The wildlife attraction wanted some publicity of its own, and it had shipped north not only the cub, but a sexy blond trainer in a tight safari suit.

Johnny would have gladly appeared with the two women and the lion cub. Columbia Pictures, however, did not want its film and its star upstaged by a blonde in a miniskirt. To placate the Hollywood studio, the trainer was told that she would not be going on the air.

The trainer became incensed, and just before airtime she primed the lion cub with a bottle of milk. As soon as Susan Hampshire handed the lion to Johnny, the cub unloaded all over the host.

At the commercial break Johnny changed his suit. Alas, the odor of *eau de zoo* hung over the host.

"How long will this smell persist?" Johnny asked the trainer.

"Oh, maybe a week."

NINE

"Olley, olley, oxen . . . free, free, free!" Joanne yelled, her voice echoing down the hallways.

Joanne had just woken up in the queen-size bed. It was eleven o'clock. Johnny had been up for hours, reading newspapers and magazines, looking for items for the monologue. Joanne padded along the beige wall-to-wall carpeting. Johnny could be anywhere. Soon after their wedding the couple had purchased the two-and-a-half-room apartment to the north of their four-and-a-half rooms, and broken through the walls. Then, when the three-and-a-half-room apartment to the south became vacant, they had bought that one too, and knocked down some more walls.

"Olley, olley, oxen . . . free, free, *free*!"

Johnny might be in his dressing room, which Joanne had carpeted with fur. He might be in the bar with its enormous wine rack. Johnny thought it looked neat, though they didn't need the bar to store bottles. His taste in wine began and ended with different flavors of Lancers. Neither he nor Joanne cooked, but he might be in kitchen number one, or kitchen number two, or kitchen number three.

"Here she comes, Gadzilla, Queen of the Gypsies," Johnny said as he came upon his bride during this morning ritual. He led her to one of the kitchens and brewed a cup of instant coffee for himself, while she had her morning tea.

Joanne had decorated this apartment around one decidedly masculine theme: John W. Carson. Johnny's favorite color was brown. There was as much brown in those ten-and-a-half rooms as in Nebraska after the spring plowing. When Joanne finished, the adjacent apartments looked like a Hershey Bar museum.

Johnny liked heavy, Spanish-looking furniture to go with brown walls, and brown rugs, and brown furs. He cut down an old butcher block for Joanne to turn into a coffee table. Before beginning work on the block, she examined it as carefully as a diamond cutter about to cut a precious jewel. She went to the Metropolitan Museum of Art on Fifth Avenue and studied the antique furniture. Then she took a gouge and chain and attacked the naked butcher block. Finally she singed it with a blowtorch until it looked positively ancient.

Joanne tried other things to make Johnny happy. She thought it would be neat if he could relax from all the pressures in a sauna. She turned the hot-water faucets on full blast in Johnny's bathroom. Before long the room was nothing but steam. Joanne's improvised sauna worked wonderfully—except the wallpaper started peeling off the ceilings.

Joanne said that she didn't want or need a child when she had Johnny; her denial was academic, since Johnny had had a vasectomy. Johnny had his toys too, spread throughout the apartment. A telescope. Weights. A videorecorder. Golf clubs. A rifle. A set of drums. Scuba equipment. *The Encyclopedia Britannica. Candy. The Naked Society. The Kama Sutra. How to Live with a Neurotic Dog*.

Joanne had her own special room, which the writer Gael Greene described as "a warren of unreorganizable clutter." Johnny called his wife's den "the squirrel's nest," after his first television program. That was a joke, but there was something peculiar about the disorder, as if, try as she might, Joanne could not get her life completely in order.

Joanne had married Johnny when celebrity had begun to affect his everyday life. A few years before, two scholars,

Donald Horton and R. Richard Wohl, had written a prophetic essay arguing that with the new mass media "[t]he most remote and illustrious men are met *as if* they were in the circle of one's peers." They called this new phenomenon "para-social interaction."

As early as October 1965 the *New York Daily News* wrote that Johnny might have "the most familiar face in America." He was on television more hours than any other performer, at what to most people was an intimate, private time of night. He did not expose himself emotionally as Jack Paar had done. He did not talk about his divorce, parade his children onto the set, or use them as vehicles for humor. In the public arena of *The Tonight Show* he attempted to put a wall about his private life.

Yet people felt that they knew him. Passers-by on the street yelled out their cornball jokes. Maître d's and waiters fawned over him. Strangers constantly attempted to be amusing, trying to turn Johnny's life into one big audition. Elevator operators perked up, saluting him with his first name. When he took his boys ice-skating at Rockefeller Center, a crowd formed around him.

At times he played the celebrity, calling the manager of an East Side movie house, asking to be allowed in without waiting in line. Just as often, however, he put on sunglasses and blended into the crowds at Giant games, or window-shopping on Fifth Avenue.

One weekend Frank Sinatra invited Johnny and Joanne to spent some time on his boat. The Carsons, Sinatra, Rosalind Russell, Freddie Brisson, and society columnist Aileen Mehle ("Suzy") headed to Westchester in two limousines. The drivers lost their way, and the group stopped to ask for directions. The local man looked at the famous passengers and offered to lead the limousines to the marina. He took them on back roads and then called a halt in front of a house far from any water. While Johnny and the others sat in bewildered silence, the man brought his wife out so that she could see his catch of the day.

Johnny had to learn to deal with this extraordinary celebrity. Together, he and Joanne created a private universe, far from the onslaughts of fans and subordinates. Joanne constructed for Johnny his own personal convent with only one acolyte. She devoted herself to Johnny and considered herself the most blessed of women. She spoke of him in words of veneration, adoration. "I'm so grateful that he married me," she said. "If he hadn't I would have followed him. I would have stood outside the studio waiting for him. I would have written him fan letters."

When people asked her to describe Johnny, she told them that she was at a loss for words. How could one describe the indescribable? To what could one compare the incomparable? She called Johnny "a husband, a father, a lover, a doctor."

Joanne hadn't finished work on the York Avenue apartment when she and Johnny had dinner with David and Joyce Susskind, in their new co-op apartment at the UN Plaza. The twin towers of the complex rose up thirty-eight stories at First Avenue and Forty-ninth Street. Susskind was as effusive and enthusiastic in private as he was in producing television programs or moderating talk shows. His subject for the evening was how much he loved this new apartment. "You have to move here," he told Johnny as they stood in the living room, looking out the floor-to-ceiling windows at a panoramic view of the city. "How can you not wake up happy living here?"

Johnny was fed up with the Con Ed crews waking him as they worked beneath his window on York Avenue. "They've been digging out there for weeks, and nobody knows what for," Carson said. "But I do. They're using it for a training ground. You know, a guy comes to work and Con Ed says, 'You don't know how to dig? Well, go over to our practice area.' "

Johnny and Joanne found their own ten-room $173,000 duplex on the thirty-fifth and thirty-sixth floors of the building. Their co-op was in the west wing of the building, and the view was even more spectacular, a sweeping panorama from the George Washington Bridge to the southern tip of Manhattan and beyond.

The Carsons were not the only prominent New Yorkers impressed by the UN Plaza, and the address became one of the most desired in the city. Truman Capote moved in and christened the complex "the compound." Senator Robert F. Kennedy purchased a six-room apartment on the four-teenth floor. Secretary of State William Rogers had his own six-room suite. Cliff Robertson, the actor, bought a place.

Joanne waited to move until October 1966, when Johnny was doing the show from Los Angeles. As soon as he left, she packed up all their belongings and had them taken to the UN Plaza. By the time she met her husband at the airport three weeks later, all Johnny had to do was to settle in.

Johnny and Joanne moved in with eight color television sets and sixteen phones. Joanne loaded up her palette with brown and began to decorate. She planned brown velvet draperies for the living room and chairs of oatmeal wool. She chose fur rugs for much of the home: wolf for the living room, cheetah for the foyer, and lamb for her dressing room. For Johnny's dressing room she decided upon draperies of what she called "tobacco and putty plaid."

Joanne became friendly with Truman Capote soon after the author gave his famous masked ball at the Plaza Hotel on November 28, 1966. Joanne was full of many of the same insecurities as her husband, and Capote was a won-drous guide into the worlds of society and glamour. "I was a little mouse," Joanne confided to Gerald Clarke, Capote's biographer. "I didn't know anything. He went through my closets and told me what to wear and what not to wear. I grew up basking in the sunlight of his approval."

Joanne called herself a "semi-active decorator." She was full of decorating ideas, but she was slow in completing her work. Six months after the Carsons moved in, the dining room and den were still cluttered with boxes and crates. Joyce Susskind remembers a party at the Carsons: "Ed

Sullivan and Jack Benny were guests. We sat on boxes at a table made up of sawhorses and Joanne served Cold Duck.''

In the fall of 1968, after two years in the building, Joanne took down some of the walls, and for months the apartment resembled Berlin in 1945. "Don't eat the sawdust, Muffie," she warned her Yorkshire terrier. A year later the walls were up, and she was covering them with dress fabrics. For her own dressing room she chose the same gray flannel cloth as several of her favorite pants suits.

Trudy Richards Moreault, a friend and neighbor, recalls another dinner party, after Joanne had completed much of the decorating. To her, the Carsons' living room looked as if Joanne had decorated it with rustic lounge furniture. It certainly was unique. Joanne had painted the foyer in Johnny's favorite "El Greco bronze." She had chosen the 832 old bricks for the fireplace and laboriously polished each one. She had placed the books in the bookshelves by the color of their jackets.

Johnny was proud of his wife's work, and he showed Don Rickles and the other guests around the apartment.

"Don't open that door," Joanne said.

Johnny pushed open the sliding doors to reveal a room full of the most bizarre accumulation of boxes, bric-a-brac, and junk.

"Hey, Barbara, come here, you have to see this room!" Rickles shouted to his wife. "It's unbelievable! Johnny Carson. He makes a million bucks a minute. And he hires George Shearing to decorate his apartment."

Johnny and Joanne gave occasional parties, but they spent most of their time alone. One of the few tradesmen she visited frequently was Buddy Hammer, a prominent furrier. When she appeared in Hammer's showroom upstairs on West Thirtieth Street, Hammer shut his office door so that Joanne could lie at peace on the furs, choosing which ones she wanted for throw rugs and bedspreads. Over the years Joanne bought several expensive coats as well.

One December Johnny called the furrier and said that he wanted to give his wife a sable for Christmas. Johnny seemed to think that buying a sable was like buying a Buick. Hammer called Joanne and secretly fitted her for a magnificent coat. Christmas morning Joanne opened her gift and gushed with thanks at Johnny's "surprise."

Johnny rarely talked of his private life, but Joanne proudly recited chapter and verse of her days with Johnny. She was not a cook, and she told of her husband dining on popcorn and a glass of milk, or Sara Lee chocolate cake three times a day, when he wasn't eating steaks. She described a typical evening *chez* Carson. She played with one of her "toys," the washing machine, wearing a bikini and a smock. In the meantime a half-naked Johnny stood over the stove popping popcorn.

Later Johnny might play with one of *his* "toys," videotaping the view or interviewing Joanne. She would rev up a Bronx accent and pretend to be a naive new arrival in the sophisticated world of Manhattan. Or, if they tired of that game, she would ask Johnny questions. "You're such a big star," she would say as Johnny videotaped her. "Can I touch you? Can I have your autograph?"

Betty Rollin was one of the first journalists to attempt to peek inside the private Johnny Carson. When she began researching her article, she found it impossible to get Johnny to open up. She talked to Joanne, who told her, "He doesn't go in for people." She talked to Art Stark: "I'm Johnny's best friend because I'm not interested in his friendship. I don't try to make contact with him." She talked to Dick, his brother: "We're not close."

In January 1966 *Look* published Rollin's article, titled "Johnny Carson, the Prince of Chitchat, Is a Loner." Johnny cared very little about reviews, but he cared a great deal about anything written about him personally.

Rollin's piece was hardly a devastating attack, but Johnny was very upset. At the time the article appeared, Johnny and Joanne's dentist invited them to his house for a party. "If we're such loners, why don't we go," Johnny said.

Johnny's dentist was great at flossing and cleaning, but his living room was not a gathering place for scintillating conversationalists. "Johnny, you keep me up at night," one man said. "I go to bed with you," quipped a lady.

"Now you know why we don't go to parties," Johnny said as they left. He felt totally vindicated. It didn't occur to him that his dentist's home was not the best place for the host of *The Tonight Show* to try out his social wings.

"I don't like to go out much," Johnny said. "We enjoy spending our time here, we have a comfortable home and we like each other's company. I'm not going to sit around in a roomful of people pretending to have a good time and saying 'Oh, isn't this fun?' when it isn't. That's silly. People say, 'Oh, but you ought to get out—you ought to go to the movies or the theater more often.' Why? I think it's a waste of time, doing things you don't really want to because people think you ought to. It always amazes me, the things people regard as comedy in the theater. Any show where the biggest laugh is 'son-of-a-bitch' isn't much of a comedy in my book. I go to see what I think I'll enjoy. For me to spend three hours in a theater because something is *charming* just isn't what I want to do."

Joanne was less reclusive than her husband. For Christmas she wanted to give the doormen and other helpers something special. She prepared snowball candles by filling coffee cups with wax, gluing the two halves together, and coating the ball with whipped wax.

Joanne thought that she had scored with her gift. But the East Side doormen are the Hessians of Manhattan. Around Christmas their smiles brighten, their steps quicken, and they dream not of snowball candles but of discreet envelopes of money.

Joanne was full of frenetic, restless energy, and she took an active role in running the co-op. She was the chairman of a cocktail party and buffet dinner in May of 1967 where the residents could meet their neighbors. Even Johnny showed up, taping the show a half hour early.

The five hundred residents of the UN Plaza were much too sophisticated to besiege Johnny for autographs or to try out one-liners in the elevator. But Johnny seemed not to want to acknowledge his neighbors.

"In the elevator I'd say good morning and he'd get behind his paper even deeper," says Mrs. Daniel Seymour, whose husband was then the president of J. Walter Thompson, the advertising agency. "He'd open his paper a little wider and scrunch back into the corner. He'd say nothing. It was a habit of his. He just didn't want to acknowledge knowing anybody. He wanted his privacy."

Joanne said hello in the elevator, though some of the neighbors found her social habits peculiar. "We had one big party, and out of the corner of my eye I noticed Joanne," recalls Joyce Susskind. "She was in jeans in the kitchen with the people who worked there."

For the most part, Joanne stayed in the apartment and communicated by telephone. On a typical day in the spring of 1968 she called Joyce Susskind to talk about the Susskinds' new baby, Samantha. She called the butcher, the florist, and Bloomingdale's. She called Mary Benny and Eydie Gorme and Bess Myerson. She called the headmaster of Johnny's sons' school. She called to find out what wine Arthur Godfrey liked so that she could send him a gift. She called the airlines to check on schedules for Johnny's next trip. She called the limousine driver to schedule a pickup. And that was only part of the list.

On *The Tonight Show* the staff wasn't sure how much influence Joanne had on Johnny, but they knew it was substantial. Associate producer Rudy Tellez nicknamed her "the killer mouse."

Joanne was clearly not happy with Bruno, who had been opposed to her marriage to Johnny. One Thanksgiving she sent him a greeting card titled "Happy Thanksgiving,

Grandma." Johnny's manager thought that the card was a dig at his attempts to control his client's professional life.

When Johnny, Joanne, and Stark flew to the Bahamas for a vacation, Joanne sent Bruno a letter berating him for the poor accommodations. The wording was couched in an exaggeratedly humorous style, but Bruno was not amused. Joanne wrote that the flight down had been long delayed, a problem that she could scarcely blame on Bruno. She said that when they were checking in, Johnny had stumbled over a couple of wheelchairs and Art had found himself between two blind guests fighting over a seeing eye dog. She concluded: "PS Johnny said to tell you your [sic] fired."

"Joanne was a weirdo," says Bruno. "She embarrassed the hell out of him, and he didn't know what the hell was going on."

Trudy Moreault, then one of Joanne's closest friends, has a similar opinion. "Joanne was not able to cope as his wife and mother," Moreault says. "Occasionally she would bring forth some great thing, like a birthday party, that was her one big accomplishment for the year. The rest was Joanne running around in her white boots in a limo trying to accomplish things. It didn't come off. She didn't have what it took to carry it off.

"Johnny liked a woman around. He told me plainly that he knew he had made a mistake even before they were married. They were living together. But there was an impetus there. She was the woman in his life and he married her."

Truman Capote, who had become a close friend of Joanne's, had yet another view. "I felt extremely sorry for his wife [Joanne]," he told journalist Lawrence Grobel in 1983. "She did a tremendous amount for Johnny. I don't think Johnny would have survived or have had remotely the career he's had if it hadn't been for her. He was *mean* as hell to her. And they lived right next door. He would holler and get drunk and start beating her and she would take refuge in my apartment. She would hide and Johnny would come pounding on my door shouting I know she's there. I would just maintain a dead silence and keep her there until he would pass out. I knew Johnny pretty well but nobody knows Johnny. When I knew him he really had no friends at all. The only time he comes alive is on camera.''

Jan de Ruth, an artist who became Joanne's close friend, said of the marriage, ''She really tried to take care of him. I think she loved him deeply. She really didn't have any-where else to put her emotions. She's not an easy person to decipher. Much that goes on does not come out through her words. Joanne was a people collector, but they usually left. She liked to spread her fingers but almost nothing stayed.''

Whatever her idiosyncracies, Joanne was quite aware of how being Mrs. Johnny Carson had changed her life. ''You just automatically know if you go out, you're going to be recognized, and stopped,'' Joanne said. ''If we went to premieres or openings, I just spent a little extra time with makeup because I knew we were going to be photographed. And you naturally wanted to look your best. But it does a strange thing to you when you're in the public eye so much. You find that you're concentrating more on yourself, and much of your attention is turned inward instead of outward. You're not as outgoing as you would be if you were in somebody's private home. When you're out in public, it's like being all polished and in a display case and rather suffocating. As Johnny always said, 'If I go out, I'm going to get nailed.' ''

Joanne had a secretary. Her name was Joanne. She looked like Joanne. She dressed like Joanne. The two women spent a great deal of time together. One of the secretary's duties was to buy clothes for Joanne. After a while the secretary was dressing better than her boss.

Joanne often went out in jeans, her hair pulled back. When she presented her credit card for a purchase, she told the salesgirl that she was Mrs. Johnny Carson's secretary.

At the same time, her secretary was taking the limousine and driving to Bloomingdale's and Lord and Taylor with her employer's consent making purchases. Joanne rarely ventured out to these places, but one day she happened to be purchasing some black mascara at Bloomingdale's. As usual, she had her hair in a ponytail and looked more like a pretty waif than the wife of one of America's most celebrated performers.

"You know you have to sign your *real* name," the salesgirl said as Joanne signed the credit card "Mrs. Johnny Carson."

"Oh, but I'm Mrs. Johnny Carson."

"No, you aren't," the salesgirl said adamantly. "You're Mrs. Carson's secretary. I know what Mrs. Carson looks like. She comes in here all the time."

Joanne finally convinced the store that she was indeed Mrs. Johnny Carson.

Joanne was always home to say good-bye to Johnny, always home to welcome him back after the show. She attempted to create ten rooms of paradise at the UN Plaza. Jan de Ruth was one of the few people invited to the Carsons' home. He watched as Joanne "tried to make Johnny as committed as she was. But there was no way to tie him up the way she wanted to, you couldn't do that with anyone."

"I tried to reach Johnny, to treat him as a human being," Joanne told journalist Karen Jackovich in 1988. "I forgot he was a star. I should have treated him as a star. If I had to do it over again, I would do it differently."

Joanne was deaf to the rumors of Johnny's philandering. Mamie Van Doren, the B-movie queen, recalls an intimate friendship with Johnny that began a month before Johnny married Joanne and lasted a decade. Van Doren necked and petted with Johnny on their midnight trysts. She says, however, that she never bestowed her ultimate honor, an award that she passed out elsewhere as often as the Girl Scouts give out cookies.

Upon her first appearance on *The Tonight Show*, Van

Doren recalls that Johnny invited her to dinner. Later the couple went to Van Doren's suite at the Plaza Hotel, where they lay in bed watching the show.

"You know, Mamie, you don't have to worry," Johnny said as the closing credits rolled down the screen and he and Mamie toasted each other with champagne. "I've had a vasectomy."

"He didn't talk about his wives," says Van Doren. "It was off and on again, and he had so many relationships. He never brought up another woman with me. I often wondered in my mind what he would do if his wife was sitting in bed with Paul Newman watching a show.

"Johnny was very oversexed. He was a man who liked to keep his body in the best shape. He prizes himself as a real lover. The reason I never went to bed with Johnny was that he didn't appeal to me, to go all the way. There was something that stopped me. It's just bad chemistry."

Alicia Bond, an Israeli actress, recalls her relationship with Johnny. "I dated him starting in 1966 in New York," says the blond former starlet. "I was dating other stars, and he was at the bottom of my list. He's not a sophisticated or interesting man. I wouldn't want to wake up and sit across the breakfast table from him. He'd tell jokes. Once we were having dinner and I wanted one of these avocados with shrimp and Thousand Island dressing. He said, 'Women always take from me. Lunch me! Gift me! Now, avocado me!' He thought he was so funny. He laughed and laughed."

Johnny spent time with his three sons on weekends, but more and more often he was performing in Las Vegas or somewhere else. In these years the main burden of bringing up Johnny's sons fell on Jody. She reportedly received $1,250 a month in alimony, and $600 in child support. She tried to be a good mother to the boys, but she was going through her own personal difficulties, and her sons were not easy. In 1964 Jody decided to put Chris, Rick, and Cory in boarding school; she feels that her sons have never forgiven her for that.

Chris was the oldest, and at fourteen, at the Nyack Prep School, he was at times like a second father to Rick and Cory. Johnny and Jody shared custody of their sons, and the boys spent much of their holidays at UN Plaza. They were a rambunctious lot, as the neighbors discovered. "We came back from our vacation after the Christmas holidays and the whole window wall facing south was absolutely glued with brown," says Mrs. Seymour, whose apartment was directly beneath the Carsons. "I've never seen anything like it, the whole thing was covered. I said, 'Oh my goodness, what has happened?' It seems that the Carson boys had been home for the holidays and had thrown chocolate sundaes out. Poor Johnny had to have special window cleaners scrape the chocolate off."

Other problems were not amusing. When Johnny had Dr. Robert Baird on *The Tonight Show* to talk about the drug epidemic, he knew no more about narcotics than did most Americans. Joanne started going to Dr. Baird's clinic in Harlem as a volunteer helper. Johnny visited the doctor's office too, and became friendly with the idealistic physician. In 1966 Johnny and Joanne's interest became a personal one. Fourteen-year-old Ricky had his own drug problem, smoking marijuana, and Johnny's second son saw Dr. Baird as a patient.

Rick, always the most troubled of the three Carson boys, needed a mother and a father who were *there*. Johnny was not only physically but emotionally absent much of the time. As for Jody, she dropped in and out of people's lives, even her own sons'. Irma Wolstein recalls the day Jody called, perhaps intoxicated, and said that she was sitting on a ledge. Wolstein spoke soothingly to her friend. After that, she didn't hear from Jody for a long time, until she received a call from Gracie Square Hospital.

"When John said he and Joanne were going to get [full] custody of the boys I had a nervous breakdown," Jody says. "I was in the Gracie Square Hospital in New York. I just flipped out. Chris went to the hospital with me. I was terribly embarrassed about having the nervous breakdown. I felt so

guilty about it. I felt I should have had more control. I felt
I shouldn't have let go.''

"It was a very hot summer day," Wolstein recalls. "She
asked could I bring her some clothes? She kept insisting I
was her only friend. I thought, That's so odd. She had no
lady friends. She knew men. When I got to the hospital,
she seemed perfectly okay, except if I tried to touch her,
she pushed me away."

Johnny and Joanne did not seek full custody, and Jody
recuperated enough to move to the Country Place, a halfway
house in Warren, Connecticut. Jody transferred thirteen-
year old Cory from Nyack Prep to the Wamago Regional
High School because "he wanted to be just a public-school
boy."

The Country Place was not a normal environment for an
adolescent boy. Johnny decided to sue for full custody. In
February 1967 Johnny and Joanne drove to Litchfield, Connecticut, for a closed-door hearing before Judge John A.
Speziale. The session lasted all day long, and that evening
The Tonight Show audience was told that "personal business" had kept Johnny from doing the show.

The judge heard testimony from Johnny, Jody, Chris,
Rick, and Cory, and a teacher who had taught the three
boys at Nyack Prep. The judge ordered that Cory return to
Nyack Prep with his brothers. As for Jody, she stayed alone
at the Country Place.

Jody still dreamed of winning her sons back. Cory wrote
his mother saying that Nyack Prep was a shambles, and he
wanted to go to another school to pursue his interest in
music. He told his mother that his current home life was a
mess. He couldn't talk to his father easily. He pretended
that he enjoyed talking to Joanne, but speaking to her gave
him headaches. He wasn't at ease and he said that he hoped
to spend a good deal of time with his mother.

When Jody read such letters and talked to her sons, she
wanted desperately to have them live with her. One evening
in Connecticut she met Don Buckley, a recently divorced
man whom she liked a great deal. They began living to-

gether, and in early 1970 Jody says that she decided to marry Buckley in part so that she could regain custody of her sons. This meant giving up her alimony, 15 percent of Johnny's gross earnings, an amount that could have made her a millionaire.

Jody was willing to forego further alimony. However, she had read in the papers about Johnny's salary. She believed that Johnny had shortchanged her by about $200,000. To settle those claims, Johnny agreed to pay Jody $13,500 a year for 30 years.

Jody had what she called her "dowry." But this marriage was no better than her first, and the couple separated after two years. For some time she kept her husband's last name, Buckley, which was about all she received out of the marriage.

For a while Jody lived in New York. One day Irma Wolstein received a phone call from Jody's analyst. "He said, 'She hasn't shown up for an appointment in two days.' I said, 'She's drunk and holed up in her house.' I went to the apartment and they wouldn't let me in. The doorman said, 'She's up there. I take the dog out.' She was drunk. She'd go in and out of these drunken things. She was a little girl who shouldn't have left home."

For years Jody drifted from place to place. Her sorority sister Zip Haslom recalls how she wouldn't hear from Jody for months. Then the phone would ring at two in the morning and she would know that it was Jody, speaking in the same flirtatious, girlish voice that had laughed at young Johnny Carson so long ago.

TEN

From the moment Johnny woke up and read the papers, he was at work. Some mornings he left early to take a singing lesson from Susan Seton, a prominent voice coach who taught Katharine Hepburn and Audrey Hepburn as well. She was one of the few people to know that Johnny dreamed of singing seriously. When he came home at night, he usually flicked on the television to check on *The Tonight Show* and then watched one of his competitors.

Everything he heard was free game for Johnny. One evening Hank Simms turned on *The Tonight Show* and listened as Johnny reminisced about mispronouncing the name of a T-shirt company as a young broadcaster in Omaha. Simms found the story very funny, particularly since it had happened to him. "He probably didn't even remember that's where it came from," Simms says. "I called him and said, 'If you're going to use my material, at least credit me.'"

Like most workaholics, Johnny dreaded vacations. In the summer of 1963 he went off to Colorado with his boys. But starting in July the following year, he spent most of his free time performing in Las Vegas. The hotels wanted Johnny to appear with *The Tonight Show*. Stan Irwin, the entertainment director of the Sahara Hotel, was an exception, and thought that Johnny could succeed as a headliner on his own.

Johnny wasn't simply going to trade on his name, giving warmed-over routines from *The Tonight Show*. His audience would be spending money to see him, and Johnny wrote new material. He went back to many of the themes of *Carson's Cellar*, lampooning TV and TV commercials. He wrote a hilarious skit about Doctor John, a kiddie-show host trying to do his TV show with a hangover. He made fun of Edward R. Murrow, that most sacrosanct figure of television journalism.

Johnny used material he couldn't get away with on *The Tonight Show*. He told the story of a wife looking at a topless show girl. "She obviously has never nursed a baby," the woman sniped.

"Are you kidding," her husband answered. "That woman could have nursed a water buffalo—in tandem."

On paper the joke didn't sound terribly funny. But that was like trying to imagine the sound of a full orchestra while reading a musical score. The joke was in the way Johnny told it. He practiced the story over and over again. Timing. Everything was timing. The audience laughed when he said "water buffalo." He waited until the laughter subsided before he said "in tandem." The joke packed a double wallop.

In the Sahara Hotel's Congo Room he broke the opening-night record set by Judy Garland. The second night the hotel turned away large numbers of people. Business was boffo during the whole four weeks. He was so successful that he could come back whenever he wanted to, and earn up to fifty thousand dollars a week. He enjoyed performing in Vegas so much that he bought a small house in the gambling capital. He played the Sahara not only during longer vacations, but on weekends. Performing was his solace, his drug, his balm. No matter how down he might be, once he got up on that stage he was Johnny Carson.

In 1964 Johnny also made his first and last appearance in a film, playing a cameo role in a debacle titled *Looking for Love*. The film disappeared quicker than a boring guest on *The Tonight Show*.

Johnny was sufficiently big now that he himself was a

target. When he and Woody Allen appeared at the Inauguration gala for President Lyndon Baines Johnson in January 1965, the two comedians made front-page headlines in the *New York Journal-American* (TV STARS' BAD TASTE AT INAUGURAL GALA). "Johnny Carson bombed," reported Dorothy Kilgallen, the New York *Journal-American* columnist who looked as if she had been born with a lemon in her mouth. "The audience was appalled into total silence as Carson took to the stage directly opposite the President's box and announced he was more effective than birth control pills and made rude remarks about Sen. Robert F. Kennedy's ninth child."

Johnny chose an appropriate forum for his rebuttal, the annual White House photographers' dinner. That evening the Washington assemblage heard a brutally acerbic Johnny Carson. "I don't know why Dorothy should take offense at a joke I made," he said. "I didn't when her parents made one! I don't see why she would object to a joke about birth control. She's such a living example for it. She's the only woman you wouldn't mind being with if your wife walked in."

Later in the year Federal Communications Commissioner Robert E. Lee was so upset by "four or five incidents" on *The Tonight Show* that he felt compelled to comment lest "the industry degenerate into indecency." Johnny hadn't even been the source of the most outrageous or most notable example. On the November 25, 1965, show, Ray Milland, the actor, told a story about doing a love scene in a swimming pool with Dorothy Lamour in *Jungle Princess*. "I had to go to the bathroom. I thought, 'Oh God, not now. Not now.' As she put her arms around my neck and started kissing me, the cold of the water of the pool did its work and I let go."

The story was presumably shocking news to Dorothy Lamour. But little children—perhaps not unfamiliar with Milland's action—were in bed, their innocence intact. The NBC press office leaked its side of the story to the media, noting that the network had received not a single protest letter, and the episode was soon forgotten.

In October 1965 NBC decided to give Johnny a party on the third anniversary of the show. Some of the staff were disappointed that NBC had the celebration at Rockefeller Center instead of renting a restaurant. Nonetheless, the program was making so much money that everyone knew that NBC would put on a spectacular spread. During the day they anticipated the event: the rarest roast beef carved by a chef; mounds of iced shrimp; caviar canapés; champagne bottles going off like forty-gun salutes; twelve-year-old scotch and twenty-year-old brandy.

After the show Johnny and the staff hurried up to the reserved room. There they found a card table spread with a paper tablecloth, Ritz crackers, American cheese, a few bottles of cheap wine, plastic cups, and a large number of smiling NBC executives singing, "Happy anniversary to you, happy anniversary to you."

If the NBC executives had set out to plan a superbly humiliating evening, they could not have done better. "Johnny was so fucking upset that it became one of the funniest, the most hysterical nights of my life," Shelly Schultz remembers. "It was something you do for a kid's sixteenth birthday. Only Johnny could have made it funny."

As Johnny gained the confidence of strong ratings, he began to assert the prerogatives of stardom. He had a proprietary interest over *his* hour and forty-five minutes each evening. More thought, energy, and talent went into the monologue and opening bit than anything else on *The Tonight Show*, but no matter how memorable the monologue, most of America didn't see it. Although the stations liked Johnny's show, local news was highly lucrative. By early 1965 neither New York nor most of the major East Coast cities carried the first fifteen minutes; of the 190 affiliated stations, only 43 ran the whole show.

On the afternoon of February 19, 1965, Johnny learned that San Francisco had joined the list of cities not carrying the opening quarter hour. NBC was glacially slow in appreciating their star's value, and the executives hadn't even informed him of the latest defection.

Instead of complaining, Johnny simply did not appear when the show began, and did not start his monologue until eleven-thirty. He joked that only "four Navajos in Gallup, New Mexico, and the Armed Forces Radio on Guam" had watched the first fifteen minutes on the program. He protested the network policy of running the shows a day late on the West Coast, joking that "in California if there's a bulletin on World War III during the show, it will have to wait."

Fed up, Johnny planned to continue his mini-strike when he returned to *The Tonight Show* on Tuesday evening. "They'll have all weekend to think about it," he said. "It isn't worth it, working to prepare material. It's an integral part of the show, a commentary on the day's events. It's not going to be put in a time capsule and placed in the Library of Congress, but a lot of effort goes into it."

The NBC executives implored Johnny to give them time to make a decision. Tuesday evening once again he came out late. "Welcome to the winter of my discontent," he said. "I would have been out sooner, but for the past couple of days I've been coming down with a fifteen-minute virus. It comes at any moment. We're looking for a cure for it without surgery."

By Friday the network had found a cure. From now on Johnny would make his entrance at eleven-thirty, letting Ed and Skitch Henderson, the musical director, fill the first fifteen minutes. On Monday Ed walked out on stage at eleven-fifteen and began *his* monologue. He was in a miserable predicament. If he did too poorly, he might lose his job. But if he did too well, he might lose it too.

Ed already had problems with his boss. Some staff members felt that Johnny was not too happy with all the money and attention Ed was getting doing commercials. Then, one evening on the show, Johnny talked about a new report on mosquitoes that preferred to bite "warm-blooded, passionate" people. Before Johnny could get in his punch line, Ed slapped his arm. He apologized during the break, but Johnny was infuriated. Ed had violated the first commandment of second bananas: Thou shalt not steal the star's laughs.

"I'll never forget that night," Bruno recalls. "The next day Johnny hit the ceiling. He said, 'Get rid of Ed!'" Johnny felt that Ed was no longer merely feeding him straight lines, propping up weak segments, remaining eternally attentive to Johnny's need. Instead, he was sitting on the couch thinking up jokes, zapping the audience with one-liners, turning the spotlight on himself.

Ed and Skitch Henderson saw the program as an opportunity. "Ed was very easy to work with," remembers the former musical director. "We came up in the hard-knock school. We wanted it to work, and I wanted visibility for the orchestra to stop it being treated like a bunch of clowns."

After one of Ed and Skitch's first outings, Johnny came prancing onto stage and said, "My job is to revive you for eight or nine minutes if it takes all night." Several nights later he began his monologue, "When I snap my fingers, you will all wake up and forget the first fifteen minutes."

Johnny could put down Ed and Skitch all he wanted. But when he sat backstage watching Ed doing *his* monologue, he came to a melancholy and shocking realization. Ed wasn't dying out there. He was getting laughs, and he was skimming the cream off the topical news of the day. "I told him, 'Look, Ed, you've just gotta cool it, you're not leaving me anything,'" Johnny said.

"Johnny was very angry," says Mrs. Mary Stark. "Art went to bat for Ed and said it would be absolute suicide to fire him. There would be no way to keep it quiet. Beyond that, Art thought Ed was the only one for the job."

Skitch Henderson observed the spectacle with dismay. "Many times I watched Johnny trying to get rid of Ed. It must have been a basic insecurity of some kind on Johnny's part. It really was so silly, because we were all trying to pull the same ship."

When NBC decided to begin *The Tonight Show* everywhere at eleven-thirty, Ed swallowed his ego, pride, and ambition, and settled down in his seat next to Johnny. He understood who he was and on what his relationship with Johnny depended. He was a salesman, and his number-one product was Johnny Carson. Over the years Ed's ringing phrase "Heeeeere's Johnny" became not only the show's signature greeting, but a perfect symbol of the relationship between the two men: the star and his announcer.

"Johnny was not the kind of guy who embraced anybody," says Bob Coe, Ed's former manager. "They were very close when they were on the set. That's how Ed has lasted all these years. That laugh that he has and that subservient attitude have really paid off."

Once they succeed, stars often drop their first managers and agents. They look on them the way many medical doctors look on chiropractors, as charlatans who massage a few bones and take credit for nature's achievement.

Johnny was upset with Al Bruno. As loath as Johnny was to admit it, Bruno had done much for him in the early years. *Who Do You Trust?* had taken months to win a large audience, and Bruno had pushed for Johnny and the show. He was a gregarious, talkative man, and he had promoted Johnny from one end of Manhattan to the other. More than anyone else, he had persuaded Johnny that he could succeed as the new host of *The Tonight Show*.

Under Bruno's aegis Johnny's salary had increased dramatically. He earned $100,000 a year from *The Tonight Show* when he began, an amount soon doubled to $200,000. In the spring of 1966 the manager helped negotiate a new contract. Under the new terms NBC paid Johnny $7,500 a week or $390,000 a year. Johnny's production company, Stage C Productions, received $7,500 a week to produce the show and for the salaries of eleven employees. Once again Johnny had almost doubled his salary, and at first he was happy. He was no longer a hired hand. His company directly controlled the producer and associate producer, four writers, four talent coordinators, and a secretary. Of the important employees, NBC hired and fired only the announcer, the music director, the director, and the associate producer.

As a performer, Johnny was a demanding perfectionist. He expected everyone to do his job, and to do it well. Unlike many stars, he didn't need hand-holding and backslapping. Most of the time he wanted to be left alone; but he did expect Bruno to do his job almost flawlessly, and he increasingly felt that his manager messed up on details. There had been the miserable vacation trip to the Bahamas, considered as Bruno's mistake. The manager reportedly scheduled Johnny to appear at the Miss Wool contest in Texas. Johnny prepared a slew of jokes about wool and sheep and sweaters. When he arrived in the Lone Star State, he was greeted by enthusiastic representatives from the Miss World contest. Bruno denies that this happened, but a series of misadventures did take place.

Johnny complained frequently of the five-show-a-week grind. So Bruno set out to develop a weekly program for his star, based on the Friars' roast that had been so important for launching Johnny. Bruno made an agreement with NBC and an arrangement with Budweiser to sponsor the program, but at the last moment Johnny backed out.

Bruno had his problems with Johnny, but thanks to his number-one client he was a powerful force in show business. Bruno and Sheils had other important clients, such as Jimmy Dean, the country-western star. In early 1963 the two men took on the management of Mike Douglas, a daytime talk-show host. Bruno could say blithely that Douglas was no competitor to Johnny, but signing Douglas was a foolish move. It was as if Bruno had suddenly forgotten how insecure Johnny was, and how he had risen from even greater obscurity than Douglas.

As his relationship with Johnny deteriorated, Bruno saw the fine hand of Joanne at work. "She wanted me out from day one," he felt. "The only thing that separated us is this young lady. I knew too many things about her, and Johnny knew that I knew. I think a girl in bed can do things to a guy.''

In February 1966 Johnny flew down to Miami Beach to headline the show at the Eden Roc Hotel for three nights. The opening-evening audience included not only those who had paid twenty dollars for the dinner show, but a busload of fidgety tourists who had gotten a bargain rate. ''I knew Miami was a swinging town when I noticed the checkroom girls were checking more wedding rings than fur coats,'' he said. He moved from one joke to the next, but the sound system was off, and the stagehands added to their sins by pulling the curtain early. Johnny was so infuriated that he refused to take a bow. He canceled the second show that evening and left Miami. He had time, however, to closet himself with Bruno and have it out with his manager.

Bruno had had arguments with Johnny before. He meekly accepted the verbal lashings as part of the job. Then, early in March, he received a short, curt letter from Johnny's lawyer abruptly severing their relationship.

Bruno telephoned Johnny at home. ''He answered the phone and he said he'd get back to me,'' he recalls. ''I have never talked to him since.''

Bruno did what he could for his other clients, but he heard that Johnny didn't want anyone associated with Al Bruno on *The Tonight Show*. His clients were loyal, but they weren't that loyal, and after a while Al Bruno was out of the business.

''I ended up with absolutely zilch,'' says Bruno, who has retired to a farmhouse in upstate New York. ''By the time we got through with his attorneys, I'd hate to say how little we got. And it was all downhill from then on. I was so depressed. I was disgusted. I'd lost a lot of faith. I thought, How could a guy do that? I had to look to other ways to establish a financial base for myself. He was so vindictive that he wouldn't let anyone I represented anywhere near the show.''

* * *

At two o'clock one morning Joanne called Bruce Cooper, who had left his job as a talent coordinator on *The Tonight Show*.

"What's wrong with the show?" Joanne asked.

"I don't want to tell you."

"You've got to tell me."

"Honey, you don't want me to tell you the truth. The first thing he ought to do is fire Art Stark. He's fucking up the show so badly. He has this father image with John, and surrounded himself with an army of yes-people."

If Joanne had called Shelly Schultz and asked him the same question, the talent coordinator would have told her that Stark was doing a first-rate job, that the show was doing fine. The fact was, however, that the staff of *The Tonight Show* had broken into pro- and anti-Stark factions. Beneath the daily activities of putting on the show, a power struggle had begun.

On one of the annual trips to Los Angeles, Art's secretary, Elizabeth Dougherty, shared a taxicab with a young and very junior secretary in Johnny's office. "She was talking about seizing power," Dougherty says. "This is a kid. I never witnessed anything like that before. Johnny was getting a stronger sense of himself, and Art was very strong. I think that Art on some level knew what was happening, but he just denied it to himself."

Art was a mercurial, often difficult man. He took a certain pleasure in his image of toughness, pride in the fact he was so sought after. He always had a dozen things on his mind, calls to return, decisions to make, people to put off. Even when he was in the hospital, he proudly noted that he received forty or fifty calls a day. Although Art got more publicity than most performers, he didn't seem to realize that the interviews, the invitations, the calls, the compliments, the stroking, were not for *him*, good old rumpled Art Stark, but for the producer of *The Tonight Show*.

Stark fired writers and other staff members with more

abruptness than grace. He pushed boring guests off the show
with a flick of his finger. "I can get small talk from stars,"
he said. "Why should I get small talk from small people?"

Stark's devotion to the show almost cost him his marriage;
he separated temporarily from his second wife, Mary. For
a time he was smoking four packs of cigarettes a day and
seemed to relax only when his young son visited him on
the set. Sometimes he appeared on a one-way street to a
nervous breakdown.

Art and Johnny shared the same mistress: *The Tonight
Show*. There, they found excitement and solace that they
could get nowhere else. When they went off on their boats
for the weekend, their minds were still working on the show.

Stark treated Johnny like a thoroughbred horse who had
to be groomed, fed, disciplined, and kept apart. Stark dealt
with the production staff. Johnny didn't even know many
of their names, yet after listening to criticism of Art he
decided to have more to do with putting on the show and
asked for a meeting of the production staff. The members
dutifully trooped into his office; and as Art hovered over
them, his arms folded, they sat there and said nothing.
Johnny didn't schedule more meetings.

Art Stark sensed that he could not depend on Johnny,
that nobody could. "If I were in trouble here, as good friends
as we are, he'd never fight for me," Stark told writer Nora
Ephron. "Unless, of course, it affected him. Which it
would. He doesn't like to be dependent."

When the reporters interviewed Stark, they usually went
to Johnny for a quote. "We're close friends," Johnny said,
"but we can be frank without getting emotionally involved.
He knows me as a performer, knows what I can do and
what I can do well. He has my interest uppermost."

But Stark's enemies on the show sat close to Johnny's
ear. Johnny's secretary, Jeanne Prior, felt that Art had become detrimental to the show. So did her boyfriend, Rudy
Tellez, who dreamed of replacing the producer. Walter
Kempley, the head writer, expressed his dissatisfaction.

Joanne talked against the producer as well, and she may have been the strongest influence.

Art Stark had meant an enormous amount to *The Tonight Show* and to Johnny's career. But Johnny had changed. He no longer felt that he needed such a powerful producer.

For Johnny, the decision was agonizing. Johnny had his reasons for firing Bruno. He had his reasons to consider getting rid of McMahon. But Art was different. He was Johnny's closest friend. They had worked together for a decade. The two men had even bought a condominium together in Fort Lauderdale. They shared confidences. The producer was loyal and devoted to Johnny. The ratings were as good as they'd ever been.

Even if Johnny decided to fire Art, it would not be simple to dump him. The producer had a two-year contract and friends in the media.

Johnny's mood depended in good measure on whomever he had talked to last. Joanne told him that he had been dealt with unfairly in the long-term contract he had signed in 1966; he needed Arnold Grant, a high-powered New York lawyer.

Grant looked over Johnny's contract and concluded that his client had been mistreated and that *he*, Arnold Grant, should seek a new contract. The public would one day become used to the spectacle of performers, especially athletes, renegotiating contracts. But in 1967 a contract was still considered a contract, and Johnny could not expect great public sympathy. Nonetheless, Grant began discussions with the network. The NBC executives did not guffaw openly when Grant asked for $2 million a year, but they did not budge, either. Johnny remembered all the slights he had suffered at the hands of the network, and he added the current negotiations to his list.

In the midst of the discussions, on April 1, the American Federation of Television and Radio Artists (AFTRA) went out on strike, primarily over the salaries of local newsmen. NBC executives and staff attempted to do the work of the striking employees. Chet Huntley, the NBC anchorman, was so opposed to the strike that he broke the picket line and vowed to start an opposing union.

Johnny did not appear to take any strong interest either pro or con. He was, however, upset that NBC had begun to play reruns of *The Tonight Show*. They had not consulted him, and were using December reruns where he joked about Christmas and the holiday season.

As the strike continued, Johnny headlined a show at Pershing Auditorium in Lincoln, Nebraska, celebrating the state's centennial. Jerry Solomon flew to New York by private jet to pick up his former fraternity brother.

Solomon, who knew practically everybody of importance in the state capital, spent the weekend shepherding Johnny around. Returning home "makes me very depressed," Johnny told an interviewer in 1960. "You expect it to be the same but it isn't. Or maybe it is, but I've changed so much it seems different. I feel very much a stranger when I go home." He had vowed never to return to his home state because, he said, people didn't treat him normally.

Solomon had asked Johnny for a donation to rebuild the old fraternity house. Johnny had turned him down; and his staff had warned Solomon not to mention the fraternity, where he even canceled a brunch.

Solomon knew that Johnny was preoccupied. He saw how he dreaded people coming up, glad-handing him all the time, bombarding him with little jokes and big compliments. But Johnny gave no indication that he was unhappy with *The Tonight Show*. At a press conference he told reporters, "I don't know what I'll do when my present contract runs out. It has two more years."

The last evening Johnny said, "I'll see you at the Phi Gamma house tomorrow morning for brunch." Solomon hadn't mentioned the fraternity once in two days. He scurried around finding a cook and inviting people, and the next morning Johnny had his brunch.

Solomon drove to the airport in the limousine to see Johnny off. "John, if I can ever be of any help to you with an insurance program, your estate planning, I'd be glad to do it,'' Solomon said.

Solomon thought he was Johnny's friend, but that was the last time the insurance salesman saw *The Tonight Show* host. He wrote him letters. He called. But it was all over. Solomon was hurt, and he tried to figure out what had gone wrong. The more he thought about it, the more he realized that he had probably upset Johnny talking about insurance. Solomon figured it was better doing business with friends than strangers. But he knew that he shouldn't have asked Johnny for anything, for anything at all.

While Johnny was in Nebraska, Arnold Grant continued his negotiations with NBC. The attorney told the network that it could not rerun *Tonight Show* episodes without Johnny's permission. NBC asserted that it was perfectly within its rights.

On April 4, Johnny's public-relations company released a statement that he was quitting *The Tonight Show*, "rescinding" his contract with the network "effective forthwith." The story was front-page news. AFTRA attempted to capitalize on Johnny's defection, making it seem that his act was one of union brotherhood.

Johnny was using the strike to push his stalled contract negotiations ahead. Along with Grant, he now had a second formidable member on his team, Louis Nizer, a prominent New York attorney. As Nizer saw it, the question of what NBC should pay Johnny was a simple matter. All one had to do was to learn how much money *The Tonight Show* earned for NBC and figure out what would be Johnny's fair cut of the pie. The network was not about to tell Nizer or anyone else what it earned from the show. But Nizer learned what the advertisers were paying per minute, which added up to approximately $25 million dollars a year in gross revenues. Johnny's lawyers reportedly asked for 25 percent, or roughly $6 million, for putting on the show, an extraordinary sum.

While Grant and Nizer negotiated in New York, Johnny

flew to Fort Lauderdale, where he lay in the sun and called himself "an unemployed prince."

"What is the price that should be paid for a rerun when it is used while your union is on strike?" he asked reporters. "That's the main point. They did not negotiate with me and they still haven't. I have the right to pass judgment on reruns before they are used."

On April 11, the AFTRA strike ended, and the NBC employees went back to work. Johnny, however, continued *his* strike. He sent telegrams to the eleven employees working for Stage C, his production company, and told them not to return, either.

Johnny flew back to New York. Reporters vied with one another to interview him. Gary Stevens received a phone call from the *Chicago Tribune*. An editor offered to pay to interview Johnny for a special five-part series. The publicist said that would cost five thousand dollars. The editor thought that Stevens meant five thousand dollars an interview, or twenty-five thousand dollars, and quickly agreed to the sum. Even Stevens was speechless. He had never heard of the press paying a celebrity for a legitimate news story, especially not such an amount. For once, Johnny was happy to meet with a reporter. He was a frugal sort, though, and he measured out twenty-five thousand dollars' worth of words, much the same words that he had given away for nothing.

Johnny did give a free interview to *The New York Times*. He said that if he returned to *The Tonight Show*, "there might also be some changes in personnel on the program." No one felt secure. Most of the staff members wondered if they would soon feel the steel blade on their necks. For the most part, their fears seemed irrational. After all, Johnny's production company hired the producer, the major writers, and talent coordinators. Johnny didn't have to negotiate with NBC to fire them, and Stark had recently signed a long-term contract. That left McMahon; Dick Carson, the director; John Carsey, an associate producer, and Milton De-Lugg, the music director who had replaced Skitch Henderson.

DeLugg was particularly worried. On television Johnny kidded with him almost nightly, creating the illusion that they were the best of buddies. The television audience had no idea that DeLugg had never spoken more than a few words to Johnny.

Art Stark read the article and began wondering about his own status. He knew what his contract said, but he knew Johnny too. Art was forceful and direct. He simply called Johnny and asked if his position was in jeopardy. Johnny told him everything was fine.

NBC had an added incentive to settle with Johnny, and settle quickly. ABC was about to mount the first major challenge to the network's sovereignty over the late night. On April 17, Joey Bishop would be hosting a show at the same time as Johnny. Bishop was a Jewish comedian from South Philadelphia with an accent as thick as a porterhouse steak. He had done well as a substitute host of *The Tonight Show*, and his fast-talking, wisecracking humor had many fans across America.

On its opening night *The Joey Bishop Show* won 40 percent of the New York audience in overnight Nielson ratings. Jimmy Dean, the country-western star substituting for Johnny, received an anemic 12 percent. Although Bishop did only half as well the following few nights, the show was still well ahead of the Johnnyless *Tonight Show*.

On April 20, Johnny agreed on a new contract that gave him twenty thousand dollars a week, plus $1 million in life insurance. Equally important, NBC agreed to absorb the salaries previously paid by Carson's Stage C Productions. Nor would he have to pay for substitute hosts, and he would be royally remunerated for reruns. This brought Johnny's take on *The Tonight Show* to over a million dollars.

During the negotiations Art kept calling Johnny every afternoon to tell him how things were going. Now, the producer thought life would return to normal. After taking his son to nursery school in the morning, he bumped into Skitch Henderson on Park Avenue. "There is something wrong," Stark said. "The prince hasn't taken my call for a couple of days."

Stark finally reached Johnny, who assured him that his position was secure. "Art, do you think I wouldn't tell you if I was unhappy with you?" Johnny asked, according to Stark.

That answer didn't satisfy Stark. "What do you want, Johnny?" Stark asked. "Is it bad news?"

Stark went to the UN Plaza apartment in the late afternoon to meet with Johnny. The two men had known each other for a decade. As he took the elevator up to the thirty-fifth floor, Stark sensed what was about to happen.

The duplex was not decorated yet, and Johnny motioned Art into the kitchen.

"You want a drink?" Johnny asked.

Stark shook his head.

"This is very difficult for me," Johnny said, trying to get the words out. "It's the most difficult thing I've ever done."

Stark stared at Johnny.

"I want to make some changes," Johnny said. "I'd like you to leave the show."

"When?" Stark asked. He knew that he was doomed, but wanted to negotiate the terms and leave with a modicum of dignity and grace.

"Now," Johnny said.

"Fuck you!"

The producer turned on his heel. He walked out slamming the door so loudly that the sound reverberated down the hall.

In a strange way Johnny thought that Art had betrayed *him*. He believed that Art had saved up all his anger and dumped on him. Johnny could have had someone at NBC tell Art that he was fired, or he could have had Arnold Grant or Louis Nizer at his side when he gave the producer the news. As Johnny saw it, he had attempted to honor his friendship by telling Art himself. And Art had turned and walked out and left Johnny alone. Johnny had no one whom he could trust completely.

Johnny knew that this would be a big story. He called Gary Stevens to alert him. "Come on over. I want to see you immediately," Johnny said, as Stevens recalls.

Stevens hurried to the UN Plaza. "You're going to hear that Art Stark has been dropped from the show," Johnny said. "I want you to know this so you can fend off these things. And all I can tell you is that Art is a very sick man."

As soon as Stark reached home, the phone began ringing. The first caller was an NBC executive, Dave Tebet. Tebet wanted the producer's tickets back for the March of Dimes benefit in Carson's honor. He figured Stark wouldn't be going.

When she heard news of the firing, Joan Rivers called Stark. She and her husband, Edgar Rosenberg, took the Starks to dinner. What had until last night been a smart social move had suddenly become an act of courage. McMahon sent an invitation to a party, but the Starks could not attend. Stark knew practically everybody important in show business. But Ed McMahon and Joan Rivers were the only performers willing to be seen socially with him.

For a couple months Art spent his days drinking at Daly's Dandelion, a restaurant owned by Skitch Henderson. "I had a car to take him home," Henderson recalls. Stark eventually produced shows such as the Junior Miss Pageant. He talked about how one always had to look ahead, but almost never publicly about Johnny. Art Stark was a broken man.

When he died in 1982, he was remembered best as the man who had once produced *The Tonight Show*. He had worked with thousands of people in his career, and his widow received many letters of condolence. Only one was from anyone who had worked with Art on *The Tonight Show*. That was from Ed McMahon. He had written a beautiful note and sent a prayer card, and Mary Stark was touched beyond measure.

ELEVEN

Soon after Johnny returned to work, *Time* began interviewing him for a cover story. During the strike he had received a surfeit of publicity, but no entertainer turned down the cover of *Time*. It was one of the great icons of success in America. Johnny posed for the sculptor preparing the cover art. He talked about the show to a *Time* reporter in great detail, and sat tight-lipped and tense as the man enumerated facts about Jody and the divorce.

When Johnny read the profile, he saw that it began at his parents' house in Columbus, Nebraska. Mrs. Carson was watching as Johnny began his monologue. "My name is Shirley Hofnagel," he said, "and I'm here to talk tonight about the wonderful progress that medical science has made in sex-change operations."

"That's not so funny, McGee!" Mrs. Carson said. She got up and went into the kitchen to make coffee, leaving Johnny's image flickering on the screen. *Time* conjectured that Mrs. Carson was pondering "the mysterious equations of show business that have enabled her son John to become the nation's midnight idol by telling silly jokes like that."

Mrs. Carson had sent out her message to the world. Johnny might make the cover of *Time* magazine. He might earn $1 million a year. But no matter what Johnny did, no matter how famous he might become, he never quite measured up.

"He comes from a very rigid, authoritarian family in Nebraska," said his New York neighbor Truman Capote. "He had to be home at a certain time, and if he was so much as fifteen minutes later, there would be terrible scenes. Once when he was drunk, he told me that his mother would throw herself on the floor and scream, 'I bore you from these loins, and you do this to me! All that pain and this is what I get in return!' I met his mother once, and she was an absolute bitch. Despite everything he's done, she's never really accepted him, and he constantly wants her approval. I think that that's what keeps him going."

"His mother was selfish and cold," Joanne Carson recalls. "No wonder he has problems dealing with women, he didn't have a nurturing, caring role model. Mrs. Carson was cold, closed off, a zero when it came to showing affection."

Johnny returned to *The Tonight Show* on April 24, 1967. Joey Bishop might have received a week of high ratings for his new show, but the return of the king of the night had put the fear of God in the comedian. To meet the challenge, Bishop hauled out a formidable, if rusty and unwieldy, weapon: Jack Paar. Bishop had gone to Paar's hotel room in Beverly Hills and begged him to come on the show.

Paar staged a one-night coup, taking over the ABC show from Bishop. As Paar chatted with Ethel Merman and Juliet Prowse, Bishop said, "You'll have to forgive me for eavesdropping."

On *The Tonight Show* Johnny appeared glad to be back. But he had the melancholy task of explaining to his audience all those headlines about him making so much money. "I really got to feeling I'd sneaked in with a couple of hired thugs and run off with this loot," he said. Johnny bantered with Buddy Hackett, one of his favorite guests, and introduced the trio of Peter, Paul and Mary. He also talked with frequent guest Mamie Van Doren.

The show was vintage Johnny, and the ratings removed

any doubt about who was king of the night. In New York *The Tonight Show* won 41 percent of viewers.

Viewers assumed that Johnny and Joey were friends. After all, Joey had substituted for Johnny six weeks a year, and they joked warmly about each other. The two comedians were no closer than ships passing in the night in a turbulent sea. Johnny gave Bishop no quarter. "I want to bury him," he said. "I wish him great success—in the storm-door business. I don't really know him, he's the competition. Does General Electric want Westinghouse to make good? This kind of success can be a very tenuous thing. A little slip, then the atmosphere of failure starts to creep in, and it grows, and it's hard to reverse it. Pretty soon you're in a slide."

The Tonight Show staff played hardball. "On Friday we would announce our guests for the following week," Bishop recalls. "NBC would call those guests and offer them two round-trip tickets to New York, and a TV set, if they'd get off my show."

Although the talent coordinators deny that they ever spirited Bishop's guests away, the mere threat of Johnny's displeasure may have been enough to dissuade many entertainers from appearing with Bishop.

Bishop improved in the ratings; but ABC had far fewer stations than NBC, and the comedian had no chance of catching Johnny. Finally ABC canceled the show. "I think two years and nine months is a long time against Carson," Bishop says. "Nobody else has come close. I don't remember being angry. I got canceled, but I gave them a good run. They were scared of me. I beat them in the Bible Belt. I'm married to the same woman and don't drink. I gave up smoking and picked up another Gideon area."

Beginning in August 1969, Johnny had a new, potent challenger: Merv Griffin. No longer would his show be syndicated on a motley patchwork of independent stations. He would now be on CBS each evening, backed by the formidable powers and money of the network.

In the battle for late-night television curiosity almost always wins the first round. The first evening Griffin won 49 percent of the audience, 39 percent of the viewers watched Johnny, and 12 percent Joey Bishop. Griffin was soon running such a distant second that he could hardly see the image of Johnny in front of him. CBS moved the show from New York to Hollywood, but that did no good, either. In February 1972 the network canceled the show.

An aura of invincible power was growing around Johnny. In 1962 he had been youthful in body and spirit. Johnny was middle-aged now, in his mid-forties, and most of the present staff hadn't known him when he was struggling and uncertain. They treated him with the distance of deference.

The Tonight Show was *his*, Johnny Carson's, and he protected his turf against assaults major and minor. In September 1968 NBC broadcast a football game between the Houston Oilers and the Kansas City Chiefs beginning at 9:00 P.M. on Monday evening. This meant that *The Tonight Show* would not begin until at least midnight.

When Johnny had started out with *Carson's Cellar*, he had suffered the ignominy of having his program pushed in and out of the schedule as a comedic filler. He was not about to have *The Tonight Show* shunted out of the way for a football game. He refused to tape the show that evening. Moreover, he refused to allow the network to fill the time period with a rerun.

"Anything is habit," he said. "If the show does not go on at the scheduled time, of course it is detrimental for the show. That is exactly the reason I am taking this stand. Pretty soon people won't know if we're there or not."

Johnny seemed unable to enjoy his triumph. Much of his success appeared tainted, or full of irony and contradictions. He had been told that Art Stark was the cause of all the unhappiness on the staff. He had fired Stark and gotten rid of Sy Kasoff, an associate producer loyal to Stark. To produce the show, he had brought in Stan Irwin from Las Vegas at $400,000 a year, almost three times what Stark had received.

The back-stabbing, the cabals, the undercutting, only

worsened. Stan Irwin was not the man to control ambitious underlings. In October Johnny called the staff together and lectured them about working together as a "happy family."

That same month Rudy Tellez married Jeanne Prior. Soon afterward, Johnny presented the newlyweds with their best wedding present by naming Rudy the new producer, a position that he had sought almost since the day he first arrived as a talent coordinator. Irwin returned to the desert sun of Las Vegas, where among other things he handled Johnny's personal appearances, a lucrative sinecure.

Tellez attempted to put his stamp on the show by opening it up more. He had Johnny skydiving out of an airplane. The producer staged a love-in at the Burbank studio, with scores of flower children plucked off Sunset Boulevard. He tried a few serious guests, but as he looked out at the nodding heads in the audience, he could almost hear them shouting, "Bring on the clowns."

The new producer discovered that it was as hard to improve the show as it was to ruin it. Tellez recalls, "I would go home some night and say, 'Wait until you see the show tonight. It's incredible. Buddy Hackett dropped his pants and the audience screamed and every guest was better than the last.' I'd turn it on and it wasn't as funny. And some nights I'd come home and say, 'Jesus, don't even watch it. It was a disaster from beginning to end. Johnny was off, the guests were boring.' I'd turn it on, and somehow it went better.

"What television does is take off all the highs, take off all the lows, and squeeze them into a little box. That's where *The Tonight Show* shines. It's the bland leading the bland."

Tellez was producing the show at a point in Johnny's career when he might have moved beyond *The Tonight Show*. "I think Johnny wanted to be another Jack Lemmon in the worst possible way," Tellez says. "But he didn't have it. There's a film intensity and a television intensity. On film he doesn't come across as a human being. On television he's this warm person you want to get to know as he sits behind the desk and just talks. On television he capitalizes on that pixie quality of his that enables the audience to say, 'That's a guy I'd like to know. Gee, that's kind of cute.' "

Walter Kempley, the head writer, had prepared more material for Johnny than anyone else had. Writing for *The Tonight Show* was like drawing oil from a deep well. One day you might start drawing up nothing but sand and water. When that happened, when there was even a little water in the oil, you were out.

Like all the writers, Kempley worked under one 13-week contract after another. He felt that he was half burned out, but when his newest contract expired, he wanted to stay. "They wouldn't renew my contract, and Johnny expected me to come to work," Kempley says. "I said, 'I'm leaving, I have no contract.' I probably could have said, 'Can you straighten it out?' But you didn't show any emotion with Johnny." And so, after five-and-a-half years, Kempley walked out the door at NBC and was gone.

One of the more intriguing writers to work on *The Tonight Show* was Nick Arnold. Arnold suffered from cerebral palsy, and his speech was difficult to understand. His head tilted to the side. He walked like a drunken sailor. But he had an original sense of humor with a healthy taint of morbidity.

Arnold tried to break in as a stand-up comedian. One of the first to appreciate his ability was Joan Rivers, who saw him perform at the Improv. "I thought it was the bravest thing," she says. "I had him come in and write jokes for me, and they weren't very good. He couldn't even hold the pencil. Then he grew and became such a good writer." Joan hired him to write for her at the munificent sum of a dollar a joke, a hundred jokes a week. In 1970 she talked Johnny into giving Arnold a trial as a monologue writer. That first evening Arnold heard Johnny telling two of his jokes, and he knew he was on his way.

The youngest writer on the staff was seventeen-year-old Jim Mulholland, who took the train in from Trenton, New

Jersey, where he was attending college. But all the writers were young and full of equal measures of enthusiasm, energy, and insecurity. Their fates were determined by Johnny's choices each day. They might think that their world was the universe, but they lived and died *The Tonight Show*.

In 1967 Carl "Doc" Severinsen became the new musical conductor. Doc, who had been sitting in the *Tonight Show* band since 1962, blew a brilliant trumpet; and Johnny appreciated the musician's talent enough to take him along on many of his shows across the country.

Doc's only weakness as a performer was that his personality was as bland as a dish of plain gelatin. He had grown up as the son of a dentist in Arlington, Oregon, a town so small that they drove the cattle down Main Street, right past his father's office. His musical ability was such that he was hired to play in big bands before he graduated from high school. After serving in the armed forces immediately after World War II, Doc resumed his musical career. He played with Tommy Dorsey. That first evening the band broke into Dorsey's theme song, "I'm Getting Sentimental over You." "I felt like my feet had left the ground," Doc recalls. "I really wasn't there for a while. I was floating."

When the Big Band era ended, Doc took a job on the NBC staff orchestra. He became part of the *Tonight Show* band, and he made extra money backing up various pop artists.

As Johnny's new musical director, Doc was out there in the public consciousness. One evening he happened to wear a tie so crazy-looking that Johnny commented on it. The audience laughed, and Doc started wearing wilder and wilder clothes. "That was at a time when there was a whole longhair clothing revolution and I identified with those people in many ways," Doc said years later. "I felt a rapport with their music and I began to dress a little like them."

Every night Doc wore a different flamboyant outfit. He

sometimes looked like a stuffed peacock whose plumage hid his bland personality. And in Doc's outfits, Johnny had as certain a laugh-getter as in Ed's drinking. They became the three amigos of late night: Johnny, the charmer with a rascal's gleam in his eye; Ed, the rotund drinking partner; and Doc, the hip musician in the coats of many colors.

Tommy Newsom, the assistant music director and Doc's substitute, was the other band member who was regularly featured on the show. Newsom's public personality was as exciting as Gatorade on New Year's Eve, but like many others on the show, Newsom was much more complex than the image he projected. A graduate of the College of William and Mary, the Peabody Conservatory of Music, and Columbia University, he was a classically trained pianist and saxophone player.

Johnny treated Newsom like a comedic punching bag. "I don't think he talked to me the first night at all, because he was totally uncomfortable," Newsom recalls of the evening in 1968 when he became Doc's substitute. "He started on me pretty fast. Probably I was a natural target. I don't ever remember getting steamed up about it. I found out that if you answer back at the expense of the star, the crowd hates you. They don't care whether you're being picked on. They're on Johnny's side. I've seen it with other people. They get too snippy with Johnny, and the crowd turns on them."

Like many powerful men, Johnny was constitutionally incapable of praising his subordinates.

"C'mon, I want to talk with you," he told Ed one evening after the show.

What the hell is *this*, the announcer thought to himself. He could see that Johnny was so nervous he was chain-smoking.

"Let's go outside," Johnny said, as Ed remembers.

The two men found an empty room.

"I have something I want to tell you," Johnny said as he lit up yet another cigarette.

Jeeze, this is it, Ed thought. I'm getting the ax. He couldn't bring himself to tell me before.

Finally Johnny spoke. "I just want to tell you that I know what you're doing. I know you're helping me out there. I know what a supportive person you are. I know that you are . . ."

As Johnny continued talking, tears rolled down McMahon's cheeks. He ran out of the room. Johnny followed him. He was crying too. "You see, goddammit," Johnny shouted, his voice echoing down the hall, "you can't take a compliment any better than I can!"

One of the talent coordinators, John Gilroy, learned what could happen when one displeased Johnny. "He [Carson] expects people to work for him 24 hours a day," says Gilroy. "He became upset with me because I wasn't in the studio when an act, Mr. Electricity, arrived early to rehearse. I had ducked out for a haircut and when I came back I could see by Carson's eyes that he was angry. I was subsequently fired from the show."

One day Johnny's brother, Dick, walked into his office with some important news. Dick said that he had decided to leave *The Tonight Show*. He had an opportunity to direct *The Don Rickles Show*, a half-hour comedy show, in the fall of 1968. "Um-mm," said Johnny reportedly, thinking of his brother's replacement. "Listen, do you think we can get Bobby Quinn to do it?"

Johnny was the sun, and everyone else rotated around him. He treated his brother no worse than he had treated Perry Cross, when the first producer wanted to leave. And as he had for Perry, Johnny hosted a going-away party for Dick.

That evening at Danny's Hideaway Johnny was drinking heavily. He had vodka in his glass on the show sometimes, but the worst of his drinking occurred off the air. Craig Tennis, a new young talent coordinator, tried to curry favor with Johnny by talking of their mutual Iowa background. Johnny didn't want to listen.

Anyone who had worked on the show for a while knew

that once Johnny got some vodka in him, the only place to be was somewhere else. Shirley Wood, a talent coordinator, made the mistake of staying at the party a few minutes too long. She ended up in a royal argument with her boss.

Most of the staff left early, like a crowd after the first act of a bad play. By default, Craig Tennis received the dubious honor of guiding Johnny out of the restaurant. Johnny didn't want to go home, but to Jilly's, a favorite hangout. The talent coordinator hailed a taxi.

"Take us to Jilly's—the *long* way please," Tennis said. The taxi driver drove around Central Park several times. After an hour he deposited his famous, inebriated passenger at the West Side bar.

"Kid, go on home," Johnny said as he sat at a table, a new drink in his hand. "I know you've got better things to do than hang around here."

Johnny never mentioned the night to Tennis.

Although some of the NBC cameramen and technicians liked Johnny, others had little use for him. He rarely berated them, or even mildly criticized their performance. He simply ignored them. He often didn't know their names. He treated them as if they were as interchangeable as the cameras.

"In all the years that I've been on the show, he has never once said hello," said one camera crew member in 1968. "He maintains that attitude with most of the other fellows, too. As for his being relaxed, I think it's a great put-on. Carson is the most uptight, nervous guy you'll ever want to meet. His short temper creates tension backstage. Everyone is sniping at everyone else."

Johnny created the atmosphere on the show. " 'Don't ever put that shit on the show again,' he'll scream," says one friend. "And then Carson will rant about how inept some of the other guests were. If those celebrities could only hear what Carson really thinks about them, there would be some dandy street fights around town."

Almost no one dared to speak on-the-record about Johnny any longer. Privately they mused endlessly about the paradoxes of the man. "I consider him the most unhappy individual I have ever met," one intimate said. "He fits the phrase perfectly—'men lead lives of quiet desperation.' He's constantly seeking gaiety without ever quite finding it."

One night when Johnny went out looking for some of that gaiety, he ended up at the Open End on the Upper East Side. The Open End was a "salt-and-pepper club," a place where blacks and whites hung out. Johnny mixed with a clientele that included athletes, jazz musicians, single women, and occasional pimps.

Johnny sat at a table with a black woman. At the bar stood Bobby Van, a nightclub owner, and his friend and associate, Ray Abruzzese.

A black man walked up to Johnny and began to argue about the woman. "Johnny was whacked out and didn't know what the fuck was happening," says Abruzzese.

Johnny and the woman got up to leave, trailed by the man. Van was worried about what might happen to Johnny. He followed the group out of the club. On the sidewalk outside the man threatened Johnny. When Van tried to intervene, the man slugged him in the eye.

As Johnny and the woman jumped into the waiting limousine, another man joined the fray and pulled a gun. "I took the gun away from one but the other guy shot two bullets at me," says Van. "I ended up getting a broken nose. I got my nose set the next day."

"Johnny just took off," says Abruzzese. "Bobby never got any acknowledgment or thanks or nothing."

Johnny's forays into Manhattan nightlife ended in more than one disaster. One evening at Voisin, an East Side restaurant, Johnny sat drinking and doing card tricks for a group that included Joanne and her friend Jacqueline Susann, the pop novelist; Rocky Graziano, the prizefighter; and Mrs. Rudy Vallee, wife of the singer. Johnny often did his card tricks or performed a string of jokes when he felt uncomfortable. He was already turning surly after a couple drinks. Jacqueline Susann was a heavy drinker too.

Johnny became so crudely insulting that, according to Susann, she told him, "You are unbearably rude. Please leave." After saying, "You're not that great a comedian," Susann picked up the best weapon at hand, a glass full of Black Russian, a sticky mix of vodka and Kahlúa, and threw it in Johnny's face.

On another occasion Johnny was sitting at the bar at Jilly's with Joanne and Ed McMahon. The door swung open, and Frank Sinatra walked in with more bodyguards and hangers-on than an Arab potentate. An aura of uncertainty, of danger, surrounded Sinatra. The room grew so quiet that you could hear the flattery drop. Johnny waited until the singer reached *his* table. He looked at Sinatra, then at his watch, and back at the singer. "Frank," Johnny said, "I told you twelve-thirty."

If Johnny had been Cinderella, forced to leave the bars and nightclubs at the witching hour of midnight, he would have had few problems. Early in the evening he was a delightful companion. One time, hoping to catch Sammy Davis, Jr., at the Living Room, he arrived to hear the opening act, a female vocalist, singing interminably. When she finally ended her set, Johnny applauded and shouted, "More, more." The woman, a vision of *The Tonight Show* dancing through her head, sang another number.

Almost every aspect of Johnny's life was different from the way it appeared to be. Johnny, the great host, was a reclusive man who rarely invited anyone to his house. Johnny, the loving husband, sought solace and comfort outside his marriage. Johnny, the caring father, lacked a deep rapport with his own sons.

Jody says that part of Rick's, Chris's, and Cory's problems when they were growing up was that they wanted their father to be the Johnny Carson they saw on television, and he wasn't.

Jan de Ruth observed the difference between Johnny, the television star, and Johnny, the person, as well. "My theory is that Johnny's a ventriloquist," says the artist. "He's one person until the show goes on. Then he sits in the background and his other self becomes a puppet that he manipulates through the show. The moment the show closes, he goes back to being himself. It takes enormous energy to do that. That's why he needs his privacy.''

''Sometime you've got to learn to trust people,'' a friend told Johnny.

''But who?'' he asked.

Johnny felt that he had been betrayed a score of ways. Everyone wanted a piece of him, made promises to him, wanted something—an autograph, a spot on the show, investment money, a contribution, a benefit performance, a moment of his attention. Everywhere the hands were out. Everywhere smiling faces and beseeching eyes.

Stan Irwin set up performances for Johnny all over the country. The heartland of America loved Johnny and felt that he was theirs. ''People waited outside to get a look at him,'' recalls Jack Eglash, who directed the music. ''It was like Sinatra and the teenyboppers. Only Johnny got them all ages, from twelve to eighty.''

One weekend Johnny flew down to Lubbock, Texas, along with his son Rick. Although he didn't like having journalists around, Johnny agreed to let Joan Barthel, a writer, and Harry Benson, a photographer, from *Life* magazine travel with him.

''How far is this place, Dad?'' Rick asked as they drove from the airport toward Lubbock in a Rix Funeral Home limousine.

Johnny said nothing. Rick, used to the impenetrable qualities of his father, sat quietly in the backseat.

After going to his suite at the Red Raider Inn and signing a few autographs, Johnny was driven to the ten-thousand-seat Lubbock auditorium. ''Holy Christ,'' he said as he looked out on the expanse of folding chairs stretching out into the gloom. Performing here was bad news enough. Then Johnny learned that this evening Texas Tech took on the University of Texas in Austin; thousands of Carson fans would be down in the capital whooping it up for the Red

Raiders. Other Carson fans would be at the final day of the Panhandle South Plains Fair watching Buck Owens of *Hee-Haw*. This was the kind of booking that had helped cost Al Bruno his job.

As Johnny digested the news, Harry Benson sought to position him for a photograph, standing alone and sullen in the empty auditorium. "He did it because it was true," says Benson. "He didn't try to manipulate or control us. There was no PR bullshit. I've spent my life photographing celebrities. Most of them are jerks. He was one of the best, not patronizing or condescending."

That evening at the Lubbock auditorium Johnny sat waiting on a folding chair in a locker room with a pink tile lavatory. Out in the sweltering auditorium the dance team of Bud and Cece Robinson performed before the lackluster crowd. Rick came back and told his dad about the oppressive heat and the pathetic crowd, some of whom were listening to the football game on portable radios. For a moment Johnny debated even going on. Then he went out onstage and, drenched with sweat, did an hour and fifteen minutes, winning a standing ovation.

On Sunday evening Johnny had another show in Dallas. In the afternoon Stanley Marcus opened his celebrated store, Neiman Marcus, especially for Johnny. Marcus was more of a showman than Johnny. He arrived in a white linen hunter's coat. Johnny sat in princely splendor between two attractive salesladies. They whispered into his ear as two beautiful models paraded past in coats, one of which was a $150,000 Kojah mink.

People were always doing favors for Johnny that he didn't request, favors that ended up obligating him. He hadn't asked that Marcus open the store. But now that the department-store magnate had gone to such trouble, it was obvious that he was expected to buy. A minor fur was probably in order. Instead, Johnny ended up buying two $225 Donald Brooks dresses for Joanne.

That evening after the performance he sat at dinner with a group that included one of his Dallas hosts. He got up

without saying even a perfunctory good-bye and walked off
to another table.

The next morning on the flight back to New York, Johnny
sat alone in the first-class section, staring out the window
through dark glasses. Barthel and Benson sat in the row
behind.

Barthel got up and moved into the seat beside Johnny.
She knew that she had material for a revealing profile, and
she wanted Johnny to know that she appreciated it. "I want
to thank you for giving us all this access," she said. "I will
write a fair piece and . . ." She talked on and on. Johnny
continued staring out the window. He said nothing. Finally
Barthel got up and went back to her own seat. As she sat
looking at him, she thought, He's got so many problems
and he's such a lonely man.

Johnny appeared to be immensely wealthy, but he had so
many hands grasping for cuts of his income that he had
serious money problems. Johnny decided that he had to get
on top of matters financially. He needed one person to
manage all of his business affairs. In April 1969 Johnny
and David A. "Sonny" Werblin announced that they were
going into partnership. Werblin had retired after a long
career that included a top executive position at MCA, the
giant talent agency, and ownership of the New York Jets
football team. He had also managed the post-football career
of the Jets' legendary quarterback Joe Namath, and Jim
Brown, the great Cleveland Brown back.

Johnny hoped to begin trading on his name. He had already lent his name to one venture, a fast-food chain called
Here's Johnny's. In March he had flown out to Omaha for
Johnny Carson Day, named by the mayor to coincide with
the opening of the first restaurant. A second Here's Johnny's
was to open in September, and then a third, a hundred
restaurants in the next year and a half. Alas, Johnny was
not destined to be the king of burgers. The chain flopped,
the spatulas were put away, and the HERE'S JOHNNY'S signs
taken down.

Werblin involved Johnny in a licensing arrangement with Hart, Schaffner & Marx to produce Johnny Carson apparel and accessories. The company, known primarily for high-quality suits, wanted to develop a new, cheaper line of attire.

FCC regulations prevented Johnny from openly plugging the clothes on *The Tonight Show*. No matter. He would simply wear the outfits on the air, a ninety-minute commercial every evening, occasionally calling attention to his wardrobe. "I went into this business because I couldn't get a fried-chicken franchise," Johnny said in his monologue.

Johnny had already had a remarkable impact on clothing in America. When he started wearing turtlenecks, men across America bought sweaters by the tens of thousands. He dressed in a Nehru jacket on *The Tonight Show*, and suddenly the jacket was mainstream America, not a Beatles outfit.

This new licensing arrangement proved to be one of the most successful in history. In the first full year alone, the company sold one hundred thousand units of tailored clothes in one thousand stores. By 1973 the company projected sales of four hundred thousand units and $50 million in sales. Over the years Johnny and Werblin each earned several million dollars from this one agreement. As late as 1982, when sales were down, Johnny still earned $262,500 in fees.

When Johnny talked about the value of his name, he was not talking abstractions. His name meant money. A man who could make millions by attaching his name to grade-2 suits was not going to sit back and let people make money off *him*. A performer who could earn twenty-five thousand dollars giving an interview was not likely to spend hours passing out witticisms for free.

Werblin's first major endeavor was to negotiate Johnny's new contract. Werblin understood that basic rule of money in America: It wasn't how much you earned, it was how much you kept. He brought in Robert A. Schulman, a Washington tax attorney, to help work out a deal that would keep Uncle Sam's hands off the lion's share. Johnny and Werblin formed a separate corporation, Raritan Enterprises, Inc., to run their joint ventures.

On July 2, 1969, *The New York Times* announced that according to informed industry sources Johnny would be earning a reported $75,000 to $85,000 a week, the highest salary in television. Johnny called the story "a gross and ludicrous exaggeration." He said that he had been earning twenty-thousand dollars a week, and his new contract offered only a "modest" increase.

Two days later *The New York Times*, in a rare mea culpa, admitted they had made a mistake. The damage had been done, however. "Mr. Carson got a 'good increase' when his contract was renewed," editorialized the Portland *Oregonian*, "and even if he now receives only $25,000 a week, it will seem ludicrous to most Americans. . . . This imbalance in monetary rewards is one of the inequities young critics of our society are griping about, we think. If so, they have a point."

Johnny became livid over talk about his salary. He and his audience took part in a calculated conspiracy: He was a hybrid, half a star, half the common man. He could joke about shopping at K mart, or eating a hamburger at a roadside stand. He could ask the stars questions that a fan might have asked. He couldn't afford to be portrayed as a rich man, as distant from the people as an air-conditioned limousine from a subway car.

TWELVE

In 1969 Charlotte Clish joined *The Tonight Show* as Johnny's new secretary. The outer office in which Clish worked was decorated in classic celebrity, framed pictures of Johnny on the cover of *TV Guide*, photos of him with Jack Benny, George Burns, and other stars. Johnny's private office resembled what *Women's Wear Daily* called a "bachelor's make-out pad." Johnny had no desk but a round marble table, a stereo, a small refrigerator, a large television, and a sensuous sofa that would have fit neatly in Hugh Hefner's living quarters.

"Johnny would come into the office at about 11 A.M., wearing a short-sleeved shirt, slacks and a jacket," Clish recalled after leaving the show. "He'd be edgy, serious, but would walk normally. But as the day progressed, he'd start standing taller as if to gain assurance in himself and get rid of the shakes. By the time he went to do his show, Johnny would be standing like a ramrod, taking huge gulps of air, swelling out his chest like a frog. Sometimes his posture was so exaggerated I thought he'd fall over backwards."

Johnny was a mass of tics and nervous gestures. One afternoon, as part of an experiment, a doctor hooked Johnny up to a portable heart monitor. The physician discovered that Johnny's heart rate more than doubled just before he went on stage to do his monologue, from 70 to 150 beats a minute.

Johnny controlled his anxiety by taking alcohol during the show. Charlotte kept his cup full. "When I first started with Johnny, he preferred Smirnoff vodka and tonic, but by the time I left, he was drinking J & B scotch and water."

On *The Tonight Show* Christmas was a time of forced joviality. Clish went around the studio badgering the staff and crew to send Christmas cards to Johnny. "It made him more pleasant to work for on those occasions," she says.

Johnny continued his tradition of handing out gifts that seemed to say, "I care enough to send the very least." One year he passed out half a dozen Nebraska steaks to his bemused staff. "I can only compare the gift to the Indian carving set that Jack Paar used to hand out," Walter Kempley says, recalling his experience with another thoughtful employer.

Each holiday season Craig Tennis gave his notorious Artillery Punch Party. One year Charlotte Clish enlivened the event by slugging a would-be suitor. The gentleman responded by slapping her right back.

Charlotte imbibed her full share of the artillery punch, but she felt it was her duty to help her boss find his way home. Johnny forgot where he had parked his car, but they headed off into the December night. The next morning Tennis asked what had happened.

"He had had a lot to drink, but he was extremely careful, the way he maneuvered his car down Fifth Avenue," Clish said.

"What do you mean, careful?" Tennis asked.

"Well, he stopped at every traffic light—regardless of what color it was."

On April 4, 1968, Tiny Tim waltzed onto *The Tonight Show* for the first time and trilled "Tiptoe Through the Tulips." Tiny Tim looked like one of the bad boys in Walt Disney's *Pinocchio* at the precise moment that he is turned into a donkey. For years he had appeared in obscure bohemian clubs in Greenwich Village like the Fat Black Pussy Cat and Page Three. He sang old, forgotten songs in a high falsetto, plucking on ukulele strings.

Johnny stared at the flamboyant singer as if he had been rendered speechless. In his hand Johnny held a short assessment of the performer and a list of questions that Tennis had prepared. *TINY TIM IS OUTSPOKEN, AND WHEN HE GETS WRAPPED UP IN A SUBJECT WILL CONTINUE WITH IT FOREVER*, the talent coordinator had written, typing out his comments in capital letters. *HE WILL, AND CAN, TALK ON VIRTUALLY ANY SUBJECT, INCLUDING IMPURITIES IN SOAP. HE IS FOR REAL, BUT WHAT HE REALLY IS, IS THE REAL QUESTION*. Tennis listed proposed questions, along with the answers that Tiny Tim would give. *HE WON'T TELL YOU HIS AGE. HE TAKES AN HOUR AND A HALF SHOWER EACH MORNING. HE IS EXTREMELY FOND OF GIRLS FROM AGE 16 TO 25*.

Johnny stuck closely to the proposed questions. Afterward, Albert Goldman wrote in *The New York Times* that Tiny "reduced Johnny Carson to his straight man with a few child-like answers; Carson, his radar scanning the house, realized immediately that Tiny Tim's obvious vulnerability made him an untouchable."

Although Tiny Tim had already received his first national exposure on the *Merv Griffin Show*, it was the appearances with Johnny that made him famous. Tiny Tim believes that "Carson felt uncomfortable with me because he didn't know how to react. I know he felt uncomfortable because of some of my beliefs."

Johnny's uneasiness was no different from his audiences'. Tiny Tim was that most unusual phenomenon in the television age: a genuine eccentric. To mid-America he appeared a man of ambiguous sexuality, yet he had an abiding interest in young women. He believed in sex only after marriage, and no birth control. He looked as if he fit in the

hippie-yippie left, yet he was a don't-step-on-my-flag conservative who had a sincere and deep interest in, and knowledge of, American popular music of years gone by.

Even as he was becoming one of the biggest performers
in America, Tiny Tim could look at himself with guileless
awareness. He sensed that his fame would last only two
years, and that one day he would be back living with his
mother in a New York City tenement. He saw that the life
of a celebrity was a matter of exchanges, and that Johnny
understood that as well as anyone. "Mr. Carson has the
mind of Perry Mason, the real Perry Mason of the books
by Erle Stanley Gardner," says Tiny Tim. "In my opinion
he's always one step ahead of his guests. His main aim is
to win. Basically he always plays to win."

Johnny held up the cover of Tiny Tim's album *God Bless
Tiny Tim*, and the record became one of the biggest hits of
1968. Tiny Tim was soon earning fifty thousand dollars a
week or more. Johnny and *The Tonight Show* staff realized
that they were riding a phenomenon. They booked him
approximately every seven weeks, and every time he appeared he was a smash.

In September of the following year Tiny Tim used the
hallowed platform of *The Tonight Show* to announce his
engagement to seventeen-year-old Victoria May Budinger.
Before the show Rudy Tellez says that he asked Tiny Tim
"what would happen if John asked you on the air to be
married on the show?" According to Tellez, Tiny Tim replied "Ooohhoooohooohooo."

Tiny Tim has a different recollection. "If someone came
in beforehand, I don't remember," he says. "I would swear
on a stack of telephone books, no way. Mr. Carson appreciated that he was the first to hear of our engagement. He
paused for a while and he asked, 'Where are you going to
get married and when?' I said, 'We're going to get married
on Christmas Day in Haddonfield, New Jersey, in Miss
Vicki's parents' house.'

"Mr. Carson thought for a few seconds. Then he said,
'Well, look, would you like to get married on our show?

We'll do it in good taste. It will be like a nighttime *Bride and Groom*.' I was familiar with that show. He said NBC would take care of the bills and pay for Miss Vicki's wedding gown. That was the key phrase. The only thing he said was, 'I can't do it on Christmas because I'll be away.' We both agreed on the seventeenth of December.''

After saying yes to Johnny, Tiny began hearing unpleasant stories about his betrothed. "There were rumors when I met her and I was falling in love with her that a few days later she was making a play for the Christy Minstrels."

Tiny Tim had no quarrel with the New Christy Minstrels, but the rumors would have given a lesser man pause. Alas, once he said yes on *The Tonight Show*, the die was cast.

"If there was no Johnny Carson, there would have been no wedding," Tiny Tim says. "I always believed Miss Vicki did not love me. I told her mother after the Carson show was already set, 'Mrs. Budinger, Mrs. Budinger, I don't believe your daughter loves me. I believe that if your daughter saw me in '66 when I was nothing, she would have smiled and walked away. I believe she wants the marriage for herself. I know the way I am, I know my beliefs are strange, I don't believe in birth control.' Mrs. Budinger said, 'She wants to do it, and we'll see what the marriage will bring.'

"So I knew Miss Vicki didn't love me. And I myself was insecure. I proposed to three different girls when I was engaged to Miss Vicki. I would say to them, 'Let's run away.' Then I said no, I cannot break Miss Vicki's heart. And I would quickly call them up and say, 'I can't do that, I already promised Mr. Carson and I would break Miss Vicki's heart. She doesn't love me, but it would be a stigma on her future.' And so I went through with it.''

Miss Vicki was not happy being married on *The Tonight Show*, either. She remembers telling her betrothed, "You better tell Mr. Carson you don't mean it, because I'm not going on television."

On December 17, 1969, the most-watched event in late-night television history took place: the marriage of Tiny Tim and Miss Vicki. There was no tougher ticket in New York than a place in the audience for *The Tonight Show* that evening.

Ed McMahon set the perfect tone for the evening, a blend of ersatz solemnity, merriment, and commerce: "We cordially request the pleasure of your company at the marriage of Tiny Tim and Miss Vicki right here on *The Tonight Show*. But right now here are some words of wisdom from Pepto-Bismol tablets."

Everything after the wedding would be anticlimactic. So Johnny stretched out the anticipation by talking first to his other guests, Phyllis Diller and Florence Henderson, who like Johnny had dressed formally for the evening. "And now here's the moment you've been waiting for," Johnny said finally. "A lot of people thought it wouldn't take place on this show."

Merrill Sindler, the set decorator, had spent three days designing and building a set that was supposed to be a Georgian English church. The yellow curtain opened on an ornate blue building surrounded by thousands of yellow and white tulips. The door opened inward to reveal the wedding party. The men wore black coats, blue pants, and ruffled shirts, a campy fantasy of the eighteenth century. The women wore purple gowns with black bodices. Miss Vicki walked slowly forward, in a gown as white as innocence, her long veil pulled back to reveal brown bobbed hair curled as tightly as wood shavings. Tiny wore a long Victorian coat, his shoulder-length hair pressed and primped by a beauty consultant.

Tiny Tim vowed to be "sweet, gentle, kind, patient, not puffed up, charitable, slow to anger, and swift to forgive." When the ten-minute ceremony ended, the newlyweds walked over to *The Tonight Show* set.

"Congratulations, Tiny," Johnny said. "And Miss Vicki, you look just as pretty as brides always look. How do you feel, Tiny?"

"I feel great. I only hope and pray I can make Miss Vicki

happy. I know I've been blessed with the most beautiful girl I've ever seen.''

Tiny Tim thanked everyone. He thanked the owner of the Ground Floor restaurant, which was providing a free reception. He thanked the clothes designer for the free outfits. He thanked the hairdresser for the free stylings. He thanked the florist for the free flowers. He thanked the King's Inn in the Bahamas for the free honeymoon.

Tiny Tim and his bride drank natural honey and milk, while Johnny and the other guests toasted them with champagne. Then Tiny Tim sang a song that he had written for his bride:

> "Oh won't you come and love me
> Oh pretty Vicki Mine,
> Oh won't you come and love me
> And be my valentine.''

Later that evening the crowd at the reception was so enormous that Tiny Tim met only a few of the guests. The newlyweds had received scores of gifts, but they were stolen, hauled off like party favors. Tiny Tim was promised a videotape of the ceremony; even that he didn't receive.

The millions who watched the show never dreamed that they were watching the beginning of the end of Tiny Tim's stardom. The wedding of Tiny Tim and Miss Vicki had been a media catharsis. America had gorged on Tiny Tim, like eating a pound of chocolate, killing its appetite for the performer.

Johnny vowed he would not make fun of the wedding, but he could not resist. On their wedding night Tiny Tim had told his bride his unique idea of a honeymoon; he and his bride would sleep apart for the first three nights of their marriage. Johnny said that Miss Vicki had hung up a DIS-TURB sign on her door.

In the following months Tiny Tim appeared on *The Tonight Show* more times, but the magic was gone. When

Miss Vicki and Tiny Tim had a stillborn child, Johnny had to ask about it, but it was all too sad. In December 1971 Craig Tennis prepared Johnny's questions for Tiny Tim's second visit of the year: *A SERIOUS QUESTION FOR A MINUTE. WHAT IS THE STATUS OF YOUR CAREER? SOME PEOPLE HAVE SUGGESTED THAT IT'S ALL OVER.*

Johnny didn't ask the question. Everybody knew the answer.

Three years later Tiny appeared on the show again, in what the staff called "a charity booking." A year later he was back for a few weeks in a New York City tenement with his mother. Miss Vicki was gone, and Tiny Tim's fame was gone. He found jobs. He made a living. He traveled from gig to gig, city to city. He was a curiosity, a not-so-golden oldie. He went on *The Tonight Show* again in the summer of 1979, another charity booking. He was fat, his belly showing, and he was not a success.

Tiny Tim figured that Johnny Carson wanted to forget him. Johnny did not show the wedding in his annual anniversary program of past highlights. "He wanted out," Tiny says. "He didn't want to be connected with the wedding."

Tiny understood that. He understood Johnny's cold eyes and what it took to stay on top. He understood because he didn't have it. And he dreamed. He dreamed of once again getting a hit record and coming back on *The Tonight Show*, sitting next to Johnny, laughing, listening to the applause.

In the summer of 1987 Tiny performed with the Great American Circus. The circus was so small that the ringmaster donned an animal outfit to perform in one of the acts. Tiny was the star of the show, and outside among the campers and trailers, he sat in his cluttered Mustang convertible in his coat of many colors, brushing his teeth, or simply waiting.

When Tiny was called, he lumbered into the tent and sang "Tiptoe Through the Tulips" and "There's No Business Like Show Business" to an audience of a few hundred, many of whom were too young to have heard of him. He was like Lola Montez, the mistress of the king of Bavaria, who in the last years of her life was a circus act, paraded through the center ring.

"Do you ever think of the past?" a writer asked him one August day on a county fairground in upstate New York. "Do you ever think what it was like when you were with Johnny and on top?"

"From morning to night," Tiny Tim said, "that's all I think about."

In the spring of 1968 Joanne became a regular panelist on a weekly quiz show, *What's My Sign?*, on Channel 11. She earned only one hundred dollars a week, but she enjoyed being back on television. Nonetheless, Johnny was her primary concern.

For Christmas of 1968 Johnny gave Joanne a writing tablet. On the leather cover in gold lettering Johnny engraved a list: "Joanne Carson: Decorator and designer. Confidante. Union organizer. Stockholder. Dog washer. Back scratcher. Counsel to the lovelorn. Workingman's friend. Sympathetic listener. Painter. Candlemaker. Part-time con artist. Friend of the needy. Corporation director. Bell Telephone's favorite. Child psychologist. Lover. . . . and all-around peachy wife."

The following Christmas Joanne returned from a trip a few days early. When she unlocked the door to the Carsons' apartment, she reportedly discovered Johnny and one of the *Tonight Show* junior secretaries in an intimate act on the living-room rug.

Joanne turned and left the apartment. She had remained deaf to all the rumors of Johnny's philandering, but this she could not ignore. While she continued to project an image of the perfect wife to the world, she sought her own private solace. Johnny may have had his casual affairs, but Joanne began a serious involvement with a race-car driver.

Sometime afterward, Johnny sat at the Unicorn restaurant in Manhattan talking with Arthur Kassel, the official photographer of the Honor Legion of the Patrolman's Benevolent Association (PBA). Kassel was an engaging young man who was sometimes useful to the rich and powerful. According to Kassel, Johnny told him that Joanne had caught him with another woman; he was worried that Joanne would file for divorce charging him with adultery. Johnny pulled a napkin and a letter from his pocket. Both had three dots on them. He told his friend that letters to Joanne had come into the house signed with the mysterious three dots. He was convinced that the three dots stood for the words "I love you," and were from Joanne's lover. He had noticed other signs, mysterious phone calls, objects and furniture missing from the UN Plaza. He was tormented by the thought that Joanne might have a lover. He asked Kassell to investigate.

Johnny had no close friends, no intimate he could turn to for help. Kassel contacted several other men and told them of his meeting with Johnny. The group of about half a dozen were either law-enforcement officers or those on the edge of law enforcement, including a precinct captain and another ranking police officer.

They attempted to take fingerprints off the mysterious letters. From the telephone company they got hold of a list of phone calls made from the Carsons' phones. They checked out calls from the phone in Johnny's separate corporate office at the UN Plaza. They prepared a grid map of Manhattan, matching the phone calls against addresses. In less than two weeks they found what they believed to be Joanne's apartment.

While Johnny waited downstairs, a police captain took the elevator up to the apartment. When the officer found that the key worked, he came back downstairs and Johnny went in. As he entered the one bedroom apartment, he saw many of the items that had been missing from the UN Plaza. He stood in the living room convulsed with pain and the agony of betrayal. He was not a man who showed his emotions, but Johnny broke down and cried. The apartment wasn't in Joanne's name, was used at least much of the time by her friend, and may have been intended by Joanne only as a place to escape her husband's violent temper, but these were nuances lost on Johnny. As far as he was concerned, his marriage was over.

On June 8, 1970, after less than seven years of marriage, Johnny changed the locks on the UN Plaza apartment. Trudy Moreault, then one of Joanne's closest friends, remembers that evening very well. "Johnny was dead drunk," she recalls. "He was inside, and she tried to get in. Joanne came into my apartment and was in the kitchen white as a sheet, red-eyed, crying. Johnny called and told me what had happened. It was dreadful, sordid. It was as if Joanne wanted to be discovered, or she wouldn't have done the things she did and told the people she told. In her complicity she wanted to get him jealous. He was doing what she thought were terrible things to her. He was having these drunken one-night stands with a lot of famous women. He did it because he thought it would be a lark, and it all turned out boring and dreary. But he did it. He said he didn't give much thought to it."

The future opened up to Joanne like a dark cavern. She moved into the Navarro Hotel, in a room overlooking Central Park. "It got to the point where I deliberately placed chairs in front of the French windows because it felt as though I was being drawn out there," she told journalist Eirik Knutzen. "I did not want to end my life. I did not want to end my life because of my curiosity. Look what I would have missed. No matter how depressed I was, I thought about my father."

For Johnny, the divorce was not easy, either. "One evening a couple months after he threw her out, Johnny called and asked to come over," says Moreault. "He talked until one in the morning. He cried. He literally cried. He was very sad. He said he gets drawn inextricably into these webs and he doesn't know how to get out, until he gets married, and then when it doesn't work, he gets a divorce. In one sense he's true and faithful in his fashion. He said that it was fine for a man to have one-night stands. He hated the idea of his second failure. He didn't want any part of Joanne anymore, yet he missed the companionship.''

Joanne discovered a world where phone calls are not returned and the answering machine sits blank and empty. Most of her friends were *their* friends, and suddenly they were not friends at all. She didn't know where to turn. She called Shirlee Fonda, a social acquaintance. Fonda offered to let Joanne stay in the five-story Manhattan town house owned by her and Henry Fonda.

"She was a friend in need and we took her in," says Shirlee Fonda. "We tried to put a little bit of sunshine back into her life. She was nothing, a shell. I'm sure she was very suicidal. I wasn't going to let Joanne be kicked more than she was being kicked. She was in love with Johnny. Why she misbehaved and got kicked out, that's her business. But she was in love with him, and because of the way he telephoned, I felt there was a possibility that they could get together.''

During Johnny's trouble with Joanne he needed a lawyer to handle the divorce. He was so isolated and so mistrustful of his professional associates that he asked Arthur Kassel to recommend a lawyer. Kassel set up a meeting with Henry Bushkin, a close friend. It would have been hard to find a less likely candidate to handle the case, a twenty-five-year-old attorney at a large New York firm. As he rode the subway into Manhattan each day, he appeared doomed to sit in back rooms poring over briefs. A graduate of Vanderbilt Law School, he was in fact an intense, ambitious lawyer, apparently in a hurry to make his way in the world.

The night before Kassel was to make the introduction, he was having dinner at the Bushkins' modest home in Queens, as he did at least once a week. Kassel was an expansive person, given to moments of extravagant prophecy and rhetoric. This evening he outdid himself. "You're going to be rich, Henry, rich!" Kassel exclaimed. "Within a year you're going to move to Manhattan. Within three years you'll move to L.A., first to a small house and then to a major house, a great house. You'll have one of the biggest law firms in the U.S., maybe the world.''

The Bushkins listened in silence to Kassel's prophecy. ''And, Judy, you know what else is going to happen? You and Henry are going to grow apart, and you'll get divorced.''

This was the strangest prophecy of all. The Bushkins had little money, but one thing they did have was a solid marriage.

''Well, Judy, should I make the introduction to Johnny tomorrow or shouldn't I?''

''Yes,'' Judy said, hoping at least part of the prediction was true.

Johnny could have had practically any attorney he wanted to handle the divorce. He chose Henry. ''I was intimidated about meeting him,'' Henry recalled years later. ''But we walked over to NBC in New York and I chatted with Carson 10 or 15 minutes. The next day I got a call from Carson. He was going through the divorce from his second wife, but I was not a divorce lawyer . . . I finally decided he was so isolated in New York, by the people representing him, that maybe I was the only guy, the only lawyer, he knew. His isolation was extreme.''

Henry was not a sophisticated Manhattan barrister, but Johnny wanted to be number one with his agents and managers and lawyers. With Bushkin, he was not only number one, he was the only one.

If Henry did well, his days of sitting on the low rung of a big New York firm were over. A more famous attorney might have attempted to play up the Carson divorce case in the media, an advertisement for himself. Henry kept the matter as quiet as possible. He did his own investigations.

For many months the news of the separation and impending divorce were kept out of the newspapers. Not until six months after Johnny locked out his wife did Aileen Mehle write in the *Daily News* on December 8, 1970, that

"Johnny Carson was served with a summons yesterday by his wife, Joanne, starting an action for separation and divorce." The columnist probably knew more about Johnny and Joanne than any other reporter in New York. She knew, for instance, about Johnny's investigation of Joanne, but she had printed nothing.

At one point Joanne charged Johnny with cruel and inhuman treatment, abandonment and adultery. She asked for seven thousand dollars a week temporary alimony. In public Johnny and his attorney mentioned nothing of any countercharges they might have made against Joanne. "There is no reason for this to be in the newspapers," Henry told a reporter. "It makes everybody's job more difficult having these problems aired in the press as a forum rather than in private or, as a last resort, in court, if need be. We're doing our utmost to keep this as quiet as possible—we're trying to work it out."

In the end Johnny agreed to pay Joanne $160,000 outright, $100,000 for 1972, and $75,000 a year from then on. He would pay until she remarried, but the alimony would end if she ever lived with a man for six months in a row.

The wrangling and negotiations lasted for more than two years from the day Johnny locked out his wife. On June 21, 1972, Joanne stood before Justice Samuel Gold in Manhattan Supreme Court to obtain the final divorce.

"Try to compose yourself," the judge told Joanne as she dabbed at her green eyes. "It is not unique. Thousands end up here."

"He told me he no longer wanted to live with me and no longer wanted to cohabit with me," Joanne told the court. "He said he wanted a divorce. He told me that on other occasions. Finally, on June 8, 1970, he changed the locks on our home, and I no longer had access. That month he was abusive and I feared for my health."

"Did you do anything to provoke your husband?" the judge asked.

"No, I was a good wife, and I didn't provoke him."

When Joanne left the courtroom that day, she went to a

Johnny Carson's first home, in Corning, Iowa *(Laurence Leamer)*

Young Johnny *(left)* and Marion Weinmann fishing in Avoca, Iowa *(Marion Weinmann)*

Johnny *(front row, far right)* and his sister, Catherine *(front row, far left)*, helping Bill Brennan *(back row, second from right)* celebrate his eleventh birthday *(Bill Brennan)*

The Carson home in Avoca, Iowa *(Morris Berndt)*

Carson's boyhood home in Norfolk, Nebraska *(Norfolk Daily News)*

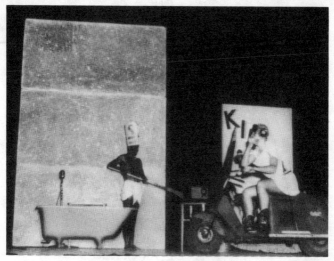

A scene from the 1947 University of Nebraska Kosmet Klub Show in which Carson played Cleopatra *(Phil Solomon)*

Carson entertains with a stripteaser at a Phi Gamma Delta fraternity function. *(Phil Solomon)*

Carson before his teeth were fixed *(CBS Photo)*

Johnny with Bill Brennan, who brought him to Los Angeles *(Bill Brennan)*

Johnny, Jody *(left)*, and Linda Williams, whose husband, Bob Lehman, directed Johnny in Carson's Cellar, his Los Angeles show *(Bob Lehman)*

Johnny, Jody, and their three sons with Red Skelton and his
family and other CBS personalities *(CBS Photo)*

A 1955 production meeting for *The Johnny Carson Show.*
Johnny is in the second row *(Bill Brennan)*

Joanne Carson in an RKO publicity show *(Wally Seawell)*

Johnny's brother, Dick *(left)*, manager Al Bruno, Ed McMahon, and producer Art Stark in Florida shortly before Johnny took over *The Tonight Show (Al Bruno)*

Johnny and his manager, Al Bruno, on Johnny's boat *(Al Bruno)*

Johnny and Joanne Carson on their wedding day *(Bettmann Archive)*

Johnny and *Tonight Show* producer Art Stark in a lighter moment *(Mary Stark)*

Johnny and Joanne Carson in 1970 *(Ron Galella)*

(Left to right) Charo, Arthur Kassel, model Ruth Leslie, and Johnny in Las Vegas *(Arthur Kassel)*

Johnny and Joanna Carson with friends Arthur Kassel and Mrs. Judy Bushkin *(Arthur Kassel)*

Johnny returns to Norfolk, Nebraska, in 1976 with Joanna Carson. *(Norfolk Daily News)*

Johnny and his mother in Norfolk, Nebraska, in 1976 *(Dale Wittner)*

Johnny with two former schoolmates at his Norfolk, Nebraska, high school reunion in 1981 *(Norfolk Daily News)*

Johnny and Faye Gordon, his elementary school teacher *(Norfolk Daily News)*

Johnny and actress Morgan Fairchild on a date *(Phil Ramey)*

Mary Jane Trokel, a television director with whom Johnny had a decade-long relationship *(Mary Jane Trokel)*

Johnny and Sally Field leaving La Scala in Malibu *(Phil Ramey)*

Johnny and Alex Mass, the fourth Mrs. Carson, with his then-lawyer Henry Bushkin and actress Joyce DeWitt *(Phil Ramey)*

Johnny and the future Mrs. Carson, Alex Mass, taking the sun at his beachfront home in Malibu *(Phil Ramey)*

Johnny and Joanna Carson with Frank Sinatra in 1982 *(Ron Galella)*

Johnny and Ed McMahon in 1982 *(Ron Galella)*

Johnny joking at the opening of the new Commercial Bank offices in 1982 *(Ron Galella)*

Johnny and Alex Mass *(Ron Galella)*

Johnny with Joan Rivers backstage at the 1983 Emmy Awards *(Arthur Kassel)*

Johnny and Fred De Cordova, *The Tonight Show* producer *(Arthur Kassel)*

Johnny and Angie Dickinson on a date in 1983 *(Ron Galella)*

Johnny's $8.9 million home in Malibu *(Phil Ramey)*

Johnny's private tennis court in Malibu *(Phil Ramey)*

In 1980 Johnny stands beside his father's 1939 Chrysler outside Norfolk, Nebraska, overcome with emotion. *(Dale Wittner)*

jeweler and had the gold wedding ring Johnny had given her melted and silver-plated; and for several years she wore the silver teardrop on a silver chain around her neck.

Johnny was one of the highest-paid entertainers in America, and he might have been forced to pay Joanne a fortune. Kassel believes that without the investigation and Henry's hard work, the settlement would have been far higher.

Johnny should have been delighted at the settlement. Nonetheless, he began joking about his ex-wife on the air. "Some performers start in a cold-water flat and work their way up to a penthouse," he said. "I started in a penthouse and am working my way down to a cold-water flat." When his monologue failed, he ad-libbed, "Hey, I need the job." The audience didn't have to be told why. In a few months he created a new element to his image: Johnny, the marital disaster, exploited by ex-wives. Joanne was so upset that she sued him for $125,000, dropping her suit when he quit his attacks.

Johnny was bitter all right, but it was about matters deeper even than money, matters that he could never joke about.

THIRTEEN

I n September 1970 Johnny was having dinner at "21" with Jack and Mary Benny; Freddy de Cordova, the new executive producer of *The Tonight Show*; and Mollie Parnis, a woman prominent in the fashion industry. Johnny had locked Joanne out of their apartment three months before. As the group sat talking, a thin, stunning brunette passed by and waved at Parnis.

"Who is that pretty girl?" Johnny asked.

"Her name's Joanna Holland," said Parnis, who knew her as a friend and occasional fashion model. The restaurant was full of attractive women, but even here Joanna Holland was special. She had the lean, sophisticated look of the East Side, but she exuded an animal vitality, an alertness like a leopard's.

"I'd love to meet her," Johnny said.

A few days later Parnis called Joanna. "Johnny Carson is going to call you," she said. "He's a friend of mine and it's okay."

Johnny called Joanna and set up a date three weeks later, on his birthday. From that evening on, according to Joanna, they talked almost every day.

Johnny had known many women in his life, but Joanna was something entirely new. Joanna was thirty-one years old, though there were those who had the impression that she was only twenty-four. To Johnny, she had all the patina of the East Side, a world in which he was still an interloper, uncomfortable, ill at ease. Unlike many models, Joanna had an elegance and grace that did not end when she opened her mouth. She spoke in a feline whisper, drawing her listeners to her. Her mother's voice had the nasal twang of New York to it, but Joanna had jettisoned anything that linked her to her modest background.

Her maiden name was Joann Ulrich and she was from Queens, New York, from an Italian-American family. She was married for a short time in the late 1950's to Alan Frendel, a Jewish businessman who later committed suicide. Sometime afterward, at a Miami country club, Joann met Tim Holland, a dashing amateur golf champion. Holland was a colorful figure of uncertain income and high style, a devotee of casinos in Monte Carlo and Biarritz. In 1960 they married, and had a son, Tim, Jr.

Holland introduced his young bride to his glamorous world of affluence. Although Joann liked the life-style, she sought stability as well, and the marriage failed.

Joann had her beauty and her wit, and one was as great as the other. Joanna says that it is "total, utter nonsense" that she changed her name to Joanna so that she would not be mixed up with Joanne. Although she insists that she was always known as "Joanna," various legal papers in the early 1970's all refer to her as "Joann Holland."

Joanna or Joann knew how to please rich older men as well as a geisha. She met Leon C. Greenebaum, a millionaire businessman and chairman of the Hertz Corporation, who was as tough in his negotiations as he was sentimental in his romantic dealings. Greenebaum was still married in name, but he and Joanna became involved.

"We all had a nice relationship with Joanna," says Adrian Lowell, Greenebaum's longtime administrative assistant. "It lasted three, three and a half years. I don't think she was working. I think that she was unemployed, but Joanna is very bright and very beautiful and had a lovely manner. I always say she probably knew all the four-letter words and never used them. She was wonderful to Mr. Greenebaum during his illness.''

Greenebaum died at the age of sixty-one on March 25, 1968. ''Joanna was in the operating room when he died,'' says Carmen, the well-known model and Joanna's close friend. ''God knows if Mr. Greenebaum had stayed alive, she would never have been attracted to Johnny.''

Marjorie Reed, another close friend, has a similar opinion. ''Leon, oh, she loved Leon,'' Reed says. ''She can't even talk about it without her eyes misting over. She adored him. She just adored him.''

The year before Greenebaum died, he wrote a codicil to his will giving Joanna either $200,000 or a cooperative apartment and money that together equaled $200,000. Greenebaum had also listed Joanna's name in his employment agreement with the Hertz Corporation. The month after his death the Hertz Corporation and Greenebaum's wife, Myra, agreed that Hertz would pay Joanna $150,000 in death benefits in monthly installments of $2,500 for five years.

Joanna was now in a strong financial position. Six months later she was close enough to another wealthy businessman, Max Kettner, for him to give her $100,000. The following April she received $40,000 more from Kettner. In all, she received at least $160,000. According to Kettner's attorney, Joanna was to use the money to redecorate her apartment.

At the age of thirty-one Joanna appeared to be a woman of independent means. That was important to Johnny. Joanna said later that Johnny ''was coming out of a bad marriage and he needed to relax—have no pressure—be with someone who was not dependent on him financially.''

Much of Joanna's money, however, was based on her relationships with two wealthy businessmen. The money would not last forever; the twenty-five-hundred dollars a month from Greenebaum's employment agreement at Hertz would run out in 1973. By then she would be an age when modeling would be an unlikely career.

Joanna set out to please Johnny. She saw that his UN

Plaza apartment was still unfinished. The duplex was full of boxes. One bathroom wall had a hole with a sign saying NEXT YEAR A MEDICINE CABINET.

Joanna found a prominent decorator for Johnny, Stephen Mallory, who worked feverishly to refurbish the apartment when Johnny was on the West Coast.

Johnny had never had a professional decorator before, and he had some lessons to learn. "We bought expensive, beautiful Porthault pillowcases for his bedroom," Mallory recalls. "One day I went to his apartment and found that his servant had the sheets ready to go out to the laundry, stuffed in the two-hundred-dollar pillowcase."

Johnny was still a boy from Nebraska, where a man might pay two hundred dollars for a bed but not for a pillowcase. He was not always comfortable with the domestic help. "One day Johnny was cleaning the toilets," Mallory says. "He said, 'Goddammit, I can clean this better than those servants.' "

Johnny had all the classic symptoms of a divorced man, ready to use women before they used him. Mallory remembers overhearing Johnny on the telephone, telling a caller that he swore he would never marry again.

"The way Johnny described to David [Susskind] as his way of dealing with women was incredible," says Carmen, who was closely involved with the producer. "He said, 'Do you want a woman tonight?' David said, 'I can get my own women. I don't need to get laid.' Johnny described to David how he told a girl, 'You're mine. You come when I call. If it's in the middle of the night, whenever. If I ever see your name in the paper, you're through. When I'm through with you, you get in the car and leave, except if I want you to stay overnight. And if I want you to stay overnight, you stay overnight.' That's how Joanna entered that relationship. She was young, but it caused resentments later."

Joanna had other involvements as well, including Kettner, who thought that he might one day marry Joanna. Richard Gully, now a Beverly Hills columnist and publicist, recalls dating Joanna whenever he was in New York. Gully, an Englishman, was a close associate of Jack Warner, the late film producer, and a *bon vivant* who took pleasure in squiring elegant ladies to exclusive restaurants. "I was doing public relations for the Riviera Hotel in Las Vegas," Gully recalls. "I invited Joanna for a weekend opening. She accepted and flew out. As soon as she arrived, she apparently called Johnny. He flew out the next day. We had dinner with Burt Bacharach and Angie Dickinson, the five of us."

Gully did not know whether he was being used or not. He was always the perfect gentleman. According to Gully, he made a quiet exit and left Johnny and Joanna to enjoy their weekend in Las Vegas.

Joanna remembers this weekend too, and Johnny's dramatic flight westward. But she says that she was not in the gambling capital on Gully's invitation.

Johnny had rarely lived alone. In March 1971 he was hospitalized with hepatitis, his first serious illness in all his years hosting *The Tonight Show*. Becoming even more irritated at life's minor vexations, he sued *Movie Mirror* for alleging that he was involved in competition with David Frost for the affection of Diahann Carroll, the singer.

One day he called his secretary, Charlotte Clish, over to the window.

"Do you hear anything?" Johnny asked as he looked down on Forty-ninth Street.

"No."

"Listen!" he said, cocking his ear. "Don't you hear that shrill sound?"

Charlotte strained to listen. "Do you mean that whistling?" she asked finally.

"Yes. And it's driving me crazy! Call up the Mayor's Office and the District Attorney's Office. See if there's an ordinance against whistling. And send somebody downstairs to find out what's causing it."

The sound was the doorman blowing his whistle for cabs, as he had every day for years. Charlotte called the District

Attorney's Office and learned that she could do nothing to stop the sound. When she told Johnny the bad news, he turned and walked away.

Charlotte returned to her typing. Suddenly a screeching noise jolted her. Johnny stood blowing into her ear with a metal police whistle.

"I just wanted you to know how it felt," Johnny said. Then he turned and walked into his inner office.

Johnny woke up on June 9, 1971, at 8:06 A.M. He looked outside and saw window washers moving their scaffolding down the side of the building. He called the front desk to complain. When he received no satisfaction, he had Henry Bushkin file a suit seeking twenty-five thousand dollars in damages and an end to window washing before 10:00 A.M. In July he dropped the action.

Johnny may have been indecisive about marriage, but he agreed to the most dramatic change in the nearly ten-year history of *The Tonight Show*: to move the show to Los Angeles beginning May 1, 1972. The decision amazed the New York staff. Tellez recalls, "Johnny had said, 'I'm never leaving New York. I love it. I'll never move to California. Those people are weak. They have no books to read. It's awful.' "

Johnny was not moving west because of a sudden love for the California sun and sand. "The main reason is the talent pool," Johnny said. "There's not much television in New York anymore. When you do five shows every week for a year, it's a little sticky sometimes to find a large number of lively people in New York."

New York was full of lively people, but lively people did not high ratings make. Celebrities did. That same medium of television that had given Johnny fame beyond fame was creating a new kind of public personality. These were the people Johnny wanted seated next to him: the actress with the hot television show, the star with the big movie coming out, the singer the kids were screaming over. That many of these guests weren't really interesting hardly mattered as long as they basked in the glow of celebrity; after one or two shots they were usually gone.

The talent coordinators were brutal in their assessments. They understood the trajectory of celebrity; they tracked it, seeking to book a guest at the height. They watched young comedians for months or even years, until they were ready; then they gave them their shot. If they didn't get the laughs, if they didn't score with Johnny, they didn't come back.

Los Angeles was the capital of celebrity. The shops of Beverly Hills were full of celebrities past their prime, faces yearning to be remembered. The exclusive restaurants were full of celebrities present, men and women who looked too small to fit their images on television or the movie screen. The agents' offices and the casting offices were full of celebrities future, young men and women striving for success, bringing with it their moment on *The Tonight Show*.

Freddy de Cordova, the new producer, had lobbied for the move to Los Angeles. As much a creature of southern California as valet parking and kiwi fruit, he was Joanne's final legacy to Johnny. Johnny and Joanne had often met Freddy socially. Joanne had been terribly impressed. The man was charming, witty. He seemed self-deprecating, yet he managed to sound little trumpets of self-promotion. Joanne kept telling Johnny that Freddy should one day take over the show.

To Joanne and Johnny, Freddy meant Hollywood. It was not, however, the Hollywood of old glamour or of great and daring films, but of an amiable, uninspired professionalism. Craig Tennis describes his former boss as "having a talent for charm which is almost staggering. He is *also* dictatorial, unpredictable, mercurial, and perhaps the most opportunistic human I have ever met." Freddy directed over twenty films, the most memorable of which was *Bedtime for Bonzo* with Ronald Reagan. He went on to become producer-director for Jack Benny.

The De Cordovas attended A-list parties in Hollywood. Freddy and Janet had a reputation for knowing where to go, when to arrive, and when to leave, skimming the top of the frivolities. The reputation was so well established that it became the basis for an apocryphal story.

The De Cordovas always attended soirees at the home of Jack and Mary Benny, whom Freddy called his "primary sponsors in Tinsel Town, as well as my closest friends." They were there the night that Jack lay dying in an upstairs bedroom. All the friends and relatives waited in the living room. Jack's wife arrived at the head of the stairs. She stood there a moment and said, "Jack has left us."

"So have the De Cordovas," replied a disembodied voice from the living room.

Freddy was a happy man. Already in his early sixties when he joined *The Tonight Show*, he was not making his career with Johnny.

Freddy brought the show fully into the aura of the Hollywood show-biz world. He contributed no great changes, no ambitious schemes. But he knew how to manage the staff, and keep the show running on an even keel. And more important, he knew how to please Mr. John W. Carson. And as long as he did, his seat was secure, twenty feet away from Johnny each evening.

That was a lesson that Rudy Tellez thought he had learned until his contract as producer was not renewed. "When I left in 1971, I realized that there was no Johnny Carson," the former producer says. "Johnny Carson was the last person who talked to him. If I was the last person out of his dressing room before the show, he'd be up. If it was Freddy, who's sometimes a very depressing, oppressive person, Johnny would be down. He takes from whoever is next to him."

A few months before Johnny moved to Los Angeles, Joanne Carson had purchased a house above Sunset Drive near the campus of UCLA. The house was reached only after making a murderous hidden turn, a turn so dangerous as to discourage all but the invited and the intrepid. Except for the distant hissing of the cars below on Sunset Boulevard, the house could have been in a wooden glen far from Los Angeles.

When she first moved in, Joanne began to decorate the house with a strange, eclectic taste. She bought a porcelain elephant and placed it on the floor. She found old carved boxes and chests, throw rugs the color of ruby wine, a wolf-hair rug, cushions, and overstuffed sofas. She said once that it looked like a "Tibetan monastery updated and placed in Bel Air." She called the house "my Shangri-la."

Joanne renewed her career in television, hosting a celebrity interview show, *Joanne Carson's VIPs*. Although the Carson name and notoriety brought great initial interest in the syndicated program, some celebrities felt that if they wanted to please Johnny, they had better not be one of Joanne's VIPs. Joanne was too hyper, too fragile, for the relentless grind of a daily show, and she soon retreated into her Shangri-la.

Truman Capote, who remained her friend, used his considerable influence to introduce Joanne to the socially elite of Hollywood. Joanne began dating a movie star, Glenn Ford, which seemed not to set well with Johnny. "Four times in the last three weeks, he has made jokes at Ford's expense," wrote Joyce Haber in her Hollywood column. "The other night Carson said: 'I watched Glenn Ford and Edgar Buchanan in bed. They certainly are a lovable pair.' And why? I called Glenn to find out. He told me, 'Ever since I started going out with Joanne, he's been taking cracks at me. Any man who can't tell the difference between Joanne Carson and Edgar Buchanan obviously needs a doctor."

Ford was sufficiently upset to discuss a lawsuit. Buchanan threatened to beat "the living shit" out of Johnny.

One evening Haber, attending a party honoring Liza Minnelli, sat down at a table with Gene Kelly. To her horror, she watched as the headwaiter led Johnny and Joanna to the table. Haber felt that Johnny didn't like her ever since she ran a veiled item in which she suggested that he was having an affair with singer Phyllis McGuire, who was often his opening act on the road.

Johnny and Joanna sat down. "Johnny turned to me and said, 'The reason I don't like you is that you're a friend of my ex-wife.'"

Joanne had signed an agreement not to embarrass her former husband by saying anything derogatory, or else she would lose her alimony. Johnny learned that embarrassment is a flower with many blossoms. "He was my first and only love and I'm still in love with the guy," Joanne told columnist Earl Wilson, on June 21, 1972, when the divorce became final. "Johnny is a genius, and I'm still his No. 1 fan but I wasn't cut out to be married to such a high achiever. For 10 years I was living on the ragged edge of his genius."

Joanne told another reporter that "it has always been part of his NBC contract not to have to do his show from the West Coast. But as soon as I moved, he moved. I think he probably felt more comfortable, just being nearby."

Joanne believed that Joanna was her clone. "The first time he met her was at a party," she reported inaccurately. "She was standing with her back to him and he went right up to her, thinking it was me."

Despite the inaccuracy of her time scheme, Joanne told Earl Wilson that she assumed Johnny wanted the divorce to marry Joanna. He was purchasing a $500,000 house in Bel Air, where they would live.

Johnny might tolerate Joanne's sentimental musings, but not when she attempted to play matchmaker. "I don't know what she's assuming, but that's not true," Johnny said. "I have no plans to get married."

The April 9, 1972, issue of the *National Insider* outraged Johnny. The Chicago-based tabloid alleged that he was moving to Los Angeles to be closer to Joanna, the woman who had broken up his marriage. The tabloid didn't seem to realize that Joanna lived in New York and had met Johnny only after his separation.

Most stars learned to ignore even the most outrageous fabrications in the tabloids. But with Henry Bushkin riding shotgun, Carson attacked, suing the *National Insider*. By the time the case was finally settled, the tabloid was already out of business.

Johnny was, indeed, thinking about getting married. But twice burned, twice cautious, especially in California, with its new community-property law. If the marriage didn't work out, Joanna would be entitled to half of the assets he earned during their years together and half of the property that they owned.

Johnny did plan to buy a house at 400 St. Cloud Road in Bel Air, a private colony above Beverly Hills and Sunset Boulevard. The estate, owned by Mervyn and Kitty LeRoy, a prominent producer-director and his wife, was scarcely a bachelor's pad. Although the stuning modern home was almost all glass, privacy was provided by a glade of trees and several acres of land.

"I was flown out to L.A., and they were living in a rented house in Bel Air down a circular drive," says Stephen Mallory. "They were looking at the LeRoy house. I was asked to decorate that. That's when Joanna said, 'I'm going back to New York.' Johnny said, 'What do you mean?' She said, 'I'm putting Timmy in school.' And shortly thereafter they married."

Johnny had certain loose ends to tie up. He closed on the house before they got married so that it would not be part of community property. "That was such a shock to her," says Marjorie Reed, Joanna's close friend. "He was very uptight about money from the beginning. When he made sure the house closed before they got married, I said, 'That projects who you are.' "

As much as Joanna's friends may have had their doubts about Johnny's commitment, some of his friends had their doubts too. "I found Joanna as someone who belonged in some European court 300 or 400 years ago, not to trap but to entrap men," says one former close associate. "I believe that Joanna plotted the marriage. I believe it was a brilliantly calculated relationship. There was a certain kind of lack of warmth between the partners. There was something that you felt, like when you're in a meeting between two bankers.''

In Hollywood middle-aged men shed wives like snakes molting their skins. Ed McMahon was as Catholic as Notre Dame. Yet he left Alice, his wife of twenty-seven years, and his four children on the East Coast. Doc Severinsen sang a swan song to his wife, Yvonne. She ended up with seventy-five thousand dollars a year, a ranch, and cars.

Although Johnny's sons were largely grown up now, their father's possible marriage was still an important matter. Twenty-year-old Rick had gone into the navy to straighten out. While in the service he had been driving around Cranston, Rhode Island, when police found his behavior suspicious. They pulled his car over, searched the vehicle, and arrested him in Cranston on a charge of marijuana possession. In 1971 it was an incident that could have happened to millions of young Americans, and Rick received probation. But this was Johnny Carson's son, and Rick's picture made the New York papers.

''Remember some time ago you were the toastmaster at a testimonial dinner to me?'' Jack Benny asked as he sat onstage at Johnny's prime-time tenth-anniversary show. ''At this dinner I said that for many years *I've* been Johnny Carson's idol.''

''It's true,'' Johnny said, looking at the aging comedian who was an authentic show-business legend.

''And all of a sudden the whole thing switched,'' Benny said, not a trace of humor in his voice. Benny stopped a moment, longer than any other comedian would have dared to pause. ''And you want to know something. It's not as much fun this way.''

Johnny still idolized Benny, but *The Tonight Show* host was himself reaching semilegendary status. NBC didn't open the prime-time schedule and build a special set for ordinary stars. President Richard Nixon sent his greetings. Governor Ronald Reagan arrived by helicopter to congratulate Johnny.

Millions of Americans picked up on what Johnny said, and what he seemed to think. No one since Will Rogers had offered such effective political commentary. When Johnny raised his eyebrow, in a subtle aside to the audience, the guest was dismissed, finished, executed, dead. Men wanted to think like Johnny, look like Johnny, dress like Johnny. *The New York Times* wrote that "probably no performer in the modern era has had as much impact on style trends as Johnny Carson." In the entertainment industry, there was no more desired an invitation than to sit next to Johnny on *The Tonight Show*. Advertisers lined up to bask in his aura, selling their beer, deodorant, and dog food to a receptive audience.

Onstage this evening sat many of the biggest comedians in the business. Benny. George Burns. Joey Bishop. Don Rickles. Jerry Lewis.

"I have a list of weeks I've substituted for you, John," said Joey Bishop. Since his failure, Bishop was back in Johnny's good graces. "This isn't your tenth anniversary. It's your sixth and my fourth."

"It's hard to believe, but I've presented close to three hundred commercials on Alpo's behalf," Ed McMahon said, attempting a moment of levity. "It's the number-one canned dog food in America."

"Whatever you do, don't do this for ten more years," said George Burns, flicking on his cigar. "You're liable to end up with NBC all your life."

"We don't see each other socially, but I've begged," yelped Rickles.

"The exciting thing about doing a show like this is that you get a chance to get together with people," Johnny mused, his head swiveling to include everyone present. "We all live here, and I rarely see Joey or Ed."

"You don't see me much, either," interjected Jerry Lewis.

"Has it ever occurred that nobody likes you?" Johnny said. Lewis appeared stunned as much by the merry laughter as by the remark. "I say it just in jest. . . . He's hurt."

"No, no, no," said Lewis, suddenly thoughtful. Unable to top Johnny's joke, he died on a sword of presumed profundity. "There can be great truth in humor. They say it's close to tragedy."

The following evening Johnny's success was celebrated in what would become an annual ritual: an opulent dinner party in the Crystal Room of the Beverly Hills Hotel. The guests included not only *The Tonight Show* staff, but also a long list of celebrities and television executives. Most of the invited guests dressed formally, except for Flip Wilson, who came as a Playboy bunny.

"And heeeeere's Johnny," Ed said, introducing Johnny as if the dinner were *The Tonight Show*.

"A lot of columnists have been asking why me and my gal haven't set a date for the wedding," he said as the elegantly attired group sat quietly. "So I think I will tell you that we were married at 1:30 this afternoon."

Almost exactly twenty-three years earlier, on October 1, 1949, Johnny had walked down the aisle with Jody in a church on the windblown streets of North Platte, Nebraska. In New York City nine years ago he had stood in a church to take Joanne as his bride. He had walked down no aisle today, run no gamut of rice and well-wishers. His bride wore a stunning designer gown. He appeared as much a part of this Hollywood world as Rosalind Russell, Lucille Ball, or any of the other guests.

As the assemblage applauded, waiters wheeled an eleven-foot-high, eleven-tier wedding cake into the Crystal Room. Even at this moment, Don Rickles attempted to heckle Johnny.

"I've got ten years, you've got ten weeks," Johnny quipped, referring to Rickles's latest attempt at a television series. "You've killed two networks. Don't kill mine. From now on, it's Armed Forces Radio for you."

Flip Wilson flounced forward in his Playboy-bunny outfit, and planted a kiss on Johnny's cheek. He then kissed the bride; and as the orchestra struck up "Anniversary Waltz,"

Johnny led Flip around the dance floor. Next Flip danced with the bride.

Hollywood had endless parties, but few authentic celebrations.

"You really surprised the hell out of all of us," said Lucille Ball, the grande dame of television comedy. "We all love you."

"On my seventeenth anniversary they gave me a one-layer cake," complained Jack Benny.

"You know how long this marriage is going to last?" asked Don Adams, the comedian. "Would you believe it's going to last ten years? Would you believe five? It's over tomorrow."

Finally Johnny had his turn again. "I hope I never get too sophisticated and too involved to say I don't appreciate all this," he said, in a voice charged with sincerity. "I never thought I'd reach the point in my life when I would have this measure of success, and to have these people say all these things. It's really what it's all about and I thank you."

Johnny and Joanna settled into the house on St. Cloud Road. The new Mrs. Carson had a style and ambition suited for the largest stage. She hired a social secretary, and she and Johnny accepted invitations that Johnny and Joanne would have summarily dismissed. She also involved herself with charity work.

Joanna had never received much publicity before. The press accounts lauded her beauty and her youth, describing her as "a former model." Soon after she married Johnny, however, a few stories appeared that had less flattering references to her past.

In March 1971 Max Kettner had sued Joanna in the New York County Supreme Court seeking to recover the $160,000 that he said he lent her. The legal process had taken many months, and now had reached public attention.

"It's the silliest thing when you're going out with someone and then you wake up and say you're moving to California and getting married and Max can't take it," Joanna says. "I didn't know anything about the suit until I came to Los Angeles and had been married a couple of months. I was outraged. I said, 'Have you gone mad?' He manufactured a story. And all of a sudden it's in the paper. There was no truth to it at all.

"I was shocked that this person said I owed him that. I was newly married. I had to hire a lawyer. It was my first lesson of public life, that people would take shots. Before that, who would care? It was dumb. I didn't have that much to do with him, either."

Despite what Joanna says now, in 1974 the New York Supreme Court noted that "on an examination before trial defendant [Joanna Carson] admitted receipt of the funds but claimed that the payments constituted a gift. She further testified that the parties had had a close personal relationship and contemplated marriage." New York civil law states that if a person gives a gift to a fiancée and the romance ends, then the gift must be returned. Kettner's lawyer, Irving Schneider, sought to amend the complaint. In May 1974 the New York Supreme Court, Appellate Division, ruled in Kettner's favor.

Kettner appeared poised to win final victory in court. This man who had so cavalierly given or lent Joanna $160,000 was now in severe financial trouble himself. He allegedly faced the prospect of other court battles, in which he was not so likely to be the winner. He left the country, a decision that pleased Joanna and her lawyer if it pleased almost no one else.

Johnny was quite possibly embarrassed by the revelations. His new marriage was not proving idyllic. In 1974, after less than two years of conjugal life, the Carsons secretly separated. Johnny moved out his clothes and other possessions and took up residence in a house in a nearby neighborhood. He had made his marital woes a national joke, but he was not ready to laugh at his latest marriage. Three months later he returned to the great house on St. Cloud, and he and Joanna resumed their married life.

Joanna devoted much of her energies to SHARE (Share Happily And Reap Endlessly), a prestigious Los Angeles charity that each year puts on an amateur theatrical attended by the Hollywood elite. The ladies spend months preparing for the show, which features a chorus line of the wives of Hollywood stars and other notables. One SHARE member remembers Joanna "lying on the floor cutting out decorations for one of our benefits." Joanna worked her way up in the organization to vice-president and finally to president. Johnny helped Joanna by appearing as master of ceremonies.

One evening Joanna invited a SHARE group to her house for a dinner party. Joanna was not the only stunning woman in the organization. "Johnny followed me into one of the other rooms," recalls one of the SHARE ladies. "He said, 'You're so beautiful.' I was really flustered. He tried to kiss me. I walked away angry. I thought that he had a lot of nerve. He said, 'I'm not through with you.' He kept his promise. After the SHARE show he sat down next to me. He said, 'You aren't ever home. I keep calling but I always get your maid.' "

On October 13, 1972, at seven-thirty in the evening, Richard and Linda Culkin were leaving a launderette near Universal Studios. They noticed Johnny talking on a pay phone in the shopping-center parking lot, far from the haunts of Beverly Hills and Bel Air. The young couple had done their wash for the week, and they decided to follow Johnny. If they were lucky, they might have a chance to talk to their idol and even get an autograph.

Johnny drove north on Lankershim Boulevard to Oxnard Street. There he took a left turn and drove into a parking lot near a Spanish-style apartment building. When Johnny slowed down, the Culkins decided to catch up to him. They didn't see Johnny get out of the car, leave a suitcase, and drive off. Nor did they see a man hurry out of the shadows to pick up the suitcase.

As the Culkins' car moved forward, a throng of police

cars descended on them. Policemen ran up, aimed shotguns at their heads, and pulled them out of their car. The officers handcuffed the hapless young couple and pushed them into a patrol car. "They threw me onto the floor and this man asked me what I had been doing," Richard Culkin said later. "When I said I had just been following Carson, he nailed me right then on my head with his fist. I was hit about 30 times in my body and face. And once they threatened they'd throw me out on the highway and I wouldn't live through the night if I didn't tell the truth. They opened the car door part way so I could hear the road pass . . . They kept saying obscene things about my wife, called me a fag and kept hitting me during most of the ride."

The Culkins had stumbled into the midst of an extortion plot. The week before, workers at Johnny's Bel Air home had discovered a fake hand grenade, binoculars, and an extortion note demanding $250,000 ("Do not insult your intelligence by dismissing this matter.") Johnny called the police. A few days later a man phoned the NBC studios and directed Johnny to a phone booth in the shopping-center parking lot. There, he was to wait with $250,000 in twenty- and fifty-dollar denominations to receive further instructions for the drop-off point.

After the extortionist, Richard Dziabacinski, a twenty-six-year-old German alien, was arrested as he tried to pick up the suitcase, the police subdued him in sufficiently exuberant fashion that he needed to be hospitalized. Richard Culkin also required medical treatment. Four days later Dziabacinski was charged with extortion and possessing a sawed-off rifle. At the same time a judge released the Culkins from jail, presumably to leave celebrity-chasing to the tabloids.

During the episode Johnny had special police protection. He had already learned to be cautious. He didn't touch any of the cakes, candies, and cookies that fans sent him. "Somebody may try to poison me," he had told his secretary, Charlotte Clish, in New York City. One day Charlotte and her assistant tried some homemade taffy that had arrived in the mail. They ended up with violent diarrhea, presumably from a laxative mixed in the candy.

Joanna continued trying to create an elegant private world in which Johnny would feel safe and happy. She did not merely buy style and image from decorators and fashion consultants. She knew what she wanted, down to the smallest detail.

The great glass house was situated among trees, behind high walls and a black electric gate. Johnny had a tennis court, where he played almost daily. He had a gym in the basement, where he worked out to maintain his excellent physical condition, and a separate house and office built next to the main house, decorated predominantly in brown with casual California-style furniture. For a time his office contained only one place to sit down, a barber chair situated in the center of the room.

The mansion on St. Cloud Road required a small troupe of helpers. Cooks. Carpenters. Pool men. Window cleaners. A full-time maid. An indoor plant service. A gardener. Cars had to be serviced: Joanna's Mercedes 450 and eighty-thousand-dollar Rolls-Royce Corniche convertible, and Johnny's Mercedes too. In 1982 Joanna's budget for household salaries was $59,360; groceries $16,926; cable television $1,443; utilities $13,522; and water $898. The round-the-clock guards at the electrical gate cost $71,000, paid for by NBC.

Johnny and Joanna were forever having problems finding and keeping good help. One German domestic took on all the airs of an aristocrat, insisting on a bottle of Johnny's finest wine each day and keeping banker's hours. Johnny threw him out one night. Another servant decided to quit of his own accord, leaving the house empty while the Carsons were in Las Vegas. Johnny refused to pay the man's final week of salary.

The Carsons were happy when they hired a friendly couple. Unfortunately the amiability was fueled on liquor.

When Johnny discovered them drunk in the kitchen one morning, he called a cab and tossed them out. Joanna left to take her son, Timmy, to school. Returning home, she discovered Johnny hard at work in the kitchen sweeping the floor. Around his forehead he wore a bandanna. Below that, he was naked.

The house on St. Cloud Road was a stage setting that Gatsby would have appreciated. But the stage was kept empty. The Carsons threw no great parties. They invited few people to their home.

The Carsons didn't accept many invitations, either. In July of 1977, when Joanna was in New York, Johnny did attend a party at the Beverly Hills home of Irving Lazar. Lazar, who looks like an aging, bleached smurf, is an agent who represents many prominent novelists, screenwriters, and directors.

A connoisseur of celebrity, Lazar had this evening invited an impressive list, including stars Tony Curtis and Gregory Peck, producer Ray Stark, director Richard Brooks, and songwriter Sammy Cahn. Even in this crowd, Johnny was the focus of attention.

Johnny said hello to Freddy de Cordova, in whose honor this party was being held. Then he worked his way through the packed living room and out the sliding glass windows, to stand alone by the swimming pool. As he stared out into the night, a waiter brought him a soft drink.

A half hour later Johnny sat at a poolside table and chatted with some of the guests. He had no jokes to tell, no anecdotes with which to regale his listeners. He was polite— no less, no more. As soon as he was able, he got up and slipped away.

Joanna tried to get Johnny to see more of the world. Her husband had never even been to Europe. Starting in the mid-1970's, the Carsons began making annual trips to England for the Wimbledon tennis matches and then to southern France, almost always in the company of Henry and Judy Bushkin. The trips to Wimbledon were set up as business excursions for NBC. Johnny believed that "it is essential to my career to be seen at such events and I customarily am shown on international television coverage as a spectator.''

Joanna loved the Hotel du Cap in Antibes. Johnny was not as enchanted by southern France. He had lived most of his adult life as a celebrity, but here on the Riviera he was just another rich American.

Johnny didn't know how to enjoy a vacation. ''One year I suggested why don't we go to this restaurant in the port of Nice,'' recalls Joanna's close friend Marjorie Reed. ''When I met Joanna at the place, I asked, 'Where's Johnny?' Joanna said, 'He's playing solitaire in his room.' ''

Another year Carmen traveled with the Carsons to Hotel Du Cap. ''Johnny was very uptight when you first met him,'' says Carmen. ''He had comments about my taking photos, and I always take photos. He didn't enjoy himself too much on the trip. He appeared to enjoy it when people recognized him.''

In Bel Air Johnny spent hours by himself in his office. The St. Cloud estate was on several acres of land, but in 1978 Johnny became upset at the sound of dogs barking day and night at his neighbors' houses. He filed suit against those nearest him: Sonny Bono, Daryoush Mahboubi-Fardi, and Raphael Cohen. Johnny wouldn't tolerate distractions.

Cohen knew that it wasn't *his* dog howling all night. And had his own list of complaints against his next-door neighbor, including tennis-court lights that beamed onto his grounds, drum playing morning and night, and loud rock music. Cohen considered Johnny—who hadn't even bothered to talk to him before filing suit—more a nasty misanthrope than a neighbor.

''Mahboubi-Fardi cross-filed against Carson and mailed a list of unbelievable questions to Carson, like what time do you go to bed, what time do you have sex?'' Cohen says. ''And ultimately Carson dropped the lawsuit.''

Being the son of a famous man is as often a curse as it is a blessing. Chris, Cory, and Rick had grown up with a double burden: children of fame and children of divorce. Johnny had been a father of special occasions, of Christmas vacations and weekends. Jody had wandered in and out of their lives like a guest.

Johnny could not give his sons the full emotional sustenance of a father's caring, but he could give them money. And as the three boys grew to manhood, he began allowing them an annual stipend, passed out each Christmas. It was not enough so that they could live extravagant life-styles, but it was enough to sustain them.

Chris had been a surrogate father to his two younger brothers, and much of his childhood had been stolen from him. Like Rick and Cory, Chris found it difficult to commit himself fully to anything, to care enough to risk failure. Of the three young Carsons, he was the only one to go to college and graduate, with a degree in psychology. He had his father's good looks, and smoldering sensual eyes that would have served him well in Hollywood. He had inherited his grandfather Kit's athletic ability, and his hopes of becoming a golf pro did not seem outrageous. He wanted nothing of Los Angeles. After college he decided to live in Fort Lauderdale, Florida. Each Christmas he flew to Los Angeles to receive his check, but his life in Fort Lauderdale was something of a mystery, even to his brothers.

Rick still presented a problem to Johnny. In February 1973, while Rick was driving an automobile registered to his father, the vehicle struck guard rails on the Connecticut turnpike. State police discovered thirty-seven Quaaludes in the car and charged Rick with drug possession, operating a vehicle while taking drugs, and driving without a license. He was put on probation.

Rick had become involved with Natalie Kosbubal, a pretty, unpretentious young woman who appeared to love him for himself and not for the goodies and perks. "Rick became abusive when he was drunk," Kosbubal says. "We had many discussions about it. I don't think Rick remembered half of what he did. I don't know if he was trying to be like his father.

"When Rick's attacks became too extreme, I called Johnny in Los Angeles and asked him to come back to New York to help. To this day I can't believe that I did that. Rick was upset. But to me, Johnny was simply Rick's father.

"Johnny acted like a regular father, a concerned father who didn't want to see two people ruining their lives. He said that before something happened, we should separate for a while. He said that if there is love there, you'll always feel that love. It will survive everything if it's strong enough. I can't believe he said that, but he did. I listened to the advice. We stopped living together."

Rick moved to Los Angeles and became an associate director of NBC's *Tomorrow Show*, his first important position in television. One of the tribulations of having a famous father was that whatever he accomplished, he could never live up to his dad, and when he failed, people clucked their lips knowingly, saying that was Johnny Carson's son. "Rick has always shown the desire to be a director, but he's afraid that people will say, 'Oh, you got where you got because your father's Johnny Carson,' " Natalie says. "He's always seemed afraid to go out on his own. The boys have all gotten money. They've never had to struggle. When someone gets to know him, Rick runs away, because he may be afraid that he's going to be seen for what he is."

Cory had a part-time job on *The Tonight Show* assisting the band, running errands, helping set up the music, and occasionally working as stage manager. Like his brother, Rick, Cory was talented enough to succeed in television. He had the kind of job he could have gotten on his own, but he was hired as Johnny's son. He dreamed, however, of becoming a classical guitarist, and he spent the rest of the day taking lessons and practicing. Some of his friends didn't even know that this lean, sensitive-looking young man was Johnny Carson's son. There was a certain resemblance, but even on the set of *The Tonight Show* new employees had to be told that Cory was Johnny's youngest son.

One day, while Cory was working as the stage manager,

Johnny rehearsed a Tarzan skit with Betty White, an actress who appears often on *The Tonight Show*, and Tommy Newsom. Johnny played an aged Tarzan, Betty, an equally aged Jane, and Tommy, the middle-aged "boy." Johnny walked on the set garbed in a grungy leopard skin, wearing a wig that looked as if a full vacuum-cleaner bag had been dumped on his head.

Cory shook his head as his father approached. "Oh, my God!" he exclaimed. "You're my father, and I can't hardly look at you."

Johnny walked up to his youngest son and put his arm around Cory. "Son," he said, as Roy Ratliff, the cameraman, listened. "You know the reason your father has to dress like this is so you can sit under a tree and play your guitar."

FOURTEEN

"**O**kay, send the kids in," Johnny said to his secretary over the intercom.

Into Johnny's office walked twenty-seven-year old Dick Ebersol, NBC's director of late-night programming, and twenty-nine-year old Lorne Michaels, the producer of NBC's forthcoming ninety-minute series *NBC's Saturday Night*.

Johnny was sweating over his monologue, his denim shirt marked by perspiration. He looked up and saw that Ebersol had shoulder-length hair, thick glasses, and a gentle, benign manner. Michaels's hair was a more conventional length, but he was wearing jeans, the de rigueur outfit of the sixties, topped by a flamboyant Hawaiian shirt and a green corduroy jacket.

"So you guys are only going to be on one night a week, huh?" Johnny said.

Ebersol and Michaels knew that they were doing their new show because of Johnny's power at NBC. Johnny was no longer happy having NBC rerun old *Tonight Shows* on Saturday evening. Less than half the NBC affiliates picked up the programs. The ratings were humiliatingly bad. NBC had even taken to handing out free spots as a bonus for advertising placed on other programs. Failure is a disease that spreads from the extremities, and Johnny wanted the reruns taken off the air.

"Well, guys," Johnny said, "I've heard about your show, and I think we've really got to talk about it. It's got similarities to mine."

Johnny was rigidly protective of his own turf.

"What we really have is a comedy-variety show as opposed to a comedy-talk show," Ebersol said.

"Well, we have variety here too," Johnny countered. He always said that *The Tonight Show* was *not* a talk show, but a variety show. To Johnny, a talk show meant William F. Buckley, Jr., or David Susskind, two talking heads speaking three-syllable words.

"You mean there's going to be no talk or interviews?" Johnny asked.

"No, none at all."

Johnny posed some more questions about the new show and then said good-bye. "Just one night a week?" he asked as his guests left the office. He didn't want to be the midwife to a show that would one day challenge his sovereignty over late night.

Saturday Night was one night a week, but one night unlike anything television had seen before. Steve Martin watched its premiere on October 11, 1975, in Aspen, Colorado. The comedian thought, Fuck, they did it. They did the show everyone should have been doing.

George Carlin was the host. The comedian said things he never would have said on *The Tonight Show*. In his closing monologue he suggested that God was only "a semisupreme being" because "everything He has ever made died." Chevy Chase anchored a satirical newscast. He quoted a mock–Gerald Ford campaign slogan: "If he's so dumb, how come he's president?" He cited a Teamster official's comment that the missing Jimmy Hoffa "will always be a cornerstone in the organization." Johnny made fun of Ford and Hoffa too, but he never went so far as not only to dance out on the precipice of bad taste, but happily, arrogantly, to step over it.

Tom Shales, the most influential TV critic in America, wrote in the *Washington Post*, "*NBC's Saturday Night* can boast the freshest satire on commercial TV, but it is more than that. It is probably the first network series produced by and for the television generation . . . a live, lively, raucously disdainful view of a world that television has largely shaped. Or misshaped.''

Chevy Chase became the first star of the show. In December 1975 *New York* magazine put Chase on the cover, calling him Johnny Carson's heir apparent. "I'd never be tied down for five years interviewing TV personalities,'' Chase said disdainfully, rejecting the dreary idea of doing the same thing every night. He made it clear that for him and his colleagues, Johnny and *The Tonight Show* epitomized the deadly formulas of commercial television.

Johnny was not an admirer of *Saturday Night*. "I've seen some very clever things on the show and they have some very bright young people,'' he told Tom Shales in remarks that he probably forgot to make off-the-record. "But basically they do a lot of drug jokes, a lot of what I would consider sophomoric humor and a lot of stuff I find exceptionally cruel, under the guise of being hip. . . . One night the show ended a minute and a half early. There were eight people—eight people—standing there onstage and not one of them could think of anything to say. They can't ad-lib a fart at a bean-eating contest.''

Johnny was incensed at a joke about a Professor Backwards, bludgeoned to death while passersby ignored his pleas of "pleh, pleh.'' He found the joke "particularly vicious,'' considering it the "kind of joke you tell at a private party. You don't tell it on television.''

Johnny was the establishment. The establishment always condemns the young for their bad taste and bad manners; what it fears is their youth, energy, and innovation. The young, for their part, imagine that they will never compromise, never settle into the routines of their elders.

Saturday Night took a few digs at Johnny. On one show Jane Curtin, as an anchorwoman, reported that *The Tonight Show* planned to go live, a change from "doing the show dead for the past fifteen years.''

Johnny was not about to promote these upstarts. Although Chase was supposedly set to be a guest host, he did not even appear as a guest until he had already left *Saturday Night*. None of the other Not Ready for Prime Time Players ever appeared on *The Tonight Show*. Gilda Radner was the next former *Saturday Night* performer to appear, and that was not until 1983.

"It was trouble between me and Johnny," says Chevy Chase. "It was not because we had any anger or rancor between us. Nobody ever came to me to talk about taking over *The Tonight Show*. It was just always in the press. At that time I didn't feel that hosting *The Tonight Show* was the direction I was going in, and I didn't voice it in a nice way. So for a while I didn't even get on the show. All I had to do was to write Johnny a letter, apologizing for any remarks I may have made, and say I think you're great, and say I want to be on the show."

By the time Chevy Chase finally hosted *The Tonight Show* in November 1986, a great deal had changed. Belushi was dead, OD'd on cocaine and heroin in a suite at the Château Marmont. Chase had had his own struggles with drugs and liquor, and was just out of the Betty Ford Clinic. Jane Curtin was starring in a situation comedy, the very form that it had once seemed the Not Ready for Prime Time Players might make obsolete by their sheer audacity and brilliance. Bill Murray, Chase, Aykroyd, and Eddie Murphy had become movie stars, doing films that were often not that much different from their elders'. Like almost everyone else in Hollywood, they came on *The Tonight Show* to promote themselves. And Johnny was still there, doing what he always did.

"It was very tough to be the guest host," says Chase. "I had just come out of a rehabilitation clinic, and I was a little nervous. The monologue was tough, because I had never done one in my life. I had put it together very fast. The most difficult were the interviews. Johnny has a philosophy about his guests. It's basically if you make your guests look good, you look good. I tell you, it's tough. He listens very carefully and he responds well, and he has obviously caught the heart of Middle America. It's tough.''

One day Craig Tennis walked into Johnny's office. ''I want to write a murder mystery using *The Tonight Show* as a backdrop,'' said the talent coordinator. ''It'll be a comedy-mystery.''

''That's an interesting idea,'' Johnny replied, as Tennis remembers. ''Who gets killed?''

''You do. Right after the monologue.''

Johnny blanched. ''Can't you have me just badly injured but recover?''

Tennis explained that he was going to research the book by asking *The Tonight Show* staff who they thought would murder Johnny. ''Listen, John, if it looks like you may live, people won't have the courage to say what they feel about you.''

Johnny laughed at the thought. ''Go ahead, kid,'' he said, giving his blessing to the project.

Tennis decided that on the night Johnny was murdered he would have as a guest Joseph Wambaugh, the writer and former Los Angeles police officer. Wambaugh would be assigned to investigate the case.

Tennis went around the studio playing Wambaugh investigating the crime. ''It took people about six seconds to get into the past tense,'' recalls Tennis. The staff took immense pleasure in their task, imagining Johnny's murder in exquisite detail. They had endless suggestions on how the deed was done. The only problem was that Tennis had more suspects than an Agatha Christie novel.

Johnny called Tennis into his office. ''How are you coming on the book, Craig?'' he asked.

''I've got a first draft, but I'm not going to show it to anyone.''

''Please don't,'' Johnny replied. ''If you've been paid any advance, I'll make it up to you. But I've had another threat on my life. I don't want people to get another idea of a way to kill me.''

* * *

While some of his staff members might take momentary delight in imagining Johnny's death, for most of them *The Tonight Show* was the apex of their careers. The jobs were lucrative sinecures, and most of the production people stayed on and on. Shirley Wood began work on the show when Jack Paar was still the host. Over the years she had grown from a sexy ingenue into a tough-spoken matron who vowed to remain on as a talent coordinator as long as Johnny remained; she in fact retired in 1988. Bob Dolce, another talent coordinator, had worked on the show for years. Bobby Quinn, the director, had begun on *The Tonight Show* as stage manager during the Paar era. Peter Lassally had been the associate producer for over a decade. (Lassally was eventually named producer, but it was a title largely without meaning, since De Cordova, as executive producer, kept the power.)

The writers, however, continued to live and die in thirteen-week cycles. Most of them came and went, leaving behind only a few anecdotes. Johnny rarely saw anything of them but their written words.

When Johnny first moved to Los Angeles, one of his main monologue writers was George Tricker, who looked more like a sumo wrestler than a comedy writer. Tricker had not graduated from high school because he had flunked English. He drove trucks and tended bar among other jobs until he began writing jokes for Joan Rivers, who got him his break on *The Tonight Show*. When the Writers Guild went on strike, Tricker returned to one of his other former professions, selling cars.

Among the writers Tricker was known as the Ox, an appellation that he lived up to as best he could. He had the only office at NBC decorated with a car tire hanging from a long rope, a furnishing more often found in the gorilla cage at the zoo.

The writers often went across the boulevard to Pepe's, a Mexican restaurant. "What can we have, Ox?" the writers asked Tricker.

Tricker ordered drinks. "Why do you do that?" asked Pancho, the bartender.

"We don't want to upset Ox," the writers said.

When a new man joined the staff, the writers told the waiter that he was not to serve him until "Ox" arrived and gave his okay. The new writer sat *sans* drink, a look of stark fear on his face, waiting to hear the heavy tread of "Ox."

Tricker thought of starting a comedy duo with another of the writers, Pat McCormick, a rotund and volatile Irishman. They would call themselves the Tornado Brothers and practice humor through terror. McCormick was a Harvard graduate, though he was about as Ivy League as Attila the Hun.

McCormick had honed his outrageousness to a fine point. He dropped his pants more often than GIs at an army induction center. At the height of the streaking craze, he dashed across *The Tonight Show* stage wearing nothing but a Johnny Carson mask. He was enough of a professional —and knew his employer well enough—to wait until Johnny finished his monologue. NBC would have stripped McCormick of his job, but Johnny went to his defense.

McCormick knew that he lived or died by the number of jokes he got on the show each evening. "We'd joke about the count for the day, who got what," McCormick says. "It was very competitive."

McCormick hung around Johnny more than the other writers did. He usually stayed to watch the monologue, unlike Tricker, who each afternoon would go down to the office of the man who wrote the cue cards to see how many of his jokes had made it. "That was your barometer of whether you were hired or fired," says Tricker. "You were safe with four jokes a day. You were borderline with three. If you went a couple days without any jokes, you were in trouble. And it always seemed to come at the time of contract renewal. I always wondered whether that was a deliberate ploy, but I think that was more writer paranoia.

"Your only jeopardy was if he didn't pick jokes. If he picked the joke and it died, that was fine. I have to give him credit for that. He figured he chose the joke. If the audience didn't understand it, that was his problem."

After a year and a half Freddy gave Tricker the message that all the writers dreaded. He was fired. Tricker knew that this was Johnny's decision. He felt, however, that the producer took peculiar delight in delivering the bad news.

Tricker had packed everything up and moved out to California to take the job. He had eight children to support. He didn't know anybody. He was desperate. He went to Johnny's office and asked to speak to him.

"I understand that you want to fire me," Tricker said, as he recalls. "But could you give me a thirteen-week cycle so I can find something else?"

"Yeah, okay," Johnny said. He hated people asking him for favors, but Tricker had couched his request irresistibly. He had not puffed himself up self-righteously to say that a mistake had been made. He had merely asked for some more time.

During the next weeks Tricker got on a roll, writing joke after joke that Johnny used. One day Tricker had a dozen jokes in the monologue, and Johnny called to thank him and tell him he was good. When the thirteen weeks were up, he was hired for a new cycle.

Tricker's good luck couldn't last forever. After another year Freddy told him he was through. This time the comedy writer knew he would get no reprieve. It had been a great two-and-a-half years while it lasted. Tricker said good-bye, took the tire down, and left *The Tonight Show* for good.

The other writers gave Tricker a trophy. Engraved on the bottom were the words:

THE LAST ANNUAL OX AWARD
To George who we will always love and fear

The entire staff of *The Tonight Show* knew that their jobs were no more secure than Johnny's will and whim. When Freddy took over as producer, Johnny gave him an autographed photograph on which he had written *Thanks,*

Freddy, after crossing out the names of the previous producers, Perry, Art, Stan, and Rudy.

"There was a ritual when you left," says Nick Arnold,
another writer who made the journey from New York to
Los Angeles. "You had to go tell Johnny. It was strange,
since all the time that you were there it didn't seem to matter
if you were there or not."

Arnold lived in a seventh-floor apartment on Sunset Boulevard, opposite the Comedy Store, the famous showcase
for new talent. During his months in Los Angeles Arnold
drank a prodigious amount of bourbon. Being a frugal sort,
he saved the empty bottles until his last evening in the City
of Angels.

Arnold threw an empty bottle out the window, watching
it sail downward, splashing into a thousand fragments on
the sidewalk. This created nary a stir. He threw a second
bottle, and a third, bottle after bottle, case after case. Still
no crowds of outraged citizenry, no patrol cars, no search-
lights scanning the sky. He proceeded to throw his furniture
out the window. Finally he stood alone, silhouetted in the
Los Angeles night, *sans* bourbon, *sans* bottles, *sans* furniture. He fell asleep on the floor.

One evening when Johnny was having dinner with Jack
Benny, Benny chastised Johnny for using dirty material on
The Tonight Show. The next afternoon he scheduled a meeting with the writers, an event the writers anticipated as if
it were an appointment for root-canal work.

At precisely two o'clock the writers marched into Johnny's office, where Johnny and Freddy were waiting.

"I can't do this filth," Johnny said.

"No, Johnny doesn't do this filth," Freddy parroted.

"Any of the filth we've submitted in particular?" asked
Hank Bradford, the head writer.

Johnny was especially upset over a skit in which he played
a doctor. Johnny was to kiss and hug a sexy woman in his
office, telling her that he liked to get as close to his patients

as possible. As she left, the camera pulled back to reveal a sign, DR. CARSON—VETERINARIAN. The camera pulled back even farther to show the sexy lady leading the patient, a chicken on a leash.

"I don't fuck chickens," Johnny said, a statement about which there was no dispute.

"Mr. Carson doesn't fuck chickens!" Freddy parroted.

"I don't do this sort of thing. I never have, and I don't ever want another sketch that suggests I do fuck chickens."

"Perhaps we could change the chicken to a beaver," Bradford suggested gently.

Johnny heaved the offensive scripts back at Bradford. Although the writers never again submitted such a skit to Johnny, they soon returned to the frequently risqué humor that was his forte and signature.

"Mr. Carson alone presides over our consciousness," wrote John Leonard in *The New York Times* in October 1975. "When *he* began making Watergate jokes, we knew it was permissible to ridicule the President, that Mr. Nixon was done for. . . . Johnny Carson is crystallized cynicism. Such, too, seems to be the mood of his constituency."

The country had backed off the passions and causes of the sixties, to a position almost as disengaged as Johnny's. His bipartisan putdown of politics and politicians reflected the mood of mid-America.

Johnny read the public pulse nightly. He saw a pattern to the course of public scandals. If Johnny got beyond the public mood, his jokes sounded partisan or petty or petulant. There came a time when such matters as Nixon's improprieties, Wilbur Mills's womanizing, or Billy Carter's drinking became rich founts of humor. Then, as often as not, the events turned tragic, or dark, and the jokes didn't work anymore.

George Tricker remembers the day in August 1973 when Judge John J. Sirica ruled that Nixon had to give up the Watergate tapes. It was the beginning of the end for the thirty-seventh president of the United States. Johnny tried some more Nixon jokes, but it was like starting a car with a dead battery.

"I think our studio audience is a good barometer of how the country is feeling," Johnny said. "Five hundred people can give you a pretty accurate indication; you can see right away what is fair game. When Agnew first got started, and nobody had heard of him, he was a great target for jokes. Then when he was in trouble, you could sense that a lot of people were pretty hard hit by that in Middle America. Wilbur Mills was funny for a while, then you find out the poor guy's an alcoholic."

Johnny was far from being a political activist. On one occasion, however, he sent thousands of people out into the street. The episode began in November 1973, when Representative Harold V. Froehlich issued a press release stating that "the Government Printing Office is facing a serious shortage of paper."

The media pay as much attention to a printed statement from an obscure congressman as garbage collectors do to a crushed can. On December 11, Froehlich issued a second press release on the same subject: "The United States may face a serious shortage of toilet paper within a few months. . . . A toilet paper shortage is no laughing matter. It is a problem that will touch every American."

This time the congressman was not ignored. On December 19, Johnny mentioned a news item about the alleged shortage. "You know, we've got all sorts of shortages these days," he said in his monologue. "But have you heard the latest? I'm not kidding. I saw it in the paper. There's a shortage of toilet paper."

The next day agitated shoppers from the Bronx to Seattle filled up their shopping carts with bathroom tissue. The hapless consumers who arrived too late found only bare shelves. Johnny attempted to calm the agitated masses. "I don't want to be remembered as the man who created a false toilet-paper scare," he said on *The Tonight Show*. "I just picked up the item from the paper and enlarged on it somewhat and made some jokes as to what they could do about it. There's no shortage."

In Chester, Pennsylvania, the world's largest toilet-paper plant continued spewing out seventy-five-hundred miles of tissue a day. Slowly Americans moved on to new anxieties, and the Great Toilet Paper Run became only a memory.

One evening Johnny had as guests Bob Hope, Dean Martin, and George Gobel. When Johnny started in network television in the 1950's, George Gobel was television's most successful comedian. By the time Johnny moved *The Tonight Show* to Los Angeles, Gobel was largely forgotten. Johnny had Gobel on dead last.

"Johnny, I'm very glad to be here and I want to tell you that without me your show tonight would have been nothing," Gobel said, slightly slurring his words. As Johnny admitted later, both Gobel and Martin were "slightly in the bag."

The audience laughed. Gobel sucked on a cigarette.

"I'm glad you saved me," Johnny said.

"You know when you come on last," Gobel said as he cradled a glass in his hand. "Do you ever get the feeling that the world was a tuxedo and you're a pair of brown shoes?"

The audience continued to laugh, though not at the right moment. Gobel finally figured out what was happening. Dean Martin was upstaging the comedian by knocking the ash off his cigarette into the comedian's drink.

Nobody dropped ashes into Johnny's drink. *The Hollywood Reporter* called him "the highest salaried performer in television history." He was so powerful and so important to NBC that in the spring of 1974 the network renegotiated his contract a year early. The new three-year contract not only gave him Monday nights off but included an extraordinary number of vacation weeks. In the first eight months of 1975 Johnny appeared only slightly more than half the time, 96 out of 179 shows.

Instead of lolling around the pool during his frequent

holidays, Johnny continued to play Las Vegas. In August 1974 he signed a contract with Caesars Palace for a reported $200,000 a week for one show a night. This represented a $75,000 increase over his salary at the Sahara Hotel for two performances nightly. The new contract made Johnny probably the highest-paid performer in Las Vegas, earning even more than Elvis Presley or Frank Sinatra. After the Caesars contract ended, he returned to the familiar haunts of the Sahara.

On October 1, 1974, NBC placed a large ad in *The Los Angeles Times* congratulating Johnny "on the twelfth anniversary of the longest-running and most successful late-night entertainment series in the history of network television." That evening Bob Howard, the NBC president, appeared onstage during the *Tonight Show*'s two-hour anniversary special.

"Do you realize that Americans have watched you for twenty-two-billion hours?" Howard asked, as if Johnny might himself have added up all the hours that viewers had tuned into *The Tonight Show*. "You've been on over thirty-five-hundred hours. That means you could stay on day and night for five months."

Howard then presented NBC's number-one star with a watch, a gift more appropriate to a retiring doorman than to the performer responsible for up to 17 percent of the network's earnings.

Whatever NBC saved on gifts, they lost each time they signed Johnny to a new contract. In 1976 the network once again signed Johnny a year early, this time for over $3 million a year.

Henry negotiated all Johnny's contracts. To NBC, the attorney was at times "Bombastic Bushkin," as Johnny characterized him on *The Tonight Show*—irascible, unruly, unreasonable, and usually victorious. That was the image that Johnny and his writers had created for Henry, a useful as well as amusing caricature. Henry patrolled the perimeters of Johnny's interests, attacking with lawsuits and threats. He allowed Johnny to keep a benign distance from the negotiations and various enemies.

Henry became a major player in Hollywood, a deal maker, one of the people in Hollywood who could make things happen. Certainly he was no longer the young lawyer who took the subway back to his home in Queens each evening.

"He stopped being himself the day we moved out here," says Judy Bushkin, his former wife. "I grew up calling him 'Hank.' I started calling him 'Henry,' because he became a totally different person."

From the way Henry moved around Hollywood, it seemed that he had been at the epicenter of money, power, and celebrity all his life. He had the great house in Beverly Hills that Arthur Kassel had predicted would be his, and was a millionaire many times over.

In Los Angeles Henry and Johnny became for each other the friend and confidant that neither man had ever had before. "I don't know if Henry can think of anyone as a friend, except for Johnny," says Judy Bushkin. "I've never known Henry to be really close to anybody except Johnny. I think that was true of Johnny as well. They had each other, and that was that."

In the world in which Johnny and Henry lived, men rarely had such close friendships. The two men worked together. They played tennis together. They went on vacations together. Joanna and Henry liked one another too. They had something in common that nobody else had: They knew what it was like being around Johnny.

Henry was always available. In his enormous private office in his Century City law firm, he kept a phone on his desk for direct calls from Johnny alone. Johnny called every day, often several times. No one else touched that phone. If it rang when Henry was out, the secretary noted in her telephone message book that "J. C." had called.

Judy Bushkin kept the nasal twang of New York in her voice, and she kept her New York skepticism as well. She lived the life of a Beverly Hills matron, but she recognized the life around her for what it was. A woman of intelligence and spirit, she experienced the "bombastic" side of her husband too. She also saw Henry's shy, private side, and she realized that Henry and Johnny had such a profound friendship because they were much alike. Henry was a man who did not seek the limelight, who shrank from publicity. He was a suspicious man who confided fully in no one.

"Henry loved Johnny and was willing to take care of him like a child," says a woman close to Henry. "He talked of him like a little person who needed to be protected. And Henry was willing to protect him from whatever came against him."

As close as the two men were, it was not a friendship between equals. Henry was on call for matters large and small. He picked up after Johnny, after his girlfriends, after his excesses. Henry was a man of great pride, and it was no easy matter working for a man who never praised him, who shrugged his shoulders almost as much at good news as at bad. At times Henry appeared like a highly paid valet. That was the price of his relationship with Johnny. This was something that even Henry's own wife didn't see.

Johnny didn't want to be bothered with the myriad business and legal details of his career. As his stockbroker, he chose Fred Kayne, a highly regarded broker at Bear Stearns & Company who rose to become the firm's West Coast managing partner.

Johnny met with Kayne for the first time in 1973. "Stocks and bonds, they're no fun," Johnny said, as Kayne remembers. "It's not like art that you enjoy. It's not like buying a house. You put your own value in that. Stocks are a boring investment. I don't like it. I don't like meeting with accountants or lawyers or with you."

Kayne appreciated Johnny's candor, and he rarely talked to Johnny about individual investments. Johnny was an extremely important client; in mid-1983 his account contained stocks and bonds worth over $8.5 million.

Kayne, a charming, personable man adept at the social nuances of Hollywood, might have become Johnny's friend; but he saw Johnny only a few times a year—and then only for lunch, tennis, or poker. Kayne simply did not feel comfortable around Johnny, and he never attempted to develop a friendship.

Kayne did well with Johnny's money, but occasionally he hit upon a loser. One year he bought stock in a company that went bankrupt, an event that merited a call to Johnny.

"I'm terribly embarrassed," Kayne said.

"You know, Fred, I'm supposed to be one of the greatest entertainers," Johnny said. "And every once in a while I have a show that's an absolute bummer. Thanks for calling."

Kayne was, however, friendly with Henry. One evening at the broker's house, Kayne, Henry, Johnny, and a few other men were playing an esoteric game of poker. It wasn't for high stakes; there was a ten-dollar limit. Johnny won pot after pot, and as the stack of chips in front of him kept on growing, he said, "I guess I can make a living. I'm not as stupid as I look."

In October 1974 the Friars of California roasted "the King Who Rules Midnight." Buddy Hackett and Bob Hope emceed, presiding over a roster of comedians and celebrities. The black-tie audience in the Beverly Hills Hilton were the elite of the entertainment industry. They laughed hardest at the inside jokes. Bob Hope introduced Burt Reynolds as star of *The Longest Inch*. Reynolds called Hope the star of *The Road to Senility*.

"What can you say about Johnny that hasn't been said —about Dick Haymes?" Pat McCormick quipped.

When Johnny stood up, he was completely rattled. He introduced his parents and his brother, but forgot to mention Joanna, who sat next to him.

So many people, universities, and organizations wanted to honor Johnny that he could have spent half his days picking up honorary degrees, placards, formal accolades, and tributes. He was very careful, for the hand that giveth honors usually seeks something in return.

In May 1976 Johnny returned to Norfolk to give the commencement address at the high school. He flew into town in a private plane accompanied by Joanna and his brother, Dick. Johnny's parents, who had retired in Columbus, Nebraska, were waiting to greet their two sons and daughter-in-law.

Nebraskans weren't the sort to gush over a home-grown celebrity, and some of the folks were aghast at Johnny's three marriages. But the town was honored by the return of its most famous son. A crowd of 4,000 or 5,000 lined the street as Johnny and Joanna rode through Norfolk perched on the backseat of a convertible.

"You don't know how terribly proud I am to be here today," Johnny told the graduating seniors and their families. "It means a great deal to me." He made a few obligatory jokes, but fifty-year-old Johnny was in a reflective mood. He told the graduates to keep a "certain child-like attitude of curiosity and sense of discovery of how everything works. Adults don't ask questions as a child does. When you stop wondering, you might as well put your rocker on the front porch and call it a day . . . Stay loose to keep from going bananas. Don't become rigid in your ideas or close the door from learning anything new. It is better to have doubts and go ahead."

After his address he asked for questions from the students.

"Did you have any idea when you were here that you would reach the heights of success that you have?" one graduating senior asked.

"Success is a relative measure," Johnny said. "I feel fortunate in doing what I want to do. When you are starting you want to move on to higher levels. By good luck I was able to move on to college, then into radio and finally into national television. However, this commencement address has made me prouder than anything I've done."

Another student stood up. "Do you find that you are

happy with what you did in life and would you change part of your life if you could?"

"I've found that there is more unhappiness than happiness in life," Johnny said firmly. "I always have doubts and concerns, with ups and downs. Then I have to sit down and examine myself. Hindsight is wonderful, but I've been relatively happy and think if I had it to do over I'd stumble along as I did."

FIFTEEN

It was Christmas Eve 1977, and Mary Jane "Emm-Jay" Trokel was alone. That wasn't the way it was supposed to be. It was raining outside her apartment in Beverly Hills. That wasn't the way it was supposed to be, either.

The telephone rang. "Hello, this is Johnny Carson," the voice said.

Emm-Jay worked occasionally as a production assistant on *The Tonight Show*. She was a tall, autumn-ash blonde with a dancer's body, a quick gait, and perpetual smile that said that life was amusing, at least to her and to anyone who was going to be around her. Emm-Jay had seen Johnny in the halls a few times, and though shyness was not her affliction, she knew enough never to try to talk to him.

"You know, it means a lot that you can come in and do the show," Johnny said.

"Well, thanks."

"Did you get the present?" Johnny asked.

"Why, no," Emm-Jay said. "But, listen, thanks for calling."

When she hung up, Emm-Jay sat and thought how amazing it was that Johnny had called. Nobody would believe it.

The phone rang again.

"Hi, this is Johnny. Are you going to be home the next half hour?"

"Sure."

Johnny's house in Bel Air was only a few minutes away. He drove up and knocked on the door. "Thanks for helping out," Johnny said. "Merry Christmas." He deposited a case of French wine and left.

Emm-Jay walked across the street to the park and spent the rest of Christmas Eve by herself sitting in the rain. Like so many others, she had come to Los Angeles to succeed in the entertainment industry. She had not moved to California directly from her home in Detroit after college. Instead, she had taught dance for a year at the University of Southern Mississippi in Hattiesburg. She was a chaperon at university functions, but she wasn't ready to play the professor. That was when people had started gossiping about her. "I heard rumors so good about myself that I decided to try them," she joked later.

As a dance instructor, she met some officers at Camp Shelby. One was a sixty-two-year old three-star general who had flown Bob Hope on some of his USO tours. The general said that he would fix Emm-Jay up with his twenty-three-year-old son. When, instead, the officer fell in love with Emm-Jay, she decided to pack up and head west.

The general used his contacts to get Emm-Jay work as an extra on a Bob Hope special. That led to a job on a game show as a production assistant, and to other positions. That was the way television worked, an itinerant mercenary army of assistants and technicians, moving from job to job, show to show.

A few weeks into the new year Johnny stopped Emm-Jay in the halls at NBC. "I'd like to talk to you sometime," he said. "You sound very interesting." Emm-Jay was a talker, yet a listener. She was feminine, yet she could swear like a taxi driver with a flat. She was part of Johnny's world of television, yet she lived outside celebrity and fame.

Emm-Jay fell in love with a Johnny who was almost gone. "We didn't go out much," Emm-Jay says. "We spent a lot of time laughing and giggling and exchanging stories. I've seen him so happy. He's happy when he's doing magic tricks or when he plays drums. He loves to diddle with his video camera. He's a very addictive man. He's charming and fun. I never experienced being put down.

"When we first became friends, he said he never wanted to get married and how I should find somebody young. He said he would never be divorced."

Emm-Jay was twenty-nine years old when she met Johnny, and she wasn't thinking much about the future. She was sexy and pretty and young, and other men pursued her. But Johnny was always in the background.

Emm-Jay thrived on the pressures of television, the easy camaraderie, the bantering, the constant undertone of stress and urgency. She became an assistant and associate director, jobs that had all the nitty-gritty work of being in charge of a show, but none of the glory and half the pay.

She was as busy as Johnny, and weeks might go by when she didn't see him. Then he would come over and they would watch television, play Monopoly or a card game, drink a bottle of wine, and be together. "I think sometimes the simplicity of the man gets mixed up with his brilliance as a performer," Emm-Jay says. "If you look at a person who does what he does, you expect someone else. Basically he is a very simple man. He's very aware of people. He's an observer. He's a little boy. He's a Scorpio too. He had other women when he was seeing me. He talked about it."

Emm-Jay was not a mercenary or greedy woman. She wanted nothing from Johnny except his love. At times Emm-Jay wished she could be more like Joanna. She blamed herself sometimes for being too strong, too self-willed, too able to take care of herself. "I don't project the image of being needy," she says. "That was my problem."

Johnny was as much a friend as a lover. "He would call at two o'clock in the morning after a fight with Joanna," Emm-Jay recalls. "Then he'd come over and sit here crying, saying how much he loved Joanna."

Emm-Jay knew all about the state of Johnny's marriage. She knew, too, about the gifts of diamonds and other precious jewels that he bestowed on his wife. Johnny gave

Emm-Jay almost nothing. One Christmas she went to Ciro Jewelers in Beverly Hills, a store that features fake jewelry, bought a necklace, and brought it home. And when her friends asked what Johnny had given her, she showed them the necklace.

Joanna fancied herself a woman of the world, willing to tolerate her husband's sexual peccadillos. "It's hard to have an affair when you're a public figure," she says. "The interesting question is how the wife finds out. I knew them all. I knew about Emm-Jay. When I confronted him, he knew how to handle it. There wasn't any pressure on my side. I'm from a different mentality. I'm certainly big enough to know that a nonembarrassing situation isn't going to hurt your family. It goes on all the time. I would think there was a little pressure on her side. I think that's when it ended. He said, 'I don't love this girl.' "

Joanna did not know as much about Johnny's personal life as she thought she did. She believed, for instance, that the relationship with Emm-Jay had started in 1980. According to Emm-Jay, her affair with Johnny began approximately three years before that; and despite what Johnny may have told his wife, the relationship continued all through their marriage.

Joanna had all the responsibilities of a Bel Air matron. She had a large house to manage. She had her charities. She had her son and mother to watch out for, and Johnny's parents as well; much of the burden of the elderly Carsons fell on Joanna.

"A lot of Johnny's problems stem from his relationship to his mother," says Joanna. "I knew that woman really well. I'd say to Johnny, 'You've got to understand where she's coming from. If you can understand her, understand what she went through. She might have done to you the most cruel things in the world, which she did, but is there not forgiveness in your heart?'

"She couldn't relate to her successful son. We got along just fine. If I didn't like her, I wouldn't have gone to Arizona and found a house for her. Basically I liked that lady."

Joanna did more than help the elder Carsons find a house in Arizona; she also supervised its decoration, as well as that of her own mother's apartment on the East Side of New York.

On June 11, 1977, she wrote a letter to Stephen Mallory, her decorator, about his work, bemoaning the fact that he had taken a pair of beautiful vases, made them into lamps, and put them into the Carsons' living room in Scottsdale. She felt that they were too good for her mother-in-law.

Joanna was primarily concerned with the way Mallory was decorating her own mother's apartment. He decorated the apartment until it personified a chic New York world further from Mrs. Ulrich than the distance between Queens and Manhattan. Joanna's mother was not an East Side socialite, and she added familiar little touches to feel at home. "I can see the kitchen window on the tenth floor when I walk past," Mallory says. "There are plants everywhere. It looks like a tenement house. In the bathroom there's a venetian blind. For Valentine's Day Mrs. Ulrich sticks cards over the venetian blind."

Mallory billed Joanna $123,970 for his services. In the spring of 1978, when she did not pay $43,058 that she allegedly owed him, the decorator sued her in New York State Supreme Court. The dispute was settled out of court.

One of the few people out of his early career days that Johnny continued to see was Merle Workhoven, one of his buddies from WOW in Omaha. In 1978 Workhoven drove out to Los Angeles to visit his daughter, Melanie.

Johnny took his former colleague and his daughter to lunch. "How was the trip west?" Johnny asked.

"Oh, just fine," Workhoven said, "except my radiator boiled over twice."

"How come?" Johnny asked.

"Well, my car's twelve years old and it's got one-hundred-sixty-thousand miles on it."

"That's reason enough," Johnny said, and changed the subject.

A week later Workhoven's daughter drove her father over to Johnny's house in Bel Air. The gates swung open and Workhoven saw Johnny "standing there grinning ear to ear."

"Worky," Johnny said, "I got you back here because I want to give you something."

"Give me something?"

Johnny handed Workhoven a set of car keys. "There's the car that goes with it right over there," Johnny said, pointing to a new blue Buick Electra, the car that Workhoven dreamed of owning. "Come on in, Joanna has baked some cookies."

Johnny didn't like to be asked for things. But if he wasn't pushed, he could be a generous man. Emm-Jay recalls him sending out anonymous Christmas baskets, a custom common in Nebraska. It was his misfortune to be treated not like a good neighbor but like a wealthy institution to be endlessly wooed. He made a $100,000 contribution to the University of Nebraska to endow four scholarships.

Later, when he and Joanna gave $1 million to the University of Southern California for the Carson Television Center, Johnny's alma mater was less than ecstatic. The clipping at the Nebraska alumni office contains the typed notation: "All of his early-life training in Norfolk, good old Univ. of Nebr. then radio in Omaha, and he gives the big gift to U.S.C. That's modern day appreciation for you!"

Although Johnny could be charitable, woe betide the promoter or entrepreneur who in a foolhardy moment tried to use Johnny's name. Earl J. Braxton startled peddling his porta-johns under the slogan "Here's Johnny!" In January 1977 Henry hit Braxton's company with a $1.1 million lawsuit. The *Los Angeles Times* reported that the company was "flushed with the success of its publicity." Eventually Johnny won the suit.

In early 1977 a series of rumors began sweeping across Westlake Village, a residential area in the San Fernando Valley. Johnny Carson was moving into the area. Johnny was building a house on Germaine Drive for his mother. Johnny was building his own house on Germaine Drive.

Nothing sold houses better than the proximity of a celebrity, and the realtors were ecstatic. Salespeople at Brown Realty, the largest real estate company in the area, told potential buyers that not only did Westlake Village boast such notable present or past residents as Walter Brennan and Virginia Mayo, they would now have the host of *The Tonight Show* himself.

On April 26, 1977, Kenneth L. Browning of the Bushkin firm called Brown Realty. "I am possibly interested in purchasing a home in the Westlake Village area," Browning told Ms. Jeanne Coffey, a salesperson.

"The price range of property in Westlake Village varies tremendously," Coffey allegedly replied. "For example, there are a number of well-known Hollywood personalities living in Westlake Village, including Johnny Carson, who has just purchased a lot."

On October 31, Joseph P. Brown, head of Brown Realty, heard over television that Johnny Carson was suing his company for $3 million. Brown, who wanted to get on with the happy business of selling real estate in a rising market, sent a letter to Johnny's home in Bel Air saying that he didn't know how the rumor had started, and he had told his employees not to mention Carson's name. "I don't believe I could have been more clear or more explicit," he wrote. He pointed out that "irrespective of how the rumor may have started, the television publicity you obtained . . . very effectively put the rumor to rest. Your approach to the problem may not have been the customary one but you can be assured that you no longer have any concern about the people in Westlake Village believing you were to become a resident in their community."

Although Johnny's problems with Westlake were at an end, he continued the lawsuit.

Johnny's name came up in the most unusual places. Arthur Kassel had moved to Los Angeles, and one day Henry called his old friend, ranting and fuming about Arthur's friends on the police force. The evening before, a police-information officer at a public meeting had named Johnny as one of the two biggest cocaine users in Los Angeles. Hollywood was rife with rumors about Johnny's cocaine use, and that he had a terrible habit, though no evidence was ever presented. Truman Capote was one of those who spread the undocumented gossip, telling journalist Lawrence Grobel in 1983 that "within the past few years he [Johnny] had to have a silver or gold thing put in his nose." It infuriated Bushkin that even the police should be repeating such stories, and he threatened a lawsuit.

Kassel calmed Henry down and negotiated an apology from Police Chief Ed Davis. "Some member of the force very improperly, without any significant knowledge, made a malicious, unfair allegation against Johnny Carson," recalls Davis, now a California state senator. "In effect, we did what was the right thing, since it was totally without basis."

Later Kassel made himself useful to Johnny once again, when he received certain death threats. He helped his friend to obtain a gun permit.

In October 1978, at *The Tonight Show's* sixteenth anniversary program, Johnny met Fred Silverman, the new NBC president, for the first time. At his previous employer, ABC, Silverman had a reputation as a programming genius. But genius in television has roughly the life span of a tsetse fly. At NBC, Silverman was having a horrendous time finding programs that won good ratings.

After the anniversary show Johnny, Silverman, and a small group dined at Chasen's, a restaurant favored by Hollywood's older set. The new NBC president wanted to have a serious discussion about the future with the network's biggest star, but he had little chance to talk with Johnny that evening.

The Tonight Show was one of the few feathers on the NBC peacock, grossing an estimated $115 million a year in advertising monies. In 1978 the show earned about $23 million, or 17 percent of the network's $122.1 million profits. Silverman believed that even *The Tonight Show* might become a problem to NBC. The show was holding steady, but only when Johnny was the host. Silverman looked at his star's salary, estimated at between $3 million and $5 million. He looked at Johnny's three-day-a-week schedule for twenty-five weeks, and four days a week for twelve weeks during the "sweeps" rating period. He looked at his fifteen weeks of annual vacation. And he decided that Johnny should work a little more.

The NBC president might have prodded Johnny privately, and left it at that. He might have given the job to Dave Tebet, NBC's vice-president in charge of hand-holding and stroking. Alas, the new regime considered Tebet an expensive frill. He had left, packing up his bottles of Dom Pérignon, his effusive notes, his myriad courtesies.

Instead, Silverman attempted to shame Johnny publicly. "I also hope there will come a moment in time when [he] will say to himself, I love [the show], and I'm going to do a little bit more," he told *Newsweek*. "He's a very competitive and professional guy. I don't think he must enjoy reading that the thing is slipping."

Silverman met Johnny on March 17, Saint Patrick's Day, in a hotel suite in New York. Silverman listened to what was the worst possible news he could hear. Not only was Johnny unwilling to work extra evenings, he told the NBC president that he was finished, tired, he wanted out. Although Johnny wanted to quit after his seventeenth anniversary show, his contract did not expire until April 1981. "That may be fine as far as you are concerned," Silverman has recalled telling Johnny. "I believe you have a contract, and you are going to continue to work."

After that, the struggle between NBC and Johnny blew up into a media feud. In April Johnny announced publicly that he wanted to leave *The Tonight Show* on September 30, after seventeen years. The announcement was important enough to merit a front-page story in *The New York Times*.

Joanna became so upset at the idea of Johnny leaving the show that she cried openly. NBC attempted to downplay the dispute, but Johnny needled Silverman much as he had his employers at WOW in Omaha three decades earlier.

One evening Johnny played Carnac the Magnificent, the mystic who, given the answer, supplies the question. Ed read the answer: "Station WKRP in Cincinnati." Then Johnny, as the Great Carnac, opened an envelope and read the question: "Where will the president of NBC be working next year?"

In May 1979 the Friars Club named Johnny Entertainer of the Year. Just five years before, the California Friars had broiled Johnny to a fine degree. That kind of roast would no longer do. He had become, as *People* called him, "the most awesome figure in entertainment, including the abbot (president) of the Friars himself, Frank Sinatra."

Tickets for the dinner in the magnificent three-tiered ballroom of the Waldorf Astoria in New York City were eagerly sought by both the celebrated and the would-be celebrated. Almost 1,500 people paid between $125 to $500 to attend. If Johnny was indeed retiring, this would be an occasion to remember. Silverman was scheduled to appear, and media watchers looked forward to a possible confrontation between the two men.

Johnny and his representatives chose the people who sat on the dais in the Grand Ballroom. Johnny was hardly gregarious, but the dais had almost as many people as Brigham Young had wives, fifty-one in all. To appear beside him, Johnny, or his minions, had selected such comedic giants as Roberta Flack, Barbara Walters, and the Egyptian and Israeli ambassadors.

Those longtime Friars whose places were usurped were upset. Milton Berle, who had founded the California Friars, had received only a printed invitation by mail. Red Buttons, the Friars' scribe emeritus, wasn't even invited. Don Rickles decided not to attend, either.

Howard K. Smith, the ABC anchorman, opened the proceedings. "President Carter says he's behind you one thousand percent," Smith said, a fair sample of the evening's wit. Few of the speakers wanted to risk Johnny's disfavor, and the program droned on. Johnny kissed and hugged the speakers after they had eulogized him.

Most of those present realized the real drama that was being played out. They watched as Johnny and Joanna made small talk with their dinner companion, Silverman. The NBC president ate his filet mignon and truffles, and said little. On several occasions he appeared to doze, only to catch himself.

"All NBC's top brass is here," said Bob Hope, the MC. "I'm sure you've seen them—refilling Johnny's wineglass, cutting his steak, kissing his ring. They never did get any dinner. They kept ordering and canceling, ordering and canceling."

When Silverman stood up to talk, the room grew hushed. The NBC president recalled how last week he had been watching *The Tonight Show* when Johnny said he had decided to stay on at least until the end of the year.

"I was so relieved I got down off the chair and put the rope back in the closet," Silverman said.

Silverman saved his barbs for Henry Bushkin, whom the *New York Post* described as "the least recognizable, but perhaps most significant man on the star-studded dais." Silverman said that he had learned that Henry's dream was to perform in the Olympics.

"I immediately made arrangements to have him participate," Silverman said. "I'm happy to announce that in Moscow in 1980, Henry will be a javelin catcher. It's the least I can do for Bushkin after all he's done for me."

Then Silverman turned to Johnny. "You're more, much more than the Entertainer of the Year," he said. "You're the entertainer of our time, you're the best friend TV ever had."

When Silverman sat down, Johnny gave him a perfunctory handshake. "There have been a lot of jokes about Mr.

Silverman here tonight," Johnny declared when it was finally his turn. "But I'm delighted to see NBC's top executives on the dais. It reminds me for some reason of another dinner—the Last Supper."

In the next months the battle over Johnny's contract became one of the most protracted, and ultimately most expensive, negotiations in the history of television. NBC held a signed contract that obligated Johnny to continue hosting *The Tonight Show* through April 1981. Moreover, the contract stipulated that for a year after that date he could not host a talk show for another network. Henry argued that California law prohibits contracts longer than seven years, and Johnny had been bound to NBC since 1972. The network lawyers pointed out that Johnny had signed three separate agreements in those years.

Whatever merit Henry's argument might have, NBC was not about to see the matter decided in court. Even if they won, they lost. The network attempted to placate Johnny. On one occasion Silverman dropped in on Johnny in Burbank for fifteen minutes of what he called "talent stroking." In a highly unusual move he left the negotiations to an outsider, Mickey Rudin, a prominent Hollywood attorney known for his association with Frank Sinatra.

Johnny was in an enviable position. At NBC, Silverman was excavating an even deeper cellar for the network. In 1979 profits dropped $16 million, from $122 million in 1978 to $106 million. In this context *The Tonight Show* reportedly represented over 20 percent of NBC's net. If Silverman did not sign Johnny or fill the time slot with an equally popular program, he might well be fired. NBC had attempted to find a suitable replacement for Johnny, but none of the possible candidates attained Johnny's ratings. To the troubled network, Johnny was as close to indispensible as a performer could be.

On several occasions executives at ABC approached Johnny about working for them. Several times the NBC negotiations nearly fell apart. Johnny wanted to shorten *The*

Tonight Show to an hour. NBC was opposed. That last half hour cost the network very little in added production costs; the advertising dollars were pure profit.

Finally, after a year of public and private discussions, Johnny agreed to a new contract. On May 2, 1980, Silverman drove to Johnny's house in Bel Air, where he met with Rudin, Henry, and Johnny to sign a historic television contract.

The three-year contract shortened *The Tonight Show* to an hour, and Johnny would do four shows a week—for which he would be paid reportedly well over $5 million a year.

But that was only the beginning. Johnny would not only be the star of *The Tonight Show*. He would be the producer and the owner of the show as well. In the sixties his company had produced the show for several years; but the whole nature of television had changed since then, and the value of old programs had increased enormously. Now Johnny and Henry would be able to sell the reruns in syndication for millions of dollars and to foreign markets as well, keeping all the money.

That was not the end of it, either. NBC agreed to buy three series and TV movies from Johnny's new, totally untested production company. *The Wall Street Journal* reported that the network would pay for at least twenty-two episodes of each series, even if it never aired a show. In 1980 half-hour programs cost roughly $300,000, and producers usually earned about a 20 percent profit. Thus, on the three series Johnny's new company could earn about $4 million. Should even one of the shows prove successful, Johnny could make tens of millions more.

In all, the production deal represented about $50 million in NBC commitments, making Johnny a major player in network television. Henry had negotiated the deal, and for his troubles he became a 10-percent owner of the new Carson Productions, Inc.

Silverman had a programming decision to make, how to fill that last half hour of *The Tonight Show*. He decided to put together an hour-long variety-talk show. Who better to host it than Steve Allen, the original host of *The Tonight Show*? Allen, in Jamaica on vacation, was unwilling to fly back early. The day after he returned to Los Angeles, the entertainer and his agent, Irvin Arthur, met with Silverman.

"Okay, here's the news," Silverman said, not wasting a minute on chitchat. "Johnny Carson eleven-thirty to twelve-thirty. Steve Allen twelve-thirty to one-thirty."

"Yes, that's a good idea," said Allen. "I don't know whether it's a good idea for me. But, yeah, I think you're thinking right about what would be exciting programming."

"Oh, I thought you were going to snap at it right away," said Silverman. The NBC president was thinking about the affiliates' meeting in which he would have to face scores of discontented station managers. "I know they'll give me a standing ovation when they hear this announcement. Carson and Allen, back to back. Goddammit, I love the idea!"

"Well, I hope we can put it together," Allen said, continuing to feign reluctance.

As Silverman led Allen and his agent out the door, he put his arms around the two men. "God, I'm so excited about this!" enthused the NBC president. "I'll check with Johnny and get back to you guys."

"You *what*?" exclaimed Arthur, the agent.

"Check with Johnny. But I'm sure there will be no problem."

Silverman checked with Johnny in a meeting that included Henry and several other NBC executives. Johnny's reaction was what Silverman called "apathetic." The next day Steve Allen learned that he would not be hosting the new show.

David Letterman became the host instead. He was a very different comedian from Johnny, playing to a younger, hipper audience. And the show was owned in part by Carson Productions.

SIXTEEN

Henry was always being approached by people wanting to do business with Johnny. In the summer of 1977 one of the firm's attorneys introduced him to Gordon Baskin, a courtly, soft-spoken businessman. Baskin had been the president of a local bank, and he was well connected to the California business community. The two men talked about various ventures in which Johnny might become involved.

Baskin set out to find investments that would make sense. If Baskin was successful, he would receive as a finder's fee a minority interest probably worth hundreds of thousands of dollars. Through his contacts he learned that KCOP-TV, an independent Orange County station, was for sale, a deal that seemed to fit in perfectly with Johnny's interests.

"I was invited to Carson's home," Baskin recalls. "I described the situation. Carson would at times be flippant, but he seemed incisive in his comments. We had found a station and a price. We had a verbal commitment from one of the biggest banks."

When the deal fell through, Baskin found another independent station in Las Vegas, KVVU-TV, for sale for $5.5 million. Baskin again arranged for a loan to buy the station. "The key to the deal was the financial condition of Johnny Carson," Baskin says. "I went to the Bank of America, with Johnny's statement. It was so heavy that I had no problem getting a commitment.''

Johnny was to receive 90 percent of the equity, with 5 percent for Henry's law firm, and 5 percent for Baskin. Henry, however, told Baskin that they needed a Las Vegas–based partner who would help them with the local establishment. Also, if they could add representatives of minorities as partial owners, they would receive special tax benefits. Thus, Henry brought in Herbert Kaufman, a Vegas executive of Wonderworld stores and, according to *Variety*, a "sub rosa producer of Strip revues" such as "Boylesque" at the Silver Slipper. To get the special tax credits, Henry lined up Forrest Chu, a Chinese-American lawyer from San Diego, another Asian-American, and a Mexican-American.

The group borrowed $4.5 million in the name of Carson Broadcasting, a newly formed corporation. To capitalize the corporation, the three main partners—Johnny, Kaufman, and Chu and his group—each put up $370,000.

"When Henry suddenly decided he wanted Kaufman and Chu to be part of this, he gave to each of them—and I use the word *gave*—one third of what Carson had," Baskin says. "Instead of Carson receiving ninety percent, he got thirty per cent, Chu got thirty per cent, and Kaufman got thirty percent. When I got the original loan commitments, I never saw Chu's or Kaufman's financial statements. I did see them subsequently."

Baskin went to talk to Henry about the deal. "Henry, there's no need, and I think it's not equitable to your client to give away these kinds of interest," Baskin remembers saying. "Take the three-hundred-seventy-thousand dollars that each one has given. You could divide that against equity, against the total deal. They were not responsible for the credit."

"Don't interfere with my clients, my business," Henry replied sharply, according to Baskin.

"Does Carson know?" Baskin asked.

"Of course, he knows everything," Henry asserted, visibly upset.

"Subsequently I was invited to go with Carson to Las Vegas a couple of times," Baskin says. "Never was I alone with Johnny Carson. Henry wouldn't even go to the bathroom when I was there. So I never had an opportunity to even make a comment."

In 1978 Baskin also interested Henry and Johnny in purchasing the Garden State Bank in Hawaiian Gardens, about twenty miles south of Los Angeles. The bank had been capitalized for a meager $700,000 and had only a little over $11 million in assets, a mere boutique sum. But the institution could grow rapidly, especially with Johnny's name associated with it. The lone office already happened to be situated on Carson Boulevard, but Johnny joked that the name Garden State "sounded like it was in New Jersey."

Johnny could have purchased the Commercial Bank on his own, without any partners, just as he could have purchased the Las Vegas station. According to Baskin, that was the original plan; the banker had approached the Bank of America to lend money to Johnny to buy the bank.

Henry was earning a reported $1.5 million a year, but wealth, *real* wealth, came not from Johnny's retainer and fees from other clients but from having equity in major business deals. Henry felt this was such a good venture that he talked to one of his law partners, Arnold Kopelson, to see if he wanted to become involved. The two men were old friends, partners from back in the New York days.

Kopelson, who deserved the appellation "bombastic" more than Henry, was a fiery, high-strung entertainment lawyer. While Henry had majored in handling Johnny Carson, Kopelson had spent much of his energy producing and packaging a series of mediocre films such as *Night of the Juggler* and *Dirty Tricks*. He was not without commercial acumen, and like Henry he had become a millionaire since moving to Los Angeles.

Kopelson thought the Garden State acquisition sounded like a good idea, as long as Johnny Carson was involved. "The man was on TV every night," Kopelson said several years later. "We felt he would be a natural draw to the institution." Kopelson brought in Michael Miller, his former law clerk. Miller, who had become successful producing syndicated television programs as tax shelters, jumped at the opportunity to be associated with Johnny Carson.

Los Angeles had "in" automobiles, "in" neighborhoods, "in" restaurants, "in" personal trainers, "in" dog beauticians. Why not an "in" bank for the big *machers* in the television and film industry? Even less affluent mortals from Anaheim to Yuba City would be able to rub dollars with Johnny.

The Bank of America loaned the group, including several other minority shareholders, about $1.5 million to buy the bank's stock without any down payment. The agreement was what bankers call "joint and several," meaning that each partner was liable for the others' obligations.

Instead of owning his own bank, Johnny was now in the middle of an extremely complicated deal. Johnny was the one shareholder with great wealth; if any of the partners stopped making payments, the bankers would be knocking on Johnny's door. Henry had parceled out the stock in such a way that made it difficult to know just how much of the stock each shareholder owned.

When Steve Peden, a lawyer at the Bushkin firm, attempted to determine ownership in 1982, he wrote that "this task has been made very difficult by the fact that there has never been an agreement reduced to writing . . . indicating which member owned which percentage of shares . . . various memos and letters . . . contain conflicting information." The attorney determined that, depending on which record one looked at, Johnny owned either 36.82 percent, 22.67 percent, or 27.72 percent of the stock. Henry owned somewhat more or somewhat less: 25.76 percent, 29.39 percent, or 27.22 percent. Henry's ownership was further complicated because he had transferred a part of his interest to other members of his firm. In any case, Johnny and Henry controlled over half of the 282,614 shares. Kopelson owned about 20 percent, and Miller less than half that. Johnny and

Henry became the co-chairmen of the board. Kopelson served as vice-chairman.

"Johnny did the bank to be one of the guys," recalls Fred Kayne, who as Johnny's broker closely observed the bank purchase. "Other people were forming banks, and it was started with the best of intentions."

Although Johnny attended a few board meetings and participated in the early decisions, he was simply not a businessman. He seemed distant, and strangely timid. One board member recalls Johnny seated next to him, whispering in his ear about matters that should be brought up, not wanting or daring to speak out.

The board members changed the name of the bank to the Commercial Bank of California. Plans were made to move the headquarters to a location in Los Angeles.

At one of the early board meetings the directors decided on the bank's new president. Gordon Baskin had been promised the position. He had been president of a troubled bank, and several of the directors had serious doubts about how the state banking regulators would feel about the appointment. Baskin thought of the men as his friends, but, nonetheless, they voted against naming him president. Baskin was a proud man, and when he was told, he appeared on the edge of tears.

In December 1979 Johnny attended a cocktail party celebrating the opening of the bank's classy new headquarters at 9255 Sunset Boulevard in West Hollywood, on the edge of Beverly Hills. In Los Angeles the opening of a small bank office is greeted with the same enthusiasm as the groundbreaking ceremonies for a 7-Eleven. But this was Johnny's bank, and over a thousand people converged on the offices for the six o'clock party. The only other star to show up was Elliott Gould. Johnny arrived at 6:45 wearing a very bankerlike blue suit and tie. Johnny even had a desk with a nameplate reading JOHN W CARSON. "I'm really enjoying this new adjunct to [show] business," he said, "although I don't think I'll cause David Rockefeller to lose any sleep."

But the bank was not all cocktail parties. Three months later, in March 1980, Johnny received a certified letter from Baskin addressed to all the board members. To make sure that Johnny read the letter, Baskin sent copies not only to his business address, but to his Bel Air home and Malibu weekend residence.

Baskin believed that the bank was headed for disaster. As a former banker and bank director, Baskin worried that he might one day be held partially responsible. His letter had the fine hand of his attorney, Rafael Chodos, all over it.

The bank had loaned out 80.9 percent of its deposits. Baskin argued that an inordinately large percentage of these deposits, $6.2 million out of $21.6 million, were in large certificates of deposits. These customers generally moved their CD's from bank to bank, seeking higher interests. If they left, the bank could be in trouble.

The loan portfolio contained a large number of unsecured commitments, some of them recently made to customers who already were delinquent on previous loans. In the past month alone, Baskin noted, "a new $1.1 million of unsecured loans was added." A number of them were to the bank directors themselves. "I just learned . . . that a new unsecured loan was made to the Bushkin, Kopelson firm in the amount of $160,000 at a favorable interest rate," Baskin wrote. "This is one of the largest loans in our portfolio. I am worried that it may represent an improper transaction under the sections of the Financial Code which forbid banks to make loans to directors, officers, or entities controlled by them." The former banker advised that all of these insider loans should be called and paid up.

Baskin felt that he was being frozen out of information about the running of the bank, particularly the itemized expense statements. "I was shocked to be told that this document had recently been declared 'off limits' at Director's meetings," he wrote. "In the context of all the other problems we have, I think it is a very big red flag waving in the wind."

Baskin was surprised that his letter created so little reaction, and he resigned from the board. Johnny may have felt that Baskin was exaggerating. Johnny was not an expert on banking, and the 1980 annual report, with Johnny's picture on the cover, showed a vibrant, growing institution, with assets up 51 percent to $29,781,000, and before-tax income up 213 percent to $133,421. The statement did admit, however, that the bank had lent $516,000 to bank directors and officers.

Baskin was still involved with Johnny and Henry as a stockholder in Carson Broadcasting. Henry and Baskin's animosity toward each other only deepened. In the spring of 1983 Baskin informed Henry and Carson Broadcasting that he wanted to sell his 280 shares in the company at the market price to the other shareholders. Baskin had a legal right to do so, but Henry considered Baskin "both foolish and greedy," and asked that he wait until the proposed sale of the company's primary asset, KVVU-TV, the Las Vegas television station purchased in 1978 for $5.5 million.

Baskin believed that KVVU might now be worth as much as $25 million. He was stunned when the Carson Broadcasting accounting firm, Fox & Company, set the market value of the company at only $2.9 million. Baskin thought he was being punished for speaking out against the management. When he refused to go ahead and sell his shares, Henry, Johnny, and the other partners filed suit against him. Baskin countersued. Baskin's judgment of the value of the company appeared vindicated when, late in 1984, Carson Broadcasting sold KVVU-TV to Meredith Broadcasting for a reported $27.5 million, netting the other partners $8,600 a share, not the $1,306 that Baskin had been offered. But that did not end the suits.

"About a year before the case went to trial, I went into an omelette parlor with my wife in Malibu," Baskin recalls. "Seated at the next table were Johnny Carson and a companion. We exchanged greetings and I said to Johnny, 'There are some things that we ought to sit down and talk about that if you don't know might be able to mitigate our problems.' He said, 'Please call me at NBC and I'll set up an appointment.'

"I called the next day. No answer. Nothing. The subsequent day my attorney received a call from Bushkin or one of his people saying keep Baskin away from Carson, it's improper, he has no right. So I never heard from Carson, and we went to trial.

"The whole business really hurt, it took much out of my life. When you take on Johnny Carson, the most powerful person in this town, who would want to deal with you? It changed my life professionally and socially. Those were some years, just making a living."

Baskin won the verdict in 1985, receiving over $2 million. Henry, Johnny, and the other partners did not let matters rest there, but appealed unsuccessfully. Baskin went on to other business pursuits, including managing the career of two track stars, Edwin Moses and Florence Griffith Joyner. But the involvement with Henry and Johnny had had a devastating impact on the former banker. In 1988 Baskin filed suit against Johnny, Henry, and the other partners, charging that they had sued him maliciously.

In March 1979, soon after the Commercial Bank opened for business, the bank made the first of many loans to Jack Catain, Jr., the president of Rusco Industries, a Los Angeles–based conglomerate involved with everything from bidets to security devices. "The first time I remember Catain coming into the picture was when his name was put on the record for loans," says Baskin. "That was at a board meeting. Henry stood up for Catain." The credit approval and loan report for the twenty-five-thousand dollar loan stated, "Mr. Catain is referred by Henry Bushkin, co-chairman of the board."

"He looked like a guy of substance," Henry told Peter S. Greenberg, a Los Angeles journalist, in 1983. Henry said that he had no relationship with Catain and knew him only because Catain had become one of the firm's clients in a divorce case handled by another attorney.

In fact, Henry had already been involved with Catain's company in at least one transaction. Like many attorneys, Henry was always on the lookout for deals of which he could become a part. While still in New York, he became the attorney for TMX, Inc., a company developing security devices for automobiles. He became a director and shareholder, and invested $150,000 of his own money. In the spring of 1977, after Henry had moved to California, TMX, Inc., granted Rusco Industries and its president, Jack Catain, an option to purchase the company.

That November the Bushkins held a party to celebrate the first anniversary of Bushkin and Kopelson's law firm. During the gala event Judy Bushkin recalls that her husband introduced a short, overweight forty-seven-year old businessman with two eight-inch scars on his neck. "Mr. Catain, this is my wife, Judy Bushkin," Henry reportedly said. According to Judy Bushkin, her husband had told her that Catain was involved in alleged organized-crime activities and that "Catain's company, Rusco Industries, was going to buy or take over TMX."

Rusco did indeed purchase TMX. But Rusco held the company only a year, selling "TMX, Inc." to "TMX Systems," a company of which Henry was a director and a shareholder and which was owned in part by Delorean Motor Cars Ltd., in which Johnny had invested $500,000. A few months later TMX Marketing Corporation borrowed about $42,600 from the Commercial Bank, a loan guaranteed in part by Henry. Henry had his hand on every one of the deals and he later asserted that he "never engaged in *any* unlawful kick-back activities."

Eight months after the Bushkin party the *Los Angeles Herald-Examiner* ran a banner page-one headline: LA CRIME LAUNDRY PROBE. "The head of Rusco Industries . . . is under investigation by the Justice Department for his alleged involvement in the finances of organized crime, according to law enforcement officials," stated the article by Jeff Gerth, originally published in *The New York Times*. "The officials say that Jack M. Catain, Jr., president and chairman of Rusco, is a key conduit in the laundering of at least $10 million in organized crime money."

Catain denied the allegations, calling them "very comical." In July 1980 he settled federal fraud charges by resigning from Rusco, under a consent settlement.

Although Catain had never been indicted, his activities had been the subject of various investigations. In 1969 he was named during the McClellan Senate hearings on organized crime as a member of the Mafia. He had repeatedly been linked to Jack P. Cerone, whom the FBI described as the Chicago crime boss.

"As far as organized crime in Los Angeles, Catain was as big as they come," says Gerald Petievich, a novelist and former Treasury agent who investigated and arrested Catain. "You're as powerful as the money you can make for the big guys, and he made a lot of money. He was laundering money, passing cashier's checks in the Cayman Islands, extortions, all kinds of operations."

In 1969, when Rusco Industries had attempted to buy Hazel Park, a racetrack outside Detroit, the *Detroit Free Press* ran a page-one story highlighting the relationships between the track officers and purported Mafia members. Anthony Zerilli, the track president, was the son of Joseph Zerilli, whom the Senate permanent subcommittee on investigations listed as the top Mafia don in Detroit. Catain admitted to *The Wall Street Journal* that "we heard some stories, and we did as much investigating as we could. . . . We went into it at length and decided, if they are, who the hell is the Mafia, what are they. I don't know and I couldn't care less."

In May 1981 the bank held a cocktail party in Jack Catain's honor. "As one of our most valued customers, we wanted to do something to express our appreciation to Mr. Catain for all he has done for us," James R. Vrataric, senior vice-president, wrote the invited guests. "He declined a gold watch and inasmuch as this Bank did not really begin until 1979, he didn't agree with having his portrait hanging in The Hall of Fame Room of the Bank. So, we decided to have a party in his honor for those who have helped him the most. He therefore gave us the names of his most valued friends and business associates.''

Catain did not invite Johnny. He did, according to the bank records, invite Ed McMahon, who said that he was unable to attend. Nor apparently could O. J. Simpson, the former football great, whose name also was on the invitation list. The forty or so other guests included people active in the worlds of business and entertainment and journalism.

The invitation to the party in the bank's penthouse mentioned only ''beverages and hors d'oeuvres,'' but the guests were treated to a buffet of scampi, chicken tetrazzini, veal, gourmet cheese, clams, and artichoke vinaigrette. The desserts included various tarts; but since it was Catain's birthday, the main treat was a birthday cake.

The bank considered its party for Catain a rousing success, opening the way for many new customers. The bank officers tallied up almost $700,000 in loans they were able to make thanks to Catain's referrals at that one party alone.

The largest loan, $100,000, was made to Catain's company, Fox Bros. Leasing, to buy a Rolls-Royce Corniche convertible. When a Rolls-Royce purchased by Catain arrived in Los Angeles on a Lufthansa freight plane, the authorities were on the alert. FBI and customs authorities employed dogs to sniff out narcotics in a vehicle that weighed 166 pounds more than a Rolls-Royce Corniche convertible was supposed to weigh. But the dogs smelled nothing unusual, and the Rolls-Royce was released.

While Johnny was becoming the part-owner of a bank, Henry, Johnny, and other show business associates became involved in a whole series of investments. Other performers wanted to be associated with Johnny and his attorney, and Henry put together deals involving various stars. Some of the investments were successful, but others were not. In

1982 they were led into purchasing KNAT-TV in Albuquerque, New Mexico. Johnny took 41 percent of the stock; Neil Simon, the playwright, 26 percent; Paul Anka, the singer, 10 percent; David Letterman, 5 percent; and Joan Rivers, 4 percent. These performers didn't fancy themselves brilliant entrepreneurs, but they expected their purchase to make at least a modest profit, not the reported $6 million to $7 million in losses in three years. By April 1985 the station was doing so badly, garnering only 4 percent of the audience, that it was shut down before being sold.

In 1981 Henry involved Johnny, Simon's then-wife, actress Marsha Mason, and several law partners in a partnership to purchase ninety-three acres of undeveloped land in Houston, borrowing a reported $23.5 million. Johnny and Neil Simon were both so wealthy that they could have put their money in bonds, blue-chip stocks, and minimalls, and lived off the interest. Instead, they were in the midst of an enormously speculative investment, hoping to build a luxury hotel and sell off land for commercial and residential development.

Johnny flew down to Texas to publicize the venture. But before even an acre could be sold, the Houston boom busted, and another luxury hotel was about as needed as a dry well.

Neil Simon and Marsha Mason wanted out. "I remember telling Johnny that Neil Simon and I had talked, and Simon had his disagreement," Joanna says. "And Johnny said, 'Well, Neil Simon is just a wishy-washy guy.' I said, 'What?' "

On December 30, 1983, Simon and Mason filed a malpractice suit against Bushkin's law firm. The couple charged that in a whole series of ventures Bushkin and his firm had failed "to adequately investigate the transactions, to adequately document the transaction, to adequately explain . . . the risks . . . and to adequately advise . . . of their interest in the transactions or of the conflicts of interest created thereby." The couple were interested more in money than revenge, and when Johnny and the other partners allowed them to get their money out of the Texas development, they dropped the suit, leaving those still involved with an even greater liability.

In 1979 Henry and Johnny decided to purchase a Las Vegas casino. No entertainer in Las Vegas had a hotel in *his* name, and the idea had an obvious appeal. But Johnny had worked in the gambling capital enough to know that outsiders did not blithely arrive, slap down their money, and walk off with a casino.

In the early days of the city the casinos had been run almost openly by the Mafia. During the early 1960's, when Johnny first played Las Vegas, the mob was still omnipresent. At that time Johnny's regular opening act was Phyllis McGuire, who had a relationship with Sam Giancana, the Chicago Mafia figure who was murdered in 1975. By the late 1970's the state was attempting to purge the casinos of mob influence, its gambling commission making sure that the on-the-record owners of the casinos were not mobsters or known associates of mobsters.

If a mobster could siphon off only a small stream of the torrent of money that flowed through a Nevada casino, the amount might be tens of millions of dollars a year. The method might be secret ownership through individuals controlled by the mob. It might be people in the counting room handing over cash receipts, skimming the profits. It could even be the maintenance contract, or construction, or kickbacks from the entertainers or the liquor.

For years the Aladdin Hotel and Casino was allegedly controlled by Mafia families in St. Louis and Detroit. In 1975 the *St. Louis Globe-Democrat* reported that the hotel was "characterized by investigators as an R & R [rest and recreation] center for organized crime figures who are often given complimentary services there."

In March 1979 a federal jury in Detroit convicted the corporation and three of its executives of allowing organized-crime figures to control the hotel. The Gaming Commission ordered the hotel sold. In the interim the commissioners commanded the owners to shut down the operation. U.S. District Judge Harry Claiborne, who would later become the first federal judge ever impeached, gave the casino a reprieve, allowing the Aladdin to remain open at least until February 1980.

Henry approached the attorneys selling the Aladdin in the name of Johnny Carson and Edward M. Nigro, an experienced casino executive who would manage the operation. Another pair, Delbert Coleman and Edward Torres, had already made a serious offer. Although the duo were prepared to pay $105 million for the Aladdin, they had certain glitches in their backgrounds that might offend the Gaming Commission. The two men had signed consent decrees in a civil case before the SEC, and Torres had once been indicted for casino skimming in a case that was later dropped. He also had the misfortune of being seen in a "chance" encounter with Meyer Lansky, a mobster and gambler.

Although Johnny had an impeccable background, his offer was not without problems. According to one close source, Henry offered a down payment of $20 million: $2 million from Johnny, $2 million from a major theater chain, $2 million from another American partner. That was all fine, but the other $14 million purportedly came from a mysterious Middle Eastern investor. That was something that the Gaming Commission might not approve, either.

A third suitor announced an interest, the National Kinney Corporation, an eastern conglomerate that owned Warner Brothers, the film and record company, and other interests. Johnny and Henry's own backup offer stood ahead of Kinney's, but the seller decided to see if the two offers could be made one.

On October 22, 1979, Johnny met with Andrew J. Frankel, chairman of Kinney, at a gathering at which Joanna was present. That day they signed an agreement to purchase the hotel should the Coleman-Torres offer fall through.

Here appeared to be a perfect mesh: Kinney's money, Nigro's management skills, and Johnny's prestige and talent. Kinney would buy the hotel, and Nigro would manage

the facility. Johnny would appear exclusively at Johnny
Carson's Aladdin in Las Vegas. He would be paid as highly
as he would have been at the Sahara, his longtime haunt.
The hotel would promote his name with "the highest standards of good taste and dignity." In exchange, Johnny
would receive five hundred thousand shares of Kinney stock,
worth over $2 million at the current price on the American
Stock Exchange.

Two hours after the meeting Joanna went to the Beverly
Hills Health Club for Women. She was so excited about
the deal that she told Emily Johns, the membership director.
From the club Joanna called her brother, Peter Ulrich, in
West Seneca, New York. Judy Bushkin told her father, Max
Beck. Fredric J. Freed, a Bushkin associate, also learned
about the agreement. Johns, Ulrich, Beck, and Freed all
hurried out and bought a total of 12,000 shares of Kinney
stock, quickly sold them, and pocketed $14,964 in profit.

This did not quite qualify the four inside traders as fledgling Ivan Boeskys, but the SEC investigated the case anyway. In the end they agreed to pay back their profits to the
previous owners of the stock.

Johnny appeared to have made a good deal with Kinney.
One old friend of Johnny and Henry was not so sure. Bob
Patty, a former government agent, had left the Treasury
Department and settled in Las Vegas. He had kept in contact
with Johnny and Henry from the New York days, and Henry
had promised that he would have a shot at becoming the
security chief of Johnny Carson's Aladdin. According to
Patty, he prepared an eighteen-page report that brought up
serious questions about both Kinney and Nigro.

The background of the Kinney Corporation had long been
the subject of rumor and conjecture. In the 1970's Kinney
had had its share of legal problems. In 1976, for instance,
two officers pleaded "no contest" for seeking to fix and
restrain trade in their building-maintenance operations. Two
years later *The Wall Street Journal* reported that executives
of Warner Brothers, a subsidiary of Kinney, were alleged
to have taken a bribe from New York Mafia figures in a

case involving the Westchester Premier Theater in Tarrytown, New York; the officials were not indicted, and Warner Communications said that its "audit committee of outside directors is making an investigation."

On December 13, the Nevada Gaming Commission rejected the Coleman-Torres bid to buy the Aladdin. One of the commissioners spoke so harshly to Coleman that he walked out of the proceedings.

Johnny believed that almost nothing now stood between him and Johnny Carson's Aladdin. The Nevada Gaming Commission was under considerable pressure to find a new owner, and Johnny was the only serious potential buyer.

Many people were interested in Johnny Carson's Aladdin. At five o'clock in the afternoon on January 29, 1980, Jack Catain sat in the lounge of the Indian Wells Hotel in the California desert talking to two men. As the three discussed various business ventures and exchanged gossip, their conversation was being monitored by undercover officers of the Los Angeles Police Department, Organized Crime Division. Catain talked about a deal he had pending with Morris Shenker, a name the police wrote down as "Schenker." Shenker, a St. Louis businessman and a longtime associate of Catain's, had alleged mob connections, and was involved in the selling of the Aladdin Hotel. Catain talked about a business deal the two men had hoped to make, building three high rises and an adjoining golf course in Las Vegas. Later in the conversation "Catain mentioned the purchase of the Alladin [sic] Hotel in Las Vegas by Johnny Carson and the National Kenny [sic] Corporation."

Nevada gaming officials feared that organized-crime figures might find a back door into the management of the Aladdin. Although Catain's name never came up publicly during the Las Vegas negotiations, he was extremely knowledgeable about the Aladdin and had had a long-term business relationship with the representatives of the sellers. About ten years before, Catain had attempted to purchase the hotel. He said later that he had backed off in exchange for "certain cash payments" given him by Morris Shenker and Sorkis Webbe, representing the group from St. Louis and Detroit, who then bought the hotel and were now selling it.

In February National Kinney withdrew from the Aladdin deal, blaming the decision on conditions that the first mortgage holder, the Teamsters Central States Pension Fund, was imposing. Others suspected that Kinney did not have enough cash, or was worried about a possible embarrassing turndown by the Nevada Gaming Commission.

Henry and Johnny were now without their financial backer. Nonetheless, the negotiations continued. The sellers were in a less and less tenable position; if the casino was shut down and its employees let go, the value of the property would decrease by millions of dollars.

On April 22, Johnny attended a meeting with representatives of the sellers in which he made his personal commitment to appear often enough at Johnny Carson's Aladdin to make the casino and hotel a success. The next day Johnny and Nigro signed a letter of intent to buy the troubled casino for $103 million, $2 million less than the previous agreement. The initial down payment was less too, $8 million, the balance payable over seven-and-a-half years.

The two sides met in Los Angeles to work out a final contract. Henry was a brutal negotiator, especially when he was dissatisfied with the terms of the deal. "The only heated discussions I was involved in were the normal kinds of negotiating," says Fred Freed, one of the lawyers negotiating on Bushkin's team. "There were no personal things, no persons screaming, saying, You did this or that. I'm not saying that didn't take place, but I wasn't part of that process."

Henry pushed the sellers to the wall, seeking a better deal. Henry could treat the sellers this way as long as they had no other offers. Only one possible problem loomed. Several months before, Wayne Newton, the singer, and his manager had announced an offer as well, and they professed still to be interested.

Johnny brushed Newton off like a speck of lint from his

tuxedo. "I think he tried to pull a cutesy publicity stunt," Johnny said. With his sleek pompadour, thin moustache, and extravagant mannerisms, Newton may have been the king of Las Vegas entertainers, but his domain ended at the city line. Over the years Johnny had made fun of Newton's extravagant public personality on *The Tonight Show*. One of Newton's old friends says that the singer was so upset at Carson's caricature that he even changed his attire and manner.

In about 1973 Newton was watching Johnny's monologue on *The Tonight Show* when he heard him say, " 'I saw Wayne Newton and Liberace together in a pink bathtub. What do you think that meant?' "

The next afternoon Newton drove to NBC and barged into Johnny's office. "I remember what I told him almost verbatim," Newton recalled in 1984. "I said, 'I am here because I'm going through a personal dilemma in my life. I want to know what child of yours I've killed. I want to know what food of yours I've taken out of your mouth. I want to know what I've done that's so devastating to you that you persist in doing fag jokes about me.'

"Carson's face went white. He said, 'Well, Wayne, I don't write these things.' I told him I'd feel better if he did, and he asked me why. I said, 'Because at least it would mean that you're not the puppet I think you are, and that you aren't just reading some malicious lines written by some writer who crawled out from under a rock. I'm telling you right now: it better fuckin' stop, or I'll knock you on your ass.'

"He said, 'I promise you nothing was ever intended in a malicious way. I've always been a big fan.' And then he went through all this bullshit about how much he likes me. He just kept talking, and it was obviously a nervous apology—but he never again told Wayne Newton jokes."

Johnny dismissed Newton, and looked to the future of Johnny Carson's Aladdin. "I think we're going to bring in a good image," he told the *Las Vegas Sun* in a telephone interview from his NBC offices. "It's good for the city. It's good for the state and it's good for the public to know that the place is not going to have people who will take advantage of it.''

Although Johnny didn't consider Newton a serious opponent, it seemed best to alert the entertainer that he was encroaching on territory where he had no business. On May 1, Kenneth L. Browning of the Bushkin firm wrote a strongly worded letter to the entertainer and sent it to Newton by overnight air. Browning wrote that the Bushkin firm had learned that, despite the Carson/Nigro letter of intent, Newton was trying to buy the Aladdin. ''This letter will advise you to cease and desist forthwith any and all conduct . . . to adversely affect the consummation of the foregoing transaction.''

Johnny and Henry had no use for Newton or anyone associated with him. Lola Falana, the singer, was involved with Newton in attempting to purchase the hotel. Years before, Johnny had seen her perform at a small night club in New York, and when he put her on *The Tonight Show*, her career took off. Falana knew it was doubtful whether she would ever be on the show again. ''I never understood quite what happened,'' Falana says. ''All I know is that my friendship with Johnny was over.''

During the lengthy negotiations in Los Angeles the Carson/ Nigro deal fell through. ''Mr. Bushkin reneged on his letter of intent,'' charged David N. Hurwitz, a lawyer for the sellers, in court testimony six years later. ''I returned to Las Vegas to report to the selling stockholders my evaluation as to the integrity of Mr. Bushkin and his partners, or lack of integrity.''

Almost immediately, on May 11, Newton and his manager, Jay Stream, signed a letter of intent to buy the casino. Newton did not have the financial clout of Johnny Carson. The selling stockholders believed, however, in Hurwitz's words, that ''Mr. Newton was extremely honorable, as compared to the prior experience we had in Los Angeles.'' Hurwitz put Newton together with Ed Torres, who just a few months before had been so unceremoniously rejected by the Nevada Gaming Commission along with Coleman. So that Torres would be more palatable to the commission, he would not technically be an owner of the Casino but would fund his 50 percent of the Aladdin from his children's trust and maintain it in their name. He would become the Aladdin's general manager.

"If you thought the zingers Carson was directing at Newton were something before, wait'll you hear 'em now," Marilyn Beck wrote in her Hollywood column. All that stood in the way of Wayne Newton was the approval of the Nevada Gaming Commission.

SEVENTEEN

At 12:02 P.M. on Monday, September 8, 1980, Henry received a phone call from Jack Catain, a man with whom he said he had no relationship. The secretary marked "w/c" after his name, noting that Catain would call again later. At 2:40 P.M. Brian Ross, an NBC reporter, telephoned the Century City offices from New York City. The attorney's secretary noted in her record book that Ross was calling "re: Aladdin breaking story." His secretary made a check mark to show that Henry had talked to the journalist.

Ross and his producer partner, Ira Silverman, were the best-known team of investigative journalists in television. In the four years since they combined forces, the two men had scored an impressive series of journalistic coups, including exclusives on the Abscam investigation. Tom Brokaw, the NBC anchorman, later called them "our Batman and Robin." They went where the action was, rushing from story to story, city to city, scoring a hard-hitting story and moving on. Although they worked for the same network as Johnny and sometimes out of the Burbank studios, they had never met him or Henry.

According to Henry, Ross told him that he was working on a story involving Wayne Newton and organized crime. Johnny had apparently ended his own attempt to buy the Aladdin, but this was nonetheless valuable information. If

Silverman and Ross could prove that Newton had ties to the Mafia, then the Nevada Gaming Commission would turn the singer down. The hotel would become available again, at a much-diminished price, to another buyer.

Three days after the initial phone call to Henry, Ross and Silverman had a confidential meeting with Lon Shepard and Joe Dorsey, two agents of the Nevada Gaming Commission. The rotund, balding Silverman pulled out a copy of a book, *The Canadian Connection*, that he had obtained from the Canadian embassy in Washington, where he lived. He pointed to a picture of Guido Penosi, an alleged mobster with purported ties to heroin smuggling into the United States. Newton had admitted to an acquaintanceship with Penosi, and the two journalists wanted to know what Gaming Commission agents had learned when they interviewed Penosi.

Ross and Silverman told the two agents that "they weren't really sure, but they had heard Newton was being black-mailed." Ross and Silverman were trying to get information, and Ross had the impression that the agents "liked Mr. Newton but that there seemed to be some kind of a Penosi-Wayne Newton connection that they didn't really know exactly what it was."

The Gaming Commission officials felt that the journalists were fishing for information, but also believed that Ross and Silverman in turn "possessed a large amount of information regarding Newton, his activities and the Aladdin Hotel." In what was a highly unusual stance for reporters, Silverman and Ross warned the agents against Newton. "They stated that licensing Newton for the Aladdin would be very embarrassing for the Board and the state," Shepard and Dorsey wrote in a confidential memo. "They also stated that they were working on an investigative report for a national news show regarding Newton, the Aladdin and o.c. [organized crime] figures, which would air nationwide in the next few weeks."

The two agents could not have been unaware of the threat implicit in Ross and Silverman's comments. The reporters

had a powerful searchlight that would be turned on Wayne
Newton, and could be focused on anyone in the state who
sought to cover up allegations against the entertainer.

A week later, on September 19, Ross called Henry again
from New York City. On September 24, he telephoned the
Century City office yet a third time, leaving the message
that he would call and would be in Los Angeles two days
later.

The next day Ross and Silverman and their camera crew
attended the Nevada Gaming Control Board hearings in
Carson City. As Silverman sat next to the camera crew,
they taped Newton saying that though Guido Penosi was a
fan and a family friend, he did not know that Penosi was
an alleged member of the Gambino organized-crime family.
The three-man board listened to the singer's testimony and
unanimously recommended granting him a license. As an
elated Newton walked to the parking lot, the NBC camera
crew trailed him. In a scene that Ross himself describes as
"tense," he confronted Newton, asking about his relationship with Penosi. The NBC crew shot footage of a now-
angry Newton refusing to be interviewed. ("I said I really
don't care what you want.")

Soon after attempting to interview Newton, the NBC team
packed up its cameras and equipment. At 3:35 P.M. Henry's
secretary noted a call from Brian Ross saying he would be
at the Westwood Marquis and "will be here at 9:15 A.M.
tomorrow."

Ross was an investigative journalist involved in a highly
serious piece of reporting. Yet he and Silverman didn't stay
in Nevada to attend the hearings the next day before the
full commission that would decide whether or not to license
Newton. Ross's four phone calls to Henry's office should
have been memorable; after all, Henry was attorney and
confidant to Johnny Carson, the linchpin of the network that
was the journalist's employer. Yet when Ross was asked
under oath about his four phone calls to Henry's office in
September 1980, he could not remember talking to Henry
even once.

At 6:10 Silverman and Ross flew out of Reno, arriving at the Burbank airport an hour later. That evening they worked on a script for their story on Wayne Newton and the mob. In the morning the two journalists arrived at Henry's office, to drive with him to Johnny's house in Bel Air.

Johnny didn't have many meetings at his house, but he listened as Ross and Silverman talked about Newton, Penosi, and other mob figures. Johnny had become very cynical about Las Vegas. He felt, as Henry remembered, "that the story that NBC had . . . probably would not have any impact whatsoever on Wayne Newton getting a license."

"You can take the whole city and drop it in Lake Mead," Johnny said, as Ross recalls. "You can't run an honest casino there. You can't do this there. I'm never going back there."

Ross and Silverman assert that they went to see Johnny to interview him, to learn if he had any useful information. Johnny didn't remember if they had even asked any questions. He stated in a deposition that he was "under the impression they were simply relating what they were doing because we had been involved in the attempt to purchase the Aladdin Hotel. And they were simply doing it as we might be interested."

On September 26, the day that Johnny met with the journalists, the Nevada Gaming Control Board approved the sale of the Aladdin to Newton. Possibly on that very day, David Hurwitz sat in an office at the closed Aladdin with Wayne Newton and several others. Hurwitz says that he called Henry in Los Angeles, and Henry told him of NBC's exposé on organized crime and Wayne Newton. Although Newton attempted to appear indifferent, Hurwitz could tell that the entertainer was "very upset."

On October 6, at 11:30 A.M. Pacific Time, Ira Silverman called Henry's office from Washington and left his phone number and a message: "Tonight . . . story on Newton & Aladdin." That evening Johnny and Henry both watched the Wayne Newton exposé on the *NBC Evening News*.

Ross and Silverman were given a healthy three minutes,

seven seconds for their story. The most telling footage was shots of Penosi and then of Newton on separate occasions apparently avoiding talking to a reporter. "Investigators say that last year, just before Newton announced he would buy the Aladdin, Newton called Guido Penosi for help with a problem," Ross said, as the camera froze on separate shots of Newton and Penosi. "Investigators say whatever the problem was, it was important enough for Penosi to take it up with leaders of the Gambino family in New York. Police in New York say that this mob boss, Frank Piccolo, told associates he had taken care of Newton's problems, and had become a hidden partner in the Aladdin Hotel deal . . . Federal authorities say Newton is not telling the whole story. . . ."

Ross concluded, "Authorities say . . . Penosi's relationships with Newton and other entertainment figures are now part of a broad yearlong FBI investigation of the investment of East Coast mob money from narcotics and racketeering into the entertainment business in Las Vegas and Hollywood. Brian Ross, NBC News, Los Angeles."

In news stories unnamed sources are like garlic; a little pinch adds to the flavor, too much and the dish stinks. Anyone who read a transcript of the story would realize that the two journalists were merely reporting what unnamed anonymous "authorities" or "police in New York" or "federal authorities" had told them. Silverman and Ross did not have enough sources or information to state their story as fact. That was a subtlety doubtlessly lost on most of the viewers, as it was on Wayne Newton, sitting watching the program in the family room of his Las Vegas house.

"I couldn't believe that something like that could be on television, much less national television," Newton said later about what was the first of three NBC stories about him. "It was just that everything I had worked for in my entire life, the reputation that I had built, never having taken a cent from anybody, never having hurt anybody, to the best of my knowledge, never, that these people could portray such a vicious lie. And I also switched channels to see if it was on one of the other networks, and it wasn't then and it never has been, just on NBC.''

The next afternoon at 3:00 P.M. Ira Silverman called Henry from Washington. The attorney's secretary made a check in her record book showing that Henry took the call.

Newton's immediate reaction was to blame Johnny and accuse him of orchestrating the NBC story. Within twenty-four hours he pulled back, and said that he didn't feel Johnny was involved. He did say, however, that an unnamed associate, presumably Henry, may have been pushing for the story. But not Johnny. "If I accused him, I'd be as wrong as NBC was last night," he said. The singer vowed to file a libel suit against NBC and the reporters, saying that "this could be a fight that could last the rest of my life."

By the time Newton filed his suit, he had once again changed his mind about Johnny, who was named a co-conspirator, though not a defendant. Johnny's name was dropped from a later complaint, but as the trial preparation began, Johnny and his role were at the very center of the singer's case.

As his attorney, Newton chose Morton R. Galane, a prominent Las Vegas lawyer. Galane had the competitive zeal of any good trial attorney, a spirit enhanced because the NBC attorney was Floyd Abrams, a New Yorker and probably the most prominent libel lawyer in America. Galane was an intellectual and a loner, a very different man from his mercurial client. He bore none of the animus toward Carson that Newton felt, but even he grew irritated when Carson did not show up for his deposition.

Galane set out to subpoena Johnny, using a Los Angeles attorney's service. Laurie Miller, the process server, decided to serve Johnny at *The Tonight Show*. According to her deposition, she arrived early enough on October 15, 1981, to obtain a seat on the aisle in the third row.

During the taping she gave a note to a security guard and asked him to give it to Freddy de Cordova. The producer read the note. ("Dear Freddy, I have in my possession a subpoena for Johnny Carson. Please arrange for me to serve him. Thank you.'') Miller saw Freddy let out a laugh and talk to an NBC page.

Nobody interrupted Johnny during a show, but during a break the page walked up to Johnny's desk and whispered to him. With that, the houselights dimmed, and as Johnny sat at his desk, a group of pages descended on the hapless Ms. Miller.

Process servers are paid by the job, and Miller was not about to be thrown out without serving Johnny. As the pages moved down the stairs, she got up, walked forward holding the subpoena, and told Johnny that she was serving him. She says that she ''dropped the subpoena over the microphone boom and it landed on the stage. I turned and said to the security guard, 'O.K., I'm through. I'll go now.' ''

At that point, according to Miller, a page grabbed her by the arm and pulled her into the aisle. ''No, he isn't served,'' the page said. ''You had a chance, but now you've blown it.''

Before she was allowed to leave, she says that a police officer stuffed the subpoena into her shoulder bag. ''There!'' she remembers him saying. ''You never served Johnny Carson. Get out of here.''

Newton's fury at Carson and NBC was fueled in part on two documents that he allegedly purchased from Michael Campion, an acquaintance, for twenty-five-hundred dollars. The documents purported to be memos from Fred Silverman to Brian Ross. ''Please pursue your current investigation regarding Newton's background and his alleged personal liaisons as per our recent information from Mr. Carson's office,'' one memo read. ''Mr. C. is to be kept advised of the progress of this investigation through my office.''

Network presidents did not usually correspond with reporters by memo. Silverman vehemently denied that he wrote the memos and called them forgeries. Las Vegas police confiscated a typewriter on which the memos may have been written. In the end the documents were not entered into the record during the trial.

Despite the questionable documents, Newton still believed that NBC had attacked him "because at that point NBC was renegotiating Johnny's Carson's contract and was trying to romance him into signing again—and Carson had tried to buy the Aladdin himself, but he obviously didn't get it." Unfortunately for that theory, Johnny had signed his new contract with NBC five months before the exposé appeared on the network.

The libel case was heard before a six-person jury in the fall of 1986. Johnny, whom Galane called "an emperor in the world in which he functioned," stood at the center of the plaintiff's case. Galane argued that Ross and Silverman had done their reports to curry favor not only with Carson but with NBC.

Galane realized that Johnny probably had fans sitting on the jury, and he was not about to attack him. "Now, Wayne Newton has not in this lawsuit once suggested improper conduct by Johnny Carson," he told the jury as the trial drew to a close. "I would venture a guess if this jury allowed itself to digress on such an issue that's unrelated to this case, the likelihood is Johnny Carson would win because everybody loves Johnny Carson. All you have to do is watch him. That's not what this case is about. This case is about the motives of Ross and Silverman in their interaction with Bushkin and Mr. Carson."

Newton testified that he had called Penosi when his daughter's life had been threatened. The singer displayed an appalling ignorance about some of his associates, but NBC was unable to show that mobsters had a secret role in the Aladdin purchase.

In December 1986 the jury found NBC and its two reporters guilty, awarding Newton $19.3 million in damages. When the singer left the courtroom, he wished everyone a "very Merry Christmas and a Happy New Year." He didn't mention Johnny Carson.

NBC appealed the verdict. In November 1987 United States District Judge M. D. Crocker ruled in Newton's favor that Ross and Silverman and NBC had shown "reckless disregard for the truth." However, the judge did not believe that NBC had damaged Newton's reputation, and he cut the verdict down to $5,175,000.

In January 1989 Newton stood before a media conference to announce his acceptance of the settlement that, now with interest, came to about $6 million. "We'll probably never know for sure [Johnny Carson's role in the NBC story]," Newton said, but he did not want to talk any longer about Johnny. Although NBC planned to appeal further, Newton believed that he had been fully vindicated.

Although Johnny lost the Aladdin, he maintained his interest in the Commercial Bank. Unfortunately Jack Catain, one of the bank's "most valued customers," had gotten himself in a bit of a jam.

In December 1981 Arthur Howard and Ray Cohen, two men associated with Catain, picked up about $2 million in counterfeit hundred-dollar Federal Reserve notes at Catain's office in Hollywood. They drove in Cohen's Cadillac to Las Vegas, where Howard was caught trying to pass the bills. Cohen was apprehended as well, and corroborated Howard's story about the source of the money.

Catain was a shrewd and careful man, and the Secret Service baited its trap with the only lure that might appeal to Catain: a lot of money and Ray Cohen, a trusted friend. When Cohen agreed to cooperate, he returned to Los Angeles, where he met Catain at the Valley Hilton Hotel and secretly recorded the conversation.

"Can we get more stuff?" Cohen asked.

"Takes time," Catain replied. "We gotta make it."

Later that day Cohen introduced Catain to an undercover agent. As the three men sat discussing a deal, Catain attempted to see if the agent checked out.

"Where are you from?" Catain asked.

"South Philly, the Second Street area."

"I knew Angelo Bruno and Frank Sandoni," Catain said, naming two deceased reputed mobsters.

The two men talked about troubles in the Philadelphia area. Catain appeared secure. He cut a deal: $100,000 in cash for $200,000 in counterfeit currency. Three days later he accepted $50,000 in cash from the agent.

Treasury agents arrested Catain at his offices and charged him with a four-count counterfeiting indictment. Within a few hours he was released on fifteen-thousand-dollar bond.

By claiming poor health, Catain was able to keep postponing his trial even as he continued his banking relationship at the Commercial Bank of California.

Johnny did not scrutinize Henry's dealings. He trusted his closest friend, and he largely let him run the ventures as he saw fit. "Henry had built a false personal image based on Johnny Carson," says one former close associate. "He appeared very insecure, very frightened. When someone jeopardizes his self-esteem, they are playing with a deadly force. He doesn't ever want to be embarrassed. It's all esteem, all image, and he guarded it with his life. He believed that together he and Johnny could take on anyone."

Henry was not the only one who found it immensely useful to be associated with Johnny. Even bankers became excited at the prospect of doing business with Johnny and his friends, and Henry moved accounts to whichever banks offered the best deals. In November 1981 Citibank took over the $2.3 million loan that had bought the stock of the Commercial Bank. Citibank thought that with Johnny Carson standing behind the loan, nothing could go wrong. Citibank considered its "inherent risk to be one of prepayment, rather than repayment."

Henry had a treasure trove of wealthy show-business clients, and Citibank was delighted at all the new business that was coming in. Henry opened a million-dollar CD for one of his other clients, Neil Simon. David Letterman opened an account, and both Marsha Mason and Paul Anka became customers of the Citibank's Fine Arts Investments. Citibank looked enviously at Johnny's $12 million investment portfolio at Bear Stearns and Simon's $8 million account, hoping to manage those as well.

Citibank was interested in developing as strong a relationship with Johnny and his friends as possible. The bank was happy to open $1.7 million lines of credit for Johnny and Neil Simon, men of such wealth that it was like putting a thousand dollars credit line on a MasterCard. Other of Johnny and Henry's associates didn't have such sterling credit, but the bank wasn't about to turn down Johnny's friends. In February 1982 Citibank opened a half-million-dollar line of credit to Kopelson. Based on Kopelson's financial statement, that was a large loan, but the bank went ahead "based primarily on our growing relationship with the law firm's most important clients and, secondly, on Arnold's own entrepreneurial activities and growth potential." In May the bank also loaned at least $1 million to Kopelson's associate Michael Miller.

Johnny had stopped showing up for most board meetings, and he was as distant from the bank as from most of his other business dealings. In the spring of 1982 Henry resigned from the board of directors of the Commercial Bank. "He told me that he was resigning as a director . . . because he could no longer use the bank to obtain loans for his clients and that it had become embarrassing to him," said Miller in a sworn affidavit.

Henry may have resigned, but the bank and the Bushkin firm were entangled in a web of personal and business relationships. In 1981 the bank paid the law firm about $114,000 in legal fees, and another $100,000 more in the first six months of 1982. The bank had lent about $1,400,000 to officers, directors, and shareholders as of December 31, 1981. A bank prospectus later admitted that at least some of these loans "involved violations of the California Financial Code or federal law and regulations."

The Commercial Bank of California was a troubled institution. At the beginning of 1982, 13.4 percent of the bank's loans, or $3,091,815, were over a month in default of payment. In the first months of 1982 officers of the bank attempted to pull in some of the more questionable loans. Jack Catain was a major problem. Tony Bazurto, the executive vice-president, wrote later, "It was always my understanding when I was first employed by the bank, and for a substantial period after that, that Mr. Catain did control a large portion of the bank. This interpretation was derived from comments made by other officers of the bank and the apparent free reign that Mr. Catain had with the bank."

On June 21, the bank sent a letter to Catain telling him that "the total direct and related indebtedness has created concern by the Bank's regulatory agency concerning concentration in one credit." His direct and indirect liabilities amounted to $374,000. The bank asked for full payment of one indirect obligation and said that it was evaluating whether he should immediately pay back another $100,000 loan.

Henry and Kopelson had been the best of friends, but the problems of the bank and disagreements at the firm strained their relationship beyond repair. In September Kopelson left the firm for good, to become more active in running the Commercial Bank. On September 13, Kopelson drove out to Johnny's house to talk to him about the situation at the Commercial Bank. Kopelson reportedly told Johnny that Henry had offered to sell his shares. "I'm staying in," Johnny said, according to Kopelson, and agreed to continue to do ads for the bank. Johnny also said that he was planning to resign as co-chairman and as a director.

After talking to Johnny, Kopelson sent a memo to Henry saying that though Johnny was resigning "he wished to keep his shares. . . . He also requested that I meet with him on a monthly basis to keep him apprised of the Bank's activities."

Kopelson went ahead a week later and bought Henry's shares. Kopelson, his wife, Anne, and Miller took over effective management of the bank. By that time the friendship between Henry and Kopelson was shattered. "Henry and Arnold were friends and partners, but they got into a real mess and began to accuse one another,'' says Marvin Landau, then a bank board member. ''That was one of the biggest problems. It got to the point that they couldn't even walk into the same room together. You're dealing with tremendous egos here. It became a joke. It was you can do no right and I can do no wrong.''

''They were both men who made too much of an investment in what people think of them,'' says another board member. ''What drove them at loggerheads was that they were trying to hurt each other's self-esteem.''

Kopelson believed that Johnny was the key to salvaging the bank. In near-desperation he turned to Joanna in an attempt to reach Johnny's ear. ''I'm absolutely sure that Johnny would have died if he had known what was going on at the Commercial Bank,'' says Joanna. ''I told him, 'You are right in the middle of a war between two ex–law partners.' I felt that Kopelson was being treated unfairly by Bushkin. When Johnny said Kopelson was lying, I said, 'He's not lying.' And Johnny was enraged with me for going against Bushkin.''

If the bank was to survive, it needed new capital. Kopelson prepared a private placement memorandum in an attempt to sell up to 265,000 new shares at $15 a share. But the financial figures in the report would make any investor leery. By June 30, 1982, the bank had loans of $3,976,766, or 13.8 percent, in default for over a month, and six-month operating losses of $254,015.

On November 30, 1982, Kopelson wrote a letter marked PERSONAL AND CONFIDENTIAL to Johnny outlining the bank's problems. The letter made the bank sound less like a financial institution than an ongoing melodrama. One of the bank's top officials ''appeared to be undergoing a nervous breakdown . . . openly sobbing claiming he was a total failure.'' Federal Deposit Insurance Corporation and California banking officials were auditing the institution, which might have to write off at least $1 million in bad loans.

If the bank's shareholders did not add more capital, the Commercial Bank would have to forfeit its charter. Johnny was the shareholder best able to cough up more capital, but the Commercial Bank was turning into an embarrassing debacle. The state regulators had discovered yet another $400,000 in bad loans that the bank's auditors had missed. To keep the bank open, Kopelson and Miller borrowed $1.5 million. Johnny kept his distance.

At the Commercial Bank headquarters Kopelson and Miller took one curious approach to their problems. They went on a shopping spree. They redesigned their penthouse offices, spending hundreds of thousands of dollars for such items as travertine tables, Oriental vases, and granite floors, a setting more appropriate for a Roman bath than for the executive offices of a small, failing bank.

Kopelson attempted to call in dubious loans. The Commercial Bank now pushed Catain harder, saying that it wanted at least part of its money, or it would take legal action. Later the bank sued Catain to pay back some of the loans.

Catain countersued and portrayed himself as an innocent dupe of the Bushkin firm. "The Bushkin firm represented me in a legal capacity as well as dealing with me as directors and owners of the bank," he told Peter S. Greenberg, a Los Angeles journalist, in a rare interview. "I guaranteed the loans on the advice of my attorneys, who were also making the loans. When they dig deep enough, they'll find out I'm clean and they're dirty."

As busy as Kopelson was managing the new bank, he still had commitments as a film producer. Each fall he took a trip to Europe. When Kopelson arrived back in New York, he received a phone call from one of the bank officers.

"Are you okay?" the man asked urgently.

"I'm fine," Kopelson replied. "What's wrong?"

"A big blue van pulled up in front of the bank. This man brought in a big basket of flowers addressed to you. It had a note attached. It read, 'Regrets on your imminent departure.' "

Kopelson was frightened. He called Arthur Kassel and spoke to his secretary. "They're going to blow up my house," she remembers him saying. Then he called Kassel at the Bushkin firm, where he was sitting with an attorney.

Kassel, who was developing the Beverly Hills Gun Club, had excellent connections with the Los Angeles Police. He called people he knew at the Organized Crime Task Force, who went over to the bank. Kassel took a suite of rooms at the Beverly Hills Hotel for Kopelson and his family and put their house under twenty-four-hour surveillance.

Kopelson ended up staying in his house, but he began carrying a .45. Gerald Pearce, a private investigator from northern California whom Kopelson hired, told him that the bank had been infiltrated by organized crime. Every time he started his car, he feared that it would blow up.

Miller carried a gun as well. One evening he came home and found a pack of matches next to his bed. Inside the cover he found the words "Personal regards, Jack Catain."

As the problems with the Commercial Bank grew worse, Henry figured out a new tax-avoidance scheme for Johnny. He still owned about 16 percent of the Commercial Bank shares; with the deterioration of the bank, the shares were worth very little. But the IRS said that the stock was valued at the price of the last major transaction. Since Henry had sold his stock for fifteen dollars a share to Kopelson, Johnny could donate the shares to the Carson Television Center at USC and take a full fifteen-dollars-a-share write-off.

The main loser in this, other than the U.S. Treasury, would be Arnold Kopelson, Michael Miller, and the other beleaguered principals of the Commercial Bank. If Johnny left the bank, crucial depositors might well follow. Kopelson and Miller prevented the transfer and sought desperately to raise more capital.

According to Henry, Miller contacted Johnny personally because he said "he was trying to get Mr. Carson to put up the money to save the bank." On February 11, Henry said that he met with Kopelson, who warned that "if Mr. Carson did not put up the money to save the Bank and if it failed, it would be known that it was 'Carson's bank' " that failed.

Citibank had happily taken over the original Commercial Bank loan and gone on to loan millions of dollars individually to the various partners. Citibank had thought that the worst prospect was that Johnny and his partners would pay up early. Now the bank found itself in the center of a rancorous dispute. Sheila Wilensky, the Citibank vice-president in charge of the loans, shuttled between the sides, a reluctant emissary. When Johnny had wanted to donate some of his Commercial Bank shares to the University of Southern California, she had dutifully and unsuccessfully asked Kopelson's and Miller's permission. And Miller had said that the investors should be putting in more money, not trying to get out.

In February 1983 Wilensky watchlisted Citibank's $2.3 million Commercial Bank loan. The banker felt that if the two sides didn't resolve their problems, the loan could become a serious problem. In the months that she had dealt with the various partners, she had come to seriously mistrust Henry and to believe that his days as Johnny's lawyer were numbered. "We are concerned that his clients could in fact be considerably unhappy with him as a result of less-than-outstanding performance in these two investments (Commercial Bank of California/Texas Land)," she wrote in her watchlist recommendation. "We perceive that our position . . . [is] likely to be Bushkin/Carson relationship-breakers."

Kopelson believed that he had been suckered into taking over the failing bank, but since he had sat on the board from the beginning, the idea of himself as an innocent dupe was not entirely credible. As the bank sank into the abyss, its debts growing deeper and deeper, Kopelson and Miller tried to find various solutions.

Finally Kopelson and Miller filed a civil suit charging Henry with fraud and fraudulent concealment under the Racketeer Influenced and Corrupt Organizations Act (RICO). The investigation by Gerald Pearce, the private detective, led Kopelson "to believe that Mr. Bushkin had engaged in a fraudulent scheme, first to obtain control of the Bank and then to use the Bank for himself and for the benefit of individuals connected with organized crime."

The suit charged that Henry had reneged on his commitment to have Johnny play an active role in the bank, attending meetings and actively promoting and publicizing the bank. They alleged in their complaint that Henry had allowed the bank to be used for loan-shark operations, and illegal kickbacks and organized-crime activities.

RICO was a formidable weapon in criminal cases against gangsters, but this was a civil case, a distinction that was easily forgotten. No matter what the outcome, once the media learned of the suit, Henry's and Johnny's reputations couldn't help but suffer.

Initially the court agreed with Kopelson and Miller's request that the complaint be kept under seal, away from public view. When the court reversed itself, Bushkin's own attorneys attempted to have the complaint resealed.

Kopelson and Miller's strategy changed when the story first appeared publicly in the *Los Angeles Herald Examiner* on March 10, 1983. Indeed, in his motion to have the case dismissed, Henry argued that Kopelson and Miller had wanted the complaint kept secret because once the news got out, Henry and Johnny "would not be willing to pay 'hush' money." Henry further charged that Johnny's name wasn't mentioned directly in the complaint because he was Kopelson's "sugar daddy," and that unless he " 'came across,' he too could be a defendant." A month later Kopelson and Miller added Johnny's name to their suit.

Kopelson and Miller might not have sued if Johnny had saved the bank with an infusion of capital. That did not mean, however, that the two men filed the suit frivolously, and they vigorously pursued the case.

Henry had other problems for—true to Kassel's prophecy—the Bushkins were going through a bitter divorce. Judy Bushkin gave one of the first depositions in the bank case. She appeared in the Century City law offices on April 6, 1983, accompanied by Arthur J. Crowley, her divorce attorney, as counsel. Henry and Arnold were there, across the table from one another.

Judy was called as Henry's witness, and she was not expected to say anything damaging to her estranged husband. She made the extraordinary admission, however, that she had been introduced to Jack Catain in November 1977 at a party at the Bushkins' house in Beverly Hills. Henry's lawyer, Henry S. Kaplan, had little choice but to pursue the matter.

"When was the first time, if at all, that you learned that Mr. Catain was involved in alleged organized-crime activities?" he asked.

"Seventy-six—seven-seven."

"And how did you obtain that information?"

"Henry Bushkin."

It had been a devastating morning, and not only for Henry Bushkin. "It was extremely traumatic," Judy Bushkin recalls. "I was very upset at having to answer certain questions. Arnold could have taken some of my answers and gone to town with them. But he remained a gentleman and didn't."

Kopelson was still involved in the movie business, and the following month he flew to France for the Cannes Film Festival, staying at the Hotel Du Cap in Antibes. While there, he received a telegram saying that the Federal Deposit Insurance Corporation (FDIC) was about to issue an "8-E" directive, removing him, his wife, and Miller as directors. Kopelson Telexed the bank that the three directors were resigning.

On May 27, officials of the FDIC walked into the Commercial Bank offices on Sunset Boulevard and took it over.

Louis Carter, the state banking superintendent, said that the bank was operating "in an unsafe and unsound condition because of substantial losses resulting in inadequate capital." The FDIC could have been liable for paying off the $24 million in deposits in the bank. To avoid that, the bank was sold to another institution, First Credit Bank of Blythe. After the Memorial Day weekend the bank opened for business as usual.

A federal judge dropped Johnny's name from Kopelson and Miller's lawsuit. "I am not surprised that the judge threw out their suit against me, for it never had any basis whatsoever," Johnny said. "Nevertheless, this meritless suit has unfairly smeared my name and reputation, so I have today instructed my attorneys to prepare to sue Kopelson and Miller for malicious prosecution."

Johnny never filed that suit. And in February 1984 Kopelson and Miller dropped their suit against Bushkin, and Henry dropped his countersuit, each side promising to "bear his own costs."

In May 1984 the FDIC filed suit against Johnny, Henry, and twenty-two other past and present shareholders and board members of the Commercial Bank. The suit, seeking at least $10 million in damages, charged the defendants with allowing the Commercial Bank to fail. The FDIC charged that the bank had allowed loans to be made to people "associated directly or indirectly with organized crime." The FDIC specifically cited Johnny for not attending board meetings and failing to "use his position, reputation, notoriety and influence to promote the business."

The same week Johnny's name was mentioned in the trial of John DeLorean on cocaine-trafficking charges. James Timothy Hoffman, the key witness against DeLorean, testified that in 1980 the auto manufacturer had boasted that he had once trafficked in cocaine with Carson. Even Hoffman said that he thought DeLorean was merely "puffing" and he did not believe him, but the charge was headline news.

Johnny immediately issued a denial. That evening on *The*

Tonight Show he told his audience, "I've been trying to contain my anger most of the day."

To pursue its case, the FDIC hired a prominent Los Angeles law firm—Finley, Kumble, Wagner, Heine, Underberg, Manley, Myerson & Casey—and paid it a fee of $1,347,671.88. Gerald Pearce, the private investigator who had worked for Kopelson and Miller, was also hired, and created "flow charts of ties" that purported to show organized-crime connections. According to court documents, "in one example, Mr. Pearce drew lines on his charts to connect Mr. Bushkin with 'the Jewish mafia' and Mr. Carson with the 'garment industry—Buffalo mafia.' " The defendant's attorney stated that "of course, Pearce had no facts to support his libelous 'theories.' "

The proceedings, which would have been of great interest to the public, were kept secret. So was the final settlement.

With the ending of the FDIC case, Johnny's legal problems with the government over the Commercial Bank had ended. He was, however, still immersed in a complicated series of lawsuits and countersuits involving payment of the Citibank loan. Kopelson and Miller had stopped paying on the loan, and Henry believed they were trying to stick Johnny with the entire burden. At Citibank Frederick S. Taff, a vice-president, felt that Henry and perhaps Johnny had "a large measure of desire for revenge" and that Henry may have wanted to push Citibank to "litigation, foreclosure, publicly for default" against Kopelson and Miller. In seeking repayment of the loan, Henry went so far as to put a lien on Kopelson's house.

"Johnny's bank," which had begun in such comradely good spirit, ended in a slough of accusations and lawsuits, tainting the reputations of everyone involved, visiting near financial ruin on Miller, and almost destroying Kopelson. In one of several suits against Kopelson a court-of-appeals judge quoted Shakespeare's *Hamlet*, saying that a " 'loan oft loses both itself and friend.' "

Kopelson was saved financially and had a certain vindication when he produced *Platoon* and received the 1986

Academy Award for the Best Picture of the Year. Miller attempted to start over again in a new business from a small office miles from Beverly Hills and Hollywood.

Johnny had come out of the various deals without large losses. That was small credit indeed for Henry, managing the affairs of the biggest television star in America in the booming years of the eighties. Johnny's name had been sullied, mentioned in the same breath with a mobster like Jack Catain, who died in February 1987 before being sentenced on the counterfeiting conviction. Johnny himself was drawn into a petty, vindictive lawsuit against Baskin and named as a defendant in a government suit for racketeering; had wasted his time in a futile attempt to buy a Las Vegas casino; was pulled into Wayne Newton's libel suit against NBC; and was sucked into a controversy with Neil Simon in which he held a potential multimillion-dollar liability over some empty landscape outside Houston.

Another star would have summarily fired his attorney. But Henry was Johnny's closest friend, and he would not listen to people criticizing him. The men shared so much in common, and knew so much about one another. Instead of getting rid of Henry, Johnny turned his problems into an item in the monologue, joking about "Bombastic Bushkin" having him invest in such winners as a Doggie-bag factory in Bangladesh and a Club Med in Beirut.

EIGHTEEN

As the Lear Jet soared high above the Nebraska landscape, Johnny did card tricks for his three companions. Henry had seen the tricks innumerable times, but he had long ago learned to give Johnny the illusion of full attention. Jim Mahoney, Johnny's cigar-smoking personal publicist, had seen Johnny's tricks too. He watched as if he were seeing the Great Houdini himself. John McMahon, the new president of Carson Productions but no relation to Ed, watched intently as well. Johnny had taken a liking to the former NBC executive, who looked somewhat like a younger version of *The Tonight Show* host.

Joanna should have been there too on this October afternoon in 1981, but instead she was in New York. She had started a business with Michael Vollbracht, a clothing designer, and was spending more and more time away from the house in Bel Air and from Johnny.

In March of that year Johnny had raged against the *National Enquirer* for printing that his and Joanna's marriage was in trouble. "This is absolutely, completely, one-hundred percent falsehood," he said on *The Tonight Show*, his voice charged with anger. "So, I'm going to call the *National Enquirer* and the people who wrote this liars. Now, that's slander—or they can sue me for slander. You know where I am, gentlemen."

The audience had applauded fervently, but alas, the Carson marriage was deeply troubled, filled with suspicions and accusations. Things were so bad that Johnny had spent September at their Malibu home separated from Joanna.

The plane glided downward toward Karl Stefan Memorial Airport, a modest strip that primarily served small private planes. Johnny pulled back from his cards and looked out the small window. "I helped build this runway we are going to be landing on," he said matter-of-factly. "After school I would haul dirt in a dump truck out here. I think I made twenty-five cents an hour."

Johnny stared down at the town where he was returning to attend a reunion of the Norfolk High School Class of 1943 and to film a ninety-minute documentary. Norfolk was a major part of the landscape of Johnny's mind. Here were the haunts of his boyhood and youth, his first triumphs as a magician, his first date.

On the tarmac waited a group of about forty people, including David Lowe, Jr., who would be directing and producing *Johnny Goes Home*. Lowe was the son and namesake of the director of *Who Do You Trust?* One of Johnny's own sons might have spent the week learning about his father's past. Instead, Johnny's nephew, Jeff Sotzing, had come along to work as a production assistant.

Norfolk had expected Johnny and a small group, not this army of filmmakers that threatened to take over the Holiday Inn. Johnny had four connecting rooms: a bedroom, a second room for his drums and card table, another room for meetings, and yet another for his bodyguard, who had his own intercom system and a private phone line. Whenever Johnny ventured out to film, he had his mobile home and an entourage worthy of a potentate.

Carson Productions paid for six of Johnny's classmates —an orthopedic surgeon, a psychiatrist, a dentist, an engineer, a business executive, and a stock broker—to return and spend the week in Norfolk. These were the men with whom he had secretly smoked cigarettes, placed a stink bomb in the ventilating system, shared first beers and first dates. They had all gone off to the service at the same time. They were all successful, all living outside Nebraska.

They could have talked with Johnny of old times and old places, of the rites of passage to manhood, of the slipperiness of memory and time. But the script didn't call for anything like that.

The men gathered at the old high school, now a junior high school, for the shooting of their scene with Johnny. The producers had found a few old-fashioned school desks, and the men were crammed into them like adults driving kiddie cars. While they talked together for the first time in almost forty years, Faye Gordon entered the room.

"Well, hello, Rascal," said the eighty-five-year-old retired schoolteacher, who had taught Johnny in elementary school. "Are you leading me to slaughter?"

Miss Gordon was a spinster schoolmarm who had devoted her life developing the penmanship and the character of thousands of children. She had lived an honorable and simple life, and could have been a character in Hamlin Garland's *A Son of the Middle Border*.

"No, you're going to do fine," Johnny declared. "You sure look pretty."

"You don't have to butter me up," Miss Gordon replied, fixing Johnny with her sternest gaze. "I'm going to do your show for you, and if you're not good, I'm going to make you stay after school."

"I've certainly done that before," Johnny laughed.

Miss Gordon had appeared on *The Tonight Show* in the mid-sixties. She had a bit of the ham in her, and as the camera whirled, she played the strict, reproving teacher working with seven hopelessly inept students.

When the camera was on, Johnny joshed with the other six men as if they had picked up without missing a step after all those years. When the camera turned off and the shooting was over, Johnny left his old friends. "He kept his privacy, kept himself a little bit at a distance," one of the six said afterward. "One or two of the guys made more effort to keep contact with him. They may have gotten a little response from him, but nothing that went very far."

At the Elkhorn River the producer wanted to shoot film of Johnny hanging from the bridge as he had done as a boy. They hired a twenty-six-car Union Pacific train to come rolling over the bridge. The train shuttled back and forth like a seasoned extra. On one take, as the twentieth car lumbered across the river, Johnny lost his grip and fell into the shallow water. One assistant wondered whether Johnny had fallen on purpose, to get some amusing film.

"It's cold," Johnny yelled as helpers ran toward him, their arms full of fluffy white towels.

"How cold is it, Johnny?" a crew member yelled.

In downtown Norfolk Johnny walked into the A. B. Nelson and Son Bicycle Shop to film another sequence. Victor Nelson, one of his high school classmates, took out an ancient account book and pointed to the August 25, 1937, listing of the bike Johnny's dad had bought for his son from Nelson's dad. Then Johnny hopped on a similar Schwinn bicycle sitting in the aisle of the tiny store. Although it appeared that the bicycle had been there for forty years waiting for a buyer, at the request of Johnny's production company Schwinn had flown the bicycle into Omaha and trucked it to Norfolk.

Johnny rode out onto the sidewalk. From among the scores of spectators, he nodded to a young girl to sit on the handlebars and wheeled into Main Street. While the police held up traffic, he rode in circles, filmed by the camera.

The crew went out in the countryside to film a sequence of Johnny hunting pheasant. Mike Fuehrer, a local young man, had been hired as a production assistant. He noticed that Johnny and his city friends had brought rifles, not shotguns. Fuehrer thought that if Johnny had shot a pheasant with a rifle, he would have been a fine shot indeed.

Fuehrer, who later became a reporter for the *Norfolk Daily News*, found the television people a strange lot. "I could never understand why they got so hyper," he said. "They pretty much led Johnny around. 'Johnny, we're going here today.' 'Johnny, do you know your lines?' ''

Monday evening Johnny attended his high school reunion. The allure of Johnny and the excitement of a special dinner-dance had brought about 80 of the 147-member class of 1943, along with their spouses, to the King's Ballroom. They were in their mid-fifties, an age when the shadow of mortality had passed over their lives. Fifteen members of the class had died; Robert Sewell had already retired from his job as a firefighter; Mary Ann Hansen had eighteen grandchildren.

The Norfolk graduates began arriving nearly an hour early for the six-thirty cocktail hour. By seven o'clock everyone was there—everyone but Johnny. The group was experiencing the feelings of nostalgia, sentiment, and melancholy common to all reunions. They had dressed in their best, and they said how young everyone looked, knowing how much they had changed. They were from towns and cities across America, and except for their Sunday-go-to-meeting clothes, they could have been an audience for *The Tonight Show*.

Johnny was driven to the ballroom in the mobile home, which was parked behind the large hall. When he finally entered the ballroom, the Bobby Mills Band was playing some classic riffs from the Big Band era, and many of the couples were dancing. Johnny moved into the room like a presidential candidate, trailed by a camera crew and two sound men maneuvering mike booms over his head. One after another, his old classmates moved forward and shook his hand.

"It was amazing seeing some of the people you hadn't seen in thirty-eight years," Johnny said afterward. "The trick was to look at their names and pretend that you weren't. Some I recognized right away and others I had to read their names. But I must be getting older or something, because the printing was so small, you really couldn't fake it."

Johnny worked his way through the room. Theodore Skillstad, the former principal, hugged Johnny. Like so many others, he was full of Johnny stories. "One day Johnny called an assembly and signed my name to it," Skillstad said.

"No, I didn't sign it," Johnny said, retreating into legalisms. "I *typed* it. Signing would have been forgery."

The elderly pedagogue was not about to argue. "Well, anyway, he called the assembly, and when everyone got there, I thought another teacher had called it. The superintendent thought I had called it. I thought he might have called it. And we sat there for a few minutes before 'the Great Carsoni' appeared onstage and cut off my tie. Well, it looked like he did. I thought that he might have, just for the laugh."

While Skillstad spun his Johnny stories, Lorraine Beckenhauer Gipe and June Korb Jaffee strolled up to Johnny wearing red-and-white baseball shirts embossed JOHNNY WHO?

For a moment Johnny appeared unsure how to take the joke.

"You had to do it," Johnny said.

"Yes, we had to do it," Lorraine said. Her younger sister had been Johnny's first love, and Lorraine had a certain bitterness toward him and the jokes he made about his adolescent romances.

Johnny had long ago learned how to push away the unpleasant and the uncertain, and to him they were often the same. The two women kissed him and exchanged a few words with him before he moved on.

While the guests sat down for an all-American meal of thick slabs of roast beef, a potpourri of salads, and vanilla and fudge marble ice-cream cups for dessert, Johnny signed autographs and posed for Polaroid and Instamatic pictures. Then he retreated to the mobile home, and everyone else, including the camera crew, had dinner.

Afterward, Dr. Gordon "Jack" Farner, a Cleveland orthopedic surgeon and the class co-president, introduced Johnny, who walked on as if the reunion were *The Tonight Show*. "I'd like to apologize for the low pay," Johnny said as everyone laughed about the dollar the production company paid them to sign releases. "Without sounding corny or oversentimental, there's a closeness or security of growing up in a small town that you don't get anywhere else. I think there's a great advantage to growing up in a community where you feel comfortable. Hell, I never remember even having to lock the doors on the house when I was living back here. Most people knew each other. There was a closeness, a security that we all miss, I am sure."

Although Johnny talked of closeness, it was not *his* closeness. As he looked out across the ballroom, he saw not only his past but his future: men and women, many of whom looked a generation older than he did. He saw not Jerry and Glenn and Art and Bette and Larry and Fred and Jack and Charlotte, friends and acquaintances of forty years ago. He saw something about which he was far more comfortable: an audience.

"As in all small towns there are certain 'nice' girls, girls that you marry and girls that you do not," Johnny said, launching into a story that he used in his Las Vegas routine. "Well, I won't use real names but, there was a girl a year younger than us, I'll call her 'Francine,' and Francine put out. At least that was going around. Well, I finally got up enough nerve . . ."

As Johnny told his story, those in the ballroom knew whom he was talking about. Some of the other men had probably had their first sexual experience with her also. She had left town years ago, had married and was a grandmother. She was as respectable as anyone in the room. Although people laughed at Johnny's bawdy recollections of his night with "Francine," it was an uneasy laughter. There were those who felt Johnny had tainted the evening.

When Johnny finished, his contemporaries gave him a standing ovation. He tried to wave off the applause, but they clapped and clapped. Then Johnny departed almost as abruptly as he had arrived.

The band continued to play, but the guests drifted out into the autumn night. It was all over, and somehow it hadn't been right. Many felt they had been used, though they weren't sure how.

The evening had ended earlier than had been expected. It happened to be Chuck Howser's birthday, and the Norfolk mortician wasn't about to let the party be over. He had several members of the class of '43 sleeping at his place, and invited a large number more to his home. The group stayed up until five in the morning.

Despite lack of sleep, Howser showed up at the Holiday Inn for breakfast. Johnny was at another table.

"Thanks for inviting me to the party," Johnny said, as Howser remembers.

"You son of a bitch. You wouldn't have come anyway."

Johnny Goes Home was supposed to begin with a shot of Johnny driving toward Norfolk on a dirt road, a plume of dust rising behind the car. Unfortunately Norfolk was not the town that time forgot but a hustling business center, with a population of twenty thousand and nothing but paved roads. Norfolk's outskirts were lined with such familiar emporiums as K mart, Wal-Mart Discount City, Shop K-O, Wendy's, Burger King, Bonanza. That was not the Norfolk that Johnny should be going home to visit. So the film crew searched until they discovered a dirt road six miles east of town that could be shot with nary a sign of modernity in the background.

Johnny drove along the dirt road, followed by fifteen other vehicles. The car was the same green 1939 Chrysler Royal that he had driven as a teenager. Bob Means, a local resident, had found the wreckage in a body shop and restored it.

As one cameraman hunched up on the floor shot footage, Johnny used the green Chrysler as a comedic prop. "It doesn't quite have the zip it used to," Johnny said. "But then, neither do I."

Beneath the jokes and the ersatz nostalgia of this drive along a forgotten road, the car was haunted by Johnny's past. This was the car that, when he was fourteen, he and his buddies had rolled out the driveway and raced along Highway 275. He had driven it the night when, in the backseat, he had sex the first time. He had driven the Chrysler when he returned home from the navy and wrecked it, rolling over and over again in a cornfield until the car lay quiet in the Nebraska night. This was the car he knew when he began to dream that terrible dream of an endless highway, the white stripe moving on to eternity.

Johnny stopped the car beside a great oak tree, tears in his eyes. Unable to continue, he stood by himself next to the Chrysler. There is no panorama of aloneness quite like the endless landscape of Nebraska. When he was himself again, the self he showed to the world, he got back into the car, and the filming continued.

Joanna was scheduled to arrive on Tuesday, but she stayed in New York. "We were having problems," Joanna recalls. "He wanted me to come in, and I didn't want to come in."

Johnny spent his free hours with Henry, McMahon, Mahoney, Lowe, and Sotzing. Henry had no work to do in Norfolk, but Johnny had wanted his closest friend to be there. The two men had been close friends for a decade, and now they shared something that brought them even closer: marital problems. Henry considered himself already separated from Judy, and he could empathize with what Johnny was going through.

Lowe was the one outsider, but he was a link with the past too, and he was invited into the entourage. Toward Sotzing, his sister's son, Johnny acted the way he couldn't to his own three sons, telling dirty jokes and joshing with the young man.

Johnny relaxed this week as much as he ever did in public. One evening over dinner at the Holiday Inn Johnny was drinking. When Johnny was drinking, there was bound to be trouble. "What are you doing tonight?" he asked the waitress.

The waitress laughed.

"Why does everyone think I'm funny?" Johnny snapped, his voice tense and urgent. "I'm not being funny."

The people in the restaurant idolized Johnny. This was not the Johnny they wanted to hear. They kept their eyes on their food and pretended nothing was happening.

"Let's go, Johnny," one of the men said.

"I want to stay here!"

When Johnny finally got up and walked out of the restaurant, he stopped in front of the Pac-Man in the hall. He looked for a moment at the electronic game, fiddling with the buttons. "In my day kids didn't get a sore hand from playing Pac-Man, but playing your man."

And then he went up to bed.

At the football pep rally Friday afternoon the Norfolk High School students had looked forward to Johnny's being part of a skit, but at the last minute he canceled. The band played *The Tonight Show* theme anyway, and a teacher filled in for Johnny. It was no big deal. Johnny was only an amusing diversion from the more important task at hand: to beat archrival Columbus.

In the evening Johnny drove to Columbus, fifty-six miles south, to watch the Norfolk Panthers play the Columbus Discoverers. In his day Johnny had not been big and strong enough to make the team, or popular enough to be chosen as a cheerleader.

Johnny was now trying to come home to a TV version of that world of almost forty years ago. If he could have suited up for the game and led the Panthers while the cameras rolled, he probably would have done so. While he could not do that, he could be a cheerleader and lead the rooters as the camera recorded his efforts.

At the game Johnny stood with the girl cheerleaders, wearing a Maroon *N* sweater and white pants. He didn't know the cheers, but he followed the five cheerleaders, playing to the camera and to the crowd. He jumped in the air and grabbed himself as if he had ruptured his back. When the camera crew had enough film, Johnny retired to the recreational vehicle.

At halftime Johnny returned and stood alone on the cinder track between the field and the stands. "This is Johnny Carson's birthday!" the public-address announcer boomed. "So let's all join in wishing Johnny a happy birthday."

The crowd sang "Happy Birthday" as Johnny stood in the track. "Johnny, not only is your wife, Joanna, here, but as a very special surprise, your brother, Dick, and sister, Catherine, are here," the announcer said, sounding like Ralph Edwards on *This Is Your Life*.

Four cake-bearers carried a three hundred-pound cake onto the field for Johnny's fifty-sixth birthday. Johnny embraced Dick's wife. "Happy birthday, sweetie," his sister-in-law said. "You can't go home without us."

"Where have they been keeping you?" Johnny asked, his voice tinged with emotion.

Johnny embraced his sister.

"Happy birthday, sweetie," Catherine Sotzing said. Then he shook hands with his brother and brother-in-law. Only then did he move to greet Joanna.

It was her husband's birthday, but Joanna did not want to be here. She thought to herself, This is weird. And as they looked into each other's eyes, Joanna felt they were saying to each other, "Now where do we go from here?"

Joanna thought she knew what this week in Norfolk had meant to him. "He wasn't himself emotionally," she says. "There was the car and everything. I think he was trying to figure out where he was and who he was and why he couldn't find happiness."

As the band played "Auld Lang Syne," the camera zoomed in on Johnny's face. His eyes were filled with tears. "You know how sentimental I am," he said. "You'll ruin my image. I'm cruel and aloof."

Johnny and the group moved off the field and into the recreational vehicle. As the Panthers fought a losing battle to the Discoverers, some of the spectators left the stands and sought out Johnny, searching from car to car in the parking lot. But the vehicle had driven off into the night.

On a Friday morning early in 1982 Johnny sat at the Polo Lounge in the Beverly Hills Hotel, only a few minutes' drive from his home in Bel Air. He rarely left the house for a breakfast meeting, but his closest advisers were with him this morning. Henry was there as always when Johnny's future was at stake. Jim Mahoney, his personal publicist, had been invited, as had Freddy de Cordova and Peter Lassally, the number-two producer.

Everyone at the table had read the article that had appeared in *The Wall Street Journal* a couple weeks earlier titled "Johnny Carson May Be Losing His Touch." The article had quoted Gerald M. Goldhaber, chairman of the communications department at the State University of New York in Buffalo, as saying that "next to ABC's 'Nightline' he's almost an anachronism, like the Queen of England."

That was a sting that had no poison in it. What hurt were the ratings comparisons showing that the other networks and independents were doing better against *The Tonight Show*. When Ted Koppel had an especially newsworthy subject, *Nightline* sometimes even beat Johnny in the ratings. The Midwest was Johnny Carson country. Yet in order to improve the ratings, WTMJ-TV, the NBC Milwaukee affiliate, pushed reruns of *Maude* in front of the program. In Minneapolis the NBC affiliate, WTCN-TV, was getting such dreadful ratings that it put reruns of *M*A*S*H* on in place of *The Tonight Show*, running Johnny's program later at night.

The Wall Street Journal was only one newspaper, but Mahoney saw the articles about the ratings troubles "spreading like a disease" from columnist to columnist, newspaper to newspaper. *The Tonight Show* was so crucial to NBC that the day after the meeting the network began airing special promos calling Johnny number one in late-night programming. Henry, who almost never talked to the press, gave a *Los Angeles Times* reporter Nielson ratings numbers showing that Johnny remained number one.

Although *The Tonight Show* was by far the top-rated late-night program, the show had lost about 815,000 viewers in the last year. Johnny was the victim of a phenomenon that practically no one of his generation would have thought possible: The networks themselves were beginning to decline. Overall ratings were slowly sinking as viewers turned to movies on HBO or Showtime, a ball game on Ted Turner's superstation in Atlanta or on ESPN, or a movie rented from the video store.

Nonetheless, Johnny was a cultural fixture in America, as familiar as the NBC peacock. "Johnny just gets better and better; everyone else gets worse and worse," wrote Tom Shales in February. "He has probably been funnier longer and more consistently than any other comedian who ever lived."

When the red light went on, Johnny was as funny as he had ever been. When the light went off, his life was full of darkness and uncertainty. His marriage was like the set of *The Tonight Show*, made to be viewed from a distance. Over the years Johnny and Joanna had gone to a psychiatrist and a psychoanalyst seeking help; and they continued to go out together, to show their public faces.

Late in February the Carsons went to dinner at a restaurant on La Cianega Boulevard. Johnny was drinking. Joanna knew the ominous signs as his temperament began to change.

After dinner Johnny and Joanna tooled off in his silver DeLorean. La Cianega Boulevard is lined with restaurants, and any weekend the police could wait and pluck drunks like ripe lemons off a tree. The police stopped Johnny not because he was obviously drunk, but because his license-plate sticker had expired.

When the police asked Johnny to walk heel-to-toe, he swayed like a sailboat adrift on a stormy sea. The police in

Los Angeles have learned to be solicitous of the foibles of the famous. Nonetheless, they put Johnny in their squad car and took him to the police station.

Johnny was less than cordial to the arresting officers. He finally agreed to a breath test that showed an alcohol level of .16 percent in his blood, more than 50 percent above the acceptable level of .10 percent.

While the officers were booking Johnny for driving under the influence, Joanna sought outside help. She would have called Henry, but he was spending the weekend on his ranch in Santa Barbara. Instead, she called Arthur Kassel, who dressed hurriedly and drove to the station.

Kassel knew more about the police than many policemen did. His kidding, ingratiating manner worked wonders on the sergeant at the desk.

"What are the chances of getting him out of here after he's booked?" he asked.

"Kassel is wanting to take him out of here," the sergeant said.

The sergeant received a phone call. "That was the chief," the policeman said, referring to Chief of Police Lee Tracy. "The chief said he wasn't going to release him because he was abusive to the cops. Arthur, you got to give us your word. If he gets behind the wheel in the next four hours . . ."

Upstairs in the lockup Johnny was singing away, oblivious to the negotiations. Finally, Johnny came tottering into the room and walked outside and into a tan Rolls-Royce.

The next day Mahoney put the best public-relations spin he could on the story. He asserted that Johnny had "abstained from hard liquor for many years but he had a little wine" to drink. He said that Johnny "can't recall ever having been ticketed for driving before, not even a parking violation." In fact, in 1973 Johnny was fined forty-five dollars for running a red light in Las Vegas. It was an incident that should have been memorable; his car smashed into another car, which in turn crashed into a third vehicle.

Johnny made his own public-relations effort. The next

evening on *The Tonight Show* Johnny had an actor in a police uniform lead him onstage. He told the "cop" that he had to do his monologue, and the officer graciously disappeared behind the curtain. The audience applauded thunderously. "You don't know how nice that sounds," Johnny said. "Would you like to be my character witnesses?"

Johnny had little choice but to talk about the arrest. "It's a strange night," he remarked. "There are other places I'd rather be. This has been what is called a slow news weekend. . . . I wish I could say I was researching my new special, 'Johnny Goes Home to the Slammer.'"

"It would be impossible to do the show without mentioning what happened this weekend," he said. "I assume you know about the reported encounter between the law and me over the weekend."

The word *reported* had on it the fine hand of a lawyer, worried lest Johnny admit anything.

"And the truth is not as exciting as what you might have read."

The truth was more exciting than the sanitized versions printed in the daily press. Johnny was a drinker who could not drink, and he had been dangerously drunk.

In the early 1980's America still had an indulgent attitude toward those who drank and drove. The members of Mothers Against Drunk Drivers felt differently. Barbara Bloomberg, the Los Angeles representative, had a son killed by a drunken driver. She had seen Johnny's soft-shoe attempt at a mea culpa on *The Tonight Show* and was not impressed. "He has made such a mockery of his arrest," she asserted. "But I'm hoping he may still come through and show some integrity."

The MADD mothers planned to show up for Johnny's arraignment in April. Joanna's presence would have added an air of sobriety and seriousness and concern. However, on that day she was in New York attending a party at the home of her good friend Marjorie Reed.

Johnny had talented lawyers who might well have found

enough technicalities to have warranted a verdict of innocence. Johnny did not want to run the gauntlet of publicity, and he pleaded "no contest" to one misdemeanor count. He could have been sentenced up to six months in jail. Instead, he was fined $603, put on probation for three years, made to attend drivers' education alcohol classes, and for ninety days allowed only to drive back and forth to work.

For Johnny, 1982 was a bad year almost any way he looked at it. It was ironic to the extreme that he was driving his sleek stainless-steel DeLorean the night of his arrest. The sports car represented his only benefit out of his $500,000 investment in the failed company. Almost every article about John DeLorean's debacle found space to mention Johnny's losses.

In Las Vegas the Sahara Hotel fired Johnny's old friend Jack Eglash as entertainment director. Johnny, upset over the abrupt dismissal, vowed never to return to the hotel-casino where he had headlined for two decades.

Hoping to sell syndication rights of old *Tonight Show* programs, Carson Productions entered into an agreement with Paramount TV. Johnny, however, reportedly backed out because *Carson's Comedy Classics* might be shown at 11:30 P.M. He was not about to compete with himself. Paramount believed that Carson Productions had reneged on the contract, and sued for $15 million.

For Carson Productions, the NBC commitments to put its programs on the air were like having chits to print money on the U.S. mint. Unfortunately Johnny's new company squandered its chits on tired concepts, producing several horrendous failures: a comedy starring Gabe Kaplan as a hard-core northern urbanite running a down-home Texas bar; Angie Dickinson in a comedy, as a clerk in a department store; Lynn Redgrave playing a high school teacher. The company finally had a hit with *Amen*, a show helped no end by being placed after the highly successful *Golden Girls*. Carson Productions did better with specials of old TV bloopers, and with a few made-for-TV movies. The company actually made a profit, arguably as much a tribute to the deal Henry had negotiated as to the programs themselves.

John McMahon, the president of Carson Productions, and Henry began having problems almost from the day that E. Gregory "Ed" Hookstratten, a Beverly Hills attorney, first negotiated McMahon's lucrative contract. McMahon hired Maynell Thomas, a stunning black lawyer at the Bushkin firm who had begun her professional career as a Playboy bunny. McMahon had the feeling that "we were doing on-the-job training for lawyers and paying huge amounts to the Bushkin law firm."

In his condominium in Century City Henry built a small screening room. After it was constructed, he allegedly wanted it charged to the company. McMahon reportedly refused and brought the matter to Johnny's attention.

"I left the company because there were some things that came up about Henry, and Johnny chose to dismiss anything about Henry's wrongdoing," McMahon says. "Henry knew that I had spoken to Johnny, and that was the end of it for me. Johnny tended to believe Henry, and I was left so vulnerable that I was finished."

Carson Productions produced the movie *The Big Chill*, an enormous popular and critical success. The new president of Carson Films, Richard Fischoff, then announced plans for seven future films, four to be produced and financed by Columbia Pictures. *Desert Bloom*, Carson Films' next venture, was critically praised but disappeared from view, and Fischoff left the company after two years. "It was Johnny's company, but Henry Bushkin was the real head," he says.

After Fischoff's departure the company made no more theatrical films.

Both Johnny and his companies required constant legal advice. In protecting their interests, Henry took the most aggressive of postures. In either late 1981 or early January 1982 a small businessman, Alex Kolis, called Bushkin's office and asked to speak to Henry.

Kolis had formed a partnership with Will Williams, a

western artist, to promote a series of paintings of Hollywood stars called "John Ford's Cowboy Kings." Although Johnny was hardly a movie hero, Williams had painted a portrait of Johnny in a ten-gallon hat. In early 1978 Kolis sent the portrait to Johnny's office, hoping that *The Tonight Show* host would have John Wayne and the other "Cowboy Kings" on his show. Johnny wrote a letter to Williams thanking him for the gift, but the old cowboy stars never appeared on the program.

Now, approximately four years later, Kolis called the Bushkin office because he was planning to develop a line of T-shirts featuring the "Cowboy Kings." Although the businessman thought that he was talking to Henry, one of his partners, Ralph Jonas, purportedly took the call. Kolis introduced himself as the head of Western Series, Inc. He said that he held the copyright on a portrait of Johnny and he wanted to reproduce it on T-shirts. He was told that Johnny would not be interested. Kolis says that he replied, "[I]n that case, I will drop the subject, good-bye." According to Jonas, Kolis threatened to manufacture the T-shirts anyway, and the attorney said that he would see him in court.

Kolis may have boasted about his plans; but if he did, it was only the vain boast of a man in his fifties struggling to make a buck as an entrepreneur. The name Western Series, Inc. may have conjured up visions of a corporate monolith, but the company consisted only of Kolis and his dreams of a world clothed in cowboy T-shirts.

The Bushkin firm allegedly called Kolis and sent a letter warning him not to proceed. Kolis says that he was out of the country when the supposed call was made and that he never received the letter.

Kolis proceeded with plans to market the other movie-star T-shirts in Europe, where a Johnny Carson T-shirt was hardly a hot item. In February Kolis says his importer told him that he was backing out of the deal because he had read that Carson was suing the businessman. Kolis was stunned to discover an article in the February 10, 1982, issue of

Variety stating that "Johnny Carson has filed suit in L.A. Superior Court against the maker of T-shirts and other products that Carson believes will bear his name and likeness. . . . The suit seeks $1,000,000 in punitive damages."

Kolis was not a rich man, and he had not made a single T-shirt of Cowboy Carson. He learned, however, what a brutal, tedious, and lengthy process the court system can be, for the innocent as well as the guilty. A year and a half later Kolis finally gave his sworn affidavit in which he said that he had never told anyone that he was going ahead with the T-shirt without Johnny's permission. Not only had he made no such T-shirts, but he had no intention of making any. He said that though he was not served with the lawsuit, "my personal name and reputation have been injured seriously as a result of this article." He asked for summary judgment, dismissing the case.

At this point the Bushkin firm dropped the case. Johnny and Henry had achieved their intention of showing that an "example should be made of defendants." In many respects Kolis was a broken man. "The suit killed me and my business before I even started," Kolis says. "And it really caused me sickness and put me on welfare for three years."

Kolis was full of the righteous anger of a little man fighting a giant. He decided to sue Johnny for malicious prosecution. "I'm a stubborn bastard," Kolis says. "And I don't feel this man has the right to just go ahead and execute anybody he can. And I use the word execute. And that's it. I mean I've got a hard-on. I'm going to get him. He's hurt me too goddamn badly."

Kolis had no money, but he was able to get a new attorney, Phil Feldman, on a contingency basis. Feldman's office was in the San Fernando Valley, not Beverly Hills, and though he was a competent attorney, he was hardly a match for the money and might of the Bushkin firm.

Feldman's associate, Ronnali Rosenfeld, prepared a passionately written memorandum marred by occasional typos and misspellings. "The question is whether John W. Carson, a rich and 'well known entertainer and television per-

sonality' can use attorneys as a private protection agency
and the press and the courts as his weapons to protect his
financial empire . . . This whole exercise in using the civil
courts . . . by filing a lawsuit, publicizing it in Variety and
dropping it years later when called up for Summary Judgment, is . . . 'despicable.' ''

Johnny's attorneys seemed to treat the Feldman firm like
a bunch of small-town hicks. Johnny reportedly stood up
Kolis's attorneys for his deposition. When it was resched-
uled, he arrived almost an hour late, wearing tennis shorts
and sneakers.

For Feldman to succeed, he had to show that Johnny was
behind the suit against Kolis. Johnny acted as if Kolis were
a gnat that Henry had swatted away. ''Mr. Bushkin informed
me they were taking action against some individual to get
a restraining order to ask him not to reproduce my likeness
on a T-shirt,'' Johnny remembered. ''It was a short conversation, something we had been through before at other
times, and that, basically, was the gist of it.''

''I expect your relationship over the years was such that
you didn't challenge the planned course of action?'' Feldman asked.

''No.''

As Kolis sat listening to Johnny, he says that he became
so ill that he had ''to pop a couple of pills.'' That was the
only time Kolis saw Johnny. The suit was thrown out of
court. Feldman appealed, but the sixty-two-year-old Kolis
had lost his last chance for revenge.

NINETEEN

Emm-Jay Trokel was in her apartment on Oakhurst Drive in Beverly Hills on Thursday November 4, 1982, when she heard someone pounding on her door. At eleven o'clock in the morning she wasn't expecting anyone, and she wasn't even dressed.

Emm-Jay knew it couldn't be Johnny. He always called before he dropped by. Almost four years had gone by since that Christmas Eve when Johnny had arrived at Emm-Jay's home for the first time. Few people knew about their relationship, though neighbors sometimes wondered what Johnny Carson was doing in the apartment complex. Emm-Jay was in her mid-thirties now, an age when even in the midst of romantic entreaties a single woman usually heard her biological clock ticking. But Emm-Jay continued her relationship with Johnny, thinking as little of the past as of the future.

The pounding continued. Emm-Jay wrapped a towel around her body and hurried to the door. A teenager stood there. "The building's on fire!" he yelled.

By then the flames had spread from the garage along the common roof to the two-story, fourteen-unit apartment building. The fire was so advanced that Emm-Jay had time only to get dressed and run out, leaving all her possessions behind. She stood on the sidewalk watching twelve engine companies fighting the million-dollar blaze. The firemen aimed their hoses on the fire, but the flames engulfed the building, destroying everything in Emm-Jay's apartment, and her car in the garage.

Emm-Jay surveyed the smoldering ruins. "Want me to go in and find something for you?" one of the firemen asked.

"Maybe my phone book," Emm-Jay said, trying to stay calm.

The fireman poked thorough the soot and rubble. After a few minutes he returned with her address book and a set of keys.

"I won't be needing these," Emm-Jay said. "They're my car keys." Even without the fire, Emm-Jay had enough problems. She was between jobs, part of that endless cycle of feast or famine in the television industry. That she could handle, if only her relationship with Johnny hadn't become a permanent crisis. His marriage was more troubled than ever, and Emm-Jay believed that Joanna knew all about her and Johnny. All she heard from him were tales of his fights with Joanna, stories of a marriage that was one bitter joke.

Sometimes Emm-Jay was afraid of Joanna, of her power and wealth. As she stood looking at the ashes, she became filled with anger. She believed that Joanna had the fire set in the garage to destroy her car as a warning. Emm-Jay went to a nearby phone booth and called Johnny. "Call her off now!" she yelled into the phone.

"Calm down," Johnny said, as Emm-Jay remembers. "Calm down."

The fire had been arson, but Joanna was in no way responsible.

"I want you to get the hell out of my life," Joanna told Johnny Saturday evening, two days after the fire.

"You got it," Johnny said.

Joanna told Johnny that "they needed time apart to sort out their lives." He was involved with another woman, and they both should think about her. But it was not only this woman that troubled her, there was Henry and the way he was managing their affairs.

Early in the year a confidant had come to Joanna and told her, "Do you realize you may be royally screwed?" The friend said that Johnny and Henry were planning a new movie-production company, of which Henry would own about 50 percent. Joanna believed that Johnny was trying to help Henry shelter money during his divorce from Judy Bushkin. But since hearing about the new company, Joanna had grown increasingly suspicious of Johnny and Henry, and saw the proposed new company as a way to hide money from her as well. "Henry was so clever and so good at the way he presented things," says Joanna. "He could sit and talk Johnny into anything. I caught them in their tracks. That's when it really hit the fan. Henry told him, 'Here's what we're going to do,' and Johnny would do it."

This evening Johnny and Joanna were like wary old boxers who knew each other's moves. They had separated twice in their marriage, the latest time a year ago. And now they were as coolly rational as if they were discussing where to have dinner. After their talk they drank cups of hot chocolate and went to bed.

Henry was already helping Johnny plan for the possibility of divorce. The two men had moved cautiously, even fearing that Joanna was wiretapping their phone conversations. If Johnny divorced Joanna, she would be entitled to half of their community assets. But if he could shelter part of his wealth, he might be able to hold on to millions of extra dollars.

In the morning Johnny packed up some of his belongings and drove out to the weekend house on Carbon Beach in Malibu. If the Carsons went ahead with their divorce, all his income from the day he actually left Joanna would be his and his alone. Thus, Johnny had to develop a clear identity as a single man living apart from Joanna. From the moment he moved out, his accountants began keeping separate books. In other ways he had to be careful as well. If he should return to the mansion in Bel Air and even once partake of marital pleasures, he might commit one of the most expensive sex acts in history.

Johnny continued to see Emm-Jay. Although he had never been particularly generous to her, she had never cared. But she was desperate now. She had nothing—no car, no clothes—and she stayed with one friend and then another, moving every few nights. Johnny offered ten-thousand dollars to tide her over until the insurance company paid off her twenty-thousand-dollar policy. Henry sent her a letter saying that the money was on its way. For the first time since the fire Emm-Jay felt relieved. But one week after another went by, and still the money did not arrive. Emm-Jay was a proud woman, and she could never bring herself to ask what had happened. She survived until she received the insurance money seven months after the fire.

One day in December 1983 Emm-Jay was flying with Johnny in his private jet. That week a story had appeared in the *National Enquirer* mentioning "a female friend in Los Angeles to whom he sent $10,000 in cash last November."

"I never got the money." Emm-Jay shrugged.

Johnny looked surprised. "I don't understand," he said, according to Emm-Jay. "Henry was supposed to give you the money."

Emm-Jay had a new car and new clothes, and she let the matter drop, believing that Henry had pocketed the ten-thousand dollars. It never occurred to her that Henry would not be so foolish as to take money Johnny intended for her. Almost certainly, Johnny and Henry had decided that during the divorce he could not be passing out ten-thousand dollars to a lover.

When Emm-Jay visited Johnny at his Malibu beach house, she found him happy to be by himself, beating away on his drums or looking out into the nighttime sky with his Questar telescope. She thought that he was happy, but she felt too that Johnny still cared for Joanna and wanted the marriage to continue.

Johnny fit well into the laid-back Malibu beach scene. He bought an expensive satellite dish, and had the house refurnished. Paintings by David Hockney and Paul Mogensen hung on the walls, along with photos of himself with various celebrities. His living room had the kind of needlepoint pillow that might have graced his mother's overstuffed sofa in Norfolk, only it didn't say HOME SWEET HOME but IT'S ALL IN THE TIMING. In his bedroom he installed Universal equipment for his daily workouts. To open or shut the window from his bed, he merely pressed a button.

As always, Johnny talked to Joanna frequently on the phone, and each week he drove over to the great house on St. Cloud Road to sign checks. When Johnny was growing up, Thanksgiving and Christmas were family times, days of good cheer, laughter, and memories. Johnny accepted Joanna's invitation for Thanksgiving dinner with one stipulation: No one else could be present, not even Cory, Rick, or Tim, Jr.

That evening the Carsons discussed many things, including Christmas gifts for *The Tonight Show* staff. Johnny, who did not like to be bothered with such details, left the choosing of gifts to Joanna, even asking his estranged wife what she herself wanted. They agreed that, as usual, she would go out and buy the present and he would pay for it.

Johnny had another serious family matter to face: the illness of his aging father, Kit. Johnny didn't want Kit to know that he was planning his third divorce, and for his father's benefit, Johnny and Joanna maintained the illusion of their marriage. On December 17, Johnny slept at the Bel Air house, though according to Joanna he did not make love to her. The next morning he and Joanna flew in Johnny's new private jet to Monterey to pick up Dick Carson and his wife, and from there to Arizona. To allay any suspicions, Johnny and Joanna stayed together in the same room at the Camelback Inn in Scottsdale.

When his parents moved into a home in Scottsdale, Johnny paid for their residence and for nursing help. Yet he was miserly in the way he passed out his emotions to his parents as to anyone else. He made the obligatory visit to his father's bedside, and the next day flew back with Joanna to Los Angeles. On their return to Los Angeles Johnny became ill; he spent another night at the house on St. Cloud.

Johnny returned for dinner on Christmas Eve with the family. His three sons almost always appeared on this day. Even Chris flew in from Florida, to visit his father and, with his brothers, to receive his annual stipend. On Christmas Day Joanna told Johnny about the $100,000 diamond-and-sapphire earrings that she had purchased as his Christmas gift.

As Joanna talked to Johnny, she felt that he wanted their marriage to continue in a manner that would "allow him to enjoy the benefits of marriage without its attendant burdens and obligations." She had had enough of that during her years with Johnny, and she wanted out.

For the third time it was not Johnny but his wife who called it quits. Jody had cried out for a divorce. In her frustration Joanne had sought other relationships. Now, Joanna was ending their marriage. "If I had given as much to marriage as I gave to *The Tonight Show*, I'd probably have a hell of a marriage," Johnny reflected. "But the fact is I haven't given that, and there you have the simple reason for the failure of my marriages. I put the energy into the show."

When Johnny went home to his house on Carbon Beach in Malibu, he thought that he was alone. He was, however, under twenty-four-hour surveillance by a team of reporters and photographers from the *National Enquirer*. The tabloid usually did not go to such lengths in its pursuit of celebrities, but Johnny had raised the publication's hackles. He had assaulted the weekly on the air, calling its staff liars for saying that his marriage was in trouble. Now, the editors intended to prove that they had been, at worst, prophetic. They wanted to shove his words back at him, on the front page of millions of copies of the tabloid in supermarkets and newsstands across America.

Early in January the rumors about the separation began in the gossip columns. Then, on January 25, 1983, the *National Enquirer* had its revenge. The tabloid headlined JOHNNY CARSON AND WIFE SPLIT: THE UNTOLD STORY. The weekly even printed a sidebar about Johnny's earlier complaint that the paper's story was "absolutely, completely, 100 per cent falsehoods."

Now that the news was out in every supermarket in America, Joanna asked Johnny to say that they had not separated. That one statement might cost him millions of dollars, and he refused. Joanna asked her husband to appear at a charity benefit. Johnny said that he would happy to do so, if she would sign a statement confirming that their separation had begun in November 1982.

A few days after the story broke in the tabloids, Sally Field arrived at Johnny's house at about 11:00 A.M. As she entered, the actress was already under surveillance by a Hollywood photographer, Phil Ramey, the kamikaze of paparazzi. Ramey made a six-figure income taking untakable photos and selling them for thousands of dollars. Some celebrities had learned simply to give up and give in, so that he could have his pictures and be gone. One of his most outrageous moments came when he climbed on the hood of the medical van carrying the body of Rock Hudson.

Ramey and another photographer tromped out onto the sand and sat down about 250 feet from Johnny's beach-level sun deck. At about 1:00 P.M. Johnny and the Academy Award–winning actress appeared on the sun deck in bathing suits. The photographers watched as she put her arm around Johnny and kissed him and as they toasted each other with wineglasses. The couple went inside in the late afternoon for an hour, returning to watch the sun set.

"The cameras were concealed in bags," Ramey recalls. "They were aimed toward Johnny and prefocused. One of us would look at the other person, and the one behind would crouch down and shoot. We sat there for four or five hours and we only got four pictures."

When Johnny and Field left the house in his black Mercedes sports car, the photographers followed them. Johnny stopped at La Scala, his favorite restaurant in Malibu. The photographers figured they already had what the *National Enquirer* wanted: a picture of Johnny with a celebrity. They didn't care now if Johnny saw them, but they wanted a few more shots.

"Ha, ha, ha." Field laughed exuberantly as she and Johnny exited the restaurant after dinner. "Oh, what a wonderful time. I loved that."

Suddenly she saw the two paparazzi clicking away. "Oh!" she gasped.

"Stop it," Johnny said. "Stop it.

"Knock it off," Johnny said firmly. "I'm telling you once and I'm going to tell you one more time. You're in trouble."

As Johnny reached for his hand bag, the two photographers fled. They had heard rumors that he carried a gun, and they didn't want to test the truth of the story.

The next week the pictures appeared in the *National Enquirer* under the heading HEEERRE'S JOHNNY WITH BURT REYNOLDS' EX-GAL SAL.

Suddenly his candid pictures meant big money, and photographers snapped him several times with Morgan Fairchild, the television actress. On one occasion he tried to escape through the back entrance of the Directors Guild Theater after a screening. The photographers were onto him. As they snapped away like hunters before a cornered prey, he raised his finger in futile anger.

For Johnny, these were the hardest of times. Not only was there the divorce, the accusations over the bank, the endless manipulations, the tabloid reporters at his heels, but his father was nearing the end. On April 8, Johnny called *The Tonight Show* off at 4:00 P.M. to fly to Arizona to be at the bedside of eighty-three-year-old Kit Carson. The next evening his father died.

* * *

Marilyn Katleman ran down the corridor at the airport in Denver. Katleman was living in Aspen, and she always made her connecting flight to Los Angeles at the last minute. She careened around the corner and saw, thank God, that the plane had been delayed.

The stunning dark-haired divorcée sat down and watched the other passengers. She had a smile on her face. She thought, Nobody knows that I've got a date with Johnny Carson tonight.

Katleman had known Johnny for a decade, having met him on a friend's tennis court when he had first arrived in Los Angeles. She was married then, and soon afterward Johnny married Joanna. Katleman knew Joanna through SHARE. She had gone to the Carsons' house occasionally, but she didn't think of either one of them as a close friend.

Now, Johnny had called and asked her out. She had seen Johnny's picture in the paper with Sally Field, Morgan Fairchild, and others, and she knew that Joanna was going out too. And she thought, Why not? Why not have dinner with Johnny?

"We had dinner at Don the Beachcomber's," Katleman recalls. "We were sitting there. Johnny warned me about dating him. He said, 'People could find out and it could get in the papers.' I said, 'I'm not a celebrity.'

"We went out quite a bit. He started sending a car for me. We went to out-of-the-way places. He came to dinner at my house one night. We went to Dick and Molly Martin's for dinner another evening.

"Johnny is very naive. Basically he's a country boy. He loves the ladies, but he's a sweet guy. He shuns the limelight. He would say, 'When I'm in a crowd of people, what do they expect? Do they expect me to solve their problems? Do they expect pearls of wisdom? I'm a talk-show host.' "

Johnny and Katleman met privately at his house three times in one week. Early one morning he walked her to a cab.

Katleman attended a celebration after the Academy

Awards. At about eleven o'clock a friend telephoned her. "You better pick up a copy of the *National Enquirer*," he said. Katleman and a friend jumped in a Rolls-Royce and drove down to Hughes Market on Beverly Boulevard.

The two women ran into the store, pulled a copy of the tabloid out of a rack, and raced through the pages. "Oh my God!" Katleman exclaimed. There was her picture as one of the dancing ladies of SHARE. She read how a bare-chested Johnny had said good-bye to her at three-fifteen in the morning, "embracing and kissing all the way." The tabloid called her a "beautiful 50-year old . . . a mother of four grown children—and close friend of Johnny's estranged wife." It quoted a "friend of Johnny's" saying that "when Joanna discovers Johnny has taken up with Marilyn, who's her friend, she is going to seethe."

Katleman knew that she had no choice but to call Joanna. "She hadn't read the article yet, and I explained how we'd gone out," Katleman says. "Joanna was very understanding. Two ladies involved in a situation." (Joanna denies that Katleman ever made the phone call.)

"After that, I went to the SHARE rehearsals. There were all these ladies dancing. Everyone wants to be in the front row. Everyone wants to chew you up, even if they're your best friend.

"Joanna pulled me aside. There we were talking, and the rest of the group watching. She said, 'You lied to me. You were at his house.' I said, 'You're making more of this than there is.' Her attitude was, How do you dare go out with my husband! There was nothing I could do.

"SHARE broke into two groups. Some of the ladies became my closest friends because they thought if anything happens between Johnny and me, they'd be on the inside.

"I called Johnny and said, 'I'm not going out with you anymore. It's not worth it.' He didn't call me again until the SHARE show was over. I liked that. We started going out again. It lasted until about August. I've often thought about it. I liked him.

"Johnny is a very kind and very nice man. He's very

sensitive. I think he loves women and is easily taken in. I think he wanted to be loved.''

Like many man going through a divorce, Johnny took a certain solace in sex. Indeed, he had always taken solace in sex. Emm-Jay had kidded with him once that she was planning to write a book. ''And what will my chapter be?'' he asked. ''The fucking years,'' she replied, with a timing that Johnny could not have bettered.

Johnny was in his late fifties, but he was hardly the aging bachelor prowling singles haunts. He was publicly, formally, legally separated now, and the women along Carbon Beach knew that Johnny Carson was available.

Malibu is one of those places, like Saint-Tropez and Aspen, where money and power go in search of youth and beauty, and sometimes youth and beauty go in search of money and power. The town sits along the Pacific Coast Highway, just north of Los Angeles. The real life of Malibu is in private homes that turn their backs on the uninvited and the curious. On the weekends someone is always giving a party that spills out onto the beach.

Johnny's property included the beach down to the waterline, but he was not known to call the police when bikini-clad maidens strode across his sand. One weekend in that summer of 1983 Johnny was sitting out on the deck surveying the scene as a tall thirty-three-year-old blonde walked along the beach, carrying a glass. She had that fresh, windblown California-girl look, as if she had little on her mind but sun and surf and a life that was nothing but weekends.

Alexis Mass was attending a gathering at the home of David Niven, Jr. Niven had just moved in, and he was celebrating his new home with an all-day party. Niven knew Johnny casually, but he had not been invited.

Alex was a woman who knew her way around various elements of society, from men of power and wealth to the humbler and ruder. Alex and Johnny talked for a while, and he accompanied her back to the party.

For years when Alex had returned home to North Hills,

in the suburbs of Pittsburgh, she had been full of stories of
her adventures, and Johnny was only the latest. She usually
dropped by to see Jim Nauman, who owns the Evergreen
Hotel and Bar, a local hangout. "She'd show up with a dirt
buster or a sophisticate," recalls Nauman. "She came back
here one time with a mercenary. Another time she told of
going on a safari as this guy's secretary. She talked too of
going out with this famous ballet dancer."

At the local laundromat that Alex's mother managed, the
ladies buzzed over the news of the ballet dancer, Mikhail
Baryshnikov.

When Alex was growing up in North Hills, she would
have seemed an unlikely candidate to become the audacious
woman who would date the expatriate Russian and meet
Johnny Carson on the beach in Malibu. She and her younger
sister lived on a street of modest houses of brick and false
brick. Her father, Alex Mass, worked as a salesman for a
valve company, traveling all over western Pennsylvania. In
his spare time he restored artwork. The Masses kept largely
to themselves.

"We would play together in grade school," remembers
Nancy Anderson Croker, a classmate. "She was real feminine, and it was very much girl play. But it seemed that
she didn't need anyone close outside her family."

In high school Alex wore her hair long and straight with
bangs, in the style of the sixties. But she was far from the
turmoil, experimentation, and excitement of that decade.
Under her picture in the 1968 school yearbook appeared the
words *Do I look all right?* For every girl impressed with
Alex's perfect dress, a boy was put off by her stylishness.
For every student who thought she was shy, someone else
thought her a snob. She had no steady boyfriend, no close
girlfriend, and she left few memories.

Upon graduation, Alex entered Carlow College, a tiny
Catholic women's college in Pittsburgh. She lasted only a
semester, letting her father believe that "she was too ambitious for school and said they weren't teaching her
enough."

Her roommate saw it differently. "She didn't do very well in school," recalls Rose Mary Carroll. "I don't think she was college material. She was into movie stars, into motorcycles, into Clint Eastwood. She seemed from a different era. She was childlike in a way. She was worried about this movie world. She put on pancake makeup every morning. Her shoes matched her purses. People couldn't relate to her, but nobody disliked her. She was in this little world of her own. And her mother and father seemed to create and support that world for her."

Alex took a job as a secretary. A stunning, intelligent young woman was not about to become lost in the secretarial pool. She had good positions in Pittsburgh as executive secretary to powerful men before moving to Boston. There, she worked as the secretary to the president of a stock company. In her spare time she volunteered in the campaign of a young, reform-minded candidate for governor, a man of such a puritan soul that he could have sailed on the *Mayflower*. When the candidate won, Alex joined the staff. "Why did we hire that blond bombshell?" asked Governor Michael Dukakis.

From Boston Alex moved to Los Angeles, where she worked for yet another powerful man as an executive secretary. She had succeeded by the standards of North Hills. Yet when she returned to Pennsylvania, she seemed discontent. She had reached the age of thirty, and her old friends were all married and had children. "Alex was never one to settle for less than perfection," says Marcia Fessler Drozd, a classmate. "She was sort of unsettled when I saw her in 1981, not certain whether she was going to stay in Los Angeles or not."

Jim Nauman saw her in Los Angeles too. "She was in the middle of looking for jobs," Nauman says. "She's always been sort of mysterious. She had a good sense of humor and a big ego, like any pretty girl. She was witty, an earthy girl, maybe naive, but maybe naive like a fox."

Strangely enough in the city of the endless face-lifts, Alex had troubles because of her looks. "I met her six months before she met Johnny," recalls Ken Schwartz, who was then working for an executive recruitment firm. "When she came in and applied, she caused quite a stir. We sent her out for a lot of interviews. She was overqualified and too intimidating for a lot of people. We sent her out for a forty-thousand-dollar-a-year job as the administrator of a Big Eight accounting firm. The senior guy said he would get all the ribbing. She was too beautiful and too poised. The next thing I heard, Johnny was setting her up in a fancy apartment on Wilshire Avenue."

"How's your love life?" Pat McCormick asked Johnny. As soon as the comedy writer uttered the words, he knew he had made a mistake.

Johnny thought a moment. "I've got to learn to rent," he said.

Johnny was in the midst of an emotional and legal donny-brook unlike anything he had gone through in his life. Joanna and Judy Bushkin had the same divorce attorney, Arthur Crowley, a lawyer with a reputation for toughness, and it was as if he and Henry were divorcing sisters.

Both couples were fighting over the date of their separations. Johnny portrayed his wife as an extravagant woman. Henry portrayed his wife as living "in a grand style fit for a queen," a mother who "eats almost every meal in restaurants and seems to have social engagements nightly" and "who does not intend to work ever." He complained about his wife's request for spousal support that included $985 a month for plant maintenance and $600 a month for an exercise teacher. While Johnny squired younger women around Los Angeles, Henry was involved with Joyce DeWitt, a star of *Three's Company*.

Johnny saved his meanest digs not for depositions but for the monologue. One evening he noted an item in the paper. Tip O'Neill, the Democratic Speaker of the House, had quipped that Nancy Reagan could leave the White House and become "the Queen of Beverly Hills." Johnny demurred. "Nancy would *not* be the Queen of Beverly Hills—I have the royal tab to prove it."

On another occasion he joked, "I heard from my cat's lawyer. My cat wants twelve thousand dollars a month for Tender Vittles."

Joanna felt that the publicity and Johnny's jokes had "increased the number of intruders upon the residence in recent weeks." Johnny had said, "I passed my house yesterday—in a tour bus." On another occasion he joked, "I'm inviting the whole audience to the house for a party after the show. I won't be there."

For much of the meanness of the divorce Joanna blamed not Johnny and his public utterances but Henry and his private counsel. "Bushkin did everything to make the whole situation full of electricity, wired," Joanna thought. "Johnny would call, very reflective, late in the evening, after he'd been drinking. He'd make proposals about the settlement and talk about the two of us getting back together. It was hard for me to take. The next day he wouldn't admit anything that he'd said. My lawyers would call and say, 'Bushkin is saying this and this.' Then Johnny would call and I'd say, 'That's not the truth. This is the truth.' He'd go back to Bushkin and say, 'Joanna says this is the truth.' And Bushkin would shoot at him so many logical reasons why I was lying.

"I told him, 'One day you will find out that I'm not lying. And that will be a sad day for you.' "

In her struggles with Johnny, Joanna had as her ally Henry's archenemy, Arnold Kopelson. Johnny claimed that Kopelson had met "surreptitiously" with Joanna in April 1983, where "privileged communication" was "extracted" from her. Kopelson may have been looking for anything negative he could find out about Henry and probably Johnny. He met several times with Joanna, including "dropping in" on her suite at the Hotel Pierre in New York as she left for Europe. He later called her in Rome to tell her that he and Miller were adding Johnny's name as a co-defendant in his Commercial Bank suit.

Johnny was loyal to Henry. Joanna seemed to be siding with their enemies. At his beach home Johnny sat down to write a note to Joanna. He wrote the few sentences over and over again. He threw several of the letters away. He accused his estranged wife of celebrating with Arnold Kopelson and said that her vengefulness would not be without cost.

In a failing marriage the matrons of Bel Air and Beverly Hills have one fundamental axiom: To spend is to save. On the day of marital judgment the wife is called in front of a judge and asked what she had spent in the waning days of the marriage. That figure will determine the divorcée's maintenance until the final decree.

Joanna asked for $220,000 a month in temporary support so that she could maintain her standard of living. To obtain that figure, she would have to prove that was the amount she spent during her years with Johnny.

The judge, whose salary was $72,000 year, needed to be told why Joanna required such a sum. Joanna and her attorney labored diligently, but even they could come up with only $107,665 in monthly expenses in 1982, not including taxes, legal costs, and interest payments on various investments.

At the Bel Air residence household salaries were $4,945 a month, groceries $1,400, automobile expenses $580, gifts of flowers $155, other gifts $12,365. Maintenance on the apartment at the Hotel Pierre in New York was $4,740, on another apartment at the new Trump Tower $2,520, and on a third apartment on Sixty-second Street in Manhattan $1,190.

Joanna described the endless travail of living a life of wealth. The couple had taken out a $2-million life-insurance policy on Johnny's life with Joanna as the beneficiary; she thought it only appropriate that Johnny continue to pay for the policy. She maintained a Mercedes 450 and a Rolls-Royce Corniche convertible. She paid the maid, the cook, the outdoor gardener, the indoor-plant service, and the servant who did the laundry but doubled as Joanna's personal aide. Joanna had a secretary as well. Her son, Tim, Jr., required $31,020 a year. The Carsons had two homes in Los Angeles, three residences in New York, and NBC paid for trips to Wimbledon and other places. But Joanna said that she spent an additional $32,340 a year traveling.

In 1982 Joanna had spent roughly $35,000 a month, or $440,000 a year, on jewelry and furs. She also spent about $5,000 a month, or $60,000 annually, on clothes and in department stores. That came to $500,000 a year simply to keep up. But Joanna did not want the court to get the wrong idea about the $60,000. "In fact, my 1982 expenses for clothing were quite low," Joanna said, "due to the fact that I purchased an extensive amount of clothing while I travelled in Europe during 1980 and 1981."

In contrast, Johnny's personal expenses were relatively modest for a man then earning about $15 million a year. Living in Malibu, he was spending about $30,000 a month, but that included $11,000 to maintain his aged mother, and roughly $10,000 in gifts.

As Johnny's response made clear, he had reached that financial Valhalla where a great deal of his life was a write-off. NBC paid for the twenty-four-hours-a-day guard service at the Bel Air residence, as well as for his life insurance. One of his corporations paid for his suite at the Beverly Hills Hotel. His corporation paid for the satellite disk that he used to receive television programs. Each summer he traveled to England to watch the Wimbledon tennis matches, but that was paid for by NBC.

Johnny did not think it proper that he would have to pay for Joanna's business travel to New York. His estranged wife's clothing business had already lost hundreds of thousands of dollars, and he felt that he had done his share. Nor did he find it appropriate to continue paying for fresh-cut flowers delivered regularly to the Bel Air house when Joanna was spending half her time in New York.

If he could help it, Johnny didn't intend to help Joanna improve her jewelry collection to the tune of $30,000 a

month. He also found the idea of shelling out $30,000 a
year to Joanna's son a bit much, especially since the young
man had already graduated from college.

When Joanna first asked for $220,000 in temporary support,
Johnny told his audience that his heroes had changed. As
a boy, he had idolized Babe Ruth. As a young performer,
he had worshiped Jack Benny. Now he had a new hero,
Henry VIII, who had beheaded two of his wives.

Joanna appeared as a sultry, sulking American courtesan,
an embarrassment in the age of women's liberation. The
divorce had become so bitter that it took until February 1984
to reach an agreement over the monthly alimony Johnny
would pay Joanna until the final divorce settlement.

Jim Mahoney, Johnny's publicist, announced that Joanna
would receive $22,000 a month, a mere 10 percent of her
original request. Joanna, in fact, received far more than
that: $35,000 in tax-free dollars a month plus about $6,600
for the New York apartments. Beyond that, Joanna received
the use of the income on roughly $2 million of community
property held in stocks and bonds. Maxwell Greenberg, one
of Joanna's attorneys, figured the agreement was worth
"about $1 million a year taxable income or about a half
million dollars tax-free."

Joanna unsuccessfully petitioned Superior Court judge
Frances Rothschild for an added $6,000 a month. Her at-
torney called it "a drop in the bucket."

Joanna's expenses were perhaps outrageous to most
Americans, but they were not exorbitant for the wife of a
man earning $15 million a year. Ellen Goodman, the col-
umnist, was almost alone in portraying Joanna's request
sympathetically. "It is only on divorce that the wife of a
rich man is reclassified as a greedy harpie who is trying to
'take him to the cleaners.' Is it more outrageous for Joanna
to be awarded $220,000 a month by Johnny than for Johnny
to be paid $1.5 million a month by NBC? If the wife of a
pauper is a partner in his nothingness, isn't the wife of a
millionaire a partner to his millions? . . . As for Johnny

Carson, if Henry the Eighth is his role model he'd better hustle. Henry died at 56. Carson is 57 and only ending his third marriage. Is there a fourth Mrs. Carson in the wings? Somebody had better lend her a history book.''

The Carsons fought their battle in the tabloids as well as in the courtroom. During the protracted struggle, the *National Enquirer* shoved Johnny's nose into the details of the divorce. A source told the paper about a secret meeting where "Joanna burst into tears. She burst out: 'Johnny, why are you being so mean to me? You're offering me $10 million after 10 years of marriage—when you make that in months.' '' The weekly quoted Joanna's friend as saying that she was "ready to list at least a dozen women who received gifts from Johnny during their marriage—including such stars as Angie Dickinson, Ann-Margret, Morgan Fairchild, Carol Wayne and black singer Kellee Patterson.'' Another article quoted sources as saying that if Johnny didn't accept a $35 million out-of-court settlement, Joanna would "put him, his girl friends and even his mother through a messy, nasty trial.'' According to the tabloid, Joanna's attorney had asked Johnny questions about a girlfriend during a deposition.

Anyone involved with the divorce knew that the *National Enquirer* had excellent sources. Then, on June 19, 1984, the tabloid ran a story about a $32 million to $42 million settlement that had purportedly been "hammered out behind closed doors.'' This time the paper was mistaken. The article was hardly as offensive toward Johnny as many of the previous stories, but Johnny sued for $51 million.

Johnny and his attorneys appeared primarily interested in finding the source or sources of the articles. The *National Enquirer*'s reporter, Sam Rubin, was not about to tell the names. Thus, Johnny's attorneys went on a futile, far-ranging quest to locate the mysterious informant(s). Johnny thought that Joanna was one possibility. She had told Johnny that there was only one possible source, and he would be surprised to learn who it was. In her deposition she said that she believed it was none other than Henry, who according to Joanna had had an "intimate friendship" with Shelley Ross, a former *National Enquirer* editor and writer. Henry called Joanna's accusation "specious and irresponsible," and swore that he was not the source.

Johnny's attorneys deposed even Joe Bleeden, the NBC publicist on the *Tonight Show*. Although Bleeden was not the source, he abruptly retired. Johnny could not even trust one of his closest public-relations advisers.

Johnny's attorneys never learned the identity of the crucial informant. The person happened to be an employee in Henry's law firm, now thousands of dollars richer. The case was eventually settled out of court, allegedly for court costs.

The real struggle in the divorce was not over temporary alimony but over the final settlement. In this, Joanna and her attorneys were the aggressors, seeking to locate every cent of Johnny's money. Joanna believed that Johnny and his attorneys were attempting to minimize or even disguise his wealth. "Of course, Bushkin and Carson lied," says Joanna. "Absolutely, they lied."

The protracted, expensive struggle took up nine volumes of records in the Los Angeles Superior Court, one of the largest divorce records in Los Angeles history. To shelter Johnny's new income, his attorneys set up several other new corporations, including Freedom Productions and Carson Tonight, Inc. Johnny admitted to Joanna's attorneys that he had formed Carson Tonight, Inc., to produce *The Tonight Show* so that he would "have a fresh start," and that Freedom Productions had been formed for the same reason. All in all, these new corporations and other accounting procedures made it difficult to determine the size of the community assets.

Learned authorities testified on the value of Johnny's image. They weighed the worth of celebrity, like medieval scholars ascertaining the weight of the soul.

The divorce proceedings continued month after month,

probably generating at least $2 million in legal and accounting fees. In July 1984 Joanna and Johnny hired retired Judge William P. Hogoboom, at two hundred dollars an hour, to determine when they had separated. Had it been when Johnny left the house in November 1982? Or was it five months later, when they proceeded with the divorce? The judge declared that "there was a complete and final separation of the parties on November 7, 1982." The judge had saved Johnny several million dollars.

For Joanna, this was a devastating time psychologically. "You're in a fight and you're being hit from every standpoint imaginable," she says. "I remember Carson calling up and saying I better accept $17 million. I laughed at him. There were the constant threats and the constant stuff on television. He'd call up and say, 'I don't know how you're getting through all this publicity.' I'd say, 'Don't worry, I'm just doing fine.' He was acting so concerned and then threatening me. It was hard for me to wake up in the morning.

"I didn't know which personality I was dealing with at a given moment. It was blowing my mind. I had to keep my sanity. My family was getting the brunt of it. It wasn't fair. I felt that Carson doesn't care. He really doesn't care. Now, I was the target for his venom. And somebody else will be the next one. I never felt protected from him when I was married, so how could I feel protected going through a divorce?"

Marjorie Reed flew out to Los Angeles to be with her friend. "Joanna was devastated," says Reed. "She never went out. She was so upset, so hurt, so saddened, by what had transpired. Every day there was something. Every day he made those miserable remarks on television, which I thought was inexcusable."

To much of the world, Joanna was a mirthless caricature of greed, diamond hard and diamond cold. In Greenwich Village a group of singers put on a Joanna Carson Benefit Concert at Folk City. They sang satirical songs, and planned to send Joanna an enormous check, at least $2' \times 5'$. The money raised was to go to another charity, however, the World Hunger Year.

Joanna pretended she didn't care, either, about the bad publicity or Johnny. She called him "Carson," as if the name "Johnny" suggested a residue of affection. But when a socialite came to the house on St. Cloud Road for a charity meeting, she saw a bulletin board devoted to clippings and pictures of Johnny with the women he was dating.

Johnny's and Joanna's attorneys finally reached a financial settlement in August 1985, almost three years after their separation. According to documents filed by Johnny's accounting firm, Ernst and Whinney, Joanna received securities and notes worth about $7.7 million, plus $12 million in other assets. This included the house in Bel Air, three apartments in New York, $4.1 million in personal property, $1.4 million in retirement plans and deferred compensation, and $2.3 million in partnerships. She would be paid alimony of $35,000 a month for five years and four months, or $2,240,000. Joanna's settlement was worth $21,940,000, a figure that probably underestimated the market value of the real estate by several million dollars.

The public considered Joanna a merciless, greedy woman who had stripped Johnny of much of his wealth. The extraordinary fact was that Johnny had paid her millions less than she might have received. According to Emm-Jay, Johnny told her that Joanna could have gotten $40 million, almost double the settlement.

The Citibank analysts who evaluated Johnny's financial statement for a loan in November 1985 might well have agreed. "There continues to be considerable hidden value in a number of Carson entities," they noted, "particularly Carson Productions Inc., balance sheet cost of $500,000 and Carson Tonight Inc., valued at a cost basis of $900.00!" Bankers use exclamation points as often as Mormons drink scotch, but these figures deserved special note. Carson Productions and Carson Tonight were probably worth well over

$40 million, and they appeared hidden on the balance sheet, like gold bars masquerading as copper.

The bank estimated Johnny's net worth after the divorce as $42 million, and that didn't even include the real value of Carson Productions and other assets. In truth, he was probably worth close to $100 million, or even more. The future didn't look bad, either. Henry had gotten his divorce too, and the two men were free to live as they wanted to live.

In 1985 Johnny's weekly salary had reached $375,000 or $19.5 million a year. And he was due for a raise.

TWENTY

Johnny sometimes talked to his neighbors, but he was not comfortable living close to other people. He purchased the house next door, but his beach house had neither the privacy nor the cachet that he felt he required, and that his income could easily afford.

Johnny decided to buy a new house. In Bel Air he had had a separate building for his office, but Joanna had stamped the main house with her style, from her glamorized Hollywood portrait in the living room to the designer pillows in the master bedroom. He now sought what for the first time in his life would be indisputably *his* house.

Johnny might have bought one of the great estates behind the gates of Bel Air, but that would have been close to Joanna, a reminder of a life he had left. He could have found a sprawling palace along Mulholland Drive, with Marlon Brando and Jack Nicholson down the street, but that wasn't for Johnny, either.

He was already in escrow on another house when he saw a fantastic glass-walled structure sitting two hundred feet above the surf on a cliff in Malibu. The house perched there in lonely splendor, as isolated from the pounding surf below as from the sky above and from the inland world of people. The house had been built and decorated by Carla and Dorn Schmidt, a couple with various business interests, including macadamia-nut plantations. If Johnny had sat down with architects and planned his own dream house, he could not have found anything any better for himself.

"Can I come back tomorrow?" he asked. He returned the next day and again that evening, and he bought the furnished residence for $8.9 million, $600,000 less than the $9.5 million asking price.

The realtor called the transaction "the largest sale ever in Malibu for a single family house," over three times the largest previous sale of $2.9 million. And this was for a single-*person* house.

Johnny was immensely proud of his new twelve-thousand-square-foot purchase. "I wish my dad was alive, because he'd enjoy it," Johnny told Emm-Jay one day. Emm-Jay wasn't so sure that this was the house for Johnny. He seemed so comfortable in his beach house, and she felt that this new place was more like a museum than a home.

When Billy Wilder, the director, walked into the gigantic living room, he asked, "Where's the desk?" The room did seem like a set for *The Tonight Show*. Paul Rosenfield noted in the *Los Angeles Times* that Johnny may have had "the unconscious intent to create a living area that's an idealized, glamorized version of the work area."

Johnny's living room had trees twenty-five feet tall rising to the glass roof, not the jungle of potted plants familiar to viewers of *The Tonight Show*. The white area rugs made a dramatic statement, as if daring anyone to soil them. The house had two outdoor pools, a giant Jacuzzi, and enough flora to seem like Hollywood's idea of the Garden of Eden before the Fall. There were also a refrigerated wine cellar for ten thousand bottles of wine, an elevator, five stereo systems, and a mirrored gym. Yet, despite the immense living room, the rest of the house was modest in size, like backstage at a theater.

The house cried out for great parties, for laughter and clinking glasses. But Johnny was not a party giver. He rarely asked his sons for family gatherings. Except for Alex and the housekeeper, the house was empty—a song that no one heard, a book that had no readers.

Robert De Niro, the actor, was one of the few outsiders to come to the house. "Uhm, ah, I'd like you to do this, uhm, movie *The King of Comedy* with me," De Niro mumbled.

"I'll do the movie if you'll do *The Tonight Show*," Johnny said.

De Niro shook his head. "I don't know how you do what you do."

"I don't know how *you* do what you do," Johnny said.

Johnny had lasted in television so long in part because he understood himself and his role in the medium perfectly. He knew that Johnny Carson, the host of *The Tonight Show*, was the character he had played for more than two decades. He believed that the audience wouldn't accept him playing anyone else. "Nobody who has played himself on TV has ever gone on to a successful movie career," he said. "Nobody." He had turned down the lead in *The Thomas Crown Affair*, a part given to Steve McQueen. He had backed away from a role in Mel Brooks's comedy *Blazing Saddles* that went to Gene Wilder.

Jerry Lewis ended up playing the title role in *The King of Comedy*, about a famous talk-show host kidnapped by a failed comedian. The movie resonated closely to Johnny's own life. He knew the frustrations of the mass psyche. He had received more than one death threat; indeed, David Chapman admitted that before assassinating John Lennon he had thought of killing Johnny simply "because he's popular. . . . Actually, I kind of like Johnny Carson."

A frustrated fan might well want to kidnap Johnny. One admirer, a former mental patient, thought that Johnny was talking directly to him. "Why won't he leave me alone!" he cried. In July 1985 NBC posted a memo in the studio warning that "several months ago we received a letter from a doctor in Sacramento which stated that . . . was on a plane heading for Los Angeles and that . . . intended to kill Johnny Carson." The doctor wrote, "You may want to advise Johnny that, at present . . . is no longer under medical supervision and, as of July 27, will no longer be under police supervision of any kind.''

Johnny was becoming ever more isolated. He didn't like talking about himself, and had almost stopped giving interviews. When the sixteen-year-old son of a friend asked to talk to him for a cable program, Johnny agreed. ''How do you do what you do?'' the young man asked. There was a long pause before Johnny replied, ''Be yourself and tell the truth.''

Johnny had just faced another challenge for supremacy of late night, this one from Fred Silverman, his former nemesis at the network. After failing to dig NBC out of the cellar, Silverman had entered the swelling ranks of independent producers. Johnny saw the ex–NBC president in a restaurant one day. ''You still in the business?'' asked Johnny, according to Silverman.

Silverman thought that Johnny was vulnerable, and he put together a syndicated show starring Alan Thicke, a Canadian television personality. Johnny had a unique perspective on the show, since Emm-Jay was associate director. In September of 1983 *Thicke of the Night* began with all the ruffles and flourishes that public relations can provide. The show was a raging success, until the ratings arrived. In December a chastened Silverman pulled the show to regroup and presumably to ponder the mystery of Johnny's continued success. The program went back on the air in the new year for a few more months, garnering ratings that *Bowling for Dollars* would have beaten. After the show left the air for good, Johnny invited his vanquished challenger onto *The Tonight Show*.

Thicke had not only had Johnny as a competitor but also Joan Rivers, who had been named the first regular substitute host in *Tonight Show* history, substituting for Johnny nine weeks a year. Rivers received strong ratings, and the overall ratings for the show were no longer a matter for worry. Moreover, NBC had climbed out of the cellar under the regime of Grant Tinker, first into second place, and then into first place, thanks in good measure to the phenomenal success of *The Cosby Show*.

Viewers across America watched Johnny not only late night on NBC, but also on the syndicated *Carson's Comedy Classics*. For that series of old *Tonight Show*s, the monologues had been cut away since they were too tied to the transitory headlines and scandals that most of the audiences had forgotten. Just who was Fanne Fox? And what did this fellow Bert Lance do? And who wanted to hear Johnny joking about Billy Carter's beer drinking?

That left a collection of skits, talks with still-famous celebrities, and bits with animals, old people, obscure characters, and kids. Despite the title, the programs were not classics like many of Jackie Gleason's *Honeymooners*, Sid Caesar's *Show of Shows*, or the early *NBC's Saturday Night*. Audiences watched because they loved Johnny and wanted more of him. "I believe in a slow build when it comes to a career," Johnny said. "Acceptance is everything."

In television acceptance was indeed everything. Johnny had reached the point where even the critics had placed him in a pantheon beyond criticism. He was Johnny Carson.

Johnny took care of himself. He was in excellent condition. In the summer of 1985, at the age of fifty-nine, he went deep-sea diving off the Florida Keys to see a seventeenth-century Spanish galleon. Tennis was his passion, and he played almost every day. When he sold his Carbon Beach house to John McEnroe for $1,850,000, he insisted on one other stipulation: that the tennis star give him six tennis lessons. Johnny was so serious about the lessons that the stipulation was included in the sales contract and the escrow instructions. Johnny no longer had his own tennis court in Bel Air, and the two men played at Pepperdine University in Malibu.

Although Johnny's new house stood on two-and-a-half acres of land, there was no place for a tennis court. So he bought the land across the street, and at a cost of several million dollars constructed one of the most remarkable private tennis courts in the world. It was not so much a court as a mini-stadium, built recessed so that passers-by could not catch even a glimpse of Johnny playing each day.

Johnny's mother died in October 1985 at the age of eighty-four. Johnny had paid for nurses twenty-four hours a day for many months, but he had not been a frequent visitor to her home in Arizona. And now the mother for whom he was never quite good enough was gone.

Johnny had shared with Emm-Jay the problem of aging parents. She had bought a house in the San Fernando Valley, and brought her parents to live with her. According to Emm-Jay, Johnny went there only once.

One time when Emm-Jay visited Johnny, she recalls noticing a yellow memo stuck to the mirror in the bathroom, reading, "Johnny, water the azaleas." Emm-Jay recognized that as Alex's handiwork, and she was amazed that anyone could get Johnny to perform such a humdrum task.

Alex was the central woman in Johnny's life. She traveled with Johnny to Wimbledon and to the French Riviera, staying at the Hotel du Cap, where Johnny had first come with Joanna. Henry and his current amour, Joyce DeWitt, were there as well, as was Bill Cosby.

"I'm tired," Johnny said one evening after dinner, as one of the group remembered. "I'm going to bed."

"Joyce and I are going to sit here," said Henry. "We'll have a cappuccino."

"I'll stay here too," Alex said. She was young, the night was young.

Johnny jumped out of his chair as if Alex had betrayed him.

Henry advised her, "Alex, you better go down before this goes further." He was Johnny's emotional valet, picking up after him.

"I think that's right," Alex said, and followed Johnny.

* * *

If Johnny sought to discard the past like reels of a half-
forgotten film, he haunted his former wives and his three
sons. They played back their memories time and time again,
seeking to understand what had happened. They were tied
to him not only by recollections and blood but by money.
One way or another, they were all dependent on Johnny's
wealth.

As the mother of their three sons, Jody had a place in
Johnny's life that could not easily be denied. Jody had
become a wanderer, moving from city to city, living in over
thirty places since her marriage to Johnny. She had several
hundred thousand dollars in the bank, plus the $13,500 a
year she received from him, enough so that she didn't have
to work. But she could not live the way she wanted to live,
the way the other ex-wives lived.

In 1983 Jody decided that she would buy a house in Los
Angeles where she could be close to Rick and Cory, her
two youngest sons. She found a place in Bell Canyon, a
mountainous area in the San Fernando Valley, for $285,000.
Johnny owed Jody $13,500 a year until 1999, or about
$200,000. If Johnny would pay her the money in a lump
sum, Jody could put it down on the house, leaving only a
small monthly payment.

"I talked to Johnny on the phone," Jody recalls. "He
said, 'Do you know what you're asking me to do?' He acted
very put upon." Through his attorneys, Johnny agreed to
pay $157,500, over $40,000 less than the expected amount.

Although Jody felt that Johnny was acting niggardly, he
was not striking a hard bargain. The interest on the $157,500
would have more than paid the $13,500 that Johnny owned
Jody each year. And in 1999 he would still have had the
principal.

Jody grudgingly accepted Johnny's proposal and looked
forward to moving into her new home. As the day of the
settlement arrived, Johnny's attorneys asked her to sign a
statement that "she accepts such sum of money as fair and
adequate resolution of all obligations of John W. Carson."

Johnny wanted to shut his wallet for good and be rid of any responsibility for the wife he had divorced three decades ago. Jody, however, smelled the rank odor of duplicity. She was suspicious of the lawyers' timing, and of the enthusiasm with which they sought her signature. She did not trust Johnny, his lawyers, her own lawyer, or even her own two sons, who wanted her to sign the document.

Jody blamed Johnny not only for their failed marriage but for her failed life. "John's made my whole life miserable one way or another," Jody says. "My whole life has been wrapped up with him. There wasn't a reason in the world why he couldn't have said, 'Of course I'll buy the house,' without having to use the children, without sending this agreement to sign, without cheating me out of forty thousand dollars. Why do all that dirty, crummy stuff? Why not be nice to this poor old lady?"

Thanks to some good investments in the stock market, Jody had enough of her own money for the down payment, and she moved into the two-bedroom house. She bought a bed, a couch, a lamp and a refrigerator, austere beginnings by any standard. The previous owner had two teenage sons, and the place needed to be painted and tidied up, improvements she felt she could not afford. She heard wild dogs howling at night. The snakes in the woods frightened her. Sometimes she was very lonely.

Rick and Cory were used to a mother who came in and out of their lives. Chris had not seen his mother for several years, and Jody and her eldest son were even more distant from one another than the miles of the continent that separated them.

In the Los Angeles area Jody became closer to her two younger sons than she had since their boyhood. But the figure of Johnny hovered over them. "When they were young, Johnny and I competed with each other for their affection," Jody says. "Now, as soon as I arrive in Los Angeles, out of the blue he buys them houses and gives them more money, thirty-five thousand dollars a year. He doesn't give them enough so they can really do something with it, make money off it, gain some self-respect. I think he wants them there under his thumb, to humiliate them, to keep them down.

"I don't think they've ever grown up. When you're in the mid-thirties, you're supposed to have your own life, and not be the boys of your parents. They are still very dependent on their parents. They act like little boys."

Neither Rick nor Cory had gotten their own jobs. They were employed by Carson Productions, Rick as a stage manager on *Amen* and Cory performing various backstage chores part time on his father's show. Although Cory was well liked on *The Tonight Show*, the staff found it curious that it was his cousin, Jeff Sotzing, who rose from a menial job to become the associate producer and seemed like Johnny's son.

Cory wasn't jealous. He was into his own thing: macrobiotics, classical guitar, ecology, New Age consciousness. From all his reading, meditation, and reflection he had decided that the parameters of life, of feeling, are always the same, whether you're Johnny Carson or the guy who reads the gas meter. He told his friends that he believed that his father had missed most of what happiness there was in life. Those who knew Cory best realized how much he loved his father, and how distant he was from Johnny.

Cory was not a fan of television. One year he gave Johnny a book calling for the abolition of television; it was as if Malcolm Forbes's son had presented his father with *Das Kapital*. Cory played the guitar hours a day, working out the intricate fingering. He performed once on *The Tonight Show*, but he was hardly another Sergovia. Sometimes he took gigs in restaurants for a few dollars a night, playing classical and other requests, and, when called upon, plucking out the chords of "Happy Birthday." At an Italian restaurant in the San Fernando Valley, Johnny came by one evening, watched his youngest son for a while, and then left as suddenly as he had arrived.

Cory had a lean, ascetic look. Dressed in jeans, he appeared the typical young graduate student, not a man who had reached the age of thirty. Cory shared with his father a shyness that could be mistaken for a quiet, willful arrogance. Like his brothers, he had no grand goals, no ambition to make his own name in the world.

Cory dated a young woman from *The Tonight Show* who became pregnant and gave birth to a child. But Cory broke up with the woman, and the matter was taken care of so that it hardly affected his life at all. "Cory's very blasé about the child," Jody says. "I don't think that any of the boys have that much of a sense of responsibility."

Jody cherished her moments with Cory, listening to him playing the guitar. She wished she could have such times with Rick too, but he appeared as troubled as ever, still desperately seeking to understand himself and his relationship with his mother and father. "Rick needs his father so much," Jody says. "He is bugged to death about it. He wants John to love him.

"Rick showed up at six in the morning after two days of partying with his father after one of the shows they were on. He was going to have it out with me. I stood up for his father.

"I said, 'Your father and I had some good times. He's not all that bad.'

"He asked, 'Why doesn't my father love me?'

"I said, 'Ricky, your father is a man, not the person you see on television. You want the father that's on television.'

"Rick said, 'Why doesn't he love me for myself?'

"I said, 'Why don't you act differently? You can't ask for something that John is incapable of giving. You have to accept what John can give and nothing more. It can't become an obsession.'"

Rick came to see his mother again just before he began work as a stage manager on the new NBC show *Amen*.

"I really love you," Jody said, as she recalls. "I hate to see you going through what you're going through."

"I'm going to be the best floor manager ever," Rick said.

* * *

Jody had hoped that in Los Angeles she would regain her
sons' loyalty and concern. She felt that she had not done
so, and she blamed Johnny and the power of his wealth.
She couldn't keep up the house payments, and in the summer
of 1986 she sold the residence. She put what few belongings
she had into her car, and headed two hours up the Pacific
Coast to Santa Barbara.

Jody didn't know anyone in Santa Barbara, but she had
read an ad in the *Los Angeles Times* for a hotel with a
beautiful fountain and attractive monthly rates. When she
arrived, she saw that the fountain was only two feet tall and
the hotel a drab complex of apartments and bedrooms, totally devoid of Santa Barbara's quaint charm. But Jody
intended to stay there only long enough to get better physically and mentally.

As the weeks went by, she did little more than go for
occasional walks. Soon it was Christmas, a time that she
had come to dread. Her sons had inherited the Carson disregard for birthdays and holidays, and she spent the last
weeks of the year largely alone.

Although Jody felt that her entire adult life had been
dominated by Johnny Carson, she was still Mrs. Buckley,
carrying the name of a man who had been merely a glitch
in her life. In the new year she decided to change her name
back to Carson. Johnny protected his name like a precious
trademark, and he was unlikely to feel happy about a third
former Mrs. Carson living in California.

Whatever Johnny may have felt, Jody noticed that the
world perked up a little at the sight of the new Mrs. Carson.
One day she took the trolley downtown, sitting her delicate,
diminutive self next to an obese matron. Jody could go days
without talking to anyone, but the woman began a conversation.

"We should get together," the lady said, as the last stop
approached. "What's your name?"

"Jody Carson."

"Not related to *the* Johnny Carson," the lady said, half in jest.

"I was married to him."

"Oh, I love him," the fat lady said, and embraced Jody.

Jody considered books her best friends, and one day she was in a bookstore, choosing her companion for the evening. She stood browsing through a book by Melvin Belli, the famous trial lawyer. When she came across a few paragraphs about Mexican divorces, she read and reread the passage. She could hardly believe her eyes. Suddenly it made sense to her why Johnny's lawyers had been so dogged about having her sign the statement saying Johnny owed her nothing else. If Belli was correct as she understood him, her divorce was not valid. She was not only Mrs. Carson in name but in fact, and Johnny, the toast of America, was a bigamist twice over. She was rich—15 percent of his gross income for all those years, and maybe a lot more.

"I feel I have a good chance to live out my old age in a measure of comfort and security like the other wives," Jody said. "That's all I want, a measure of security."

Jody didn't react precipitously. Impressions were important, and when she went to see a lawyer, she had to look right, with a new hairdo and the appropriate matronly dress. "I have to go in with the proper attitude, very together and very proper," she said.

For the moment she was content to anticipate a rich future. "I realize that I've had practically everything tried on me that can be tried," she said. "I'm old enough so I'm not vulnerable to men any longer, to flirtation. I like living alone. I don't need a partner. All I need now is security. I want all the money I can get."

Jody told practically no one about her discovery, but she felt that Johnny knew that she had found out. On *The Tonight Show* when Johnny talked about a Reno divorce, she was positive that he was speaking directly to her. She thought that her phones might be bugged, and she was sure that she was being followed.

Jody spent hours on the telephone talking to an author writing Johnny's biography. She needed to talk, and he was ready to listen to her. "If I'm rubbed out, you'll know who did it," she said. "My life isn't worth a plug nickel." At first she didn't trust the writer, either, not completely, and sometimes she felt that he was working for Johnny, passing on her every word. As the months went by, she didn't talk so much about all the money that she was going to get from Johnny, and as that dream slowly receded, so did much of her energy, her aspiration, and her bravado.

In July 1987 the author called her, as he did every few days. "Alex talked to Rick and Cory," she said in a voice shaking with apprehension. "She told them Johnny is going to sue me for slander and see to it that I don't get any more money."

From that day on Jody didn't answer the phone, even if it rang a hundred times. She remained on at the hotel for almost two years, and did not move out into an apartment until the late spring of 1988. Often in the evenings she sat watching *The Tonight Show.* When Johnny joked about his ex-wives and all they had gotten from him, she laughed too.

The second Mrs. Carson also watched *The Tonight Show.* Joanne had been Mrs. Carson from the day she arrived in Los Angeles as a new divorcée two decades ago, and she had never relinquished her name. She still lived in her sprawling house in a private wooded enclave above Sunset Boulevard. Despite all those years that had passed, she had not finished decorating to her satisfaction, and the garage was full of boxes and bric-a-brac, treasures and trash.

Joanne had an irresistible impulse to trust the wrong people. Guests walked off with her valuables. Investment counselors and "savvy" friends put her money in ventures that went wrong, losing hundreds of thousands of dollars. Robbers entered the house, tied her up, locked her in a closet, and got away with her jewelry. But Joanne had long ago learned to block out the unpleasant.

Joanne moved from project to project, person to person, phone to phone, in perpetual motion, dressed usually in warm-ups, a lit cigarette in her hand. When she was friendly with someone, she often crushed them with her intimacy and assaulted them with her goodness. She was best with those who were needy. When Paul Newman's son, Scott, had a drug problem, she spent hours with him, and she remained his friend until he died.

Joanne began studying at International College, a tutorial institution in Westwood. She received a master's degree in psychology in 1976, and a Ph.D. in nutritional biochemistry and physiology in 1981. Joanne titled her thesis "The Wisdom of the Body," and dedicated it to several men, including Johnny, "who gave me support, guidance, and wisdom."

Through her studies Joanne had decided that hypoglycemia, or low blood sugar, had caused her divorce. The symptoms included emotional swings, weight gain, headaches, anxiety, depression—a checklist of life in urban America. "I attribute everything that went wrong to the problem, one hundred percent," she said in 1983. "If I knew then what I know now, I would still be married to him."

In the fall of 1981 Joanne renewed her television career as a field reporter on *Alive and Well*, a cable show devoted to better health and nutrition. This gave her an opportunity to promulgate her view that "90 percent of the American population is suffering needlessly from this condition [hypoglycemia]."

This time Joanne sought her own celebrity. "I want a cover," she told Eirik Knutzen, who was writing an article for *TV-Cable Week*. "The last cover I did was still tied into Johnny. I want a cover on my own." She was still, however, "Joanne Carson—Johnny's Ex," as the short-lived weekly called her on its cover.

After a year and a half Joanne once again ended her career in television. She kept busy counseling people, and managing her house in short bursts of frenetic energy.

Joanne was always there to welcome Truman Capote when he made his occasional visits to Los Angeles. Truman had tried to turn Joanne into a swan, but she was better not straying far from her nest on Sunset, better still when she had someone to nurture.

After Truman published his famous "La Cote Basque story" in *Esquire* in November 1975 and was no longer invited to the great homes of Manhattan, he came to Joanne. He wandered around her house saying again and again, "But they know I'm a writer. I don't understand it." The following November he spent a drunken Thanksgiving in Joanne's Shangri-la. When the turkey was finally served, Truman's lover, John O'Shea, spat in another guest's face and collapsed on the floor.

In his declining years, as Truman Capote fought liquor and drugs and despair, he stayed with Joanne at least once a year in a doll-like two-room suite off the kitchen. She prepared health foods, watched him swim in a pool as heated as a bath, and let him have the run of her house and her life.

Truman was back in late August 1984. Early Saturday morning Joanne entered the little bedroom to wake him, as she had so many times. He was as white as a blank sheet of paper. She felt his pulse. His heart was fluttering. She believed in nutrition as a magical talisman, and she went to get Truman breakfast.

"No, stay here," he said.

"Are you all right?" Joanne asked.

"No, I'm not. But I soon will be."

"Truman, I think I should call the paramedics."

Truman knew Joanne. She wanted the world to be right, her home to be his haven, his life to be whole. He held her there with his words. He talked and he talked, and as the hours passed, his voice grew weaker. Joanne asked again to call a doctor, but Truman said no. Truman was suddenly cold. Joanne reached out for a blanket and held him in her arms.

"Mamma," Truman said. And he was dead.

Joanne called the paramedics and lied to them, saying that Truman had died in his sleep. She kept his room as a shrine, just the way he had left it. She thought of him all the time. She thought of Johnny too, and said that she still loved him.

Joanne's dog, Cinnamon, died at Christmas 1987. Joanne held the dog in her arms the way she had held Truman. To help her through her grief, she decided to have a New Year's Eve party. She had workmen string the trees in her garden and entryway with hundreds of tiny lights, like fireflies. She filled the house with candles. For her party she wore a warm-up suit, and flitted from guest to guest taking photographs, never stopping for more than two or three minutes. She took photographs of Robert Blake, who wore old jeans, and Esther Williams, who dressed with the panache of an aging star. Alan Thicke had made it to the party too, and she took pictures of Johnny's former competitor and his entourage as well.

Just before midnight Joanne flicked on the television set in the living room. The guests watched Johnny celebrating New Year's Eve on *The Tonight Show.*

In December 1986 Joanna Carson walked into a Manhattan store and bought needlepoint pillowcases that read ANYONE WHO SAYS MONEY DOESNT BUY HAPPINESS DOESNT KNOW WHERE TO SHOP. She had a house in Bel Air and an apartment at the Pierre. She had a Rolls-Royce and a Mercedes. She could buy whatever she wanted to buy and go wherever she wanted to go.

When she returned to her suite at the Pierre Hotel one evening in September 1986, she discovered that thieves had stolen sixty-five thousand dollars worth of jewelry. The robbers had taken a bracelet, some earrings, two rings, and four watches. Two months later she went to a party at Trump Tower for Harry Winston, the jeweler. This time she wore some *real* jewelry. "The thieves didn't get *everything*," she said as she sipped champagne.

Joanna was a stunning woman who enjoyed charity balls

and fancy dinner parties. She always managed to have a date on her arm. The newspapers linked her name to everyone from Julio Iglesias, the famous singer, to an Arab prince, to a television producer. But there were no other Johnny Carsons waiting in the wings.

Joanna knew what an emotional price she had paid and what a struggle it was to go on sometimes. She had money, but money couldn't help on that day in October 1986 when her mother was struck by a car as she crossed a street in Manhattan. Joanna had money, but money couldn't heal her feelings, or assuage the pain. She had money, but money couldn't change the way the world thought of her.

Joanna believed that Johnny had cheated her in the divorce, and she contemplated suing her former husband, though a few million dollars more would change her life not an iota. She sought vindication, to redeem her image and her life. She sought revenge, not realizing that the only true revenge is no revenge at all, but to go on and to forget.

In February 1987 Joanna attended a luncheon for a Mexican lady who had read all about the infamous Mrs. Carson. The lady listened to Joanna and watched her closely. "I can't believe it," she said. "I always perceived you as so tough."

Joanna started to laugh. "I'm the least tough person I know," she said.

"You're nothing like your image."

"People thought I was going to get Mr. Wonderful. I even have friends in New York who thought that. When they say it, I laugh at them."

• • • • • • • • • • • • • • • • • •

TWENTY-ONE

Early one evening in May of 1986 Brandon Tartikoff, NBC's entertainment president, called Johnny at his home in Malibu to tell him some amazing news. Joan Rivers would be starting her own late-night talk show on the new Fox Broadcasting network.

Johnny could hardly believe it. Years ago he had given Joan her big break. Now, she subbed for him eight weeks a year, his only regular guest host. Joan had said time and time again how appreciative she was. She had even dedicated to him, in part, her autobiography, a volume that sat prominently on his coffee table.

Joan's move was professionally surprising as well. Johnny was a connoisseur of comedians, and he considered Joan perfect as an occasional spicy contrast to his blander, meat-and-potatoes comedy. But she was too raw, too fevered, as a steady diet.

Johnny had hardly digested the news when the telephone rang again. This time he heard Freddy de Cordova's familiar voice. The comedienne and her husband, Edgar, had just called the executive producer to tearfully tell him that her show would begin in October, opposite *The Tonight Show*.

As Freddy relayed the conversation, one of Johnny's other phones rang. Joan was on the line, wanting to break the news to him. "I'm not taking her call," Johnny told Freddy.

"It was a little late in arriving . . . about three months late."

In an instant, Johnny shut Joan out of his life as if snapping a book closed. He didn't talk to her that day, or the next morning, when she called again before her press conference. He canceled her last two weeks of guest hosting, and according to Joan he has never spoken to her again.

In the next few weeks Johnny acted as if Joan's sole mistake had been a social faux pax. If only she had called before, he would have wished her well, as he had David Brenner. A regular on *The Tonight Show*, Brenner had told Johnny beforehand that he would be hosting a syndicated late-night show.

Joan wrung her manicured hands in remorse. She had wanted desperately to tell Johnny first. "Johnny, it has nothing to do with you," she would have said. "It's the treatment I've been getting from everybody else."

Johnny considered Joan as a de facto opening act, a performer whose primary function is to prepare the audience for the emergence, or in this case the reappearance, of the headliner. Joan, however, had not sat gingerly on Johnny's seat, but jumped up and down, creating attention, occasional pandemonium, boxes of outraged letters, and strong ratings.

As much as Joan enjoyed hosting the show, she had a running battle over the bookings. She had wanted to enliven a program that at times, she felt, was not so much produced as embalmed. When she sought to have Pee Wee Herman, Cher, and Lily Tomlin as guests, the producers acted as if she were proposing an hour with Run-D.M.C. and mud-wrestling from the Tropicana. Joan had nothing against such frequent guests as Bob Hope and Burt Reynolds, but she found many of them as exciting as warmed-over macaroni and cheese. "We had to beg to have American Olympic athletes on, and the audience went crazy," Joan says. "We had Mary Lou Retton on, and they bumped her to put on someone else. They didn't like me because I was arguing all the time.

"I did nothing wrong when I left. I called everyone before the news was released. I don't know what they thought, that I was a woman and I couldn't leave. They wouldn't give me a two-year contract. We had found there was list of potential replacements for Johnny, and I wasn't on that list. And then Fox came to me with an offer of fifteen million dollars. Who wouldn't leave?"

"Why shouldn't I go," Joan said at the time, "with somebody who really *wants* me, who will give me a three years' on-the-air commitment?"

Joan had considered *The Tonight Show* her show-business home, but now at NBC she was a pariah, her raucous laugh like a leper's bell. Her closest friend on the program was Peter Lassally, who had been passed over when Freddy became producer. For years Joan had watched Lassally standing in the wings, an understudy who never received a call, while Freddy took his nightly turn in the spotlight. Joan needed a producer for her show who had the ability to forge an original and successful program. Her first choice was Lassally, and she discussed with him the possibility of joining her.

On *The Tonight Show* Lassally's friendship with Joan had become as much a liability as hiccups to a contralto. Lassally told Johnny of Joan's offer. "He used me to show Johnny that he was really on his side." Joan says. "We had brought up our children together, taken their children to Europe with us. And he said, 'See, Johnny, she asked me to leave, and I'm staying with you.'

"I was in shock. I couldn't believe it. The Lassallys turned their backs on us in Spago one evening. They were having dessert, and she leaned so far away from me that she got whipped cream on her sleeve.

"Everyone on the show was scared to stay in contact with me. Ed McMahon was the only one who went over and kissed me and wished me well."

Johnny was not one to stand blithely by as Joan attempted to lure away his top staffers. Joan and her minions tried to

employ other *Tonight Show* personnel, most notably Jim
McCawley, the highly regarded coordinator who booked
comedy acts on the show. "We wanted to bring him over,"
Joan recalls. "We got him a lot of money at Fox. I had to
talk to Barry Diller, the head of Twentieth Century-Fox.
After that, he went to Carson and traded our offer for more
money."

As the weeks went by, Johnny developed as strong an
antipathy toward Joan as he had toward any performer in
his long career. He tried to keep quiet about her, but couldn't
resist making her abortive phone call a theme in the monologue. One evening he noted that the president of NBC,
Grant Tinker, had "tried to call [Alfred] Hitchcock, but
Hitchcock hung up on him." On another show he mentioned
Gorbachev's problems in the Soviet Union. "It's all my
fault," Johnny said. "He called me . . . but I hung up on
him."

Johnny saw himself "in total contrast" to Rivers. "I am
not going to ask Joan Collins her age," he said. "Joan
[Rivers] can get away with that." Johnny was the most
disciplined comedian in America. When he edged out onto
the precipice of nastiness, his studio audience told him so,
scolding him with their clucking that he was not *their*
Johnny. If Joan succeeded with her new show, Johnny's
idea about the nature of television was wrong. It would be
as if overnight mid-America changed its favorite food from
steak and french fries to Szechuan chicken and sour cream.

When Joan had first appeared on *The Tonight Show*,
Johnny had seemed to her like a warm, laughing, generous
father. He had anointed her, told her she was funny, told
her she would be a star. She had "always fantasized this
big, wonderful, warm relationship." Joan said later that that
relationship had never developed; Johnny and Joan had a
brilliant telegenic rapport, but as soon as the camera was
off, Johnny was like a blank television screen, hardly ac-
knowledging her presence.

Back in the New York days Johnny had invited her to
his fortieth-birthday party. At the time Joan had been ex-

cited, considering it a big moment in her life. Now, looking back, she thought how sad it was; Johnny seemed to have no friends, only managers, lawyers, a few performers, his producer, and assorted lackeys, the myriad attendants of stardom. Joan had helped scores of people in her career, but the day would come when she would look at her own life and wonder who was she to criticize. What friends would she have left but various retainers and assorted helpers?

Joan was a show-business provincial who knew little beyond the entertainment worlds of Las Vegas, Hollywood, and New York. She was, however, singularly perceptive about herself and television. "Television lies," Joan says. "Don't give me this nonsense that television tells the truth. Excuse me. Look at Johnny. He's totally isolated but he has great charm, boyishness, on the air."

Joan saw what she and Johnny had in common. "I think we are both basically loners and terribly shy," Joan says, "both pretending to ourselves that the tremendous warmth and rapport we had on camera extended into real life."

Each time Joan stepped before the audience, a garish masquerade fit over her thin and vulnerable self. She hungered desperately for approval, and she saw her career as a relentless struggle, a storm of defeats broken only by occasional moments of bright, transitory victories.

In a media age Joan's gift for publicity was a valuable asset, but it was an asset of fire that could scorch and burn as well as warm and comfort. In the first weeks after the announcement Joan entered talking. She told the story of Johnny hanging up on her everywhere from *People* to *Playboy*. Taping the audio version of her autobiography, she broke into tears as she read aloud the chapter on doing *The Tonight Show* the first time.

When *The Late Show* starring Joan Rivers debuted in October, *People* pictured Joan on the cover under the title JOAN RIVERS GOES TO WAR. Her weapons were a motley array of ninety-nine stations, including independents, and the six Fox flagship stations, hardly a formidable arsenal.

Moreover, half of Joan's shells would fall on empty fields, since in most places she went on the air at 11:00 P.M., a half hour before *The Tonight Show*. In any case, Fox's plan was not to defeat Johnny but merely to stay on the same field with him and win respectable ratings, roughly half Johnny's.

On the evening of October 8, 1986, Joan Rivers stood alone before several hundred clapping, stomping fans in the newly refurbished theater at the Fox Broadcasting studios in Hollywood. The camera zoomed in on her fevered countenance. She clapped back at the audience, holding her arms straight out.

"I have a whole monologue—which I won't do tonight," Joan said, when the applause finally died down. She was too wired, too frenzied. Joan hugged several members of the audience, and then retreated to her desk.

Joan spent the hour with David Lee Roth, Elton John, Pee Wee Herman, and Cher, a group that she could not book together on *The Tonight Show*. They assaulted the airwaves, and even Pee Wee Herman talked about sex. In their energy and audacity Joan and her guests set themselves apart from Johnny's middle-aged civility. Joan sought a younger audience, and it was as if she thought vulgarity was the province of youth. As the program ended, Joan stood next to Elton John playing the piano. "The Bitch is back," he sang, and Joan joined in. "I can bitch, I can bitch . . . I can bitch, I can bitch better than *you*!"

Johnny knew that it was no great accomplishment to create controversy and excitement the first evening. When he took over *The Tonight Show*, he had deliberately underplayed. He did not zap the audience with all the one-liners he had saved up for months, nor did he load the program with special guests. After all, a game consists of more than one play.

On *The Tonight Show* Johnny alluded to his new competition in his monologue. "There are a lot of big-time confrontations this week," he said. "Reagan versus Gorbachev, the Mets versus the Astros, and me versus *The*

Honeymooners' lost episodes." Johnny had Richard Pryor and Sean Penn as his guests. They were a powerful draw, and Johnny interviewed them with his usual politeness.

Joan did better in the ratings that first evening than almost anyone had imagined. She even beat Johnny in New York and San Francisco. For a few days it looked as if Johnny might have the most formidable competitor in a quarter of a century. But within weeks the ratings began their slow decline.

Joan could indeed bitch better than Johnny, as she had sung out her first evening. But night after night, guest after guest, Joan couldn't be her caustic self. She was *nice* to her guests, and it was often a bore. Although Joan was excellent at ad-libbing, she necessarily had a list of proposed questions and answers before her. She went through it as if passing an exam, often barely connecting with the person seated beside her.

Joan Rivers is to insecurity what Domino's is to pizza, and as the ratings declined, she became more and more uncertain. During the commercial breaks four or five people would run up to her, as if she were a boxer between rounds. The hairdresser touched up her hair. The makeup artist touched up her lips. Her husband, Edgar, the executive producer, touched up her ego.

Finally, after eight months, on May 15, 1987, Fox pulled the plug. The audience applauded with fervor. And Joan, who would talk about anything, said that she could not talk about leaving, since matters were still being negotiated.

On *The Tonight Show* Johnny mentioned Jim Bakker, the deposed evangelist, and his mascara-laden wife, Tammy. "Don't worry about Tammy Bakker," Johnny said. "She just got an offer from Fox Broadcasting. . . ."

The audience laughed, as if they had been let in both on a private joke and public vindication. "I've been saving that one for a long time," he said as the applause subsided.

A week later Rivers stood before an audience in the 1250-seat Circus Maximus at Caesars Palace in Las Vegas. "First of all," Rivers said as the welcoming applause died down, "you are looking at a woman who has finally been able to make Johnny Carson happy."

From Joey Bishop to David Brenner, Dick Cavett to Alan Thicke, Johnny always invited the vanquished back on the show. But not Joan. "When I was fired, everyone said that Johnny should have had me back the same night, if he was smart," says Joan. "He should have opened the door and brought me back. I did nothing to hurt Johnny, and instead Johnny tried to kill me in this business. Johnny wouldn't let me on *The Tonight Show*. He wouldn't let me on Letterman."

Johnny didn't have to send out a memorandum. Everyone who worked for Carson Productions knew how he felt, but Johnny was not the Stalin of show business, able to destroy careers on a whim. Joan found out who her friends were, or more accurately, who her friends weren't. The phones stopped ringing. The invitations stopped coming. The agents had other deals to make.

Joan had seen how quickly one can fall, but this was darker even than her own pessimistic imagination. It was like a biblical judgment, a terrible penance for a crime she didn't commit. Edgar was a sick man, and he blamed himself. He felt that he was dragging Joan down.

"My husband had a breakdown and killed himself," Joan says. "After it happened, I understand that someone called Johnny and said, 'Have Joan on now.' And he said, 'No way!' And when I heard about it, I got so angry. I wouldn't have gone on anyway. Long after that I was booked on a show, and Carson was supposed to be on. And he said, 'If she's on, I won't be on.' "

Joan gave an interview to *People* and went back to work. She signed on to the only television show that would have her, *Hollywood Squares*.

Almost no one knew how fragile Joan was, how intense her anger, how deep her despair. She kept busy, busy, busy. She took over the role as the mother in Neil Simon's *Broad-*

way Bound. After the show each evening she performed stand-up at Michael's Pub. Busy, busy, busy.

Joan had her good days and her bad days, and though she could talk about Edgar's death now, she could hardly mention Johnny's name without crying, and she tried to forget. When she appeared at Caesars Palace in October 1988, she looked out at a room with no empty seats, she heard the guffaws and shrieks of an audience that had come to laugh, and felt that finally she was back.

One Sunday late in June, Johnny and Alex were at the house in Malibu. Normally at this time of year Johnny took several weeks' vacation and usually flew to Wimbledon to watch the tennis finals. This summer of 1986 Johnny felt haunted by an inexplicable desire to return to Avoca, Iowa, the first hometown that he remembered.

"Why don't you go?" Alex asked.

"Okay," Johnny said.

Johnny ordered up the Gulfstream jet, and on Monday he and Alex flew to Omaha. From there Johnny rented a white Ford Taurus and drove on the interstate to Avoca, forty-five minutes away.

It had been fifty-three years since that October day in 1933 when he had left Avoca. As they entered the town of twelve hundred residents, Johnny could see that it was too small to be rimmed by fast-food franchises, discount stores, and gas stations. The interstate ran nearby, making Avoca close enough to Omaha that people went there to do their major shopping.

"You won't know where your house is," Alex said. Avoca had changed very little, and Johnny drove down Main Street, his memory honing in perfectly on the two-story white frame house on the corner of Cherry Street. The gingerbread trim was gone, and it wasn't as big as in his memory, but other than that he could have been walking in the past.

At about 4:00 P.M., Johnny parked the car on the broad,

tree-lined street, and he and Alex walked up to the front door and knocked.

"Hello, my name is Johnny Carson, and I used to live here," Johnny said almost shyly to the middle-aged, slightly rumpled man who answered the door. "Can I come in?"

"Yes," said Morris Berndt, as if he were used to Johnny Carson knocking on his door on a summer afternoon.

Berndt, a junior high school teacher, usually wasn't home at this hour, but summer vacation had begun. He had been reading a newspaper in the living room.

Berndt, who had heard that Johnny had once lived in the house, showed his guests into the living room, where two of his children had fallen asleep on the floor watching *The Muppets Take Manhattan* on a video. Johnny noticed that the living room had the same dark wood paneling as half a century ago. His mother had been a stickler for neatness, and the living room had been a genteel, decorous place. The Berndt living room was not that tidy. The television set was its focal point, the chairs scattered around the room facing the screen. The Berndt boys, used to sleeping with background noise, did not wake up.

Johnny's mother could have walked into the kitchen and started dinner, perfectly at home. Upstairs, the main difference was that the French doors had been removed. Almost the only major change in fifty years was the television set.

Berndt, a polite and modest man, waited until Johnny stepped outside to ask, "Do you mind if I videotape?"

"No," Johnny said. Berndt got his video camera out, and the schoolteacher taped Johnny as he stood outside talking about playing underneath the porch, a discovery that the Berndt boys had made as well. He followed Johnny with his camera as he walked into the backyard, around the swing set, and stood on the front sidewalk saying good-bye.

The neighbors, who had quickly spotted Johnny, started descending on the house. One of the ladies, Jan Niemann, asked Johnny if he would mind stopping by to say hello to her mother, Ruth, who had just gotten out of the hospital.

Johnny said that he wouldn't mind at all, and he drove over to see the elderly lady. He visited the fairgrounds too, where the swimming pool had once stood.

When Mrs. Berndt returned home from work, Johnny had left. "I want to show you something on television," Morris Berndt said, and sat his wife down in front of the set.

"My gosh, that's Johnny Carson in our driveway," Laurie Berndt said.

By that time Johnny was already up at the Embers restaurant, eating a six-ounce steak while Alex nibbled on a hamburger. Then they drove to the Omaha airport, and returned to Los Angeles.

The next morning Donald Nielson, the editor of the *Avoca Journal-Herald*, received a slew of phone calls about Johnny's visit. Nielson was usually concerned with such matters as getting pictures of the Rotary Club meetings and ads for the Farmer's Mart. But this was big news.

Nielson called *The Tonight Show* in Burbank and was told that Johnny was in Malibu. The editor called Carson Productions and was told the same thing. The sightings kept coming in, and Nielson asked the Associated Press to check out this possible imposter who had foisted himself off on the good people of Avoca. Charlie Barrett, the NBC media representative, told the AP authoritatively that Johnny was in Malibu. Not until Wednesday morning did Nielson learn from Jeff Sotzing in the *Tonight Show* offices that Johnny had indeed visited his old hometown.

Three weeks later, when Johnny returned to *The Tonight Show*, he called Morris Berndt to tell him that he would be mentioning his visit that evening. Johnny talked to the Berndts' children, Andrea and Aaron, who had suffered the ignominy of sleeping through the famous visit.

The boy from next door happened to be visiting the Berndts. Even he got a chance for a few words with Johnny. The youth went home and bragged to his mother, who scolded him for making up stories.

That evening Johnny held up the front page of the *Avoca*

Journal-Herald. "It was like touching base somehow," Johnny said, "where you lived and the first thing you remember."

"We have a new president of the network, Mr. Robert Wright," Johnny told *The Tonight Show* audience during his monologue on November 12, 1986. "Well, apparently he announced his intention of laying off three hundred employees, part of the general cost-cutting program. A lot of nervous people around here . . . Freddy de Cordova will no longer be able to save on batteries by plugging his pacemaker into the electrical outlet."

Over the years Johnny had joked about NBC and its parent company, RCA. But he had never imagined that giant RCA would be purchased by another corporation, General Electric, which had a reputation as a mean, lean corporation that had little use for sentimental indulgences like tenure. NBC employees were not happy, but they could hardly look enviously toward ABC or CBS, where new management was paring payrolls with equal speed. As the networks' share of the audience steadily declined, the orders at all three networks were the same: Protect the bottom line. That meant even *The Tonight Show*.

Roy Ratliff handled the one camera that focused only on Johnny's head each evening. Ratliff had a ranch in the countryside, but he loved his work and cared about the way Johnny looked. If Johnny's clothes weren't just right, he would motion to the stage manager. Ratliff liked the hours too. He would do *The Tonight Show*, and that would be it for the day. Under the new management the camera crew worked Johnny's show for three-and-a-half or four hours, and then hurried off to do other shows. If things had been a little loose before, they had gone to the opposite extreme.

"The way it is now, you're supposed to take these people," Ratliff said. "That's their attitude. You're just a number. Before, people played together and worked together and enjoyed themselves. Now, if you look sideways, if you're five minutes late, they're going to discipline you.

When that red light comes on, you're there. That's what matters.''

In the early evening of December 30, 1986, two *Tonight Show* employees carried a dummy wearing jeans and an NBC cap to the roof of the NBC studios in Burbank high above the city. Ratliff stood below with a hand-held camera. As they heaved the dummy off the roof, Ratliff filmed it, letting it fall as close to him as possible.

The next evening, New Year's Eve, Johnny was going to play the tape, saying, "This is the first NBC employee of the new year thrown out by General Electric." It would have been a funny bit, but the production staff was told that Johnny was not going to do it, and it was not shown the next evening.

The week before Christmas 1986 Johnny's publicist confirmed that Johnny had asked Alex Mass to become his fourth wife. The shopkeepers and salespeople along Rodeo could have guessed as much. Alex had become a familiar figure to them as she began bedecking herself in all the trademark clothes of wealth. She wore heavier makeup and heavier jewelry, until she looked like a youthful clone of Linda Evans. "Watching the transition of Alex was frightening," says an actress who saw Johnny and Alex frequently. "The person goes because only one life lives there."

In March 1987 Mort Wells came to town. Johnny loved to reminisce with his old friend about the days in Omaha when Mort had his own band on WOW, and Mort was looking forward to going out to the house in Malibu. When he didn't hear back from Johnny, he figured he knew what was wrong. The newspapers were running stories that Johnny's son Chris had fathered an illegitimate daughter in Florida. The mother, Tanena Love Green, thirty-five years old, married, and black, was supposedly living in a rat-infested house trailer in Fort Lauderdale.

"Johnny didn't call, and I suspected why," Wells says. "I finally called Drue, his secretary. Drue said, 'We can't hardly even talk to him. He's so mad he could kill these people.'

"I got to talk to Johnny. He said, 'I have to apologize. I hope you come back soon so we can spend some time together. I would have liked to have you come out and see the house. But I'm crawling the walls. I'm so goddamn mad I could kill. Her lawyers are trying to attach my holdings.''

Unlike Rick and Cory, Chris had tried to get away from the shadow of his father. When he graduated from the University of Miami in 1972 with a degree in psychology, he stayed in Florida. Johnny's publicists said that Chris was a golf pro, a fiction that even his mother believed. But Chris hardly had to work, since in those years Johnny paid his eldest son $12,000 to $15,000 tax-free dollars a year, enough for a small walk-up apartment, a few pieces of furniture, and a Datsun.

Chris was frugal by necessity as well as by nature. One day when he was looking for a pair of pants at a flea market on Oakland Boulevard, he was attracted to the saleslady, a striking black woman named Tanena Love. Chris got the woman's phone number and invited her out.

"He was a caddie when I first met him," Love says. "He wore the same clothes all the time. He had four pairs of pants. He lived in this second-floor apartment with crooked wooden steps. He had a bedroom and not even a full living room. He had a pole for his clothes."

Chris says that Love would appear and disappear, and he saw her infrequently over the next few years. Her memories are far different, of a close, intense platonic friendship, ending when she married and moved away.

When Tanena returned to Fort Lauderdale in 1985, Chris met her again at the flea market. He was a little better off now. Johnny was paying him $35,000 a year tax-free, and had bought him a $119,000 condominium not far from his old apartment. Chris's main extravagance was a twenty-two-hundred-dollar big-screen television that sat in his living room.

"Do you want to be a daddy?" Tanena asked one day, as Chris remembers.

"I don't think so. I would rather not." The fact that Tanena was married didn't seem to enter into their discussion.

The two met again. "I wasn't kidding about that, and I really would like a child," she said.

"Well, I'm not too interested in being a daddy," Chris recalls saying. According to Tanena, Chris said that he wanted to father her child and to have a wife and family.

Though Tanena was still married, she and Chris began a sexual relationship. "I liked him because he was so lonely," Tanena says. "His life wasn't normal to me. I'd bring him things over for the holidays, food and things.

"He would talk about his upbringing. He lives in the past. He lives in high school. He's always talking about when he was a little boy, and his bicycle. He never talks about now. He repeats himself over and over again.

"He looks at *The Tonight Show* like it's a religion. He doesn't miss a program. He mentioned that was his father. But it was like a joke. Carson is a common name. I thought he was this great fan who imagined himself to be the son. I knew he wasn't worldly, and I thought he pretended that Johnny was his father.

"Chris is like someone who's never been weaned. It's like he's never found closeness anywhere. He needs company. He wanted love from his father. He would do anything to get love from his father, or attention from his father."

During the Thanksgiving holiday Tanena brought a turkey dinner to Chris's house and told him she was pregnant.

Chris had lost contact with his mother and hadn't talked to her for half a dozen years. He had little choice but to call his father.

"What were you doing fooling around with a married lady?" Johnny responded, as Chris remembers.

"It was a rather stupid mistake," Chris replied. "I was

in a sense invited to have sex with her. I thought with the use of contraceptives there would be no child."

"Looks like you are in pretty hot water."

Cristal Love Carson was born July 3, 1986. Chris asked his father's help in getting a lawyer. Once the blood test proved that Chris was the father and he made it clear that he would take no parental responsibility, the legal case became a simple one. It was a matter of how much money Chris would have to pay to support his daughter. Chris believed that he should pay whatever was the minimum amount. Beyond Johnny's stipend, he earned a few hundred dollars a year giving golf lessons. "I don't give a great many because I hope to be out playing a little bit, playing golf," he said in his deposition. He was taking flying lessons, and wanted to get his private license. In the summer he planned to drive up to New England and play golf there.

The court ordered that Chris pay $175 a week to support the child, whom Chris did not see. However, in the spring of 1987 Tifinie Wessell saw a man enter the Green Star Trailer Park, where she and Tanena had trailers. Wessell was sure that it was Chris Carson. When the man spotted her, he hurried off in his old car. A week later the man entered the park again. Tanena had asked the old lady to watch over her trailer, and when Mrs. Wessell went to the door, the man ran off.

Johnny had his son's scandal to worry about, but he could always retreat into the sanctuary of *The Tonight Show*. He had a few friends—Henry, of course, and Buddy Rich. Johnny played the drums as well as a lot of journeyman drummers; Buddy played the drums like nobody else in the world. Johnny was the most calculated and diligent of performers; Buddy had never taken a lesson or practiced in his life.

Buddy was an aberration of nature, God's marvelous mistake. At the age of four he had performed on Broadway, and he had never stopped performing. He was a man of violent temper and stormy ego, who raged and ranted, living his life as loud and fast as he played his drums. Johnny loved Buddy Rich for what he could do and for what he was. And when Buddy suffered a brain tumor and was in the UCLA Medical Center, Johnny reportedly sent Buddy and his wife, Marie, a check for twenty thousand dollars.

The surgeons removed the tumor, and seventy-year old Buddy left the hospital. He was a tough man, but on April 2, 1987, he died of a heart attack.

Johnny was one of the first to hear the news. "The worst I've ever seen him was the day Buddy Rich died," recalls Roy Ratliff. "He did the show that day, but he blew up doing his skit. The next day he canceled."

The memorial service for Buddy was held at the Chapel of the Palms at Westwood Memorial Park. Buddy had known practically every major figure in the music and entertainment world since the 1940's, and many of them were present. When Frank Sinatra, Jerry Lewis, and Mel Torme spoke, they told show-business recollections of times good and bad. Johnny spoke fewer words than the others, but he spoke from the heart and told no anecdotes.

"I think that people who knew Buddy only through his music miss the better part of the man," Johnny began. "For a guy who professed to dislike sentimentality he was one of the most sentimental people I have ever met. For a man who often on the outside appeared to be rough, tough, sometimes hostile, even impenetrable, he was one of the most vulnerable human beings I've ever met. And for a guy who often seemed to live within himself and pretend to be fiercely independent, he was probably the most loving and caring person I have ever met.

"I think I can say that Buddy was not afraid of dying. He was simply afraid of living and not being able to play his drums. I loved Buddy Rich, like most of you people here, and I'm going to miss him terribly."

Johnny found it hard to continue. "So, dear friend, thanks for the memories and the music, and most of all thank you for making our lives more full and complete by letting us be a part of yours."

* * *

On *The Tonight Show* everyone treated Johnny with overwhelming deference. These people had worked for Johnny
for years. Freddy was in his late seventies, and producing
The Tonight Show was not only the best job he ever had,
but the last. Peter Lassally would almost certainly retire
when Johnny left, as would Bobby Quinn, the director. They
did not want to change the show that was their golden cow;
and since *The Tonight Show* had shrunk to an hour, there
was little room for experimentation, or the luxury of spontaneity.

Johnny's success had spilled over onto many lives, nowhere more generously than on Ed's. The two men didn't
even bother pretending that they were the same carousing
drinking buddies they had been so many years ago in New
York. Ed's closeness to Johnny ended when the television
camera went off. Whereas Johnny drove himself to the
studio, Ed traveled in his own limousine, and as soon as
the show was taped, he was off to his next appointment.

Ed's daily stint on *The Tonight Show* was little more than
a pit stop as he raced around Los Angeles from one activity
to another. He had become the great huckster of the television age, shilling products with the same enthusiasm that
he had so many years ago applied to the Morris metric
vegetable slicer on the Boardwalk in Atlantic City. He was
Everyman writ big, spokesman for beer and dog food, not
champagne and caviar. Even the successful syndicated show
that he hosted, *Star Search*, was every man's dream in
America of the eighties, being plucked from obscurity and
whisked to stardom in Hollywood. Ed had fulfilled that
dream, making incredible sums of money. In 1981, for
instance, he was the spokesman for thirty-seven banks
across America; they paid him between $15,000 and
$100,000 a piece; and that was nothing compared to the
checks he received from Budweiser, Alpo, and other major
corporations.

As an announcer, Ed was no different from his peers than
one dog food is from another. But thanks to sitting next to

Johnny, he anointed a product. Years ago he had made peace with himself and his role as second banana, and the millions that he had earned were only part of the wealth of his life. He had his own star on Hollywood's "Walk of Fame" next to W. C. Fields, and he gave generously of his time to a myriad of charities. In 1986 he and his second wife, Victoria, adopted a five-day-old infant. Even for Los Angeles, this was a strange spectacle: sixty-three-year-old Ed, with the body of the Goodyear blimp, seated in the backseat of a limousine changing diapers. But he took to fatherhood again, measuring out formula like a chemist. His marital happiness did not last, and he would soon be embroiled in a divorce every bit as bitter and publicized as Johnny's from Joanna.

Doc Severinsen did not join Ed in the fatherhood sweepstakes, but he too had a new, younger wife, and a career that had been blessed immeasurably by his association with Johnny. He was married for the third time, and it was no wonder that Johnny sometimes joked about Doc's marital woes. The trumpeter had five grown-up children, three of his own from his first marriage, and two more from his second wife's first marriage whom he had adopted. Like Ed, he used the celebrity that the show gave him and went off with members of the band across America giving concerts. He formed his own jazz band, Zebron, which performed in concert halls and intimate clubs. He was a great trumpet player, but he was more dependent on Johnny and *The Tonight Show* than Ed. When Johnny retired, Doc would almost certainly leave too, putting the glory days of his career behind him.

Ed and Doc understood perfectly their roles on *The Tonight Show*. They were there for Johnny, and they were always ready. On the show Johnny was most comfortable talking with unknowns, young comics, or up-and-coming performers. He still was not always comfortable interviewing the biggest stars of his age or performers who paraded their hipness.

In May of 1987 Eddie Murphy appeared on the show to promote his new film, *Beverly Hills Cop II*. Murphy was about as different a personality from Johnny as two comedians could be. The night before his appearance Murphy had been hanging out in his hotel with friends, including Chris Jackson, a twenty-seven-year old fledgling comedian.

Jackson did his Prince imitation, rolling around on his knees, singing in falsetto. Murphy laughed his patented laugh, like an asthmatic having an orgasm. "That's the funniest thing I've ever seen," Murphy said.

"Can I go with you tomorrow, Eddie?" Jackson asked as he left the hotel room, thinking about the free buffet.

"Yeah," Murphy said, "You can go if you do the Prince imitation."

"You're jerking me!"

"Be here at four-thirty."

The next afternoon Murphy and his entourage drove out to the studio in his limousine. The comedian walked onstage to a thunderous ovation.

"What were you doing ten years ago?" Johnny asked.

"Stealin' somebody's bike."

"Do you remember?" Johnny asked, as if he hadn't heard right.

"Yeah, I'm twenty-six and we'd go and steal bikes," Murphy said. Then he looked out in the audience. "Remember and they caught us and . . ." Murphy was talking to his friends as if Johnny were an unwanted observer. "Not Woody. Whose Mother came . . ."

"Did you have a *gang* with you here tonight?" Johnny asked.

"I brought my *friends*."

"Are you pretty much of a loner?"

"I'm not a loner at all. I'm telling you, we walked in the place today and you should have saw the people in the back saying, 'Who are all these Negroes coming in?' "

The audience exploded in laughter.

"What's interesting is that it was Floyd, the shoeshine

man, who said that," Johnny said, referring to one of the few blacks at NBC.

Murphy laughed as if amused at something besides Johnny's joke. After the showing of a clip of *Beverly Hills Cop II*, the comedian's stint with Johnny was about up. Johnny asked a few last questions about Murphy's sudden wealth.

"You know what I'm saying," Johnny said. "You walk down the street and you see something in the store window and you say, 'Man, look at that.' "

"I do that sometimes."

"Now what would catch your eye?" Johnny asked, leaning toward Murphy, who earned millions a picture. "A watch? A coat?"

Murphy was convulsed in laughter. "What do you like? What catches your eye?" he said mimicking Johnny. "Look at that shiny ring. Hey, Amos, get a load a that coat. That's a mighty big watch there.

"Hey, where's Chris Jackson at?" Murphy asked. "Do you know a guy called Chris Jackson?"

"Do I know who?" Johnny asked, momentarily bewildered. He had almost lost control of this interview, and now this.

"Where's he at?"

"Chris Jackson?" Johnny asked, looking around for help.

"This guy does an imitation of Prince that is the funniest," Murphy said as a tall, husky black man walked onstage.

"Is this Chris Jackson?" Johnny asked, as if it might be Lech Walesa or a member of the Vienna Boys' Choir.

"Come here, Chris," Murphy said.

"Come here. I don't . . . I don't know," Johnny stuttered. "How're you doing?"

"Everybody, Chris Jackson," Murphy said, introducing his friend.

Jackson got down on his knees. "You don't have to be beautiful," Chris sang. It was not exactly a world-class Prince imitation, but Murphy doubled up in laughter. Johnny

laughed almost as hard, but abruptly ended the segment
when Jackson finished and walked offstage.

Afterward, Jackson hid in the men's room, afraid that he
was going to be thrown out. A band member happened upon
the young comedian there. "You were great," he said.
"I've never seen that happen before." Jackson decided it
was okay to come out.

Early on the afternoon of Saturday, June 20, 1987, Judge
William Hogoboom and Mrs. Hogoboom drove up the Pacific Coast Highway to Malibu. A few weeks before, Johnny
had called the retired judge and asked him to officiate at
Johnny's marriage to Alex. Johnny had met the judge when
Hogoboom had ruled on his separation from Joanna, but he
had not seen him since that day.

Johnny and Alex walked with the judge and his wife to
the garden. Johnny's brother, Dick, was the only other
person present. Alex's parents took part in the ceremony
on a speaker phone. Alex wore a white gown and carried
a bouquet of pink roses. Johnny wore a conservative double-
breasted blue suit and tie.

The judge had married scores of couples before, and he
moved Johnny and Alex assuredly through the ceremony.
Afterward, the party drank champagne and Alex cut the
wedding cake, and then it was all over.

"It's such a magnificent spot," Judge Hogoboom recalls.
"If you were designing a motion picture, you couldn't possibly make a believable scene out of it. It's so fantastically
beautiful and it's in exquisite taste, nothing flamboyant.

"It's perfect, and to have no one there, no friends, it felt
a little bleak. I felt a little sorry for them, sad. I thought
about all the people I would have had if it had been my
wedding.

"I just hope he's happy."

Alex and Johnny flew to London to attend the Wimbledon
tennis tournament. Afterward, they traveled to the Medi-
terranean for a cruise on a $6.5 million, 147-foot yacht,
Parts V, that rented for $49,000 a week.

Johnny invited Henry and his new love, Mary Hart of *Entertainment Tonight*, to go along. He also invited his brother, Dick. One evening, according to one source, the tender of the *Parts V* took the group into Juan-les-Pin, for sightseeing and shopping. "The boat will be here at eleven-thirty to pick you up," the captain said to Johnny as they left. "But please take the walkie-talkie if you want us earlier or later."

Johnny gave the bulky walkie-talkie to Henry, who went off with Mary. Henry told the sailor that he would like to be picked up at twelve-thirty, but to call for Johnny at eleven-thirty.

Johnny was always punctual, trained by the unforgiving times of television. Johnny, Alex, and Dick arrived back at the dock at eleven-thirty and found no boat. Henry had the walkie-talkie, and Johnny was upset. With his new wife and brother, he walked back into town.

At about twelve-thirty Johnny and his group met Henry and Mary at the dock. "Where'd you go?" Henry asked innocently.

"We left," Johnny said. "That son of a bitch wasn't here on time."

"I'm sorry, Mr. Carson," said the young British captain. "I was seven minutes late and you're weren't here, and we've waited for you since."

"If I'm paying fifty fucking thousand dollars, you better be on time!"

"Mr. Carson, you're on holiday," the captain replied. "It's the south of France. I apologize. I was seven minutes late. But we were getting a Telex from our office in London."

Johnny got on the tender, but he was still fuming. "I'm not sailing with this guy anymore. We're getting off this boat in the morning and checking into the Hotel Du Cap."

When the tender reached the ship, four adults spent two hours convincing one adult that he was making a great deal out of nothing.

Almost from their wedding day, Hollywood was full of

rumors that Johnny's newest marriage was in trouble, that Johnny couldn't tolerate Alex's extravagances. "I think he's incapable of having a normal relationship with a woman," says one close associate. "They hadn't been married for two weeks when he said to her, 'You do that goddamn thing one more time, and you won't be married three weeks.' When you hear this, you want to get up and pretend that it never happened."

When Emm-Jay first heard that Johnny had gotten married, she was angry and upset. She had known him for close to ten years, and she had nothing to show for it. She was going to be forty years old.

In the fall she flew to Paris to be the associate director on a special live syndicated show, *The Search for the Titanic*. She had never been in Paris before, but she had little time to see the Louvre or walk along the Seine. According to Emm-Jay, Johnny called her in Paris and chatted with her.

Emm-Jay worked long, difficult hours, and when the show was broadcast, she collapsed and passed out. For a moment her heart stopped, and she had a vision of life passing away, a vision of endless water. When she woke up, she knew that she had to live for herself.

"I think of it now and I realize I'm far happier than any of them could ever be," she says. "They are possessed by things that are meaningless. I have friends that are there for me. That's my answer to why he's not happy. He's not happy within himself. He thinks people care for him because he's Johnny Carson. He's insecure. I feel sorry for him. It's absurd having achieved all this and really to have nothing."

At Christmas Emm-Jay went to Burbank to see Johnny on the set of *The Tonight Show*. Bob Hope was backstage waiting to go on. Hope's whole public life had become a commemoration of his career, a ritual in which Hope, the person, had long ago disappeared. Emm-Jay had the feeling that people had begun to treat Johnny the same way. "I walked away and I thought, Johnny is really a very nice person, but he's totally in another world," Emm-Jay said. "He has no idea what's going on, and it's kind of sad."

On New Year's Day Emm-Jay heard Johnny's voice on her answering machine. She thought for a moment, and didn't call back.

Johnny and Henry were splitting up. That was the extraordinary gossip that began circulating over breakfasts at the Polo Lounge, lunches at Le Dome, and dinners at Spago. The news was passed on from person to person, weighed and examined and evaluated, and those who knew Hollywood best said that it was impossible. Johnny and Henry had one of the best marriages in Hollywood, a personal and professional relationship that had brought great wealth to Johnny and a considerable fortune to Henry. Johnny had never had a friend like Henry. Maybe Henry was not going to have as much to do with some of Johnny's activities, but as for a breakup, well, it was frankly impossible.

The rumors had begun after Johnny decided that he wanted to sell Carson Productions, of which Henry owned 10 percent. Johnny was not an empire builder like Merv Griffin, who wanted his name on hotels and great business enterprises. He was an entertainer.

When Johnny told Henry of his plans to sell the assets, the attorney disagreed. He thought that Johnny should wait a couple years. They should build up the company, move ahead with a bunch of new projects, and *then* sell. Henry had a reputation for being totally bloodless and uncaring, but he was more concerned with the people who worked for Carson Productions than Johnny. He didn't think it was right to let them go and sell off the assets. Johnny was tired of all the problems.

Johnny was adamant, and Henry had learned long ago that when Johnny made up his mind, he had better do what Johnny told him to do. "Henry was running around like crazy trying to sell it," says one top television executive. "They were asking something like $70 million. We looked at it, but it wasn't worth shit. They owed Ed Weinberger such a big cut of *Amen* that it was unbelievable. They were running an enormous deficit on *Mr. President* because of George C. Scott's salary. I asked their financial guy, 'How the fuck could you make these deals?' He said, 'Henry makes these deals, and we have to suffer with them.' ''

Fred Kayne was the obvious person to handle the sale. But though Kayne was still directing Johnny's investments, he had left Bear Stearns & Company, and Henry passed the sale on to Michael Klein, the managing director and a man Henry trusted.

"After Bear Stearns looked at it, they decided that it wasn't worth as much as they had thought originally," says Kayne. "They blamed Bushkin that the company wasn't in the shape it should have been."

Klein developed a list of problems and difficulties stemming in his opinion from Henry's management of Johnny's affairs. Klein could not take on Henry alone. He approached his close friend E. Gregory "Ed" Hookstratten, a powerful Beverly Hills attorney who represented sports and television figures. Hookstratten already knew a good deal about Henry and Carson Productions thanks to another friend, John McMahon, who had left Carson Productions unhappy with Henry.

Klein and Hookstratten reportedly presented their case to Johnny. Over the years others had come complaining about Henry, most notably Johnny's own wife Joanna. If he had wanted to fire Henry, he could have found ample reason, from the Commercial Bank mess to the embarrassing failure to buy the Aladdin. The two men had gone through their divorces together, and that had made them even closer. Johnny had always turned a deaf ear, but now he could not ignore the relentless drumbeat of criticism. As for Henry, he had grown weary beyond weariness of dealing with Johnny. Johnny had one last meeting with Henry, and with that their seventeen-year relationship came to an end.

"Johnny carries a tight suitcase," McMahon had said years earlier, and no one who watched *The Tonight Show* that evening would have imagined that he had lost the one close friend he had ever had. Johnny was shut off now, like a vault that has no combination. Johnny and Henry were kindred souls, and Henry kept his own feelings to himself as well. He told an acquaintance that he had never been Johnny's friend. He had been his lawyer, lackey, hired gun, tennis partner, beard, bartender, adviser, and therapist. But he had not been his friend.

Johnny seemed to want to purge himself of anyone or anything that had to do with Henry. Maynell Thomas, the top attorney at Carson Productions, was one of those who suffered. Thomas had not gotten along with Ed Weinberger, the producer of *Amen*—the company's one hit—and the most important creative person in the company. Another employee might simply have been cast out with severance pay. But since Thomas had spent so many years working for Johnny, Henry had spent several months negotiating a lucrative contract for Thomas as an independent producer associated with Carson Productions.

When Johnny learned of the proposed contract, he reportedly blamed Henry, considering it totally unnecessary, an albatross that any new owner would have to pick up. "I didn't understand what happened," Thomas said. "I think I got caught in the earthquake going on between Henry and Johnny. My entire career was for his company, and I feel I wasn't appreciated for what I did. I think that Alex may have had something to do with it. If he thinks Alex has his best interests in mind, he's wrong. As for Johnny, I don't think that he has any concern for human life. He's hurt so many people, his own family, his own children. He's not a protector. I always thought he was different. He always treated me with such passionate concern. Then one day I tried to talk to him and I called and Alex answered the phone. I don't know if she ever gave him the message. He's a very unhappy man. He doesn't have anybody now but the gatekeeper."

In December Fred Kayne drove out to Malibu. Although Kayne believed that Alex was behind Henry's firing, Kayne was nonetheless surprised to see Johnny's new wife sitting in on this meeting. Joanna had never attended Johnny's business meetings. "They said that they were going to handle their money a different way," Kayne said. And so, after thirteen years, Kayne was no longer managing Johnny's money.

"I had the feeling that his attitude is always, What did you do for me yesterday?" Kayne says. "He's always looking at it that way. He really doesn't appreciate."

The Wall Street Journal called the ending of Johnny and Henry's association "one of the more unpleasant Hollywood splits since Lewis left Martin." A central problem in untangling the relationship was Willowbrook West Ltd., the ninety-three undeveloped acres in Houston that stood there barren, unused and unwanted—at least not at the prices the partners were seeking. Henry had already been sued once for malpractice by Neil Simon over the fiasco, but that was not the end of Henry's problems.

Johnny was stuck with millions of dollars in potential liability. For several years the United Savings Bank of Texas had been trying to get the various partners to pay up. As in the Commercial Bank deal, Johnny and the other partners signed a note that each would be liable for the entire amount if the other partners defaulted. In December Johnny's company, Carson Tonight, went ahead and purchased the entire note from the Texas bank. Now, it would be Johnny and his attorneys knocking on the doors of the other partners, including Henry, if they could not sell the land for the $18.5 million that they had shelled out.

Johnny was not about to swallow such an enormous loss. His attorneys filed a malpractice claim against Henry's law firm, alleging that Henry had a conflict of interest, representing not only Johnny but the developer, Bill Bird, and Bird Development Company. Then, in seeking repayment, on May 6, 1988, Carson Tonight sued Henry, his law partners Jerry K. Staub and John Gaims, and several others, for $16,672,711, plus attorneys fees, costs, and whatever further relief the court judged fair.

Bushkin, Gaims, Gaines & Jonas had been one of the most prominent entertainment law firms in Hollywood. Its exquisite offices were unlike any others in Century City. But in the wake of Johnny's leaving, the firm closed its doors. The various partners and associates moved off into other firms and other offices.

When Arthur Kassel, one of Henry's many former friends, heard that the office would be shutting down, he had one immediate reaction. "Maybe I can buy some of the furniture," he said.

Any attorney makes enemies. But Henry had, unfortunately, made few friends. Mary Hart of *Entertainment Tonight* had been with him when he was the legendary "Bombastic Bushkin," but she was soon gone.

"I don't know if Henry can think of anyone as a friend except for Johnny," says his former wife, Judy. "It was absolutely a real friendship between John and Henry. That's why it's very, very sad. I don't think either one of them has close men friends, anyway. I think they had each other and that was it. Now, they basically have nobody.

"Henry has burned a lot of bridges over the way. One of these days it was going to catch up with him. I knew it was going to happen sooner or later. People get so caught up in playing God in this town. They think they're indestructible, but they're not. Nobody is."

Johnny had called Henry several times a day. Now, the phone in Henry's private office was silent. Johnny and his business affairs had taken up vast amounts of Henry's time. Now Henry had a free schedule. Johnny's prestige had brought many clients to the firm of Bushkin, Gaims, Gaines & Jonas. Now, there was no longer even a firm.

No one felt as much a sense of vindication as Joanna Carson. She heard that Johnny was telling people that she had been right all along.

TWENTY-TWO

To Johnny, *The Tonight Show* was everything. When the Writers Guild went on strike in March 1988, the show shut down and he had nothing to do except walk across the road to his private tennis court. But as much as he loved to play tennis, that took no more than a couple hours. He usually read a lot, but almost always to prepare for the show. He and Alex could have gone to Europe, China, or Brazil, but Johnny didn't like to travel. He had been talking about retiring for years; but if the ratings of the twenty-fifth-anniversary show were any indication, he had practically an endowed chair. The fact was that he liked the routine of *The Tonight Show* and didn't want to change a thing.

A few weeks earlier CBS had announced that in January 1989 Pat Sajak, the host of *Wheel of Fortune*, would have his own late-night show opposite *The Tonight Show*. And many people believed that Johnny would not even contemplate retiring until Sajak had gone the way of all his predecessors.

Hookstratten had become Johnny's lawyer; and if the Beverly Hills attorney had had his way, Sajak would not even have entered the late-night sweepstakes. Hookstratten had been representing Sajak as well as Johnny, and he had advised the game-show host not to accept the CBS offer. Sajak sought advice from Alan Rothenberg, another prominent entertainment lawyer. "Pat was suspicious," Rothenberg says. "I called Hookstratten and asked him to send over the files. And then we negotiated the CBS deal."

Johnny and Alex spent a weekend in San Diego visiting the city's famous zoo. Johnny had made the San Diego Zoo even better known by often featuring its animals on his program, and the zoo administrators gave the couple a special tour. In early April the Carsons flew to Washington, D.C. Johnny wasn't a sightseer, and the couple spent much of the time in their suite at the Four Seasons Hotel in Georgetown and appeared to be perfectly happy together.

Soon after his return to Malibu, Johnny decided that if the strike lasted much longer, he would consider going back on the air, writing his own material. It was a challenge that few performers of Johnny's stature would even have contemplated.

For several days Johnny and *The Tonight Show* staff discussed the pros and cons. Johnny was in a bad mood. The ratings of the reruns were touching bottom. His production company was paying the salaries of idle *Tonight Show* employees, a generous gesture but one that could not go on much longer. Even so, Johnny had not written most of his own television material since *Carson's Cellar* four decades ago. He might get by for a night or two with jokes that he had squirreled away, but what if the strike lasted?

Hookstratten tried unsuccessfully to negotiate a separate contract with the Writers Guild. On May 3, Johnny announced that, writers or no writers, he was going back to work. "There are numerous *Tonight Show* staff members, many have been with us for over 20 years, who are in danger of losing their jobs if this strike goes on much longer," Johnny said. "I can't let that happen. I also can't turn my back on the *Tonight Show* audience, who have remained loyal these 25 years. It's time to get back to work."

Johnny admitted later that he was having problems with Alex at home. He had become so irritable that he snapped back even when she asked if he wanted a cup of coffee. "I really believe one more week off and my marriage would have been resolved by small-arms fire," he said.

Johnny had become part of the emotional fabric of millions of American lives, and he was far from the only one to miss the show. "Where people once needed a mug of warm milk before bed, many now require a nightly flagon of Johnny Carson," wrote Tom Shales in the *Washington Post*. "Deprived of this necessity some of us become dour, gruff and cranky."

On Wednesday, May 11, Johnny drove to the studio in Burbank to tape the first *Tonight Show* in over two months. The tickets for the show were long gone, the fans not concerned with picketing writers.

The Tonight Show staff knew what an unusual evening this would be. Many of them stayed for the taping of the show. At 5:20 Freddy walked out to begin warming up the audience. "Good evening, ladies and gentlemen," the executive producer said. "And welcome to what I believe is a very special evening, which will be hosted by a young comedian in whom I have enormous faith. I believe he is talented as a comedian. He's a very pleasant personality. He's proven to be a fine writer. And his name is Johnny Carson."

As Freddy went through this litany each evening, he usually got a few gasps of disappointment before he mentioned Johnny's name. He fooled no one this evening. Then, as he always did, Freddy introduced Doc Severinsen by talking about the musician's string of decrepit racehorses. Doc burst onto the set, to the applause of recognition and a stunning riff from the band.

"Are you there?" Doc yelled. "Right now we're going to bring out a gentleman who's going to come out here and explain how we put on *The Tonight Show*; that is, if he isn't too stoned to remember. You know who I'm talking about, the one and only Eeeeeeeeedddddd MccccMahon!"

"Hi Ho!" Ed yelled as he rumbled onto the set. "Hi

ho!'' To the audience, Ed McMahon was as familiar as Johnny. When they turned on the tube, he was either sitting next to Johnny, hosting *Star Search*, or shilling Budweiser, Alpo, or the product of the moment. They got their mail and there his face was again, promoting a magazine sweepstakes.

"You sound terrific!" Ed told the audience. "I'm going to pay you a nice compliment. I know what night it is. I haven't had a drink yet this evening. I will very shortly. It's Wednesday night. Right. You sound like, sound like, a Friday night crowd."

The audience whooped it up at this compliment.

"Friday night is the greatest night in all of show business," Ed continued in his sonorous baritone, his voice charged with enthusiasm. "See, the audience is better on Friday night, turning on the actors, who perform better. So you'll see a better show, like you will tonight."

Ed never changed his spiel. The audience could have been passed out in their seats, and he would have called them a "Friday night crowd." He was a masterful salesman. He sold the audience the idea that it was singular, that it was about to see not just another evening, another show, but a unique performance. When the audience clapped and hooted and yelled, it would be applauding not only Johnny but itself.

"Guess who showed up after the strike?" McMahon asked. "The man who appears in the title of the show will actually host his own show tonight."

The audience applauded.

"We have less than a minute to go," McMahon continued, looking up. He had done this thousands of times, but even he appeared a bit nervous. "I always thought having a lot of time off would be great. It's miserable. It's terrible. I'm ready. We're almost thirty seconds. I'll be over there."

Ed walked over to the side of the set and took the detachable microphone in his hand. "All right, are you all ready for a great show?" he asked rhetorically.

"Let's get this baby cranked up," he said over the applause. "I want to see if I still remember. Yeah. It's like riding a bicycle. You never forget. Face this way. I'm going to make a lot of notes."

"Five." The last seconds were counted off.

"Four."

"Three."

"Two."

"One."

The theme music burst forth. "Frrrrrrrooooom Holly-wood, *The Tonight Show* starring Johnny Carson. This is Ed McMahon, along with Doc Severinsen and the NBC orchestra, inviting you to join Johnny and his guests, Joe Piscopo, bird-expert William Toone, and a musical tribute to Irving Berlin. And now, ladies and gentlemen, *Heeeeere's Johnny!*"

As Johnny stepped from behind his curtain, the audience stood and clapped and whistled and cheered. Ed waved his arms, calling for even greater applause.

Johnny stood awash in adulation, the applause mounting. "Thank you very much," he said finally.

"Welcome back, Johnny!" someone shouted.

"Thank you very much," Johnny replied over another burst of applause.

"A lot of people asked me, Why did you decide to come back? I'll be honest with you. I just could not stay away any longer with all the things that are going on in the country."

Twenty-five years ago Johnny's monologue had been a witty aside to the serious events of the day. Now, it often seemed that the front-page news read like *Joe Miller's Joke Book*. In the sixties Johnny wouldn't have thought of rudely satirizing such religious figures as Billy Graham, Norman Vincent Peale, or Bishop Fulton J. Sheen. They had given way to the likes of Jimmy Swaggart, Jim and Tammy Bak-ker, and Oral Roberts. Johnny had cracked his Kennedy jokes, but that was nothing like the material the Reagans provided. And now, during Johnny's weeks off, Donald

Regan, the former chief of staff, had revealed in his book that Mrs. Reagan had regularly consulted an astrologer.

"We finally have a clue now as to what the hell the loony-toon things that have been coming out of Washington," Johnny said. "We apparently have a new cabinet officer, the secretary of Health, Education and Soothsaying. Astrologers say that the Reagans' rising sign is in the house of Aquarius. Nancy's sign, I think, is in the house of Adolfo."

The audience laughed and laughed. For years Americans had been reading headlines as an exercise in disillusionment. Johnny exorcised part of their bitterness with laughter. As the audience grew more alienated from politics, Johnny had to take longer setting up the jokes. Other than Ronnie and Nancy, he couldn't be sure that his audience knew the players in Washington.

"Donald Regan, the former chief of staff and former secretary of the Treasury, came out with a book. And in it, according to Regan, every appearance that the president made was planned according to astrological signs. Did you know somebody named Joyce Jillson? She came out and said this was extremely important because, and I quote Miss Jillson, 'The president performs at his best during a full moon.' "

Johnny couldn't top the truth. Johnny milked the subject for several more jokes. When his writers prepared the monologue, he treated a failed joke like a rotten fish, tossing it away. These were *his* jokes this evening. He acted reverentially toward his material, setting each joke up perfectly, never disdaining the joke with a saver.

"I really believe now that if Jim and Tammy Bakker had read their horoscope, they would not be in the trouble they're in. I checked on Jim Bakker's horoscope. At the exact time of the affair with Jessica Hahn, apparently Jim's moon was rising when it shouldn't have been."

When Johnny had first hosted *The Tonight Show*, he wouldn't even have attempted such a joke. Now, in part because of Johnny, television audiences had become comfortable laughing at sexual humor that once would have been relegated to the lounge rooms in Las Vegas.

"We are very happy to be back," Johnny said.

The red light went off, and the television monitors showed a series of soundless commercials. Johnny stood alone before the studio audience. "Thank you very much, you made it much easier," he said as the applause died. Usually Johnny said only a few words, but tonight he wanted to speak longer.

"I'll be very honest with you. I was very nervous tonight. When you haven't worked in ten weeks, you tend to get out of rhythm. I don't think I've been so nervous since I emceed the first Academy Awards. You made it very nice."

The audience applauded again. "Astrology was too much," Johnny said. "I had to come back for that."

"I got a joke for you!" someone yelled.

"You got a joke?" Johnny said, his voice an amused echo. "How's it go?"

"What did one earthquake say to the other earthquake?" a man yelled.

"What did one earthquake say to the other earthquake?" Johnny repeated, his voice twanging out the words. "I don't know, Andy, what did . . ." Johnny fell into the character of George Kingfish Stevens, the conniving con man on the *Amos 'n' Andy* radio show that he had listened to as a boy.

"It's not my fault!" the man yelled.

The audience laughed and jeered in equal measure.

"We'll take anything we can get," Johnny said. "Thanks for coming out."

Johnny sat down at his desk. Its decorations were always the same—two pencils, a little box, the lighter. "Well, Andy, here we are at the lodge hall," Johnny said to himself. That was how George Kingfish Stevens set up the scene at the Mystic Knights of the Sea in *Amos 'n' Andy*.

A small group of *Tonight Show* staff members gathered

around the edge of the set. Johnny took a puff on a cigarette, and hid the cigarette from view. In the sixties he would smoke on-camera, but not in the health-conscious eighties. He tapped his pencils on the desk as the band played the introduction.

When the red light turned on again after the commercial, Johnny and Ed bantered for a few minutes. Ed showed Johnny and the viewers photos of his two-and-a-half-year-old daughter. Johnny raised his eyebrows in mock despair. Then Doc offered up photos of his dog. ''We've probably got a pretty big audience tonight, and this is the stuff we're giving them,'' Johnny complained. It was his show, though, and he knew that the audience wanted to see the photos, wanted to know what Doc had been doing, wanted to think of themselves as part of an extended television family.

Johnny did a bit about Pete Rose's incident with an umpire that had gotten the Cincinnati Reds manager suspended. It was vintage Carson, first showing the original tape of Rose confronting the umpire, then running a second tape of Johnny and an actor dressed as an umpire replaying the incident in supposed slow motion.

For the next segment Johnny introduced Bill Toone of the San Diego Zoo. Johnny asked about the baby condor born at the zoo, and then showed film footage that included shots of copulating condors, a first for American television.

Joe Piscopo, Johnny's other guest, had first gained attention on *Saturday Night Live*. Since then he had made a couple films, but he had become famous appearing in Lite Beer commercials. In Johnny's era, comedians did commercials in order to work; in the eighties, some comedians worked in order to do commercials. Such television advertisements were mini–situation comedies, and the audiences sometimes watched the commercials more attentively than they did the shows.

Piscopo waddled on stage dressed as an obese rap singer, looking like the world's largest bowling ball. He stood there and, along with three black singers, performed a rap song about his appearance on *The Tonight Show*. The song's primary feature was the repetition of the name "Joe Piscopo."

Piscopo merited a few minutes talking to Johnny. Johnny adeptly sucked some entertainment out of the segment, and sent Piscopo on his way.

The show's finale featured Doc and the band playing a tribute to Irving Berlin. "They asked someone what Irving Berlin's place was in American music," Johnny said. "And someone said, 'Irving Berlin *is* American music.' He's an absolute genius. He's a hundred years old this week. And we thought to have Doc and the band wish Mr. Irving Berlin a happy birthday."

The band began its medley. "Easter Parade." Johnny tapped on the desk and listened as intently as anyone. "Oh How I Hate to Get Up in the Morning." Here was American popular culture at its greatest. "There's No Business Like Show Business." People would sing these melodies as long as there was love and hope and joy.

An elderly black tap dancer wearing a top hat and tails appeared from behind the curtain. He tapped to the music of "Putting on the Ritz," his feet elegant instruments of movement and sound. The audience watched mesmerized at the old dancer from an era when entertainment was something worth getting dressed up for. The audience had come as if they were at home watching the tube. They wore shorts, running shoes, toreador pants, jeans, and T-shirts, surfer swimming trunks, sports shirts with the sleeves cut off. The old man danced on, but the next melody began, and there was no time for a bow.

"Alexander's Ragtime Band." "This is the Army, Mr. Jones." "God Bless America." These were great songs. Berlin had understood the emotional cadences of American life.

"I really hope you enjoyed the show," Johnny said as the hour ended. "No matter what the reviews are, we shall return tomorrow night."

The audience stood and applauded, the music and the

laughs still resonating. If Berlin was American music, Johnny was American television. He understood his audience and his time as well as Berlin had. He was not a hundred years old, but in the span of television he was as old as the composer.

After the show Johnny usually drove home by himself in his Corvette. He traveled west on the Ventura Freeway, still crowded with the last remnants of the rush hour, then along the Pacific Coast Highway to his great house on Wild Life Drive. By the time he reached home, the sun was slowly falling into the Pacific, and the ocean was streaked with golden rays.

So long ago he had dreamed that nightmare of an endless highway, the road stretching on to eternity. He traveled on an endless highway now, night after night, the endless road of *The Tonight Show.*

His mother and father were gone. Henry was gone, connected to him only by lawsuits, accusations, and memories. Cory and Rick rarely visited any longer, and Chris was far away. Jody was gone. Joanne was gone. Joanna was gone. Emm-Jay was gone too.

It was dark now even in Malibu, and on the East Coast and Midwest, *The Tonight Show* was beginning. America had missed Johnny, and millions of added viewers were tuned in this evening. From mansion to tenement, apartment to farm, college dorm to retirement home, America waited.

''Heeeeere's Johnny,'' Ed yelled, and everything seemed normal again.

RESEARCH NOTES

King of the Night is based primarily on over 700 interviews that I personally conducted, and thousands of pages of legal documents. I also relied on various books, newspaper and magazine articles, videotapes of various shows in which Johnny Carson appeared, and other archival material. In two-and-a-half years of work I conducted research in Los Angeles; New York City and upstate New York; Omaha, Lincoln, North Platte, and Norfolk, Nebraska; Avoca, Corning, Red Oak, Clarinda, and Shenandoah, Iowa; Las Vegas, Nevada; and Pittsburgh, Pennsylvania.

These research notes are not a sentence-by-sentence accounting of my various sources, but a listing of the major sources and interviews. I interviewed some of my major sources as many as fifteen or twenty times, and in some cases many times more. Of course, I do not and cannot list the many off-the-record interviews that I conducted.

ONE

PAGE

1 Description of twenty-fifth-anniversary show: author present.

2 *over five thousand times:* NBC promotional material for the twenty-fifth anniversary.

2 *over 21 million:* Nielsen ratings in *Los Angeles Times,* October 7, 1987.

7 Description of twenty-fifth-anniversary party: author present; also,

The Official Pictorial History of Queen Mary by Robert O. Maguglin, p. 27.

15 *"Gatsby, like . . ."*: quoted in "Profiles: Fifteen Years of the Salto Mortale" by Kenneth Tynan, *The New Yorker*, February 10, 1978.

15 *"That god damned."*: *Long Day's Journey into Night* by Eugene O'Neill, Yale University Press edition, p. 149.

TWO

16 *Johnny Carson stood:* author interviews with Bill Brennan and Marion Weinmann.

16 *One time:* letter from Ruth Klug to Johnny Carson, July 26, 1986, courtesy of *Avoca Herald*.

16 *Each summer:* based on articles and advertisements in the *Avoca Herald*, September 8, 1932.

17 *Season tickets: Avoca Herald*, June 8, 1933.

17 *" 'Kit' has a . . ."*: *Avoca Herald*, June 30, 1932.

17 *Kit played:* author interview with Edwin Doll.

18 *"The father was . . ."*: author interview with Bill Brennan.

18 *The Carsons are:* Genealogical information is from a book that Alex Haley gave to Johnny Carson, as cited in Tynan.

20 *Few people:* author interviews with Mabel Gaskill, Helen Andrews, and Jim Logan.

21 *only a month:* records of Red Oak School District.

21 *In May 1933: Avoca Herald*, May 4, 1933.

22 *"Mrs. Carson . . ."*: author interview with Mrs. Leach.

22 *"I'm sure he . . ."*: author interview with Peggy Leach Ebles.

22 *"H.L. 'Kit' . . ."*: *Avoca Herald*, October 5, 1933.

23 *"We washed . . ."*: author interview with Orvie Fisher.

23 *Norfolk was:* description of Norfolk and Nebraska in the 1930's based primarily on *Nebraska: A Guide to the Cornhusker State*, the Federal Writers' Project Guide to the State and *History of Nebraska* by James C. Olson.

25 *high-water mark: Norfolk Daily News* centennial edition, July 9, 1966.

25 *"There comes . . ."*: interview in *Rolling Stone*, by Timothy White March 22, 1979, as reprinted in *Chicago Tribune Magazine*, April 29, 1979.

26 *"a little snip . . ."*: interview with Mrs. Stella McNeely for *Time* cover story, May 29, 1967.

27 *"We were . . ."*: interview with Dick Carson for *Time*, May 29, 1967.

27 *"I hooked . . .":* interview with Johnny Carson conducted by Jim Brodhead for *Time*, May 29, 1967.

27 *"He picked . . .":* author interview with Dr. Alan Landers.

27 *"I was walking . . .":* author interview with James Cochran.

28 *"I sat . . .":* author interview with Lorraine Beckenhauer Gipe.

28 *"I was trying . . .":* off-the-record author interview with one of Johnny Carson's high school friends.

28 *"There's a mean . . .":* author interview with Bill Bridge.

28 *"I have a feeling . . .":* author interview with Larry Sanford.

28 *"It showed . . .":* quoted in *Here's Johnny* by Nora Ephron, p. 56.

29 *"He could be . . .":* interview with Mrs. Carson conducted by Dave Wilkinson for *Time*, p. 58. May 29, 1967.

29 *"seen anything . . .":* quoted in interview in *Playboy*, December, 1967, p. 256.

29 *"Mother, do you . . .":* quoted in Ephron, p. 58.

30 *"Johnny had . . .":* author interview with James Cochran.

30 *"I can't say . . .":* quoted in interview in *Playboy*, December 1967.

31 *"used to keep . . .":* *Lincoln Star*, January 17, 1964.

31 *"Nobody in our . . .":* quoted in Ephron. p. 52.

31 *"His mother . . .":* author interview with Jody Carson.

32 *"He told me . . .":* author interview with Jody Carson.

32 *"John was . . .":* author interview with Chuck Howser.

33 *"We had paint . . .":* interview with Johnny Carson quoted in *Viewpoint*, Northeast Technical Community College, October 1981.

33 *"He somehow . . .":* author interview with Dr. John Busch.

33 *"Miss Walker drew . . .":* author interview with Jennie Walker, and Ephron, p. 50.

34 *"Johnny was . . .":* author interview with Dale Raasch.

34 *"His dad had . . .":* author interview with Duane Demaree.

34 *"Egley bawled . . .":* author interview with Fred Egley.

35 *"The first time . . .":* *Playboy*, December 1967.

35 *"As in all small . . .":* reporter's notes of Karen Jackovich on assignment for *People*, 1981.

36 *"One of our . . .":* author interview with Bob Hall.

36 *"It was a . . .":* author interview with Mary Jane Beckenhauer Bentley.

36 *"John and I . . .":* author interview with James Cochran.

37 *"Johnny was . . .":* author interview with Dr. John Busch.

37 *"One night . . .":* author interview with Chuck Howser.

38 *"I, John . . .":* quoted in *Time*, May 29, 1967, cover story.

THREE

39   Description of Carson's trip to California based on Tynan.

40   *Sixty-one credits: Time,* May 29, 1967, cover story.

40   *"We were putting . . .":* author interview with Jules Arceneaux.

40   *"One night . . .":* author interview with Jim Cochran.

41   *"It practically . . .":* interview with Carson for May 29, 1967, *Time* cover story.

41   *"Jesus, what . . .":* interview with Carson for May 29, 1967, *Time* cover story.

42   *Johnny has rarely:* author interview with Jody Carson.

43   *"I walked . . .":* interview with Carson for May 29, 1967, *Time* cover story.

44   Description of Carson's apartment in Columbus based on author's off-the-record interviews.

45   *"I'd go down . . .":* author interview with Bob Hall.

45   *"Johnny was . . .":* author interview with Jerry Calhoun.

45   *"Johnny didn't . . .":* author interview with Charles Thone.

46   *In 1936: Daily Nebraskan,* November 11, 1948, and November 18, 1949.

46   *"Be sure to . . .":* recording provided by Dee Devoe.

47   *"a police court . . ." Daily Nebraskan,* November 24, 1946.

48   *"You can let . . .":* author interview with Dee Devoe.

48   *"What might . . .": Daily Nebraskan,* May 8, 1948.

49   *"That summer . . .":* author interview with William Butterfield.

49   *"Gasoline was . . .":* interview with Bill Wiseman, Jr., in *TV Guide,* July 30, 1966.

50   *"I would have . . .":* author interview with Marge Alexis Todd.

50   *fall of 1948: Daily Nebraskan,* November 11, 1948.

51   *During the war: Lincoln Journal and Star,* May 13, 1962.

51   *"He was always . . .": Time* interview with Mrs. Minier conducted for May 29, 1967, *Time* cover story.

52   *"I was very . . .":* author interview with Merle Workhoven.

53   *"I said I'd . . .":* author interview with Jody Carson.

54   *"fun but a . . .":* author interview with Jerry Calhoun.

56   *"My sorority . . .":* author interview with Marge Alexis Todd.

56   *"I remember . . .":* author interview with Jody Carson.

57   *"There are many . . .":* quoted in *Here's Johnny* by Nora Ephron, p. 65.

FOUR

58   *His salary: Playboy,* December 1967.

58   Description of wedding from undated newspaper clipping from Omaha newspaper.

59   *"I had . . ."*: author interview with Jody Carson.

59   *The Omaha papers: Omaha World-Herald,* August 14, 1949.

60   *Johnny was present: Omaha World-Herald Magazine of the Midlands,* February 2, 1975.

60   *"It had to . . ."*: *Omaha World-Herald,* September 15, 1976.

61   *"My experiences . . ."*: *Omaha World-Herald,* September 16, 1976.

62   *"Most deejays . . ."*: author interview with Merle Workhoven.

63   Description of plains humor based in part on author interview with Roger L. Welsch.

63   Audiotape of *Squirrel's Nest* courtesy of Dick Scott.

64   *"The pressures . . ."*: author interview with Jody Carson.

64   *"Hot damn . . ."*: author interview with John and Barbara Haslom.

64   *"We went . . ."*: author interview with Jerry Solomon.

65   *"Do you think . . ."*: author interview with Mort Wells.

65   *Joe Kirshenbaum:* author interview with Joe Kirshenbaum.

66   *"We started . . ."*: interview with Johnny Carson for documentary *Omaha TV: The Early Years.*

66   *"Please get . . ."*: interview with Johnny Carson for documentary *Omaha TV: The Early Years.*

67   Carson's stories of early years in Omaha based on documentary film of *The Early Years* of Omaha television.

68   *"The station . . ."*: author interview with Merle Workhoven.

68   *Johnny managed: Omaha World-Herald,* May 2, 1983.

69   *Johnny dubbed:* author interview with Dick Scott.

69   *Mrs. Wolcott:* author interview with Mrs. Wolcott.

70   Audiotape of Christmas *Squirrel's Nest* courtesy of Dick Scott.

FIVE

73   *"John, I've got . . ."*: author interview with Bill Brennan.

73   *"He owed money . . ."*: *Omaha World-Herald,* August 27, 1984.

73   Log of KNXT-TV New Year's Day schedule courtesy of John Condon.

74   *"I remember . . ."*: *Chicago Tribune,* May 3, 1967.

74   *"The Meinigers . . ."*: interview with Mr. and Mrs. Keith Meiniger.

75   Description of early years of Los Angeles television based primarily on KTLA documentary on the station.

77   *"I shoved . . ."*: author interview with Bob Lehman.

77   *"He was . . ."*: author interview with Bill Baker.

77   *"He had . . ."*: author interview with Jody Carson.

78 *"John said . . .":* author interview with Jerry Solomon.

78 *"Ladies and . . .":* description of *Carson's Cellar* and the *Johnny Carson Show* based on scripts courtesy of John Condon, and interviews with Condon, Lehman, Baker, Peter Leeds, and others.

81 *On one program:* author interview with Bill Baker.

81 *"It was a . . .":* author interview with Peter Leeds.

82 *"If he can . . .":* author interview with Phil Weltman.

82 *"Aubrey said . . .":* author interview with Phil Weltman and James Aubrey.

83 *The young comedy:* author interview with Bob Weiskopf.

83 *"When does . . .":* author interview with Bob Lehman.

83 *"They hired . . .":* author interview with Bob Lehman.

84 *"The show . . .":* author interview with Bob Weiskopf.

85 *"You look . . .":* "Carson Rides the Crest" by Philip Minoff, undated, untitled clipping in Lester Sweyd Collections, University of Southern California Library.

85 *"None of . . .":* author interview with Bill Brennan.

85 *"One day . . .":* author interview with Red Rowe.

86 *"The longest . . .":* *Los Angeles Times,* March 18, 1972.

86 *"I used . . .":* author questioning of Red Skelton during Orange County press conference.

87 *"Personally, the . . .":* *Chicago Tribune,* May 4, 1967.

88 *"J. B. Derkin of . . .":* Based on transcript of *The Tonight Show* for May 13, 1987.

89 *"I think . . .":* author interview with Seaman Jacobs.

89 *"He was . . .":* author interview with Margaret Ferraro.

90 *"I knew . . .":* author interview with Jody Carson.

SIX

91 *"Brennan went . . .":* author interviews with Bill Brennan and Mort Green.

91 *"When I . . .":* author interview with Jody Carson.

92 *"I'm sitting . . .":* author interview with Mort Green.

93 *"All the time . . .":* author interview with Jody Carson.

93 *"Carson was . . .":* author interview with Mort Green.

94 *"the rest . . .":* *New York Times,* July 24, 1955.

94 *"You've got to . . .":* author interview with Bill Brennan.

94 *"One of the . . .":* *New York Herald Tribune,* July 11, 1955.

95 *"Did you hear . . .":* author interview with Mort Green.

96 *"I'd have . . .":* *New York Herald Tribune,* April 11, 1956.

96 *One day Johnny . . .":* author interview with Hank Simms.

98 *"It was kind . . .":* author interview with Cal McKinley.

98   *Weltman used:* author interview with Phil Weltman.

99   *One evening the:* author interviews with Jody Carson, Jack Narz, and Mary Lou Dawson, the former Mrs. Narz.

100   *"Many people . . .":* author interview with Jody Carson.

100   *"Johnny got . . .":* author interview with Seaman Jacobs.

100   *"I was seeing . . .":* author interview with Jody Carson.

102   *Bruno and Sheils:* author interviews with Al Bruno and Tom Sheils.

102   *"I always felt . . .":* letter to Carson read to author by Phil Weltman.

102   *"John was so . . .":* author interview with Don Fedderson.

103   *Johnny's friends:* author interview with Bob Lehman.

103   *"When we were . . .":* author interview with Jody Carson.

SEVEN

104   Description of *Who Do You Trust?* based on the scripts of the series provided courtesy of Roy Kammerman.

106   *"That son of . . .":* author interview with Roy Kammerman.

107   *"Do you want . . .":* author interview with Hank Simms.

107   *Television had: Tube of Plenty* by Eric Barnouw, pp. 165–67.

108   *Johnny talked:* interview with Ed McMahon conducted by Eirik Knutzen in March 1982.

108   *"It was my . . .": Los Angeles Herald Examiner,* July 7, 1979.

109   *"I was responsible . . .":* author interview with Bob Coe.

110   *"When Al Bruno . . .":* author interview with Jody Carson.

110   *"Jody waits . . .": New York Sunday News,* July 13, 1958.

111   *"Once I admired . . .":* author interview with Marsha Hunt.

111   *"I always felt . . .":* author interview with Jill Corey.

112   *"It was so . . .":* author interview with Jody Carson.

112   *"I wasn't in . . .":* author interview with Dr. Tauber.

112   *He called:* author interviews with Dr. and Mrs. Wolstein.

113   *"He has a . . .":* author interview with Dr. Ben Wolstein.

114   *"The night . . .":* author interview with Jody Carson.

115   *"On September 30":* date of separation from legal papers supplied by Jody Carson.

115   *"He had . . .":* author interview with Red Rowe.

115   *"I don't think . . .":* author interview with Dr. Tauber.

116   *"That's the lowest . . .": Playboy,* December 1967.

116   *"There was this . . .":* author interview with Jody Carson.

117   *He even subbed:* Earl Wilson column in *New York Post,* October 12, 1958.

118   *"Don't be . . .":* author interviews with Gary Stevens and Al Bruno.

119   *"He came out . . .":* author interview with Al Bruno.

119   *He hit: TV Guide,* March 24, 1962.

119   *"One Christmas . . .":* author interview with Stu Billett.

120   *He shot:* author interview with Lila Garrett.

121   *"You say . . .":* New York Journal-American, July 1, 1962.

121   *Rayfiel was:* author interview with David Rayfiel.

122   *"We would go . . .":* Johnny Carson in interview by David Frost quoted in *New York Daily News,* February 24, 1970.

123   *"I got a . . .":* author interview with Don Fedderson.

123   *"Johnny was . . .":* author interview with Bob Coe.

123   *"They all protected . . .":* author interview with Harriet Van Horne.

124   *"Joanne says . . .":* interview with Joanne Carson conducted by Eirik Knutzen.

126   *As a first:* author interview with Wally Seawell.

126   *"I thought . . .":* interview with Joanne Carson conducted by Eirik Knutzen.

127   *"notably free . . .":* TV Guide, March 24, 1962.

128   *"There were . . .":* author interview with Jack Narz.

128   *"I helped . . .":* author interview with Jody Carson.

128   *"She used . . .":* author interview with Bob Coe.

129   *"Johnny tried . . .":* author interview with Al Bruno.

EIGHT

130   *"The Tonight Show . . .":* author interview with Tom Poston.

131   *"What band? . . .":* quoted in *The Tonight Show* by Robert Metz, p. 75.

132   *"The captain . . .":* quoted in Metz, *The Tonight Show,* p. 116.

132   *"most talked . . .":* quoted in *New York World-Telegram,* September 21, 1962.

134   *"A new funnyman . . .":* quoted in *New York Daily News,* June 29, 1958.

134   *"It's almost . . .":* quoted in *New York Post,* December 20, 1957.

134   *didn't "need . . .":* quoted in Ephron, p. 33.

135   *"A lot of . . .":* author interview with Al Bruno.

137   *"About your wife . . .":* quoted in *TV Guide,* March 24, 1962.

137   *"Whether you . . .":* quoted in *New York World-Telegram,* September 21, 1962.

138   *He called Hank:* author interview with Hank Simms, confirmed by Al Bruno.

139   *"It can be . . .":* quoted in *New York Herald Tribune,* August 6, 1962.

139   *"We would sit . . .":* quoted in Ephron, p. 37.

139   *"Tom Sheils . . .":* author interview with Jack Narz.

140   *"the nervousness . . .":* author interview with Perry Cross.

140   *"Good luck . . .":* author interview with Skitch Henderson.

140   *When Shelly:* author interview with Shelly Schultz.

141   *What am I . . .: Time* interview with Carson, May 29, 1967, cover.

141   *"I don't come . . .":* quoted in *TV Guide,* June 8, 1963.

142   *"I wonder how . . .":* author interview with Tony Bennett.

142   *"I thought . . .": Omaha World-Herald,* October 3, 1962.

143   *"Here was a . . .":* author interview with Shelly Schultz.

144   *"You have to . . .":* Carson interview in *Players,* winter 1965.

146   *"If you book . . .":* Carson interview conducted by NBC publicity department for twenty-fifth anniversary of *The Tonight Show.*

146   *"You're kind . . .":* quoted in *TV Guide,* June 8, 1963.

147   *"for it . . .":* Carson interview quoted in *TV Guide,* June 17, 1964.

147   *"The ratings . . .":* Carson interview for May 29, 1967, *Time* cover story.

148   *"It's for the . . .": New York Times,* November 18, 1982.

148   *He had even had:* "Johnny Carson, the Prince of Chitchat Is a Loner" by Betty Rollin, *Look,* January 25, 1966.

149   *"like the . . .":* author interview with Shelly Schultz.

149   *One day:* author interview with Perry Cross.

150   Description of going-away party based on interviews with Bill Bridge and William Butterfield.

151   *"I can get . . .":* interview with Bruce Cooper.

153   *"If one fails . . .":* author interview with Walter Kempley.

153   *Television Magazine:* as reported in *New York Times,* April 26, 1964.

154   *On one occasion:* author interview with Shelly Schultz.

154   *As Johnny took:* interview with Walter Kempley for May 29, 1967, *Time* cover story.

155   *The bird was:* author interview with Shelly Schultz.

156   *"After about a . . .":* author interview with Skitch Henderson.

156   Description of Carson wedding from *New York Journal-American,* August 10, 1963.

157   *"I flew down . . .":* author interview with Jody Carson.

159   *"Where are the . . .":* author interview with Jeanne Prior.

160   *"In everybody's . . .":* author interview with Jeanne Prior.

161   *"How are we . . .":* quoted in *Johnny Tonight!* by Craig Tennis, p. 107.

162   Description of Joan Rivers's first night on *The Tonight Show* based on author interview and *Enter Laughing* by Joan Rivers pp. 365–73.

163   *Sometimes Johnny:* Metz, pp. 222–23.

NINE

164 *"Olley, olley, oxen . . ."*: Joanne Carson as quoted in "The Improbable Private Life of Mrs. Johnny Carson" by Gael Greene, *Ladies Home Journal*, July 1966.

164 *"Here she . . ."*: quoted in Greene, *Ladies' Home Journal*, July, 1966.

165 List of books from "Johnny's Like Folks" by Gael Greene, *New York Herald Tribune*, January 16, 1966.

165 *"a warren . . ."*: Greene, *Ladies Home Journal*, July 1966.

166 *"[T]he most remote . . ."*: "Mass Communication and Para-social Interaction: Observations on Intimacy at a Distance" in *Psychiatry*, 19 (1956) as quoted in *No Sense of Place: The Impact of Electronic Media on Social Behavior* by Joshua Meyrowitz, p. 119.

166 *"The most familiar . . ."*: *New York Sunday News*, October 24, 1965.

166 *One weekend*: "My New Life: Joanne Carson" by Jody Jacobs, *Harper's Bazaar*, March 1972.

167 *"I'm so . . ."*: quoted in Ephron, pp. 205–06.

167 *"They've been . . ."*: quoted in Ephron, p. 213.

168 *"I was a . . ."*: quoted in *Capote: A Biography* by Gerald Clarke, p. 435.

168 *"Ed Sullivan . . ."*: author interview with Joyce Susskind.

169 *"Don't open . . ."*: author interview with Trudy Richards Moreault.

169 *Hammer shut*: author interview with Buddy Hammer.

170 *"He doesn't . . ."*: quoted in "Johnny Carson, The Prince of Chit-chat Is a Loner" by Betty Rollin, *Look*, January, 1966.

171 *"Johnny, you . . ."*: quoted in Ephron, p. 200, and author interview with Nora Ephron.

171 *"I don't like . . ."*: interview with Carson for May 29, 1967, *Time* cover story.

172 *"In the elevator . . ."*: author interview with Mrs. Daniel Seymour.

172 *"We had . . ."*: author interview with Mrs. Joyce Susskind.

172 *typical day*: *Newark News*, May 26, 1968.

172 *"killer mouse"*: author interview with Rudy Tellez.

172 Thanksgiving card and letter shown to author by Al Bruno.

173 *"Joanne was . . ."*: author interview with Al Bruno.

173 *"Joanne was not . . ."*: author interview with Trudy Moreault.

173 *"I felt extremely . . ."*: interview with Truman Capote by Larry Grobel in *Conversations with Capote*, p. 194.

174 *"She really tried . . ."*: author interview with Jan de Ruth.

174 *"You just automatically . . ."*: quoted in Jacobs, *Harper's Bazaar*, March 1972.

175 Description of Mamie Van Doren's involvement with Johnny Carson based on *Playing the Field* by Mamie Van Doren and author's questions to Van Doren on *The Tom Snyder Show*.

176 *"I dated him . . ."*: author interview with Alicia Bond.

177 *"We came back . . ."*: author interview with Mrs. Seymour.

177 *drug problem:* author interviews with Dr. Robert Baird, Jody Carson, and other, off-the-record interviews.

177 *"When John . . ."*: author interview with Jody Carson.

178 *"It was . . ."*: author interview with Irma Wolstein.

178 *Cory wrote:* letter courtesy of Jody Carson.

179 *"He said, 'She . . ."*: author interview with Irma Wolstein.

179 *"Her sorority . . ."*: author interview with Zip Haslom.

TEN

180 *singing lessons:* author interview with Susan Seton.

180 *"He probably . . ."*: author interview with Hank Simms.

181 *Sahara Hotel's: Variety,* July 29, 1964, and July 30, 1964.

182 *"Carson bombed . . ."*: *New York Journal-American,* January 19, 1964.

182 *"degenerate into . . ."*: quoted in *New York Journal-American,* December 15, 1965.

183 *"Johnny was so . . ."*: author interview with Shelly Schultz.

184 *"Four Navahos . . ."*: quoted in *New York Post,* February 21, 1965.

184 *"They'll have . . ."*: *New York Post,* February 21, 1965.

185 *"I'll never forget . . ."*: author interview with Al Bruno.

185 *"My job is . . ."*: quoted in Greene, *New York Herald Tribune,* January 16, 1966.

185 *"I told him . . ."*: Carson interview for May 29, 1967 *Time* cover story.

185 *"Johnny was . . ."*: author interview with Mrs. Mary Stark.

185 *"Many times I . . ."*: author interview with Skitch Henderson.

186 *"Johnny was not . . ."*: author interview with Bob Coe.

186 *NBC paid:* Ephron, p. 142.

187 *Bruno made an agreement:* author interview with Al Bruno and documents shown author by Bruno.

187 *"She wanted . . ."*: author interview with Al Bruno.

188 *"I knew . . ."*: quoted in *New York Herald Tribune,* April 3, 1966. Account of Eden Roc incident also based on *New York Post,* February 28, 1966, and *Variety,* March 2, 1966.

188 *curt letter:* letter shown author by Al Bruno.

188 *"He answered . . ."*: author interview with Al Bruno.

189 *"What's wrong . . ."*: author interview with Bruce Cooper.

189   *"She was talking . . .":* author interview with Elizabeth Dougherty.

189   *40 or 50 calls: Rocky Mountain News TV Dial,* February 6, 1966.

190   *"I can get . . .": Detroit News,* January 27, 1966.

190   *"If I were . . .": New York Post,* January 24, 1967.

190   *"We're close . . .": Telegram,* Toronto, week of March 11–18, 1966.

191   *two-year contract: New York Post,* April 14, 1966.

192   *"makes me . . .":* quoted in *Lincoln Journal,* May 8, 1960.

194   *"there might . . .":* quoted in *New York Times,* April 17, 1967.

195   *"There is . . .":* Metz, p. 250, and author interview with Skitch Henderson.

196   Description of firing based on Art Stark interview with *Newark Evening News,* October 26, 1967, and author interview with Mrs. Mary Stark.

197   *"Come on . . .":* author interview with Gary Stevens.

197   *Tebet wanted:* Ephron, p. 151.

197   *Ed McMahon and:* author interviews with Mrs. Mary Stark and Joan Rivers.

ELEVEN

198   *"My name . . .": Time,* May 29, 1967.

199   *"He comes . . .":* interview with Capote in Clarke, p. 436.

199   *"His mother . . ."* conversation with Joanne Carson by an acquaintance.

199   *Bishop had:* Ephron, p. 152.

200   *"I want . . .":* quoted in "Notes Toward an Article on Johnny Carson" by Neil Hickey, *TV Guide,* October 24, 1967.

200   *"On Friday . . .":* author interview with Joey Bishop.

200   *"I think . . .":* author interview with Joey Bishop.

200   *The first:* "Battle of Talk Shows" in *Newsweek,* September 1, 1969.

201   *In February:* Metz, p. 268.

201   *In September: New York Times,* September 2, 1968.

201   *"Anything is . . .": New York Times,* September 10, 1968.

201   *To produce: New York Times,* May 30, 1967.

202   *In October:* "On the Air" by Bob Williams in *New York Post,* October 25, 1967.

202   *"I would go . . .":* author interview with Rudy Tellez.

203   *"They wouldn't . . .":* author interview with Walter Kempley.

203   *"I thought . . .":* author interview with Joan Rivers.

203   *two of his jokes:* author interview with Nick Arnold.

204   *"I felt . . .":* "Doc Severinsen" by Zan Stewart, *Down Beat,* November 1985.

204 *"That was . . ."*: *San Francisco Chronicle,* July 5, 1981.

205 *"He started . . ."*: interview with Tommy Newsom by Eirik Knutzen in June 1988.

205 *"C'mon, I . . ."*: Timothy White interview in *Rolling Stone,* March 22, 1979.

206 *"He expects . . ."*: quoted in "H-e-e-r-e's Johnny" by Kay Gardella in *New York Daily News,* February 21, 1971.

206 *"Listen, do . . ."*: *Here's Johnny,* by Robert Lardine, p. 33.

207 *"Take us . . ."*: Tennis, p. 209, and author interview with Craig Tennis.

207 *"In all the . . ."*: quoted in "Johnny-on-the-Spot" by Bob Lardine, *New York Sunday News,* September 8, 1968.

207 *"Don't ever . . ."*: Lardine, *New York Sunday News,* September 8, 1968, and author interview with Lardine.

208 *"I consider . . ."*: quoted in Lardine, *New York Sunday News,* September 8, 1968.

208 *Johnny sat:* author interviews with Bobby Van and Ray Abruzzese.

209 *"You are . . ."*: quoted in *Lovely Me: The Life of Jacqueline Susann,* by Barbara Seaman, p. 198.

209 *Johnny was sitting:* Ephron, p. 196.

209 *"My theory . . ."*: author interview with Jan de Ruth.

210 *"People waited . . ."*: author interview with Jack Eglash.

210 *One weekend:* "Here's Johnny! Out There" by Joan Barthel, *Life,* October 10, 1969.

211 *"He did it . . ."*: interview with Harry Benson.

212 *"I want to . . ."*: interview with Joan Barthel.

213 *the company sold:* New York Times, December 17, 1972.

213 *As late as:* document filed in re: the marriage of Joanna Carson and John W. Carson, Superior Court of California, Case No. D088654. exhibit A, p. 2.

214 *"a gross and . . ."*: *New York Times,* July 3, 1969.

214 *"Mr. Carson got . . ."*: quoted in the *New York Times,* July 4, 1969.

TWELVE

215 *"bachelor's make-out pad . . ."*: *Women's Wear Daily,* May 19, 1971.

215 *"Johnny would . . ."*: quoted in *Here's Johnny* by Robert Lardine, p. 150.

215 *physician discovered:* Tennis, p. 25.

216 *'When I first . . ."*: quoted in Lardine, *Here's Johnny,* p. 89.

216 *"It made him . . ."*: quoted in Lardine, *Here's Johnny*, p. 162.

216 *"I can only . . ."*: author interview with Walter Kempley.

216 *"He had had . . ."*: Tennis, p. 210.

217 Craig Tennis's questions from *Tiny Tim* by Harry Stein, p. 104.

217 *"reduced Johnny . . ."*: "And He Keeps His Ukulele in a Shopping Bag" by Albert Goldman, *New York Times*, April 28, 1968.

218 *"Mr. Carson has . . ."*: author interview with Tiny Tim.

218 *"what would . . ."*: author interview with Rudy Tellez.

219 *"If there was . . ."*: author interview with Tiny Tim.

219 *"You better . . ."* *Ladies Home Journal*, June 1972, quoted in *New York Daily News*, May 24, 1972.

220 *"We cordially . . ."*: tape of *Tonight Show* for December 17, 1969, at Museum of Broadcasting.

220 *Merrill Sindler*: author interview with Merrill Sindler.

220 "sweet, gentle . . ." based on videotape of *Tonight Show* for December 17, 1969, viewed at Museum of Broadcasting.

222 *A SERIOUS . . . .*: Stein, p. 110.

223 *"From morning . . ."*: author interview with Tiny Tim.

223 *"Joanne Carson . . ."*: Johnny's Ex-wife Tells Her Story" by Linda Francke, *McCall's*, January 1973.

223 *Johnny sat*: author interview with Arthur Kassel.

224 *Kassel contacted*: author interviews with Kassel, two former police officers, and an off-the-record source.

225 *"Johnny was . . ."*: author interview with Trudy Moreault.

225 *"It got . . ."*: one of several lengthy interviews by Eirik Knutzen conducted in 1983.

225 *"One evening . . ."*: author interview with Trudy Moreault.

226 *"She was a . . ."*: author interview with Shirlee Fonda.

226 *The night before*: author interviews with Arthur Kassel and Judy Bushkin.

227 *"I was intimidated . . ."*: quoted in "The Off-Camera Carson" by Paul Rosenfield, *Los Angeles Times*, July 6, 1986.

228 *She knew*: author interview with Aileen Mehle.

228 *cruel and*: New York Times, January 15, 1971.

228 *"There is no . . ."*: quoted in *New York Post*, December 8, 1970.

228 *"Try to . . ."*: *New York Daily News*, June 22, 1972.

229 *For several years*: Francke, *McCall's*, January 1973.

THIRTEEN

230 *"Who is . . ."*: author interview with Mollie Parnis.

230 *Johnny called*: author interview with Joanna Carson.

231 *Joann met Tim*: *People*, February 28, 1983.

231   *"We all had . . .":* author interview with Adrian Lowell.

232   *"Joanna was . . .":* author interview with Carmen.

232   *"Leon, oh . . .":* author interview with Marjorie Reed.

232   *a codicil:* codicil to will dated November 20, 1967.

232   *Hertz would pay:* consent agreement signed to the Hertz Corporation on July 12, 1968, and filed in Surrogate's Court, New York County.

232   *Six months:* author interview and correspondence with Irving Schneider, attorney for Max Kettner; author interview with the former Mrs. Max Kettner; court documents in *Max Kettner* v. *Joanna Holland Carson,* New York Supreme Court, Appellate Division, May 19, 1974, supplement, second series, pp. 408–09; and *New York Daily News,* February 1, 1973.

232   *"was coming . . .":* as told to Marilyn Funt, quoted in *Johnny Carson: An Unauthorized Biography* by Ronald L. Smith, p. 167.

233   *"We bought . . .":* author interview with Stephen Mallory.

233   *"The way . . .":* author interview with Carmen.

234   *"I was . . .":* author interview with Richard Gully.

234   *hospitalized: New York Times,* March 8, 1971.

234   *He sued: John W. Carson* v. *Daily Mirror, Inc.,* filed in Supreme Court of the State of New York, County of New York, Index No. 4600/72, April 1972.

234   *"Do you . . .":* Lardine, *Here's Johnny,* pp. 157–58, and author interview with Lardine.

235   *Henry Bushkin file: John W. Carson* v. *Harold L. Glasser, 860 West Tower, Inc. and Douglas, Gibbons, Hollyday & Ives, Inc.,* filed in Supreme Court of the State of New York, County of New York.

235   *"Johnny had . . .":* author interview with Rudy Tellez.

235   *"the main . . .":* Los Angeles Times, April 30, 1972.

236   *"having a . . .":* Tennis, pp. 75–76.

237   *"When I . . .":* author interview with Rudy Tellez.

238   *"Four times . . .":* Lardine, *Here's Johnny,* p. 103.

239   *"Johnny turned . . .":* author interview with Joyce Haber.

239   *"it has . . .":* Francke, *McCalls,* January 1973.

239   *"The first time . . .":* Francke, *McCall's,* January 1973.

240   *"I was flown . . .":* author interview with Stephen Mallory.

240   *"That was . . .":* author interview with Marjorie Reed.

241   *left Alice: Rolling Stone,* March 22, 1979.

241   *She ended:* Smith, p. 170.

241   *probation: New York Times,* October 14, 1971.

241   Description of *Tonight Show* tenth-anniversary show based on videotape at the Museum of Broadcasting.

242   *"probably no . . .": New York Times,* December 17, 1972.

243 Description of tenth-anniversary party based primarily on *Variety*, October 4, 1972.

244 *"It's the silliest . . ."*: author interview with Joanna Carson.

245 *"On an examination . . ."*: *Max Kettner* v. *Joanna Holland Carson*, Supreme Court, Appellate Division, First Department, May 14, 1974, pp. 408–09.

245 *He left*: author interviews with Irving Schneider and the former Mrs. Max Kettner.

245 *secretly separated*: statement of decision by William P. Hogoboom, judge pro tempore, in re: the marriage of Joanna Carson and John W. Carson, May 8, 1985.

246 *"lying on . . ."*: *People*, February 28, 1983.

246 Account of extortion attempt based on *Los Angeles Times* and *New York Times* coverage in 1972.

248 Expense figures for Bel Air residence based on Exhibit F, p. 1, in re: the marriage of Joanna Carson and John W. Carson.

249 *Johnny discovered*: Tennis, p. 205.

249 *July of 1977*: Tynan, *The New Yorker*, February 10, 1978.

249 *"it is essential"*: declaration of John W. Carson in re: the marriage of Joanna Carson and John W. Carson.

250 *"One year . . ."*: author interview with Marjorie Reed.

250 *"Johnny was . . ."*: author interview with Carmen.

250 *filed suit*: *John W. Carson and Joanna Carson* v. *Salvatore P. Bono, Daryoush Mahboubi-Fardi, and Raphael Cohen*, filed October 31, 1978, in Superior Court of the State of California, County of Los Angeles; and interview with Raphael Cohen.

251 *February 1973*: *New York Post*, February 1, 1973.

251 *"Rick became . . ."*: author interview with Natalie Kosbubal.

253 *"Oh, my . . ."*: author interview with Roy Ratliff.

FOURTEEN

254 Description of Carson's meeting with Dick Ebersol and Lorne Michaels based on *Saturday Night* by Doug Hill and Jeff Weingrad, pp. 16–17.

255 *"Fuck, they . . ."*: Hill and Weingrad, p. 93.

257 *"It was trouble . . ."*: author interview with Chevy Chase.

257 *"It was very . . ."*: author interview with Chevy Chase.

258 *"I want . . ."*: author interview with Craig Tennis and other off-the-record interviews with *Tonight Show* staff.

259 Description of George Tricker's tenure on *The Tonight Show* based on author interview with Tricker.

260 *McCormick had*: author interview with Pat McCormick.

262 *"There was . . ."*: author interview with Nick Arnold.

262 *"I can't . . ."*: Tennis, pp. 95–96.

263 *"Mr. Carson . . ."*: New York Times, October 29, 1975.

264 *The episode: New York Times,* February 3, 1974.

265 Description of *The Tonight Show* featuring George Gobel based on tape of the tenth-anniversary special viewed at Museum of Broadcasting.

265 *"the highest . . ."*: Hollywood Reporter, February 25, 1974.

265 *slightly more: New York Daily News,* September 12, 1975.

266 *highest paid:* reported by Joe Modzelewski for *People,* August 5, 1974.

267 *"He stopped . . ."*: author interview with Judy Bushkin.

268 *"Stocks and . . ."*: author interview with Fred Kayne.

268 *over $8.5 million:* Kayne deposition in re: the marriage of Joanna Carson and John W. Carson, March 22, 1984.

269 *"I'm terribly . . ."*: author interview with Fred Kayne.

269 *In October: Variety,* October 23, 1974.

270 *"You don't know . . ."*: Norfolk Daily News, May 24, 1976.

FIFTEEN

272 *"Hello, this . . ."*: author interview with Emm-Jay Trokel.

275 *"It's hard . . ."*: author interview with Joanna Carson.

276 *On June 11:* a copy of letter in author's possession.

276 *"I can see . . ."*: author interview with Stephen Mallory.

276 *In the spring: New York Times,* May 5, 1978.

276 *In 1978:* author interview with Merle Workhoven.

277 *$100,000 contribution: Lincoln Star,* December 23, 1977.

277 *"flushed with . . ."*: Los Angeles Times, September 16, 1977.

278 *"I am possibly . . ."*: Kenneth L. Browning declaration in *Carson* v. *Brown Realty.* WEC-50685, 1987, p. 10.

278 *On October 31:* Joseph P. Brown declaration in *Carson* v. *Brown Realty,* p. 3.

278 *"I don't believe . . ."*: letter from Joseph Brown to John W. Carson, November 21, 1977.

278 *one day:* author interview with Arthur Kassel.

279 *"Some member . . ."*: author interview with Senator Ed Davis.

279 *In October:* Fred Silverman deposition in *Wayne Newton* v. *National Broadcasting Company; RCA, Brian Ross, Ira Silverman, Paul Greenberg, William Jack Small,* vol. 20, p. 4154.

280 *Johnny's three: New York Times,* December 22, 1977.

280 *"I also hope . . ."*: quoted in Gary Deeb "Silverman v. Carson" reprinted in *Valley News,* March 31, 1979.

280 *"That may be . . .":* Silverman deposition in *Wayne Newton* v. *NBC, et al.,* p. 4155.

280 *In April: New York Times,* April 20, 1979.

281 *"the most awesome . . .": People,* May 21, 1979.

282 *"President Carter . . .": New York Post,* May 10, 1979.

282 *"the least recognizable . . .": New York Post,* May 7, 1979.

283 *"talent stroking":* Silverman deposition in *Wayne Newton* v. *NBC et al.,* p. 4157.

284 *NBC agreed: The Wall Street Journal,* June 4, 1980.

285 Description of the Steve Allen's abortive television show based on Silverman deposition, in *Wayne Newton* v. *NBC, et al.,* p. 4160, and author interview with Irvin Arthur, and information confirmed in author interview with Steve Allen.

SIXTEEN

286 *summer of 1977:* author interview with Gordon Baskin.

286 *KCOP-TV:* "Johnny Carson in Syndicate Aiming to Buy TV Station," *Variety,* February 8, 1978.

286 *"I was . . .":* author interview with Gordon Baskin.

287 *"sub rosa . . .": Variety,* June 28, 1978.

287 *To capitalize:* Baskin and declaration of Henry Bushkin in *Bushkin, et al.* v. *Baskin,* October 23, 1984.

288 *capitalized:* annual report of Commercial Bank of Los Angeles for 1980 and "Th-e-e-e-re Goes Johnny!" by Peter S. Greenberg, *Los Angeles Magazine,* August 1983.

288 *"sounded like . . .":* Greenberg, *Los Angeles Magazine,* August 1983.

288 *$1.5 million:* petitioner statement in re: the marriage of Judy Beck Bushkin and Henry I. Bushkin in Superior Court of the State of California, County of Los Angeles, March 6, 1984.

288 *"The man was . . .":* quoted in Greenberg, *Los Angeles Magazine,* August 1983.

289 *When Steve Peden:* memorandum to Arnold Kopelson, Henry Bushkin, et al. from Steve Peden, May 21, 1982.

290 *"Johnny did . . .":* author interview with Fred Kayne.

290 *In December: Los Angeles Times,* December 12, 1979.

290 *"I'm really . . .":* quoted in "David Martin's Headliners" in *New York Post,* December 14, 1979.

291 *His letter:* letter from Gordon Baskin to all members of the board of directors of the Commercial Bank of California, March 25, 1980; interviews with Baskin and Rafael Chodos.

292 *"both foolish and . . .":* Bushkin declaration, in *Herb Kaufman,*

John Carson, Henry Bushkin, et al. v. *Gordon Baskin, Adriana A. Baskin,* October 23, 1984, p. 4.

292 *"About a year . . .":* author interview with Gordon Baskin.

293 *"Mr. Catain is . . .":* credit approval and loan report for Jack Catain, March 30, 1979.

293 *"He looked like . . .":* Greenberg, *Los Angeles Magazine,* August 1983.

294 Henry Bushkin's involvement with TMX based on his declaration in support of motion for summary judgment in *Kopelson and Miller* v. *Henry Bushkin and John Carson,* August 1, 1983.

294 *"Mr. Catain . . .":* deposition of Judy B. Bushkin in *Kopelson and Miller* v. *Henry Bushkin,* United States District Court, Central District of California, April 6, 1983.

294 *"never engaged . . .":* declaration of Henry Bushkin in *Kopelson and Miller* v. *Bushkin and Carson,* August 1, 1983, p. 8.

294 *"The head . . .":* "Rusco's Catain Under Investigation by U.S." by Jeff Gerth in *New York Times,* June 12, 1978.

295 *In 1969:* 1986 U.S. Secret Service arrest report of Jack Catain obtained by author with a Freedom of Information request.

295 *"As far . . .":* author interview with Gerald Petievich.

295 *"We heard . . .":* quoted in *Wall Street Journal,* May 26, 1969.

295 *"As one . . .":* letter from James R. Vrataric, senior vice-president of the Commercial Bank of California, May 13, 1981.

296 *bank records:* hand-printed invitation list to the party.

296 *$700,000 in loans:* undated memo titled "business from cocktail party, May 21, 1981."

296 *largest loan:* loan approval and credit report, May 5, 1981.

296 *arrived in:* internal FBI document dated February 4, 1982, obtained by author with a Freedom of Information request.

297 *In 1982: Wall Street Journal,* June 12, 1985.

297 *In 1981:* "Why Johnny Carson, 'Bombastic' Bushkin Are Pals No Longer" by Daniel Akst in *Wall Street Journal,* May 2, 1988.

297 *"I remember . . .":* author interview with Joanna Carson.

297 *On December 30: Neil Simon and Marsha Mason Simon* v. *Bushkin, Gaims and Gaines, a law partnership, Bushkin, Kopelson, and Gaines, a law partnership and Does 1 through 20,* filed December 30, 1983 in Superior Court of the State of California, County of Los Angeles.

298 *"characterized" . . .:* "Shenker Call in U.S. Inquiry into Webbe Dealings," *St. Louis Globe-Democrat,* February 25, 1975.

299 *The two men:* "Kinney and Carson Plan a Casino Deal" by Jeff

Gerth, *New York Times*, October 26, 1979, and "Coleman, Torres Declared Unsuitable to Buy Aladdin" by Al Delugach, *Los Angeles Times*, December 15, 1979.

299 *On October 22:* memorandum of understanding among Edward Nigro, Johnny Carson, and National Kinney Corporation dated October 22, 1979, filed in *Carson and Nigro* v. *National Kinney Corp.*, April 24, 1980.

300 *Joanna went: Time*, July 16, 1980, and *New York Times*, July 1, 1980.

300 *Two years later:* "Two Warner Communications Officials Accused of Taking Bribe That Is Linked to Mafia Figure" by Stanley Penn and Jim Drinkhall in *Wall Street Journal*, November 20, 1978.

301 *"Catain mentioned . . .":* Los Angeles Police Department Organized Crime Division, internal reporting document dated January 29, 1980, 1700 hours.

301 *"certain cash . . .":* "Rusco Directors to Study Charges Against Catain" by Al Delugach, *Los Angeles Times*, June 13, 1978.

302 *On April 22:* testimony of David Hurwitz in NEWTON v. NBC, U.S. District Courts, November 12, 1986, pp. 3304–05.

302 *The next day:* Hurwitz testimony, *Wall Street Journal*, April 25, 1980, and *Los Angeles Times*, April 25, 1980.

302 *"The only heated . . .":* author interview with Fred Freed.

303 *"I saw . . .":* *Penthouse* interview with Wayne Newton, June 1984.

304 *"This letter . . .":* letter from Kenneth L. Browning to Wayne Newton, May 1, 1980, plaintiff's exhibit 480 in *Newton* v. *NBC*.

304 *"I never understood . . .":* author interview with Lola Falana.

304 *"Mr. Bushkin . . .":* testimony of David Hurwitz, in *Newton* v. *NBC*, November 12, 1986, p. 3307.

304 *Hurwitz put:* Hurwitz testimony, *Newton* v. *NBC*, pp. 3310–13.

305 *"If you thought . . .":* "Carson's Aladdin Bid Fails as Newton Gets his Wish" by Marilyn Beck, *Valley News*, May 8, 1980.

SEVENTEEN

306 The accounts of Henry Bushkin's phone calls based on office record of incoming calls for September 8, 19, 24, 25, and October 6, 7, 1980, plaintiff's exhibits 502, 507, 616, 518, 556, and 557, in *Newton* v. *NBC*.

306 *"our Batman . . .":* "TV's Toughest Reporters" by Jane Alice Karr, *US*, June 1, 1987.

306 *According to Henry:* Henry Bushkin deposition in *Newton* v. *NBC*, November 10, 1986, pp. 3138–40.

307   *"they weren't . . .":* memorandum to Garry Reese, supervisor, from
       Agents Shepard and Dorsey, September 12, 1980, plaintiff's exhibit
       105 in *Newton* v. *NBC.*

307   *"liked Mr. Newton . . .":* Brian Ross testimony in *Newton* v. *NBC,*
       November 25, 1986, p. 5222.

308   *not remember:* Brian Ross testimony in *Newton* v. *NBC,* November
       26, 1986, p. 5481.

309   *"that the story . . .":* Bushkin deposition, in *Newton* v. *NBC,* No-
       vember 10, 1986, p. 3142.

309   *"You can take . . .":* Ross testimony in *Newton* v. *NBC,* November
       26, 1986, p. 5455.

309   *"under the impression . . .":* Johnny Carson deposition in *Newton*
       v. *NBC,* November 10, 1986, p. 3177.

309   *"very upset":* Hurwitz testimony in *Newton* v. *NBC,* November 12,
       1986, p. 3318.

310   *"Investigators say . . .":* transcript of NBC broadcast, plaintiff's
       exhibit 258 in *Newton* v. *NBC.*

310   *"I couldn't . . .":* Wayne Newton testimony in *Newton* v. *NBC,*
       October 21, 1986, p. 719.

311   *"If I accused . . .":* *Las Vegas Times,* November 8, 1980.

311   *Newton filed: Las Vegas Sun,* July 28, 1981.

311   *name was dropped: Las Vegas Sun,* August 19, 1981.

311   Description of Laurie Miller's attempt to serve a subpoena based on
       her declaration, October 21, 1981, in *Newton* v. *NBC.*

312   *"Please pursue . . .":* *Las Vegas Review-Journal,* December 9,
       1982.

313   *"because at . . .":* quoted in *Penthouse,* June 1984.

313   *"an emperor . . .":* Mort Galane in *Newton* v. *NBC,* December 10,
       1986, p. 6966.

313   *"I would venture . . .":* Mort Galane in *Newton* v. *NBC,* December
       8, 1986, pp. 6560–61.

314   Account of Jack Catain's arrest based on U.S. Secret Service files
       obtained under a Freedom of Information Act request.

315   *"inherent risk . . .":* Citibank memorandum to file re: John W.
       Carson & Associates, from Sheila Wilensky, assistant vice-presi-
       dent, September 18, 1981.

315   *million-dollar CD:* Citibank memorandum, September 18, 1981.

316   *half-million-dollar line:* Citibank memorandum to file re: Arnold
       Kopelson, February 17, 1982.

316   *"based primarily . . .":* Citibank memorandum, February 17, 1982.

316   *"He told me . . .":* Michael Miller declaration in *Kopelson and
       Miller* v. *Bushkin,* U.S. District Court, August 1, 1983, p. 8.

316 *$114,000:* private placement memorandum of the Commercial Bank of California, p. 42.

316 *$100,000:* private placement memorandum of the Commercial Bank of California, unnumbered last page supporting documentation.

316 *"involved violations . . .":* private placement memorandum of the Commercial Bank of California, p. 41.

317 *"It was . . .":* memo from Tony Bazurto to Arnold Kopelson, February 20, 1983.

317 *"the total . . .":* letter to Jack Catain from the Commercial Bank of California, June 21, 1982.

317 *"he wished . . .":* memorandum to Henry Bushkin from Arnold Kopelson, September 13, 1982.

317 *"Henry and Arnold . . .":* author interview with Marvin Landau.

318 *"I'm absolutely . . .":* author interview with Joanna Carson.

318 *financial figures:* private placement memorandum, p. 3.

318 *"appeared to . . .":* letter, Arnold Kopelson to Johnny Carson, Personal and Confidential, November 30, 1982.

319 *$1.5 million:* Greenberg, *Los Angeles Magazine,* August 1983.

319 *"The Bushkin . . .":* Jack Catain in an interview with Peter S. Greenberg, *Los Angeles Magazine,* August 1983.

320 *prevented the transfer:* Greenberg, *Los Angeles Magazine,* August 1983.

321 *"he was trying . . .":* declaration in support of motions for summary judgment of Henry Bushkin in *Kopelson and Miller* v. *Bushkin,* August 1, 1983, p. 9.

321 *"if Mr. Carson . . .":* Bushkin declaration, August 1, 1983, p. 9.

321 *"his clients . . .":* memorandum to file re: watchlist recommendation Bushkin, Carson, et al., February 23, 1983.

322 *"to believe . . .":* declaration of Arnold Kopelson in *Kopelson* v. *Bushkin,* August 1, 1983.

322 *" 'came across' ":* motion to dismiss in *Kopelson and Miller* v. *Bushkin,* May 16, 1983.

323 *"When was . . .":* deposition of Judy B. Bushkin in *Kopelson and Miller* v. *Bushkin,* April 6, 1983.

323 *"It was . . .":* author interview with Judy Bushkin.

324 *"in an unsafe . . .":* "State Takes over Ailing West Hollywood Bank" by Al Delugach, *Los Angeles Times,* May 28, 1983.

324 *"I am not . . .":* *Los Angeles Times,* August 23, 1983.

324 *"associated directly . . .":* *Los Angeles Times,* May 27, 1984.

324 *"use his position . . .":* *Los Angeles Times,* May 27, 1984.

324 *name was mentioned:* New York Times, May 26, 1984.

325 *$1,347,671.88:* letter from Mark Rosen, deputy general counsel of FDIC, to author, May 25, 1988.

325 *"flow charts":* FDIC v. *Carson, et al.,* May 1984, U.S. District Court, defendants' brief, p. 41.

325 *"a large measure . . .":* memorandum to file re: Carson, Bushkin, Kopelson, Miller and Smith signed by Frederick S. Taff, September 6, 1985.

EIGHTEEN

327 *As the Lear:* author interviews with John McMahon and Karen Jackovich.

327 *"This is . . .":* quoted on *CBS Evening News* with Dan Rather, transcript, March 18, 1981.

328 *September:* petitioner's trial brief re: date of separation in Joanna Carson and John W. Carson, July 11, 1964, and Judge Hogoboom statement of decision, May 8, 1985.

328 *"I helped build . . .":* reporting of Karen Jackovich for *People* in 1981.

329 *"well, hello . . .":* reporting of Karen Jackovich for *People* in 1981.

330 *Schwinn had flown:* author interviews with Mr. and Mrs. Victor Nelson.

330 *Mike Fuehrer:* author interview with Mike Fuehrer.

331 *Norfolk graduates: Norfolk Daily News,* October 20, 1981; reporting of Karen Jackovich for *People*; videotape of *Johnny Goes Home,* NBC documentary on Carson's return to Norfolk; and author interviews with eight of those present.

332 *Johnny appeared:* author interview with Lorraine Beckenhauer Gipe.

332 *"I'd like . . .":* videotape of *Johnny Goes Home.*

334 *The evening had ended:* author interview with Chuck Howser.

334 *the wreckage:* author interview with Bob Means.

335 *"We were . . .":* author interview with Joanna Carson.

335 *already separated:* declaration of Henry I. Bushkin in re: the marriage of Judy Beck Bushkin and Henry I. Bushkin.

336 *he canceled:* "Carson Skids into Cheering Debut" by Susan Darst Williams in *Omaha World Herald,* November 24, 1981.

337 *"Happy birthday . . .":* videotape of *Johnny Goes Home.*

337 *"He wasn't . . .":* author interview with Joanna Carson.

338 *"On a Friday morning. . . ." . . .* Carson: *Los Angeles Times,* February 8, 1982.

338 "spreading like . . .": *Los Angeles Times,* February 8, 1982.

339 *815,000: Los Angeles Times,* February 8, 1982.

339 *"Johnny just . . .":* "Carson, the Magnificent" by Tom Shales in *Washington Post,* February 2, 1982.

339 *psychiatrist:* Judge Hogoboom statement of decision, May 8, 1985.

340 *alcohol level: Los Angeles Times,* March 3, 1982.

340 *"What are . . .":* author interview with Kassel.

340 *"can't recall . . .": New York Daily News,* March 1, 1982.

340 *an incident: Los Angeles Times,* August 28 and September 12, 1973.

341 *"He has made . . .":* Marilyn Beck column in *Los Angeles Daily News,* March 25, 1982.

342 *Johnny, upset: Variety,* January 20, 1982.

342 *Paramount believed: Variety,* October 27, 1982.

343 *"we were doing . . .":* author interview with John McMahon.

343 *"It was Johnny's . . .":* author interview with Richard Fischoff.

344 *Johnny wrote:* letter from Johnny Carson to Will Williams, February 15, 1978.

344 *"[I]n that case . . .":* declaration of plaintiff Alex Kolis in *Alex Kolis v. John W. Carson,* C504521, Superior Court of California. September 25, 1987.

344 *sent a letter:* Rauer L. Meyer of Bushkin, Kopelson, Gaims and Gaines to Alvin Kolis, January 22, 1982.

345 *"Johnny Carson has . . .": Variety,* February 10, 1982.

345 *"my personal name . . .":* declaration of defendant Alex Kolis in support of the motion for summary judgment, in *John W. Carson v. Western Series, Inc., Alvin Kolis, et al.,* October 21, 1983.

345 *"example should . . .": John W. Carson v. Western Series, Inc., Alvin Kolis, and Does 1 through 25,* complaint for unauthorized use of name and likeness, etc., February 1, 1982.

345 *"The suit . . .":* author interview with Alvin Kolis.

345 *"The question . . .":* memorandum of points and authorities in *Alex Kolis v. John W. Carson,* September 25, 1987.

346 *"Mr. Bushkin . . .":* deposition of John W. Carson in *Kolis v. John W. Carson, an individual, and Does 1 through 100,* in Superior Court of the State of California, County of Los Angeles, June 9, 1986.

346 *"to pop . . .":* author interview with Alvin Kolis.

NINETEEN

347 *Emm-Jay was:* author interview with Mary Jane Trokel and "Arsonist Suspected in Blaze in Beverly Hills," *Los Angeles Times,* November 5, 1982.

348 *"I want you . . .":* Judge Hogoboom statement of decision in re: the marriage of Joanna Carson and John W. Carson, May 8, 1985.

349 *"Henry was so . . .":* author interview with Joanna Carson.

350 *"a female friend . . .": National Enquirer,* December 6, 1983.

351 *Johnny accepted:* Judge Hogoboom statement of decision in re: the marriage of Joanna Carson v. John W. Carson, May 8, 1985.

352 *"allow him . . .":* Joanna Carson's trial brief in re: the marriage of Joanna Carson and John W. Carson, July 11, 1984, p. 3.

352 *"If I had . . .":* quoted in Rosenfield, *Los Angeles Times,* July 6, 1986.

353 *Ramey and:* author interview with Phil Ramey and tape recording of discussion between John Carson, Sally Field, and Ramey and the other photographer.

354 *On April 8: Los Angeles Times,* April 12, 1983.

355 *Katleman ran:* author interview with Marilyn Katleman.

356 *"embracing and . . .": National Enquirer,* April 19, 1983.

357 *Niven had:* author interview with David Niven, Jr.

358 *"She'd show . . .":* author interview with Jim Nauman.

358 *a salesman:* author interview with Alex Mass.

358 *"We would . . .":* author interview with Nancy Anderson Croker.

358 *"she was too ambitious . . .":* quoted in "Walk Along Malibu Beach Pays Off 'Tonight' " by Virginia Miller, *North Hills News Record,* February 6, 1987.

359 *"She didn't . . .":* author interview with Rose Mary Carroll.

359 *"Why did we . . .": Wall Street Journal,* July 18, 1988.

359 *"Alex was . . .":* author interview with Marcia Fessler Drozd.

359 *"She was in . . .":* author interview with Jim Nauman.

360 *"I met her . . .":* author interview with Ken Schwartz.

360 *"How's your . . .":* author interview with Pat McCormick.

360 *"In a grand . . .":* interrogatories in re: the marriage of Judy Beck Bushkin and Henry Bushkin.

361 *"Nancy would . . .":* quoted in *Johnny Carson* by Smith, p. 202.

361 *"increased the . . .":* declaration of Joanna Carson in re: the marriage of Joanna Carson and John W. Carson, September 13, 1983, p. 2.

361 *"Bushkin did . . .":* author interview with Joanna Carson.

361 *"dropping in . . .":* Kopelson deposition in *Kopelson* v. *Carson,* as quoted in "Carson Claims Smear, Says He will Sue Pair" by Al Delugach in *Los Angeles Times,* August 12, 1983.

363 *"due to the . . .":* declaration of Joanna Carson in *Joanna Carson* v. *John W. Carson,* September 13, 1983, p. 5.

363 *paid for by:* declaration of John W. Carson in re: the marriage of Joanna Carson and John W. Carson, October 14, 1983.

364 *Jim Mahoney:* AP, September 23, 1983.

364 *"about $1 million . . ."*: "Joanna Carson's $500,000 Support Figure Disputed" by Myrna Oliver, *Los Angeles Times*, February 24, 1984.

364 *"It is only . . ."*: Ellen Goodman in *Los Angeles Times*, October 26, 1983.

365 *"Johnny, why . . ."*: *National Enquirer*, October 25, 1983.

365 *"ready to list . . ."*: *National Enquirer*, December 6, 1983.

365 *"hammered out . . ."*: *National Enquirer*, June 19, 1984.

366 *"intimate friendship . . ."*: Joanna Carson declaration in libel suit *John W. Carson* v. *National Enquirer*, May 2, 1985.

366 *"specious and . . ."*: Henry Bushkin declaration in libel suit *John W. Carson* v. *National Enquirer*.

366 *"Of course . . ."*: author interview with Joanna Carson.

367 *"there was . . ."*: Judge Hogoboom statement of decision in re: *Joanna Carson* v. *Johnny Carson*, May 8, 1985, p. 6.

367 *"You're in . . ."*: author interview with Joanna Carson.

367 *"Joanna was . . ."*: author interview with Marjorie Reed.

368 *According to documents . . .*: Citibank memorandum to file re: John W. Carson, October 25, 1985. When Joanna Carson was read the figures, she said that they were about correct.

369 *$375,000:* Citibank memorandum.

TWENTY

371 *"the largest . . ."*: *Los Angeles Times*, November 25, 1984.

371 *"I wish . . ."*: author interview with Mary Jane Trokel.

371 *"the unconscious . . ."*: Rosenfield, *Los Angeles Times*, July 6, 1986.

371 *"where's the . . ."*: Rosenfield, *Los Angeles Times*, July 6, 1986.

372 *"Nobody who . . ."*: Rosenfield, *Los Angeles Times*, July 6, 1986.

373 *"You still . . ."*: *Los Angeles Times*, March 18, 1983.

373 *first regular:* "For the 'Tonight Show,' Joan Rivers Is the Next Best Thing to Johnny Carson" by Frank J. Prial, *New York Times*, July 31, 1983.

374 *summer of 1985: Los Angeles Times*, August 14, 1985.

374 *stipulation: Los Angeles Times*, August 18, 1985 and *Parade*, April 7, 1985.

377 *"John's made . . ."*: author interview with Jody Carson.

381 *"I feel . . ."*: author interview with Jody Carson.

382 *" Alex talked . . ."*: author interview with Jody Carson

383 *"I attribute . . ."*: Joanne Carson interviewed by Eirik Knutzen, March 12, 1983.

384 *He wandered:* Clarke, p. 471.

384 *spat in:* Clarke, p. 476.

385 *For her party:* author present.

385 *Joanna walked:* New York Daily News, December 28, 1986.

385 *she discovered:* New York Daily News, September 28, 1986, and New York Times, September 28, 1986.

385 *"The thieves . . .":* New York Daily News, November 10, 1986.

386 *"I can't believe . . .":* author interview with Joanna Carson.

TWENTY-ONE

387 Account of Joan Rivers phone call to Johnny Carson based on author interview with Joan Rivers, and Fred de Cordova's account in his autobiography, *Johnny Came Lately.*

388 *"Johnny, it . . .":* "Can I Talk?" by Joan Rivers, *People,* May 26, 1986.

388 *"We had to . . .":* author interview with Joan Rivers.

389 *"He used me . . .":* author interview with Joan Rivers.

390 *"total contrast":* Rosenfield, Los Angeles Times, July 6, 1986.

391 *"I think we . . .":* People, May 26, 1987.

393 *"First of . . .":* Los Angeles Times, May 21, 1987.

395 Johnny Carson's dialogue based on his account of the trip on *The Tonight Show,* July 22, 1986.

396 *Berndt, who had:* author interview with Morris Berndt and videotape of Carson visit

397 *The next morning:* author interview with Donald Nielson and *Avoca Journal-Herald,* July 3, 1986.

398 *Ratliff handled:* author interview with Roy Ratliff.

399 *In the early:* author interviews with Roy Ratliff and Scott Morris.

399 *Wells came:* author interview with Mort Wells.

400 *Johnny paid:* Chris Carson depositions in *Tanena Love Green* v. *Christopher Carson,* February 4, 1987, and July 1, 1987.

400 *"He was a caddie . . .":* author interview with Tanena Love Green.

401 *"Do you want . . .":* Chris Carson depositions in *Tanena Love Green* v. *Christopher Carson,* February 4, 1987, p. 38.

402 *spring of 1987:* affidavit of Mrs. Tifinie Wessell.

403 *"The worst . . .":* author interview with Roy Ratliff.

403 *"I think that . . .":* tape of John Carson's eulogy.

404 *In 1981:* Wall Street Journal, July 8, 1981.

406 *"That's the funniest . . .":* author interview with Chris Jackson.

406 *The comedian walked:* tape of Tonight Show.

408 *"It's such a . . .":* author interview with Judge Hogoboom.

410 *"I think of it . . .":* author interview with Mary Jane Trokel.

412 *"After Bear . . .":* author interview with Fred Kayne.

413 *"I didn't understand . . ."*: author interview with Maynell Thomas.

414 *"They said . . ."*: author interview with Fred Kayne.

414 *"one of the . . ."*: Daniel Akst, *Wall Street Journal*, May 2, 1988.

414 *In December:* verified complaint for breach of guaranty, *Carson Tonight, Inc.* v. *Henry Bushkin, Jerry K. Staub, John Gaims, Hugh G. Pike, Jon E. Anderson, Neil Block, and Does 1 through 50,* filed May 6, 1988.

414 *on May 6, 1988:* verified complaint in *Carson Tonight, Inc.* v. *Henry Bushkin et al.*

415 *"I don't know . . ."*: author interview with Judy Bushkin.

TWENTY-TWO

417 *"Pat was . . ."*: author interview with Alan Rothenberg, confirmed by Pat Sajak.

417 *"There are . . ."*: *Hollywood Reporter*, May 4, 1988.

418 *"I really . . ."*: author present for *The Tonight Show*.

418 Author present for *The Tonight Show*.

BIBLIOGRAPHY

Allen, Steve. *The Funny Man*. New York: Simon and Schuster, 1956.

Allen, Steve. *Funny People*. New York: Stein and Day, 1981.

Allen, Steve. *The Question Man*. New York: Bellmeadows Press, 1959.

Arlen, Michael J. *The Camera Age: Essays on Television*. New York: Penguin, 1982.

Barnouw, Erik. *Tube of Plenty: The Evolution of American Television*. Oxford University Press, New York: 1975.

Bedell, Sally. *Up the Tube*. New York: Viking Press, 1981.

Berger, Phil. *The Last Laugh: The World of Stand-up Comics*. New York: Limelight Editions, 1985

Brown, Les. *Television: The Business Behind the Box*. New York: Harcourt Brace Jovanovich, 1971.

Cather, Willa. *My Antonia*. Boston: Houghton Mifflin, 1918.

Charbonneau, Jean-Pierre. *The Canadian Connection*. Ottawa: Optimum Publishing, 1976.

Clarke, Gerald. *Capote: A Biography*. New York: Simon and Schuster, 1988.

Cole, Barry, ed. *Television Today: A Close-up View*. New York: Oxford University Press, 1981.

Corkery, Paul. *Carson: The Unauthorized Biography*. Ketchum, Idaho: Randt & Company, 1987.

De Cordova, Fred. *Johnny Came Lately*. New York: Simon and Schuster, 1988.

Ephron, Nora. *And Now Here's Johnny*. New York: Avon, 1968.

Federal Writers' Project. *Iowa: A Guide to the Hawkeye State*, compiled and written by the Federal Writers' Project of the Works Progress

Administration for the State of Iowa. Saint Clair Shores, Michigan: Scholarly Press, Inc., 1977.

Galonoy, Terry. *Tonight!* New York: Warner, 1974.

Gitlin, Todd. *Inside Prime Time*. New York: Pantheon Books, 1983.

Gitlin, Todd, ed. *Watching Television*. New York: Pantheon, 1986.

Goldsen, Rose K. *The Show and Tell Machine*. New York: Dial Press, 1977.

Grobel, Lawrence. *Conversations with Capote*. New York: New American Library, 1985.

Grote, David. *The End of Comedy: The Sit-Com and the Comedic Tradition*. Hamden, Connecticut: Anchor Books, 1983.

Gurewitch, Morton. *Comedy: The Irrational Vision*. Ithaca, New York, and London: Cornell University Press, 1975.

Hill, Doug, and Jeff Weingrad. *Saturday Night*. New York: Vintage, 1987.

Kern, Edith. *The Absolute Comic*. New York: Columbia University Press, 1980.

Lardine, Robert. *He-e-e-ere's Johnny.* New York: Award, 1975.

Lauter, Paul. *Theories of Comedy*. New York: Doubleday, 1964.

Lorence, Douglas. *Johnny Carson: A Biography*. New York: Drake, 1975.

Maguglin, Robert O. *The Queen Mary: The Official Pictorial History*. Long Beach, California: Sequoia Communications, 1985.

Mayer, Martin. *About Television*. New York: Harper & Row, 1972.

Make 'em Laugh: Life Studies of Comedy Writers. William F. Fry and Melanie Allen. Palo Alto, California: Science and Behavior Books, 1975.

McNeil, Alex. *Total Television: A Comprehensive Guide to Programming from 1948 to the Present*. New York: Penguin, 1984.

Metz, Robert. *The Today Show*. Chicago: Playboy Press, 1977.

Metz, Robert. *The Tonight Show*. Chicago: Playboy Press, 1980.

Meyrowitz, Joshua. *No Sense of Place: The Impact of Electronic Media on Social Behavior*. New York and London: Oxford University Press, 1985.

Olson, James C. *History of Nebraska*. Lincoln and London: University of Nebraska Press, 1955.

O'Neill, Eugene. *Long Day's Journey into Night*. New Haven and London: Yale University Press, 1956.

Pound, Louise. *Nebraska Folklore*. Lincoln: University of Nebraska Press, 1959.

Rivers, Joan. *Enter Talking*. New York: Delacorte Press, 1986.

Rollin, Betty. *Am I Getting Paid For This?* New York: New American Library, 1986.

Seaman, Barbara. *Lovely Me: The Life of Jacqueline Susann*. New York: Morrow, 1987.

Smith, Rolland. *Johnny Carson: An Unauthorized Biography*. New York: St. Martin's Press, 1987.

Steiner, Gary A. *The People Look at Television: A Study of Audience Attitudes*. New York: Alfred A. Knopf, 1963.

Tennis, Craig. *Johnny Tonight!* New York: Pocket Books, 1980.

Van Doren, Mamie, with Art Aveilhe. *Playing the Field: My Story*. New York: G. P. Putnam's Sons, 1987.

Welsch, Roger L. *A Treasury of Nebraska Pioneer Folklore*. Lincoln: University of Nebraska Press, 1966.

Welsch, Roger L., with Linda K. Welsch. *Catfish at the Pump: Humor and the Frontier*. Lincoln and London: University of Nebraska Press, 1986.

INDEX